ELUSIVE UTOPIA

ANTISLAVERY, ABOLITION, AND THE ATLANTIC WORLD
R. J. M. Blackett, Edward Rugemer, and James Brewer Stewart, Series Editors

ELUSIVE UTOPIA
THE STRUGGLE FOR RACIAL EQUALITY IN
OBERLIN, OHIO

GARY J. KORNBLITH AND **CAROL LASSER**

LOUISIANA STATE UNIVERSITY PRESS
BATON ROUGE

Published by Louisiana State University Press
www.lsupress.org

Copyright © 2018 by Louisiana State University Press
All rights reserved. Except in the case of brief quotations used in articles or reviews, no part of this publication may be reproduced or transmitted in any format or by any means without written permission of Louisiana State University Press.

Louisiana Paperback Edition, 2021

Designer: Barbara Neely Bourgoyne
Typeface: MillerText

Cover image: "Bird's Eye View of the Town of Oberlin."
Drawing by A. Ruger, 1868. Oberlin College Archives.

Library of Congress Cataloging-in-Publication Data
Names: Kornblith, Gary J. (Gary John), 1950– author. | Lasser, Carol, author.
Title: Elusive utopia : the struggle for racial equality in Oberlin, Ohio / Gary J. Kornblith and Carol Lasser.
Other titles: Struggle for racial equality in Oberlin, Ohio
Description: Baton Rouge : Louisiana State University Press, [2018] | Series: Antislavery, abolition, and the Atlantic world | Includes bibliographical references and index.
Identifiers: LCCN 2018012614| ISBN 978-0-8071-6956-8 (cloth : alk. paper) | ISBN 978-0-8071-7015-1 (pdf) | ISBN 978-0-8071-7016-8 (epub)
Subjects: LCSH: Oberlin (Ohio)—Race relations. | Oberlin (Ohio)—History—19th century. | Antislavery movements—Ohio—Oberlin—History—19th century. | Abolitionists—Ohio—Oberlin—History—19th century.
Classification: LCC F499.O2 K67 2018 | DDC 305.8009771/23—dc23
LC record available at https://lccn.loc.gov/2018012614
ISBN 978-0-8071-7624-5 (paperback)

for Russell, Max, and Simon,
who grew up in Oberlin

CONTENTS

List of Maps | ix
List of Charts and Tables | xi
Acknowledgments | xiii

Introduction | 1
1 Envisioning Utopia | 9
2 The Arrival of African Americans | 33
3 An Experiment in Racial Integration | 58
4 Means and Ends in Oberlin Abolitionism | 84
5 Fighting for Equal Rights in the Civil War Era | 110
6 The Postwar Pursuit of Black Political Power | 147
7 Race and Opportunity in the Late Nineteenth Century | 173
8 Temperance, Gender, and the Racialization of Respectability | 196
9 Utopia Forsaken | 224
   Epilogue | 253

Notes | 259
Index | 313

Illustrations follow page 134

MAPS

"Map of the Western Reserve including the Fire Lands in Ohio," published by William Sumner, 1826 | 9

"A Plan of Oberlin Colony," drawn by Hiram Davis, 1835 | 18

Map of Oberlin in *Atlas from the 1857 Map of Lorain Co. Ohio from Actual Surveys by John F. Geil* | 79

"Diagram of the Burnt District in Oberlin," published in *Oberlin Weekly News*, March 17, 1882 | 197

"Map of Oberlin Village," published for Louis E. Burgner, circa 1920 | 237

CHARTS AND TABLES

CHARTS

2.1. Birthplace of Adult Residents of Russia Township by Race, 1850 | 51

7.1. Mean Real Estate Assessments by Race of Oberlin Taxpaying Households, 1865–1900 | 176

7.2. Median Real Estate Assessments by Race of Oberlin Taxpaying Households, 1865–1900 | 176

7.3. Occupational Distribution of Oberlin Men by Race, 1870 | 177

7.4. Occupational Distribution of Oberlin Men by Race, 1900 | 177

7.5. Racial Composition of Real Estate Assessment Quintiles, 1860 | 193

7.6. Racial Composition of Real Estate Assessment Quintiles, 1900 | 194

TABLES

2.1. Russia Township Taxpayers by Assessment Quintile and Race, 1850 | 52

7.1. Population of Oberlin, with Breakdown by Race, 1860–1900 | 175

7.2. Distribution of Taxpaying Oberlin Households across Real Estate Assessment Quintiles, Sorted by Race of Household Head, 1865–1890 | 185

7.3. Mobility Out of the Lowest Real Estate Assessment Quintile after Ten Years, Sorted by Race (1865, 1870, 1875, 1880 Cohorts Combined) | 192

CHARTS AND TABLES

7.4. Mobility Out of the Lowest Real Estate Assessment Quintile after Twenty Years, Sorted by Race (1865, 1870, 1875, 1880 Cohorts Combined) | 193

ACKNOWLEDGMENTS

When we first envisioned this study two decades ago, we had no idea it would take us so long to complete. But Oberlin is a community with a complicated history. As we struggled to make sense of how and why the town evolved from a utopian experiment in racial integration to a more typical American community riven by racial bigotry and a color line, we benefitted immeasurably from the help, advice, and knowledge of dozens of Oberlinians and scholars far and wide. We sincerely thank everyone who assisted us in this endeavor. This book belongs to you as well as us, though of course we assume full responsibility for errors that have made their way into the finished text.

Three gifted, generous individuals inspired us from the beginning of the project and repeatedly aided our efforts along the way. Marly Merrill warmly welcomed Carol to the study of Oberlin women when she arrived at the college in the early 1980s. Together they edited the correspondence of Lucy Stone and Antoinette Brown Blackwell, and they formed a close friendship that flourishes to this day. For this book, we have drawn extensively on Marly's vast knowledge of nineteenth-century Oberlin and we turned to her for smart and insightful comments on various drafts. She has provided us with sustained and sustaining encouragement throughout the writing process.

Phyllis Yarber Hogan is a grassroots historian of the highest order. Phyllis grew up in Oberlin, and her knowledge of the African American experience within the community is unsurpassed. She was the prime mover behind the formation of the Oberlin African-American Genealogy and History Group and also a key figure in the establishment of Juneteenth festivities in Oberlin, a community-based initiative designed to honor and celebrate

ACKNOWLEDGMENTS

Oberlin's black heritage and achievements. Above all, Phyllis is a wise and candid truth-teller. Over many years, she has sought to educate us about how Oberlin looks to people raised here without wealth or white privilege. She keeps us honest, and we regard her as our toughest critic. She has read and critiqued much of the manuscript, and it is definitely better as a result. Phyllis is our activist hero.

The late Patricia Holsworth was an indefatigable researcher and genealogist extraordinaire. With awesome dedication and diligence, she singlehandedly compiled a detailed genealogical database that encompassed over seventy thousand Oberlin residents, from the earliest settlers forward. It is a goldmine for historians as well as genealogists, and Pat was remarkably generous in making a computerized copy of the database available for our use without restriction. As an expert in reading nineteenth-century handwriting, she was able to decipher words and names that left us mystified, and she made linkages between multiple sets of records that required levels of patience and persistence much greater than ours. Plus she possessed a wonderfully dry sense of humor. We miss her deeply and wish she had lived to see this book in completed form.

Over the years, we hired a small army of students to help us with archival research, the digitization of census and tax records, the retrieval of materials from electronic databases, and a failed attempt to create a dynamic historical map using GIS software. Among those who performed these often unexciting yet utterly essential tasks were Tom Anderson-Monterosso, Jeffery Cristiani, Trish DeCoster, Nick Gliserman, Jen Graham, Max Kotelchuck, Nayeem Mahbab, Ben Master, Braden Paynter, Steve Prince, Cory Rogers, Natalia Shevin, and the amazing Ben Weber. We thank them for their contributions to this project, and we thank Oberlin College for financial grants that helped underwrite the cost of their fine work.

We also thank all the students in Carol's "Oberlin History as American History" course, whose projects over the years helped us make sense of the puzzle that is Oberlin history. We thank, too, Kurt Russell and his Oberlin High School students who partnered with Carol's students, and Principal William Baylis for his essential support.

In pursuing our research, we benefitted immensely from the expert guidance and supportive assistance of Oberlin College's talented librarians, archivists, and technologists. Reference librarians Megan Mitchell and Jen Starkey never seemed to tire of our asking them for help in tracking down

ACKNOWLEDGMENTS

obscure resources. Our frustrations became their challenges, which they met with cheerful enthusiasm. During the past decade, Associate Director of Libraries Alan Boyd promoted the digitization of local newspapers, an initiative that saved our tired eyes from yet more time at the microfilm reader. So did the work of volunteer Elizabeth Rumics, who labored assiduously on an index to those newspapers in the years before the digitization project began. Head of Special Collections Ed Vermue and his assistants, Lindsey Felice and William Tully, were always happy to pull from the shelves nineteenth-century volumes that rarely made their way to the reading room. Heath Patten performed digital magic on problematic images. It would be impossible to overpraise the staff and the holdings of the Oberlin College Libraries.

The Oberlin College Archives are also superb. Much credit belongs to Roland Baumann, who served as the college archivist from 1987 to 2008. Roland is a historian of Oberlin in his own right, and he has kindly shared with us his extensive knowledge of relevant source materials and his views on our overlapping scholarly interests. We also thank Tammy Martin, who for many years helped Roland in supporting researchers. Since becoming the college archivist in 2008, Ken Grossi has warmly welcomed us and has reached out to townspeople as well as students to make the archives' rich holdings increasingly accessible to all. We are deeply grateful to Ken, Associate Archivist Anne Salsich, and Archival Assistant Louisa Hoffman for their enthusiasm and their prompt responses to our sometimes obscure requests.

On the technology front, we thank the highly skilled and user-friendly staff of the Oberlin College Center for Information Technology, who rescued us from computer problems on more than one occasion. We are especially indebted to Albert Borroni, director of the Oberlin Center for Technologically Enhanced Teaching (OCTET), who is one of the nicest guys in the world.

Under the resolute leadership of Patricia Murphy, the Oberlin Historical and Improvement Organization evolved into the Oberlin Heritage Center while we were working on this book, and we greatly appreciate the help we received from the center's staff members, including the late Pat Holsworth, Maren McKee, Prue Richards, and Liz Schultz. Liz (who recently succeeded Pat Murphy as the center's executive director) and the late Ron Gorman shared with us the findings of their own research on Oberlin and the Underground Railroad; we thank them for their enormous generosity.

Not everything relevant to Oberlin's history is available in Oberlin itself. We thank the staffs of the Lorain County Records Retention Center, Lorain County Engineer's Office, Lorain County Probate Court, Lorain County Recorder's Office, Elyria Public Library, Lorain County Historical Society, Library of Congress, National Archives, Baker Library at Harvard Business School, and the Rare Book and Manuscript Library of Columbia University for welcoming us to their repositories or for supplying us or the Oberlin College Archives with copies of materials in their collections. Special thanks to Jan Blodgett and John Wertheimer, who tracked down materials for us in the Davidson College Archives; Dan Feller, who responded quickly to an inquiry about one of Andrew Jackson's correspondents; and Craig Thompson Friend, who shared with us a fascinating letter about Oberlin that he discovered at the Library of Congress.

George Dick, Nancy Hendrickson, A. G. Miller, and Maggie Robinson kindly shared with us documents they had in their possession as a result of research on their own family histories or on property they had acquired. Art Holbrook, Bob Longsworth, Rob Thompson, Marilyn Wainio, and John Willis also shared research findings with us, as did Brent Morris, whom we first met when he was a graduate student working on his doctoral dissertation. Out of that dissertation emerged Brent's fine book *Oberlin: Hotbed of Abolitionism*, from which we have greatly profited.

We thank the commentators and audience members who supplied feedback on papers and presentations we gave before different groups and at different venues while we pursued this project, including the annual meeting of the Society for Historians of the Early American Republic in 2001, Kendal at Oberlin in 2002, the Oberlin African-American Genealogy and History Group in 2002 and 2005, the Great Lakes Colleges Association Black Studies Conference in 2003, the American History Research Seminar at the Institute of Historical Research in London in 2004, the Cleveland Civil War Roundtable in 2005, Case Western Reserve University in 2006, the Israeli Seminar on American Studies at Tel Aviv University in 2007, the Oberlin Heritage Center in 2009, the "Ohio Goes to War" Conference at Cleveland State University in 2011, Oberlin Community Services in 2012, and a gathering jointly sponsored by the Oberlin African-American Genealogy and History Group and the Oberlin Public Library in 2015. We also thank Wendy Kozol, Kelly Verda, Mira Walter, and Sandy Zagarell, who listened to us discuss our research at length in private conversations. We are grateful to Jack Glazier and Charles Peterson for pointing us toward resources that we otherwise might have missed.

ACKNOWLEDGMENTS

Almost last but certainly not least, we thank the many friends and colleagues who read drafts of various chapters and offered us encouragement and constructive criticism as we struggled to shape our research findings and interpretive analyses into a coherent manuscript: Pam Brooks, Tom Dublin, Doug Egerton (who published four books of his own during the time we labored on this one), Ron Gorman, Phyllis Yarber Hogan, Pat Holsworth, Steve Prince, Cory Rogers, Liz Schultz, and Amy Dru Stanley. Deborah Kaplan and Marly Merrill deserve special commendation for reading drafts of the manuscript in its entirety. Their attention to style as well as substance was most valuable.

We are thrilled to have this book appear in the Louisiana State University Press series on Antislavery, Abolition, and the Atlantic World, edited by Richard J. M. Blackett, Edward Rugemer, and James Brewer Stewart. We are deeply grateful to Nikki Taylor for her insightful referee's report for the press; we benefitted greatly from her sharp advice in making final revisions. We thank Derik Shelor for copy editing the manuscript with extraordinary care and professional precision; he saved us from mistakes both large and small, thereby enhancing not only style but also substance. Finally, we thank our dear friend Jim O'Brien, who prepared the index, and Editor in Chief Rand Dotson, Managing Editor Lee Campbell Sioles, and the other members of the LSU Press staff who guided the transformation of our manuscript into a handsome book. We feel very fortunate to have had so much expert assistance in bringing this project to fruition.

ELUSIVE UTOPIA

INTRODUCTION

Utopian experiments enjoyed remarkable popularity in nineteenth-century America. Before his premature death in 1854, the indefatigable Scottish-born investigator A. J. Macdonald compiled information on sixty-nine efforts to construct utopias, religious and secular, in the United States.[1] Modern-day scholars have identified well over a hundred intentional communities planted before the Civil War, including initiatives launched by Dunkers, Moravians, Spiritualists, Transcendentalists, Fourierists, and Associationists.[2] These experiments engaged Zoarites in Ohio, Rappites in Pennsylvania, Owenites in Indiana, Shakers across several states, and both white abolitionists and enslaved blacks in the short-lived Nashoba settlement in Tennessee. Many of these communities struggled from the beginning and quickly succumbed to a mix of internal conflicts and external forces. A small number flourished, enjoying economic success and ideological cohesion for several decades. Some maintained their original structure and mission; others evolved toward mainstream norms, growing distant from their founding visions.

In his mammoth *History of American Socialisms*, published in 1870, John Humphrey Noyes, the charismatic leader of a famous utopian community in Oneida, New York, observed astutely that the timing of these nineteenth-century communitarian experiments "lies parallel with the line of religious Revivals."[3] For Noyes, the formation of utopian communities, which he termed "Socialism," went hand in hand with "Revivalism." As he explained, "They are to each other as inner to outer—as soul to body—as life to its surroundings."[4] Citing in particular the vigorous evangelical labors of Charles Grandison Finney, Noyes specified the period between 1831 and 1834 as the time "when the American people came . . . near to a surrender of all to the Kingdom of Heaven."[5] Significantly, the Oberlin colony emerged at precisely that historical moment, and Finney played a key role in its development.

Yet Noyes did not include Oberlin among the utopias that he chronicled. Why? Certainly the community that took root in the clay soil of northeastern Ohio displayed all the characteristics of the "utopian mentality" later outlined by the great social theorist Karl Mannheim. The founders of Oberlin were inspired by an idea that was "situationally transcendent," and they sought to produce "a transforming effect upon the existing historical-social order." They imagined a future "bursting the bonds" of the present, in a community brought together by shared commitments to changing the world.[6] Perhaps what confounded Noyes was the profound enlargement of the utopian vision that Oberlin embraced in its earliest years, transforming its mission and placing it on a historical trajectory different from nearly all of the era's other communitarian experiments.

As deeply religious Christians committed to saving the American West from the forces of sin and corruption, Oberlin's founders organized their colony around a school that would educate and send forth ministers and teachers to spread a millennial message between the Appalachian Mountains and Mississippi Valley. The colony's first settlers signed a covenant pledging to "feel that the interests of the Oberlin Institute are identified with ours, and do what we can to extend its influence to our fallen race."[7] They believed they could thereby usher in the Kingdom of God on earth. But their efforts took on a new, more socially disruptive meaning when, in 1835, the trustees of the Oberlin Collegiate Institute "resolved, that the education of the people of color is a matter of great interest, and should be encouraged and sustained in this institution."[8]

In the wake of this action, Oberlin, both school and town, became an experiment dedicated to radical racial egalitarianism. Oberlinians believed that they followed the teachings of Christianity in their embrace of racial equality and that, by ridding the world of the sins of slavery and color prejudice, they would bring about the redemption of humankind. Their intentionally interracial community sought to eradicate the bigotry that held back people of color from full realization of their religious, political, and personal freedoms, modeling the path to full racial equality. "Abolition was for a long time thought to be the sole idea and aim of Oberlin," wrote 1838 college graduate Michael Strieby, who organized his life around the quest for equal rights and social justice.⁹ Oberlin's students and residents joined together to make their sanctuary community famous—even notorious—in their challenge to the American racial hierarchy. Their pursuit of racial equality ultimately transmuted Oberlin's primary mission from sacred to secular.

This book takes seriously how the inhabitants of Oberlin, both white and black, related to and acted upon their changing understandings of racial justice across the long nineteenth century—from the community's founding in 1833 through the early 1920s. While many scholars have explored Oberlin's antebellum history, this study concludes not with the Emancipation Proclamation nor with the Union victory in the Civil War, nor even with the ratification of the Thirteenth, Fourteenth, and Fifteenth Amendments, but rather with the advent of legally enforceable residential segregation and the exclusion of people of color from the ranks of the town's elected officials in the early decades of the twentieth century. Although the community's founders certainly did not intend, and probably never anticipated, the imposition of a "color line" in Oberlin, its appearance after the Civil War changes our understanding of the Oberlin story.[10]

Our focus on the *town* of Oberlin also differentiates this work from several existing studies that trace the pioneering path of Oberlin College in desegregating higher education and preparing a cadre of African Americans for leadership in American society.[11] We note that, for the period we study, blacks rarely exceeded 5 percent of the students enrolled at Oberlin College, while fully 20 percent of the town's residents were persons of color in 1860, a proportion that has remained fairly steady up to the present. We look at the shifting politics and population of this decidedly multiracial community in an effort to document, analyze, and contextualize changes in racial attitudes and behavior across the long nineteenth century.

In our work, we have viewed blacks and whites as active participants in shaping their own histories, seeing in their interface a struggle for definition of themselves, the town in which they resided, and the meaning of racial equality. We seek to understand how and why the white successors to the leaders of "the town that started the Civil War" came to view black poverty as the result of personal failings, endorsed racially differentiated education in local public schools, and supported segregated army training facilities. We have attempted to listen carefully to the voices of local black activists, first in their critical efforts to mobilize abolitionists of both races before the Civil War and subsequently in their struggles to maintain a distinctive black political presence in the face of local whites' retreat from the active pursuit of racial equality.

This book examines nearly a century of Oberlin history. It begins with a new look at Oberlin's early years, finding in the different backgrounds of its black and white residents the roots of their divergent social, economic, and political trajectories. In the mid-1830s, the community's white founders decided to welcome people of color to their fledgling utopia. Over the next quarter century, Oberlin attracted individuals and families of color interested in education and activism in a community that boasted integrated common schools, an integrated central church, and a college open to both men and women, regardless of race. Unlike their white counterparts, who migrated mainly from New England and the mid-Atlantic states, most of Oberlin's early black settlers came from the Upper South. Many were impoverished former slaves, including fugitives who had escaped bondage illicitly, but others were longstanding free blacks or the relatively wealthy, mixed-race children of slaveholding fathers. With racial heterogeneity came other important distinctions. In particular, white and black Oberlinians understood their mutual commitment to antislavery activism in different terms. The black men and women who came to Oberlin in its early years prodded the town's white evangelicals to make good on their promises to defend the community against the incursions of those who would re-enslave people of color. In 1858, Oberlin's antislavery movement achieved an unprecedented degree of cross-racial unity in opposition to an effort by slave hunters to return freedom seeker John Price to bondage.

Oberlinians carried their militant abolitionism, separately and together, into the Civil War, which culminated in emancipation and, by 1870, the guarantee of equal civil and political rights under the Constitution, regardless of race. Yet these important victories masked patterns of racial inequality that persisted and often deepened in the postwar era—in Oberlin as elsewhere in the United States. Ironically, Oberlin's most accomplished people of color frequently left the confines of Oberlin when afforded new opportunities to pursue success and status in the broader world that opened to them during Reconstruction, particularly in Washington, D.C. For African Americans who remained in Oberlin and for new residents of color who came to town after the Civil War, however, an economic gap between the races remained and even expanded.

INTRODUCTION

The enfranchisement of black men proved a tool inadequate to the task of constructing full equality, particularly as the leaders of evangelical Oberlin took up temperance as their next battle, seeking, as they saw it, to free the sinful from the enslavement of alcohol. Increasingly conflating class, color, and respectability, the white leaders of Oberlin's temperance crusade unwittingly promoted a stigmatization of race, impervious even to the efforts of those people of color who sought vindication in the reclamation of respectability. By the beginning of the twentieth century, deteriorating national conditions, along with new "scientific" approaches to race that identified supposedly innate and unbridgeable differences, prompted white disillusionment with the goal of achieving racial equality even in Oberlin. As the college retreated from its commitments to social equality, the town's white leaders failed to heed local black voices that urged resistance to the rising tide of racial inequality. The "color line" came to Oberlin perhaps later than much of the country, but by 1920 its presence was undeniable.

To tell this story we have constructed a largely chronological narrative that draws on private correspondence, newspapers, pamphlets, organizational records, and memoirs, as well as more quantitative sources, especially census materials and tax lists. Our book consists of nine core chapters. The first traces the evolution of Oberlin's communitarian ideal from its evangelical origins through its embrace of radical racial egalitarianism in 1835, even in the absence of African American participants. Chapter 2 tells the stories of black people who moved to antebellum Oberlin, providing accounts of their individual experiences and offering a collective social profile of the town's early residents of color. Chapter 3 then examines how black and white people lived together in this antebellum community where most people avowed a commitment to social justice. Here the focus is on quantitative and qualitative evidence that illuminates the extent—and limits—of integration in a town proclaiming its racial radicalism. The participation of Oberlinians in the great struggle for abolition is the subject of the fourth chapter, including analysis of the town's most famous antislavery event, the Oberlin-Wellington Rescue. The involvement of two Oberlinians of color in John Brown's raid on Harpers Ferry also receives attention.

The fifth chapter traces the struggle for racial equality during and immediately after the Civil War, attending especially to the impact of the war at home in Oberlin, including its influence on the campaign for black suffrage.

Changes in the quest for racial equality following the achievement of political equality are the subject of the sixth chapter; during Reconstruction, the storied interracial unity of Oberlin receded into myth as political priorities differentiated by race came to the fore. Chapter 7 unpacks quantitative data teased from census records and tax lists to identify racially distinct patterns of economic achievement and social mobility after the Civil War, underscoring the impact of the departure of Oberlin's most successful people of color while demonstrating the deepening of economic inequality between whites and blacks in the late nineteenth century. Chapter 8 looks at how the temperance movement created a new local politics that, while pioneering a route to national prohibition, succeeded in the local marginalization of black political concerns at the same time that it racialized whites' perception of social respectability. The final chapter describes how, in the early twentieth century, the concerted efforts of Oberlin's small black elite to claim respectability for themselves—and thereby to foster the larger cause of equality for all African Americans—proved unsuccessful in the face of the national progress of a "color line" that branded blackness itself as suspect.

In seeking to answer the question of why Oberlin's experiment in radical racial egalitarianism failed, this book offers a number of reasons. First, the utopian vision formulated by white people in the absence of people of color naturalized white norms, unintentionally imposing limits on the possibilities for a truly multiracial vision. Although blacks and whites worked together effectively in the fight against slavery, they proved unable to construct an enduring egalitarian community. Second, in the wake of the Civil War, many of the most successful people of color in Oberlin took advantage of new opportunities to pursue careers outside of Oberlin, leaving behind less privileged African Americans who lacked the social and economic capital to succeed independently. Third, most black people came to Oberlin with fewer resources than their white counterparts, and they and their successors rarely found in Oberlin opportunities to close the original gap. Then, too, white political leaders in post–Civil War Oberlin failed to comprehend the importance of threats to equality that local black political organizers identified in the backlash against the quest for full racial equality. In addition, the temperance movement of the late nineteenth century reinforced class differences and promoted the racialization of respectability in Oberlin, thereby hobbling efforts for African American advancement. No single factor can account for Oberlin's retreat from its original commitment to radical racial

INTRODUCTION

egalitarianism, but in the end a combination of historical dynamics deflated and defeated the founders' utopian vision.

What can this Oberlin story tell us about the wider world? Perhaps most important, it can expand our understanding of how well-meaning people who believed themselves allies in a struggle for racial justice failed to comprehend their roles in the reinscription of racial inequality. The inability of Oberlin's white reformers to recognize their continuing racial privilege after the abolition of slavery and achievement of black male suffrage hindered the progress of local African Americans, deepening racial distrust, segregation, and inequality in the community. Whether consciously or not, white Oberlinians used their power to exert control over the town and its resources. Black people paid the price.

In 1926, Professor of Theology Kemper Fullerton, looking both forward and backward, urged Oberlin to reclaim its commitment to racial egalitarianism. He told listeners in the college chapel, "Racial antagonism is more menacing today in this country than at any time since the Civil War." He then pointedly challenged, "If the problem of the relationship of the white and colored race cannot be worked out in a just and satisfactory way in Oberlin, a place dedicated almost at its birth to the cause of emancipation, it cannot be worked out in the nation at large." He continued with an ominous prediction: "In that case, this problem can only mean a terror and a suffering to the nation at large which will be incalculable. The agony of the Civil War will be slight in comparison."[12] Today, at a moment when the Black Lives Matter movement collides with the pledge of a reactionary president to "Make America Great Again" by reinvigorating white supremacist tendencies in American culture, we find in Fullerton's words a chilling reminder of what is at stake.

Oberlin's quest for racial equality across the long nineteenth century began in utopian aspiration and ended in accommodation to the racist norms of mainstream American society. Yet the outcome was not inevitable, and neither is our future. We write as white twenty-first century residents of Oberlin who are committed to the principles of racial egalitarianism notwithstanding the setbacks and disappointments documented in this study. Although we do not believe that history offers up neat, formulaic lessons for later generations, we do believe that people can learn from past mistakes and missed opportunities. As beneficiaries of white privilege in our own lives, we aim to be as fully conscious as we possibly can be to the limits of our vision and to the enduring threats faced by persons of color. We must listen carefully to each other as we confront the structural obstacles that continue to block the path toward genuine racial equality in Oberlin and throughout the United States. As Bernice Johnson Reagon, inspired by the great social justice warrior Ella Baker, has written, "We who believe in freedom cannot rest."[13]

1

ENVISIONING UTOPIA

"Map of the Western Reserve including the Fire Lands in Ohio," published by William Sumner, 1826. Cleveland Public Library.

The location was inauspicious. Three decades after Ohio had achieved statehood in 1803, Russia Township in Lorain County was covered with little more than swamps, woods, and wildlife. Although Native Americans had resided in the area for millennia before Europeans "discovered" North America in the sixteenth century, by the middle of the eighteenth century the territory along the southern rim of Lake Erie between the Cuyahoga and Sandusky Rivers was nearly devoid of human habitation—the disastrous consequence of epidemic disease and military conflict.¹ In the decades following the War of Independence, Euro-Americans flooded across the Appalachian Mountains into the Northwest Territory, but few chose to settle in Russia Township, where dense clay made plowing difficult.² In 1830 the twenty-five square miles comprising the township boasted a total population of only 216 individuals residing in forty-one households.³

Beginning in 1833, however, hundreds of new migrants made their way to this desolate place to create the Oberlin colony. Motivated primarily by a deep sense of Christian purpose, these early colonists—initially all white—aspired to construct a utopian community that would serve as a model for the United States and the world. In 1835 they took another radical leap. In open defiance of the antiblack racism that pervaded the so-called free North as well as the slave South, they made a public commitment to racial egalitarianism and determined to include people of color as full participants in their social experiment. They would stand not only against slavery, but also for the eradication of color prejudice in their community and throughout American society.

Oberlin's story begins with John Jay Shipherd, a religious visionary and Oberlin's founding father. Born in 1802 into a well-to-do, politically prominent, white, slaveholding family in upstate New York, Shipherd from his youth desired to preach the gospel. In 1827 he took his first ministerial position in Shelburne, Vermont, and the next year he became general agent of the state's Sabbath School Union. In 1830 he decided on a bolder course.⁴ "[I]t now seems to me the finger of Providence points *westward* even to Mississippi's vast val[l]ey, which is fast filling up with bones which are dry, very dry," he explained to his parents. "The Lord of the harvest says 'Whom shall I send, & who will go for us?' The heart of your unworthy son responds: 'Here am I send me.'"⁵

Accompanied by his wife, Esther, and their young children, Shipherd departed for Ohio's Western Reserve in late September 1830. On their journey they stopped in Rochester, New York, where Charles Grandison Finney, the foremost evangelist of the Second Great Awakening, was leading a gigantic religious revival.⁶ On October 7 the family arrived by steamboat in Cleveland, Ohio. Before the week was out Shipherd found employment as minister of the First Presbyterian Church in nearby Elyria, a village of roughly seven hundred people.⁷

By his own admission, John Jay Shipherd was not a gifted preacher. Although during the summer of 1831 he engineered a religious revival in Elyria, his success proved short-lived. When he called his congregation to forsake the corrupting pleasures of intoxication in favor of the holy cause of temperance, several church members objected. They regarded imbibing alcohol as a right of frontier living, not a sin, and they undertook to drive Shipherd from his pulpit. By early fall he was out of a job.[8]

From these difficulties emerged Shipherd's plan to found a small, intentional community dedicated to the glorification of God and the Christian conversion of humankind. His main collaborator in this audacious enterprise was Philo P. Stewart, a friend from Shipherd's youth who, with his wife, had taken up residence in the Shipherds' house in 1832. Stewart, like Shipherd, felt called to help save the American West, and he had served as a missionary to the Choctaw Indians in Mississippi before moving to Elyria to prepare for ordination under Shipherd's supervision.[9] Taking inspiration from the late Pastor John Frederic Oberlin's celebrated ministry among the rural inhabitants of Ban de la Roche—a remote region of Alsace, France—Shipherd and Stewart imagined a religious colony of their own design in the wilds of Ohio.[10] "O! tho[ugh]t we, how would God be honored in the influence of his religion upon the world, if it were divorced from Mammon, & wedded to simplicity & true wisdom!" Shipherd wrote his brother in August 1832. "Now, said we, let us gather some of the right spirits, & plant them in the dark Valley, to give such an example as Pastor Oberlin's flock, & they will make our churches ashamed of their unholy alliances with earth."[11]

The colony would be named after Pastor Oberlin and its focus would be education. "To promote useful education at home & abroad," Shipherd explained, "schools shall be established . . . from the infant school up and as high as may be, at least, as high as the highest High School. The hope is that we may have, eventually, an institution which will afford the best education for the Ministry."[12]

Lacking financial resources but brimming with confidence in God's beneficence, Shipherd and Stewart researched possible sites for their projected community. They soon decided on a heavily forested section of Russia Township, roughly nine miles southwest of Elyria. The location that they selected was conveniently uninhabited, which meant that they would not encounter resistance from established residents who failed to share their utopian vision.[13] Shipherd and Stewart could, in effect, approach the territory as a "tabula rasa."

The land on which Shipherd and Stewart wanted to establish the Oberlin colony was not free for the taking, however. It was owned by Titus Street and Samuel Hughes, two merchants from New Haven, Connecticut, whose local sales agent was Eliphalet Redington, the postmaster of Amherst, Ohio, which bordered Russia Township. Although Redington was eager to sell the seven thousand acres in question, Shipherd and Stewart lacked sufficient funds to make the purchase. So they devised a two-pronged strategy for moving forward. Shipherd would go east to raise money, recruit colonists, and negotiate a deal with Street and Hughes. Stewart, with Redington's help, would prepare the site in Russia Township for human settlement in anticipation of Shipherd's success.[14]

Shipherd departed Elyria in late November 1832. He traveled by horseback through upstate New York and then on to New Haven, stopping regularly along the way to make appeals for financial support. The initial response was discouraging. After two months on the road, he had raised less than $200. Once he reached New Haven the situation brightened. Impressed by Shipherd's dedication—and lacking other prospective buyers—Street and Hughes offered him generous terms. On the condition that construction would begin promptly, they agreed to donate five hundred acres for an educational institution, and they further agreed to sell land to incoming settlers at the bargain rate of $1.50 per acre. The contract was signed on February 16, 1833.[15] From that date forward, Shipherd found it much easier to raise funds for the fledgling enterprise. By the time he returned to Ohio in September, contributions and financial pledges to the Oberlin colony totaled over $3,600.[16]

Equally important as raising money was recruiting colonists. Shipherd carried with him on his eastward journey a statement of intent and obligation that he asked prospective colonists to endorse. Remarkably similar to the documents that served as founding charters of Puritan communities in seventeenth-century New England, the Covenant of Oberlin Colony consisted of twelve propositions that together defined the mission of the colony and specified the obligations of its members. In sharp contrast to the individualistic and acquisitive values that dominated much of American society in the 1830s, the Oberlin covenant prescribed a profoundly communitarian and ascetic way of life.[17]

The covenant opened with dire observations about "the degeneracy of the church and the deplorable condition of our perishing world." To reverse this trend required concerted human effort, beginning in the Mississippi Valley (broadly conceived to include Ohio) and spreading across the globe. The covenant's first proposition identified the colony's main purposes: to glorify God and to do good in the world. Thereafter followed six propositions emphasizing the importance of self-denial and self-discipline. Although colonists would own property in their own names, they were expected to behave as if they possessed that property in common. They were to purchase and consume only what they needed for subsistence and basic comfort; any excess goods or income should be applied to the higher purpose of serving God and evangelizing others. All forms of extravagance were to be avoided. The "smoking[,] chewing and snuffing of tobacco" was expressly prohibited "unless it be necessary as a medicine," and colonists were expected to forego culinary indulgences such as tea, coffee, and anything else "simply calculated to gratify the palate." Likewise, colonists were to "renounce all the world's expensive and unwholesome fashions of dress" and to reside in plainly furnished houses. By living simply and frugally, the colonists would "add to our time, health, and means for service of the Lord."[18]

Alongside personal restraint, the covenant emphasized communal obligation. The eighth proposition declared that "we all as the body of Christ are members of one another" and specified as a collective responsibility the care of the ill, the poor, and those without family guardians. The ninth and tenth points highlighted the importance of education and tied the colony's fate to the success of the Oberlin Institute, the projected school for training ministers. Finally, the last two propositions reiterated the importance of piety, mutuality, and service to the Lord and pledged the signatories "to provoke each other to love and good works."[19]

Although to a twenty-first century reader the covenant's precepts may seem a prescription for rigid social conformity and the repression of both individual freedom and cultural diversity, it is important to recognize as well the optimistic and inspirational dimensions of the Oberlin colony's original mission. Like John Winthrop and other founders of the Massachusetts Bay colony two centuries earlier, Shipherd and Stewart sought to establish a "city upon a hill" that would serve as a model of virtue and generosity for humankind to emulate.

At the start of his eastward journey, Shipherd had hoped to convince "about 50 families of the Lord's peculiar people" to make the trek to northeastern Ohio to join the Oberlin experiment.[20] Although he fell short of this goal, the folks who signed on to the project did so with enthusiasm. One of the first persons to make a commitment was Theodore S. Ingersoll, a farmer living in rural Ogden, New York.[21] After learning of the successful negotiations with Street and Hughes, Ingersoll wrote Shipherd, "I have not sold my farm yet; but am making every calculation as if I had: trusting that the Lord will send somebody to buy in his own time which I shall be satisfied with." Ingersoll also sought to interest others in the enterprise. "I am now trying to obtain 2 or 3 females to go to Oberlin as school teachers & other useful employments," he reported. "I see the hand of the Lord in the work, & in the efforts I am making & believe it will go forward."[22]

Back in Ohio, Stewart and Redington prepared to welcome the anticipated colonists. They arranged to have land cleared, and they enlisted a "Board of Trust" to oversee the launch of the Oberlin Institute. The board consisted of leading citizens of Lorain County, and at a meeting on March 8, 1833, they hired Peter Pindar Pease of nearby Brownhelm Township to clear land for the Institute. In April, Pease and his family moved into a log cabin that he had constructed on colonial land, making them Oberlin's first residents.[23] The board subsequently agreed on the basic layout of the colony, applying a grid pattern with a public square at the center.[24]

By the time Shipherd himself took up residence in Oberlin with his wife and children in September 1833, the colony comprised about a dozen families as well as a few unattached individuals—perhaps fifty people in all.[25] The energy level was high. While women were attending to food preparation, childcare, and other family needs, men were busy felling trees, burning brush, and erecting houses. In the spring of 1834 a recently arrived female settler wrote to friends back east, "Things about us are all going on so briskly *one* cannot well feel *sleepy*."[26] As James Harris Fairchild explained in his memoir of growing up in Lorain County during this era, "The forests were a vast store house of material for building and fencing, and for fuel.... The pioneer found his best friend in the forest but the friendship was one of stern conditions, yielding its advantages only to the brave hearted."[27]

Oberlinians' weekly religious services and general assemblies followed the model of early New England. On October 15, 1833, the colonists voted to allocate the expenses involved in building roads and surveying land "according to the number of acres each Colonists [*sic*] shall have taken up." They also agreed to buy fifty acres for a parsonage and appointed a committee to draft a petition for an "act of incorporation for the Oberlin Colony." A week later they voted to petition relevant authorities for a post office, but they also decided that "Mr. Saxton be not admitted as a member of the colony."[28] Although the early colonists wanted to establish effective communication with the outside world, they also wished to draw a moral boundary around their community that would exclude persons they considered unsuitable for their righteous enterprise. (The precise nature of Mr. Saxton's offense remains obscure.)

Staffed by a lone teacher, the Oberlin Institute opened for instruction on December 3, 1833. Ten days later Shipherd wrote his father, "We now have 34 boarding scholars & expect 40 for the winter." He observed with satisfaction, "Nearly all our visitors (& they are not few) express surprise that so great a work has been wrought here in so short a time. God be praised!"[29]

In a prospectus issued the previous August, Shipherd declared, "The grand (but not exclusive) objects of the Oberlin Institute are the education of gospel ministers and pious school teachers." The school would be open to both males and females, and to both young and old. It would offer course work at the secondary and collegiate levels plus post-graduate training in theology. The pedagogy would be unusual: manual labor would complement instruction in the literary arts. "The system of education in this Institute will provide for the body and heart as well as the intellect," Shipherd explained, "for it aims at the best education of the *whole man.*" Male students would perform "a variety of agricultural, horticultural, and mechanical labors," while women would do work "suited to their sex," such as "[h]ousekeeping, the manufacture of wool, the culture of silk, the appropriate parts of gardening, particularly raising and fitting seeds for the market, the making of clothes, &."[30]

Manual labor would not only promote the spiritual and physical health of students; it also would help them earn the funds necessary to pay for an Oberlin education. For similar reasons, students would enjoy a twelve-week annual vacation during which they could pursue gainful employment, such as teaching school. By this means, Shipherd argued, "students may do much good . . . and become acquainted with *common things*; and earn money for their support in term time."[31]

Compared to the covenant of the Oberlin colony, Shipherd's prospectus for the Institute seems remarkably modern. Whereas the covenant pointed backward to colonial New England's ideal of an intensely religious and culturally homogeneous community of true believers, the prospectus pointed forward to an era when American colleges and universities would be considered engines of social mobility and democracy. A circular issued in March 1834 underscored the Institute's goal of accessibility: "The grand objects of the Institute are, to give the most useful education at the least expense of health, time, and money; and to extend the benefits of such education to both sexes; and all classes of community as far as its means will allow."[32] Yet in Shipherd's mind the purposes of the colony and the Institute were complementary. He wanted people of varied backgrounds to join the Oberlin enterprise, but he expected them, once they signed on, to practice and promote a shared set of millenarian Christian values. Out of diversity would emerge solidarity and selfless commitment to a common religious mission. The ultimate objective of the Institute's educational agenda was to hasten the arrival of God's Kingdom on Earth.

On December 23, 1833, the colonists approved two petitions to the Ohio state legislature. One memorial requested passage of an act to incorporate the colony as the Oberlin Society; the other asked for passage of an act to legally incorporate the school as the Oberlin Collegiate Institute.[33] The colonists sought to establish their related projects on a firm legal foundation. The legislature responded favorably to both memorials in late February 1834, but it inserted the term "Presbyterian" into the act of incorporation for the Oberlin Society, as if the Society were a church rather than a civic body.[34] Initially the colonists seemed happy enough with this outcome. Six months later, however, they sought to draw a sharper distinction between civil and religious authority within the community.

On August 19, 1834, Oberlinians gathered to form "The congregational Church of Christ at Oberlin," and in September they adopted "Articles of Faith & Covenant" that would bind all church members. This document encapsulated the evangelical, optimistic, and egalitarian dimensions of the Second Great Awakening. While it affirmed a belief in Adam's original sin, it emphasized the munificence of Christ's atonement and the potential for universal salvation. To achieve grace, the articles proclaimed, "the Sinner must be born-Again" by means of a "moral change, produced by the Influence of the holly [sic] Spirit operating on the mind through truth." Yet grace was available and accessible to everyone, not just to an elect few (as had been the belief of seventeenth-century Puritans). "[M]en are free & voluntary in all their conduct," the church's founders agreed, "and the offer of salvation is freely made to all men." In other words, although God ruled supreme, He was not only merciful but also an equal-opportunity savior. Consequently an individual's fate was in his or her own hands: "those who perish under the light of the Gospel perish by voluntarily rejecting its offers of eternal life."[35]

Significantly, the church was self-styled Congregational, rather than Presbyterian, the denominational term employed in the state charter for the colony. Yet the line separating Congregationalism and Presbyterianism was exceedingly thin in the Western Reserve in the early 1830s. Under a Plan of Union adopted in 1801, New England Congregationalists and Presbyterians had agreed to collaborate on missionary activities in the Northwest, and that agreement remained in place three decades later.[36] It should come as little surprise, then, that members of Oberlin's newly established Congregational Church voted to apply for admission to the Cleveland Presbytery.[37]

The decision to establish the Congregational Church reflected the founders' belief that the government erected under the state charter of the Oberlin Presbyterian Society was secular in character. But concern remained about the charter's adequacy as a basis for civil authority. In October 1834 a committee established by the Oberlin Society petitioned the state legislature for incorporation as a "Town and Village." While the Ohio Senate acted favorably on this request, the bill subsequently died in the House of Representatives. For the next two decades Oberlinians would muddle through on the basis of the original charter.[38]

Early Oberlin's spatial arrangement reflected the founders' communitarian ethos. The colony was square in shape, with each side nearly three miles long and the whole expanse comprising approximately fifty-five hundred acres. The colony was bisected by the North-South and East-West roads (today's Main and Lorain Streets) that crossed at the community's center. Within a half-mile of this intersection were clustered dozens of the residential dwellings on lots that were three to eighteen acres in size. Immediately to the southwest of the intersection was the public square, which in turn was bordered on the south by the Institute's combined boardinghouse and classroom building. Surrounding this compact town core were square and rectangular lots ranging in size from 40 to 169 acres. Most of the colony's thirty-five families (as of late 1834) owned both a small central lot and a larger plot of land on the periphery that they farmed for food and income.[39]

In the Oberlin covenant, colonists pledged to "hold in possession no more property than we believe we can profitably manage for God as his faithful stewards."[40] The implication was that nobody would accumulate great

"A Plan of Oberlin Colony," drawn by Hiram Davis, 1835. Oberlin College Archives.

wealth. How egalitarian was early Oberlin in practice? Surviving auditor's records provide data on the distribution of taxable property within the community in 1835. Leaving aside the Institute's holdings, a parcel reserved for a future parsonage, and land still held by the New Haven merchants Street and Hughes, there were 4,611 acres of real estate valued for tax purposes at $13,834. This real estate, along with personal estate assessed at $499, was distributed among sixty-three taxpaying units (sixty-one independent proprietors and two partnerships). Some people were considerably better off financially than others. The richest quintile (20 percent) of taxpayers owned 46 percent of the assessed property, while the poorest quintile owned only

1 percent.[41] By modern standards, however, Oberlin was quite egalitarian. In the United States today, the top 20 percent of households own nearly 90 percent of all household wealth.[42] Even by early nineteenth-century standards, wealth in early Oberlin was rather evenly distributed. The gini coefficient for Oberlin tax listings in 1835 was .46, compared to .56 in Chester County, Pennsylvania, in 1800–1802, and .78 in Boston, Massachusetts, in 1830.[43] (Gini coefficients range from 0 to 1—the smaller the coefficient, the more equal the distribution of values.)

Integral to the Oberlin colony's successful launch was the popularity of the Institute, which drew students from near and far, including Massachusetts, New Hampshire, Vermont, New York, Pennsylvania, Michigan, Ohio, and even—in one instance—Louisiana.[44] Yet high demand almost proved the Institute's undoing. In order to attract "the *common people*," tuition and fees were set lower than at preparatory schools in the East.[45] It was expected that subscriptions from benevolent donors as well as the value added by the manual labor required of students would allow the Institute to achieve financial stability. But during its first year of operations, more students flocked to the school than it could comfortably accommodate, while the revenue stream proved inadequate to meet basic expenses, including faculty salaries. By the fall of 1834 the trustees of the Institute faced a major fiscal crisis. They debated among themselves whether to scale back the Institute's mission and size in an effort to lower costs or, alternatively, to expand the enterprise in an attempt to generate more income and achieve economies of scale.[46] A majority of the board favored the latter strategy, and in late October the Institute admitted its first students at the collegiate level.[47] A month later John Jay Shipherd departed on a journey to hire more faculty—as well as a president—and to raise additional funds for the school.[48]

Shipherd's trip lasted six months and resulted in a fundamental redefinition of the colony's utopian mission. Seizing opportunities to put the Institute on a firmer financial footing, Shipherd entered into agreements that added racial egalitarianism to the mix of evangelical Christianity and communitarianism that had informed his original vision for the colony. As a consequence, not only the Institute but also the community at large became an experiment in racial integration based on the then-radical idea that people of color were equal to whites in both natural ability and human rights.[49]

Upon leaving Oberlin in November 1834, Shipherd headed toward Cincinnati, the largest city in Ohio and—more importantly for Shipherd's purposes—the home of Lane Seminary.[50] Chartered in 1829, Lane Seminary, like the Oberlin Institute, sought to save the American West from sin by preparing young men for the ministry. Lane's president was Lyman Beecher, a renowned Congregational minister from New England who stood alongside Charles Grandison Finney as a leader of the Second Great Awakening. Although Beecher's fame had attracted large amounts of money and large numbers of students to Lane, when Shipherd reached Cincinnati in December 1834 he found the school embroiled in controversy.[51]

Among the students who had enrolled at Lane Seminary with the intention of studying under Beecher was the charismatic Theodore Dwight Weld. Born in 1803—a year after Shipherd—Weld had experienced a spiritual rebirth in 1826 upon hearing Finney preach in Utica, New York.[52] Thereafter Weld threw himself into spreading the Lord's message and promoting religiously inspired social reforms, including temperance and manual-labor education.[53] In late 1832 he embraced the cause of the immediate abolition of American slavery. Influenced by the British abolitionist Charles Stuart and the American abolitionist William Lloyd Garrison, among others, Weld came to believe that slavery was not merely an oppressive system of labor but a vicious sin that contravened the holy order of the universe.[54] "No condition of birth, no shade of color, no mere misfortune of circumstances, can annul that birth-right charter, which God has bequeathed to every being upon whom he has stamped his own image, by making him a *free moral agent*," Weld reasoned. "He who robs his fellow man of this tramples upon right, subverts justice, outrages humanity, unsettles the foundations of human safety, and sacrilegiously assumes the prerogative of God."[55]

At Weld's initiative, over the course of eighteen evenings in February 1834, dozens of students at Lane publicly debated how good Christians should address the sin of American slavery. More particularly, they framed the issue as a choice between, on the one hand, support for immediate abolition and, on the other hand, support for "the doctrines, tendencies, and measures of the American Colonization Society," which included the removal of free blacks to Africa and—at most—the very gradual emancipation of slaves. After the first nine evenings of debate, a vote was taken on the question "Ought the people of the Slaveholding States to abolish Slavery immediately?" The students voted "yes" by an overwhelming margin. After the next nine evenings of debate, all but one answered "no" to the question of whether the American Colonization Society was "worthy of the patronage of the Christian public."⁵⁶ But the Lane students did not stop there. In early March they formed the Anti-Slavery Society of Lane Seminary, and over the next several months they raised the banner of immediate abolition and organized a lyceum, library, and several schools to benefit Cincinnati's black population.⁵⁷

While Garrison and other "immediatists" celebrated the Lane students' actions as noble and inspiring, the local gentlemen who dominated Lane Seminary's Board of Trustees viewed them as scandalous and inflammatory. Cincinnati bordered the slave state of Kentucky, and Cincinnati businessmen profited from their commercial dealings with slaveholders. Moreover, the city had a history of racial conflict. Over the course of several days in August 1829, white mobs had viciously attacked African Americans, prompting hundreds to flee for their safety.⁵⁸ Members of Lane's board considered abolitionist agitation against the "peculiar institution" unpatriotic and threatening to the social order. President Beecher, a colonizationist, sought to quiet the controversy at Lane, but while he was away from campus on a fundraising trip during the summer and early fall of 1834 the trustees took matters into their own hands. After circulating a report highly critical of the students in August, the board on October 10 issued an ultimatum: the students must either stop protesting slavery and stop helping local blacks, or they must leave Lane.⁵⁹

Within a week thirty-nine students announced their decision to withdraw, and others subsequently followed their lead.⁶⁰ "Free discussion being a duty, is consequently a right, and as such is inherent and inalienable," the so-called Lane Rebels explained. "It is *our* right. It *was* before we entered Lane Seminary: privileges we might and did relinquish. . . . But this *right* the institution 'could neither give nor take away.'"⁶¹

News of the upheaval at Lane was the reason Shipherd headed first to Cincinnati in late 1834, rather than to New York or New England. He was himself an abolitionist—he belonged to the Western Reserve Anti-Slavery Society—and also an admirer of Theodore Dwight Weld, whom he had tried unsuccessfully to woo to Oberlin as a mathematics professor the previous summer.⁶² On his arrival in Cincinnati, Shipherd was warmly welcomed into the home of Asa Mahan, a local minister and the only Lane trustee to side with the Rebels.⁶³ Shipherd learned from Mahan—if he did not already know—that the prominent New York merchants Arthur and Lewis Tappan had offered to support the Rebels financially wherever they chose to pursue their training after Lane. For the time being, many of them were studying together under an *ad hoc* arrangement in nearby Cumminsville, Ohio. Shipherd promptly invited the Rebels to relocate to Oberlin, along with Mahan—to whom Shipherd offered the Institute's presidency—and John Morgan, a professor whom the Lane board had fired for his abolitionist sympathies.[64] In a letter to his brother, Shipherd observed, "I trust God has put my hand on a golden chain which I shall be able to link to Oberlin & thro' it bind many souls in holy allegiance to our Blessed King."[65]

The Lane Rebels, Mahan, and Morgan had their own agenda. They informed Shipherd that they would accept his invitation on two conditions: first, that the Oberlin Institute pledge not to interfere with the right to free speech, and second, that the Institute open its doors to blacks as well as whites. Shipherd agreed without hesitation. The Rebels also raised the possibility of recruiting Charles Grandison Finney to join them in Oberlin as professor of theology. Again Shipherd responded positively. Having thus concluded negotiations in Cincinnati on a very promising note, he and Asa Mahan departed for New York City in mid-December to solicit money from the Tappans and other potential benefactors, and to entreat Finney to transfer his base of operations from the nation's largest metropolis to a fledgling community in the backwoods of northeastern Ohio.[66]

Although Shipherd was general agent for the Oberlin Institute and the most respected figure in the Oberlin colony, he acted without institutional authority in agreeing to the terms set by Mahan, Morgan, and the Lane Rebels. He quickly sought official sanction for his efforts. In a letter dated December 15, 1834, he asked Nathan P. Fletcher, a fellow trustee of the Institute, at the next board meeting "to secure the passage of the following resolution, viz. 'Resolved, That students shall be received into this Institution *ir*respective of color.'" Shipherd supplied a two-part rationale for the motion. His first reason was moral: "because it is *right prin*ciple, & *God* will bless us in doing right." His second reason was financial: "because thus doing right we gain the confidence of benevolent & able men who probably will furnish us some thousands." Without passage of the resolution, he added, "Bros. Mahan & Morgan will not accept our invitations." Equally important, Shipherd wrote that he himself would quit working for Oberlin if the board rejected his motion: "I should have *no heart* to labor for the upbuilding of our Seminary, believing that the curse of God would come upon us as it has upon the Lane Seminary, for its unchristian abuse of the poor Slave."[67]

To Shipherd's mind, the Cincinnati agreement was a modern miracle. When reports of the deal reached Oberlin, however, many of his heretofore-loyal followers reacted with dismay and alarm. "A general panic & dispair [sic] seized the Officers[,] Students & Colonists," Nathan P. Fletcher later recalled. "P. P. Stewart . . . at once proclaimed Br[other] Shipherd Mad!! . . . [D]espondency brooded with Sable distrust o[v]er almost every Soul, because the Christian patrons made it a condition in their donations that Color[e]d people should stand equal in the privileges of the Institution—many students said that they would leave & Br[other] Stewart s[ai]d he would not stay."[68]

The Board of Trustees scheduled a meeting for January 1, 1835. On December 29, the president of the board—the Reverend John Keep of Cleveland—decided to move the meeting's location from Oberlin to Elyria.[69] A committed abolitionist, Keep sought to insulate the trustees' deliberations from the racial fears roiling the colony.[70] On the eve of the meeting, two petitions circulated among Oberlinians. One petition declared, "We, Students of the O. C. Institute, hereby certify our view as to the practicability of admitting persons of color to the Institution under existing circumstances." Beneath this statement were two columns, one labeled "In favour" and the other "Against." A total of fifty-eight students (thirty-seven males and twenty-one females) signed their names to this document: twenty-six in support of admitting blacks and thirty-two in opposition.[71]

The other petition, signed by colonists as well as students, asked the board to meet in Oberlin, rather than Elyria, in order "that your deliberation may be heard and known on the great and important question in contemplation." At the same time they declared that their minds remained open to Christian persuasion. "We feel for our Black brethren," they wrote. "We feel to want your counsels and instructions—we want to know what is duty—and God assisting us we will lay aside every prejudice and do as we shall be led to believe God would have us do."[72] Among the thirty-two Oberlinians (all male) who signed the second memorial were seven students who listed themselves "In favour" and three students who listed themselves "Against" the admission of blacks on the first petition. Evidently Oberlinians were not only divided between themselves but, in some cases, even *within* themselves over the question of whether they should permit persons of color to join their virtuous community.[73]

The trustees were no more united on this point than the students and colonists at large. At the meeting on January 1—held in Elyria, as Keep directed—the seven board members in attendance voted unanimously to appoint Mahan president and Morgan professor of mathematics and natural philosophy. But they refused to grant Shipherd's "wish that students may be received into this Institution irrespective of color."[74] According to Nathan P. Fletcher, who supported Shipherd's proposal, Philo P. Stewart's "wicked conduct" poisoned the board's deliberations.[75] By an undisclosed margin, the trustees voted "That this Board do not feel prepared till they have other and more definite information on the subject to give a pledge respecting the course they will pursue in regard to the education of people of color: wishing that this Institution should be on the same ground in respect to the admission of students with other similar institutions of our land[.]"[76]

Although they were comfortable educating women alongside men, a majority of the board hesitated to challenge the racial hierarchy of contemporary American society by educating blacks alongside whites. The trustees wanted to save the American West, but most of them wanted to do so only for white Euro-Americans like themselves, not for non-white "others."

News of the board's recalcitrance reached Shipherd in New York City in mid-January, by which time he had reached a tentative accord with the Tappans and other wealthy benefactors to bankroll the Institute on the condition that Finney serve as its professor of theology, an appointment which the great evangelist would accept if assured that the faculty (not the trustees) would exercise internal control over the school and that he could spend the winter months away from Oberlin. But the whole arrangement would unravel if the board blocked the admission of black students.[77] In a letter dated January 19, Shipherd bluntly informed his fellow trustees, "It should be known that br[other] Finney is in favor of educating at Oberlin colored persons who are worthy, & indeed, he says he would not join any institution where they were excluded—so says br[other] Mahan—so says br[other] Morgan—so say I." Shipherd added that he found the board's failure to endorse his proposed resolution "surprising & grievous to my soul." Yet he sought to avoid a full-scale confrontation by reassuring members of the board that the admission of *suitable* blacks would not trigger revolutionary upheaval. "I did not desire you to hang out an abolition flag or fill up with filthy stupid negroes," he explained, "but I did desire that you should say you would not reject promising youth who desire to prepare for usefulness because God had given them a darker hue than others."[78]

Seeking to win over the board through Christian persuasion, Shipherd presented his case at some length. For the most part he emphasized the religious basis, not the economic benefits, of admitting students of color to the Institute. Thus he posited, "*All Christians* agree that [colored youth] ought to be educated & fitted for the full privileges of freemen." The question was how to achieve this goal most efficiently—by educating them "in connexion with whites" or "in a separate school." In support of an integrationist approach, Shipherd cited the absence of available black colleges and enumerated a handful of precedents for the admission of students of color at predominantly white institutions—albeit only on an occasional basis.[79]

While Shipherd acknowledged the social reality of color prejudice, he regarded such prejudice as morally reprehensible and therefore not a legitimate basis for institutional policy. Most boldly, he openly addressed the possibility of black and white students engaging in interracial romantic relationships. Without defending "amalgamation" (as interracial sex was then called), he minimized the threat it posed to the Institute and its reputation. "There is no more danger of intermarriages among our white & colored youth than there is of fornication among our white sexes," he declared, "& yet we *risk* that sin among them to gain important ends."[80]

For Shipherd the issue of racial prejudice was deeply personal. "I was bro[ugh]t up with blacks & slaves & would choke with thirst before I would drink from the same cup as them," he confessed, "but God has shown me that it was an *unholy pride* & *sinful predjudice* [sic] which I dare not cherish longer through fear of his displeasure." Having seen the light, he would not retreat into the darkness of bigotry. "I do not believe that God will bless us if we suffer a *worldly expediency* to control us so far as to withhold the right of education at our Seminary from our colored brothers," he concluded. "If my dear brethren of the Board cannot consent to this, I cannot *conscientiously* consent to labor any longer for the building of the O. C. Institute. If *right, eternal right*, its glory, must forsake it[,] *I* must forsake it too."[81]

On January 27, Shipherd dispatched a separate missive to the Oberlin colony as a whole. Framed like a sermon, this "pastoral letter" recalled the utopian sensibility of the covenant. "[P]ermit me to exhort you to be 'the Lord's *peculiar* people zealous of good works,'" Shipherd wrote. "I would not have you *needlessly* singular, but I would have you actually singular, even among the churches, if they continue as they now are. Far better to be unlike them, and all on earth, than to be unlike Christ." Shipherd beseeched the colonists to act bravely in order to speed Christ's Second Coming: "Fear not brethren to *lead* in doing right. There must be a mighty overturning before he whose right it is shall rule over all nations; & the servants of God will have to turn much upside down as Paul did before all will be right."[82]

Moving from this general summons to the specific concerns at hand, Shipherd offered twenty reasons for welcoming people of color into the Institute and the colony. The first reason drew upon the colonizationists' rationale for the removal of blacks to Africa: "They are needed as ministers, missionaries, & Teachers for the land of their fathers, & for their untaught, injured, perishing brethren of our country." Subsequent reasons, however, echoed the abolitionists' arguments for immediate emancipation: "God made them of one blood with us. . . . They are our *neighbors*, & whatsoever we would they should do unto us, we must do unto them or become guilty before God." As he had in his letter to the Board of Trustees, Shipherd explicitly addressed the question of miscegenation. "Intermarriage with the whites is not asked, & need not be feared," he assured the colonists. "None of you will be compelled to receive them into your families, unless like Christ, the love of your neighbor compel you to." Again, religious logic was paramount. Only near the end of his list did Shipherd mention the financial implications of the decision, and he argued that material factors reinforced the moral case for admitting blacks: "The men of money which would make our institution most useful, cannot be obtained if we reject our colored brother."[83]

In his pastoral letter to the colony, Shipherd announced publicly what he had repeatedly conveyed in private since first striking the deal with Mahan, Morgan, and the Lane Rebels in Cincinnati: his future involvement with Oberlin depended on the Institute's acceptance of students of color. "Such is my conviction of duty in this case," he wrote, "that I cannot labor for the enlargement of the Oberlin Collegiate Institute, if our brethren in Jesus Christ must be rejected because they differ from us in color." The choice facing the trustees and the colonists was stark. Either accept racial integration or bid farewell to Reverend Shipherd, the colony and Institute's founding father.[84]

The board reassembled on February 9, 1835. This time it met in Oberlin, rather than Elyria, and nine trustees attended—two more than on January 1. After an opening prayer, the trustees debated the Institute's admissions policy, failed to reach a consensus, prayed again, and adjourned until the next morning.[85] On February 10 they made the fateful decision that would open the Oberlin Institute to African Americans and align both the school and the community with the cause of immediate abolitionism. But the board stopped short of approving Shipherd's original proposal to admit students "*ir*respective of color"—a policy already adopted by the Oneida Institute in upstate New York.[86] Instead, by a 5–4 margin, the trustees voted "That the question in respect to the admission of Students into the Seminary be in all cases left to the decision of the Faculty & to them be committed also the internal management of its concerns."[87]

In adopting this formulation, the trustees affirmed their respect for the faculty's autonomous power and authority over most institutional operations—Finney's foremost condition for taking up an appointment at Oberlin—while they dodged Shipherd's arguments for racial equality. Yet they could not ignore the plight of African Americans completely. In a separate resolution, the trustees cited "fears entertained on the one hand [that our colored population] will be left unprovided for, as to the means of a proper education, and on the other that they will in unsuitable numbers be introduced into our Schools, and thus in effect forced into the Society of whites." The board did not want Oberlin to become too closely identified with blacks, much less to become a predominantly black school. The most the trustees were willing to proclaim officially was "That the education of the people of color is a matter of great interest and should be encouraged & sustained in this Institution."[88]

That was enough to satisfy Shipherd, Mahan, Morgan, Finney, the Lane Rebels, and the Tappan brothers.[89] But the board chose not to announce in the antislavery press that blacks would be welcome to attend the Institute. Instead, on February 12, Keep sent the *New York Evangelist* a short statement publicizing the appointment of Finney and Morgan and referring vaguely to "Other important arrangements . . . to carry into effect the great designs of those benevolent individuals in your city who have given *substantial* proof of their sympathies for the great west, in their pecuniary benefactions to Oberlin."[90]

Three months elapsed between the trustees' meeting in February and the first appearance of Lane Rebels in Oberlin. The Rebels were in no rush because the Institute was out of session and they had other matters to pursue. In late April, fifteen Rebels participated in the initial meeting of the Ohio Anti-Slavery Society in Putnam. Though not present, Asa Mahan and Charles Grandison Finney—both now identified with the Oberlin Institute—were appointed officers of the society.[91] Mahan sent the Anti-Slavery

Society a letter endorsing its goals as "the principles of eternal truth and rectitude." "I am an abolitionist," he declared openly. "In every station and relation in life, I would be known as such, while a single slave groans beneath the oppressor's yoke, or bleeds beneath the oppressor's scourge."[92] Although Shipherd had assured the Institute's trustees that he "did not desire you to hang out an abolition flag," the man whom he had selected to head the school was eager to do just that.

Mahan and his family took up residence in Oberlin in early May. Shipherd returned to the colony later in the month, and Finney and Morgan followed in June. Attracted by Finney's appointment as well as the low cost of tuition, roughly two hundred prospective students converged on the Institute before the summer term began in early July.[93] The colony was hard pressed to absorb the invasion. "[T]he Colonists, and every family here, practice much self-denial in order to accommodate as many [students] as possible," observed a visitor in mid-August, adding that a building boom promised to relieve the situation. "The square is surrounded by about 40 neat frame houses, painted white, and many are erecting," he reported. "The college buildings are in progress as fast as possible. Besides a temporary building, they have completed a large boarding-house, two and a half stories high, and another building, 80 by 36 feet, three stories high, with two wings, will be completed in the next month. Another, 80 by 40 feet, to be called Colonial Hall is erecting."[94]

Not all Oberlinians embraced the new regime. Although Philo P. Stewart welcomed Shipherd back to the colony with—in Shipherd's words—"a kiss which I never saw him give to his wife," two other trustees who (like Stewart) had opposed the admission of black students resigned their positions.[95] Yet the grand inauguration of Mahan, Finney, and Morgan on July 1, 1835, signaled the return of harmony to the Institute and the colony. The ceremony took place on the central square under a huge tent provided by Finney's New York supporters and topped by a banner proclaiming "HOLINESS UNTO THE LORD." Mahan and Finney each addressed the assembled multitude. Mahan offered a critique of classical education and argued that students would be better served by learning "practical, available knowledge." Finney focused on the failings of contemporary ministerial education. "Young men now come out from the seminaries with very little knowledge of the forms of heresies now prevailing," he complained. "They are more like *great babies* than like men harnessed for the work of the Lord." Oberlin's theological department would aim higher.[96]

Although neither Mahan nor Finney raised the issue of racial equality in his inaugural address, the process of "abolitionizing" Oberlin was already well under way. A week before, on June 25, a large gathering of students, faculty, and townspeople had founded the Oberlin Anti-Slavery Society. The decision to launch the society grew out of a midday "concert of prayer" dedicated "to the down-trodden people of color." "We did not 'fast for strife nor debate;' but to 'undo the heavy burdens and let the oppressed go free,'" Reverend Shipherd explained in a letter to the *New York Evangelist*. "In the afternoon we formed an Anti-Slavery Society, enrolling 230 members—nearly all who were present. Indeed, when the motion to resolve ourselves into an Anti-Slavery Society was decided by rising, the congregation came up en masse, arm and soul to this good work of God." Only one person remained seated.[97]

The founders of the Oberlin Anti-Slavery Society promptly adopted as their own—nearly verbatim—the constitution drafted by Theodore Dwight Weld for the Anti-Slavery Society at Lane Seminary. Remarkably progressive by the standards of the era, this document not only called for the immediate end of slavery, but also for the repudiation of color prejudice and the attainment of racial equality in the United States. "Our object," the constitution boldly proclaimed, "is the immediate emancipation of the whole colored race within the United States: The emancipation of the slave from the oppression of the master, the emancipation of the free colored man from the oppression of public sentiment, and the elevation of both to an intellectual, moral, and political equality with the whites."[98]

According to the constitution, chattel slavery should be abolished because it violated the slave's God-given rights as "a moral agent, the keeper of his own happiness, the executive of his own powers, the accountable arbiter of his own choice." It also destroyed family relations among the enslaved and "expose[d] to pollution a million of females." Indeed, as a system of oppression, slavery encouraged baneful behavior by everyone caught up in its web of iniquity. "[Slavery] excites the enmity of the oppressed against the oppressor, goads to desperation and revenge, provokes insurrection, and perils public safety," the constitution warned. At the same time, "It tends to blunt the sensibilities of all who exercise authority over the slave, and to transform them into tyrants." The persistence of human bondage in the United States contradicted the nation's founding principles and "expose[d] the nation to the judgments of God."[99]

Even more radical than the document's attack on slavery was its critique of color prejudice. Most white northerners in the mid-1830s opposed human bondage in principle yet recoiled at the prospect of sharing equal rights and opportunities, much less the same accommodations, with people of color.[100] The state of Ohio prohibited blacks from voting, prevented them from serving on juries or testifying against whites, and barred them from attending public schools.[101] The founders of the Oberlin Anti-Slavery Society openly challenged this status quo. By their account, although presently "impoverished, disfranchised, and trodden into the dust," blacks were not naturally inferior to whites; they were instead the blameless victims of white oppression. The Oberlin Anti-Slavery Society's constitution took moral aim at the injustice of American racism (though it did not employ that modern-day term). "It is a part of the tyrant to inflict penalties upon the innocent; and when the victim is powerless, friendless, long oppressed, and already heart broken, it is the part of a fiend," the document declared. "We cannot hold our peace, while these, our brethren, are immolated upon the altar of prejudice and pride."[102]

What was to be done? The constitution emphasized that the interrelated goals of abolishing slavery and eliminating color prejudice could only be rightfully achieved by peaceful and lawful means. It specifically denied any intention of encouraging slave rebellions, making war on the slave states, or even appealing for "congressional interference" with states' rights. "Even if Congress had power to abolish slavery," the document explained, "our principles 'show us a more excellent way.'" That way involved "approaching the minds of slave holders with the truth, in the spirit of the Gospel" and making "appeals to [their] pecuniary interests." It also involved mobilizing popular opinion and "concentrating public sentiment against the system."[103]

In making their case for radical change, the founders of the Oberlin Anti-Slavery Society sought to defuse fears that abolition would unleash social chaos. "By immediate emancipation, we do not mean that the slaves shall be turned loose upon the nation to roam as vagabonds and aliens," the constitution assured an imagined white audience, "nor [t]hat they shall be instantly invested with all political rights. . . . But we do mean—that instead of being under the unlimited control of a few irresponsible masters, they shall receive the protection of law." Upon emancipation, ex-slaves would "be employed as free laborers, fairly compensated" and enabled "to worship God according to the dictates of their consciences, and to seek an intellectual and moral equality with whites." The process would require "benevolent and disinterested supervision," and it would take time. But the result would be a fundamental and thoroughgoing transformation of the American social order.[104]

Most of the 230 people who joined the Oberlin Anti-Slavery Society at its inception were newcomers to the colony. They included Asa and Mary Mahan and their two daughters; Charles Grandison and Lydia Finney and one of their children; fourteen Lane Rebels; and several dozen new students planning to attend the Institute. Yet at least eighty veteran students and colonists (including children) also enrolled in the Oberlin Anti-Slavery Society. Significantly, fully one-third of the students who had expressed opposition to the admission of black students in late December now endorsed the abolitionist cause. So did Philo P. Stewart. In the space of six months, these dedicated white evangelicals had overcome their antiblack prejudice and embraced the vision of a racially integrated school and a racially egalitarian society. In the summer of 1835 Oberlin—the Institute and the colony together—was reborn as a Christian community explicitly dedicated to the principle of racial equality.[105]

Notably absent from the roster of the Oberlin Anti-Slavery Society's founders was Theodore Dwight Weld, the erstwhile leader of the Lane Rebels. Setting aside his theological studies, Weld had accepted an appointment as agent and lecturer for the American Anti-Slavery Society, and throughout 1835 he toured Ohio and eastern Pennsylvania spreading the abolitionist message. His reputation as an orator attracted sizable audiences wherever he went, but his radical views often provoked violent opposition. About his experience speaking at a church in Circleville, Ohio—near the center of the state—Weld reported, "At the second lecture, the mob gathered and threw eggs and stones through the window. One of the stones was so well aimed that it struck me on the head and for a moment stunned me. Paused a few minutes till the dizziness had ceased, and then went on and completed my lecture."[106]

In November Weld came to Oberlin, where he received a much warmer reception. Over the course of three weeks he lectured nightly to large and enthusiastic, though physically uncomfortable, audiences. "Our meetings are held in one of the new buildings," he wrote Lewis Tappan. "It is neither plastered nor lathed and the only seats are rough boards thrown upon blocks;

and you may judge something of the interest felt at Oberlin on the subject of abolition when I tell you that from five to six hundred males and females attend every night, and sit shivering on the rough boards without fire these cold nights, without any thing to lean back against, and this too until nine o[']clock."[107]

Two decades later, James Harris Fairchild, a freshman at the Oberlin Institute in 1835, still marveled at the intensity of Weld's presentation. "Weld came among us to lay open the treasures of his anti-slavery magazine—to equip the young warriors for their winter campaign; and more than twenty long, dark November evenings he illuminated with the flashes of his genius and power," Fairchild remembered in 1856. "Under such influences, Oberlin became . . . thoroughly 'abolitionized,' whatever it may have been before. Students, and Faculty, and citizens, set themselves vigorously about their appropriate work."[108] During the winter of 1835–1836, dozens of Oberlin students went forth from the colony to speak and organize against slavery and to teach in black schools.[109] Oberlin and abolitionism became inextricably linked in the public mind.

Yet there was one major element missing from Oberlin's commitment to racial egalitarianism in 1835: the involvement of people of color. The founding members of the Oberlin Anti-Slavery Society were all white. When Theodore Dwight Weld gave his fiery lectures at Oberlin in the fall of 1835, quite likely only two African Americans resided in the colony. Would people of color come to Oberlin in substantial numbers just because white people said they were welcome? If blacks came, would whites and blacks live together in harmony? Could Oberlinians resist the hegemonic racism of American society, or would they bow to mainstream cultural, political, and economic pressures? It was one thing to envision a racially egalitarian utopia; it was another thing to turn that vision into a viable, lived reality.

❋2❋

THE ARRIVAL OF AFRICAN AMERICANS

When the trustees of the Oberlin Institute agreed to open the school to qualified applicants regardless of race in 1835, no persons of color resided in the colony. Yet over the next twenty-five years blacks moved to Oberlin in ever increasing numbers. By 1860, African Americans comprised 20 percent of the town's total population—five times the proportion in Philadelphia, and more than ten times the proportion in New York City and Boston. This chapter examines how and why people of color came to Oberlin, describes their initial impressions and early involvement in community life, and compares the economic profiles of the town's black and white populations at mid-century. In the space of a generation, Oberlin evolved from an all-white enclave composed mainly of migrants from New York and New England into one of the most socially diverse communities in the United States.

Evidently unaware of the precedent set by the Oneida Institute in upstate New York, Reverend John Keep in January 1836 wrote philanthropist Gerrit Smith that the Oberlin Institute was "the only institution in our Country . . . where *prejudice* is so far conquered that colored people are admitted, to the full enjoyment of all & the same privileges as others." "Among the present students," Keep added, "are two, from Virginia of color, & they are as well received, & treated as others."[1] The students to whom he referred were the brothers Gideon and Charles Langston, probably the first African Americans ever to set foot in Russia Township.[2]

Born free in 1809 and 1817, respectively, Gideon and Charles were mixed-race sons of Ralph Quarles, a wealthy white Virginian planter, and Lucy Jane Langston, a former slave manumitted by Quarles in 1806.[3] The brothers grew up on their father's plantation in Louisa County in the Virginia Piedmont. Their parents' relationship, though not legally recognized, was public knowledge, and Quarles openly embraced his paternal responsibilities. He not only taught Gideon and Charles how to raise tobacco, but also personally tutored them in the fundamentals of the liberal arts. Boldly transgressing the hardening lines of Virginia's race-based caste system in the early nineteenth century, Quarles raised Gideon and Charles to become gentlemen farmers like himself.[4]

But as persons of color Gideon and Charles Langston could not follow in their father's footsteps after his death in early 1834. In his will, Quarles bequeathed the bulk of his estate—including over two thousand acres plus bank stock but not his slaves—to Gideon, Charles, and their younger brother John in equal shares.[5] Only Gideon was old enough at the time to claim his portion, however, and rather than remain in Virginia, where opportunities for free blacks had contracted rapidly since Nat Turner's rebellion in 1831, the three brothers embarked for Chillicothe, Ohio, where their half-brother William Langston was already established.[6]

When Gideon, Charles, and John Langston reached Chillicothe in the fall of 1834, African Americans comprised roughly one-tenth of the town's population and boasted a rich tradition of collective action. Although concentrated in low-paying occupations, local persons of color managed to support two black churches (African Methodist Episcopal and African Baptist) and their own school. In the summer of 1834, they founded the Chillicothe Colored Anti-Slavery Society, an early auxiliary of the American Anti-Slavery Society.[7]

Most likely Gideon and Charles learned about the Oberlin Institute's adoption of a color-blind admissions policy from other members of Chillicothe's black community. Leaving younger brother John in the care of a white family with longstanding ties to their parents, Gideon and Charles made their way to Oberlin in time to enroll for the fall term that began in early September 1835. They entered the Institute's preparatory department—akin to secondary school—and participated in the manual labor regimen required of all Oberlin students. They worked, studied, and dined alongside white students without causing a stir.[8]

At some point in late 1835 or early 1836, Charles Langston signed the constitution of the Oberlin Anti-Slavery Society.[9] Both he and Gideon joined Oberlin's Congregational Church in March 1836.[10] A few months later, when the Institute opened a satellite preparatory school in Sheffield, Ohio, the Langston brothers transferred to that location. Charles would return to Oberlin for further study between 1841 and 1843, and younger brother John would arrive in 1844.[11] Subsequently both would play prominent roles in Oberlin's campaign against slavery. In 1835–1836, however, Gideon and Charles Langston were noteworthy mainly for the extent to which they did *not* stand out in a community seeking to transcend the racial prejudice of the wider society.

The third student of color to come to Oberlin was James Bradley, a refugee from the Lane Seminary. His background was markedly different from the Langstons' comfortable upbringing. According to a brief autobiography that he wrote in 1834, Bradley had been born around 1805 "somewhere in Africa, far back from the sea." At a very young age he was stolen from his mother, transported to the African coast, and then shipped across the Atlantic Ocean to Charleston, South Carolina, where he was put up for sale. After a short stint with a different owner, he was bought by "a Mr. Bradley, by whose name," he explained, "I have ever since been called."[12]

For the next dozen years or so, James worked as a field hand and experienced physical beatings and other hardships common to plantation slavery, though by his own account he "never suffered for food, and never was flogged with the whip." At about age fifteen he moved to the Arkansas territory with his owner, who promptly died, leaving James to his widow. At that point James began, in his own words, "to contrive how I might buy myself. I used to sleep three or four hours, and then get up and work for myself the remainder of the night." At first he wove horse collars out of husks and sold the collars at fifty cents apiece. He gradually accumulated enough money to purchase pigs. To feed the pigs he raised corn (as well as tobacco) on unclaimed federal land near his mistress's plantation. Selling his pigs at a profit, he accrued $160 over five years. "With this money," he recalled, "I hired my own time for two years," an arrangement that he subsequently extended for another eighteen months. In 1833 he purchased his freedom for "about seven hundred dollars" and immediately "started for a free State." Once he reached Cincinnati, he learned about Lane Seminary and applied for admission. He had taught himself to read while a slave, and though he lacked adequate preparation for standard coursework, he was accepted as a special student.[13]

As an ex-bondman and the only person of color enrolled at the institution, James Bradley boldly advocated immediate abolition in the famous Lane

Debates of February 1834. To those who questioned whether "slaves [could] take care of themselves if emancipated," he answered: "They have to take care of, support themselves *now, and their master and his family into the bargain*; and this being so, it would be strange if they could not provide for themselves, *when disencumbered from this load*."[14] When the Lane trustees moved to suppress abolitionist activism at the school six months later, Bradley joined with the other Lane Rebels in quitting the institution.[15] In early 1836 he traveled to Oberlin to resume his education.

Accompanying Bradley was Hiram Wilson, a white Lane Rebel who recounted their perilous journey in a letter to Cincinnati abolitionist Amzi Barber dated March 25, 1836. First Bradley and Wilson "took a deck passage on the steam boat Navarino" from Cincinnati to Marietta, Ohio. While on board, Wilson engaged in moral arguments over slavery with a "floating aristocracy of Southerners." On one occasion an angry slaveholder took "out his pistol & swore if I came where he lived & preached my sentiments he would shoot me down as quick as he would a *mad dog*." On a separate occasion "a slaveholder came up on deck & began to question Bradley about his free papers." Fortunately, another passenger intervened on Bradley's behalf and "bid the slaveholder be gone from the deck." "Sir," Bradley's defender declared, "we have paid for the deck & you have no business to intrude."[16]

After landing in Marietta, Bradley and Wilson traveled overland the rest of the way to Oberlin. "We excited much notice as we passed together thro' the country," Wilson explained. "At one place where we staid over night *big Guns* were fired at the door in honor to us in the evening." At a later stop, Bradley and Wilson were welcomed warmly by all the members of a local family except "the eldest son," who stayed overnight at a neighbor's rather than share space with a person of color. "The next morning early he returned [and] I bade him Good Morning," Wilson recounted. "He broke out in a Rage.... Do you regard us as N——s here or *white people*," the son asked, and he angrily threatened Bradley's life. "He then flew up stairs & in a minute came down & was coming towards Bradley with a drawn sword." Alerted by the boy's mother, his father intervened, "disarmed him & bid him be gone from his door." With calm restored, Bradley and Wilson "staid till after breakfast & family devotions in which Bradley led in an affectionate, melting manner."[17]

The intrepid duo reached Oberlin on March 19, 1836. "It would have done you good to have been here & seen the cheerful & hearty welcome of Bradley,"

Wilson wrote Barber. "All things are moving finely here, the institution is full & overflowing & they are about starting another school preparatory to this at Sheffield."[18] Like Gideon and Charles Langston, Bradley transferred from Oberlin to Sheffield when the new branch of the preparatory department opened there in the summer of 1836. Yet he only stayed for one term, and he never returned to Oberlin to pursue a college degree. What became of him in later years remains a mystery.[19]

A total of twenty African Americans—fifteen males and five females—entered the Oberlin Institute between 1835 and early 1840, the first five years of color-blind admissions. Comprising less than 2 percent of all enrollees at the Institute during this period, these students of color rarely played a significant role in the wider community.[20] The foremost exception was former bondman Sabram Cox, who made Oberlin his permanent home and went on to become an important local figure over the next half century.

Cox was born enslaved in Virginia in the early 1820s. After his first owner died while Cox was still a boy, his new owner took him to Tennessee and then to Shelbyville, Illinois. Although Illinois was officially a "free" state, bondpersons brought into Illinois did not automatically gain their freedom and lacked legal standing to sue for their liberty.[21] Twice Cox attempted to escape. The first time he was captured and returned to his owner. The second time he was captured and jailed, but his owner failed to show up to claim him. As a result, he was eventually allowed to go free, and he made his way to Alton, Illinois, where, in his mid-teens, he became a drayman, building his own modest yet profitable enterprise. Cox also met and may have worked for Elijah Lovejoy, the controversial abolitionist editor and publisher. After Lovejoy died at the hands of an angry mob in November 1837, Cox reputedly rescued Lovejoy's press from the Mississippi River and attended to his burial. Cox then sold his carting equipment and skipped town.[22]

In the spring of 1839 Cox traveled to Oberlin with Climson and Nathaniel Meachum, sons of John B. Meachum, pastor of the African Baptist Church in St. Louis. In a letter addressed to the treasurer of the Oberlin Institute, Reverend Meachum described Cox as "a steady, industrious, and seriously inclined young man." "He is as yet no professor of religion," Meachum acknowledged, "but I do hope and trust that he is not far from the Kingdom. By his own industry, perseverance, & economy, he has saved a considerable sum of money and now having attended to his family affairs, he has of his own accord gone to Oberlin to study under you."[23]

Cox enrolled in the preparatory department in the fall of 1839, and, though he never received a degree, he continued as a student for ten years. His lack of prior schooling hindered his progress, and he sought the assistance of other students. In 1844, one of them described Cox's plight with a mixture of sympathy and condescension: "A colored man by the name of Cox, a grown man and an ex-slave, who is trying to get an education, and with his whole life up to manhood spent in slavery, ignorance and degradation, he finds it hard work, and he has enlisted me with my fresh knowledge of books, to help him. So I spend all the time I can spare, trying to get the rudiments of Arithmetic into his rather dull and untutored mind."[24]

Soon after his arrival in Oberlin, Cox emerged as a leading activist in the fight against slavery. In 1841 he took part in a successful ploy to stop slave hunters from seizing a group of fugitives on their way to freedom in Canada.[25] According to a narrative published four decades later, Cox and six other Oberlin men of color served as decoys, pretending to be the hunted slaves and heading off from town in a covered wagon "driven by two white persons, whose mission was to testify in court that the passengers were free Oberlin people."[26] When the wagon reached Elyria, an attorney acting on behalf of the slave hunters interrupted its journey and had the decoys taken into custody. For several hours Cox and his black compatriots—all in disguise, one as a woman—were held as prisoners in an overheated tavern.[27] The story continues:

> Cox was sitting next to the fire, well muffled with rags, so as to conceal his identity. At length, however, the fire became so warm that he was forced to remove some of the wraps about his neck. As he did so he was suddenly recognized by a former fellow student in college.
>
> "By heavens!" exclaimed the latter, "if there ain't Cox, of Oberlin!"
>
> Amid the general consternation the facts of the deception became known. And now was the turn of the prisoners. Turning to the constable, who had performed the arrest, Cox made some remarks to him which were certainly not ambiguous in their nature, for they made such an impression upon him that the same night he "folded his tent and silent stole away" from the town.[28]

Cox and the other decoys were subsequently acquitted of all charges while the real fugitives escaped.[29] Cox would continue to play a major role in local antislavery efforts over the next two decades, while he established himself as a widely respected figure in the Oberlin community—and a neighbor of Charles Grandison Finney on West Lorain Street.[30]

Of the women of color who settled in Oberlin during its early years, the best documented is Martha Janey. Born in Chillicothe in 1798, she married Joseph Janey, a man of color, around 1820, and in 1830 they resided with five children and another man of color in Seneca Township in northwestern Ohio.[31] The family relocated to southern Michigan in the mid-1830s, but then Joseph either died or deserted his wife and progeny. Martha arrived in Oberlin in 1838 with three children in tow: Elizabeth, Emeline, and Thomas Jefferson Janey. They moved in with William Ferris, a man of color whom Martha subsequently married. The children attended Oberlin's public schools in the early 1840s, and Elizabeth also attended the preparatory department of the Oberlin Institute.[32] Yet in 1847 townspeople turned against William Ferris for promoting unorthodox views on abolition. According to a notice placed in the *Oberlin Evangelist*, "A public meeting of the citizens of Oberlin" held on February 15, 1847, denounced as "evil" his "influence as a speaker" traveling "about the country, speaking on Anti-Slavery." "We do most earnestly protest against his being encouraged," the meeting resolved, "and request those friends to whom he may come, to see to it that the cause of Anti-slavery be not injured by such an advocate."[33] In the aftermath of this contretemps Ferris disappeared from Oberlin, and in 1850 Martha married again—this time to Godfrey Gaskins, a black sailor.[34]

As Oberlin's reputation for welcoming people of color spread, the number of African Americans who chose to make the town their permanent residence began to rise. The federal census of 1840 listed only four households headed by persons of color in Russia Township—2 percent of the total. By contrast, the federal census of 1850 reported that people of color (including those listed as "mulatto" as well as "black") comprised 8 percent of the township's household heads (28 of 337).[35]

A large proportion of the African Americans who settled in Oberlin during the 1840s came from the Upper South.[36] Many were legally free on arrival, but the town also prided itself on protecting fugitive slaves from recapture. Some came as individuals, others in family groups. Teasing information about their journeys to Oberlin from surviving records can be challenging. Take, for example, the case of David Gordon. He first appeared on the tax rolls for Russia Township in 1843, assessed for a horse and a cow but no real estate.³⁷ He was listed in the 1850 federal census as a forty-year-old "mulatto" without occupation who had been born in Maryland. At that time he resided with three other mixed-race individuals—a forty-five-year-old woman, a nine-year-old girl, and a twenty-two-year-old man—none of whom shared his last name.³⁸ How did he make his way to Oberlin? Circumstantial evidence suggests that he migrated as a youth from Maryland to Ohio with his natal family. The federal census for 1830 listed one William Gordon as head of a household of seven persons of color residing in Plymouth Township, Ohio.³⁹ This was probably David's father—the same William Gordon who in 1860, at age eighty, lived with David in Henrietta Township.⁴⁰ Yet the circumstances under which the Gordon family left Maryland remain obscure. Largely for an economic reason—the substitution of wheat for tobacco as the state's most profitable crop—slavery declined rapidly in Maryland in the early decades of the nineteenth century. While it is possible that the Gordons were fugitive slaves who escaped to Ohio illicitly, it is also possible that they were legally manumitted and then departed Maryland as free persons of color.⁴¹

Like David Gordon, John and Mary Campton settled in Oberlin in the early 1840s, bringing with them three children. They hailed from Raleigh, North Carolina, where all members of the Campton household were listed as free persons of color in the 1840 census. Upon the family's arrival in Oberlin in 1843, John purchased a small parcel of land and established himself in business as a skilled carpenter and joiner.⁴² By 1850 Mary had given birth to three more children, John had bought a second parcel of land, and the family resided comfortably on East Lorain Street. John Campton's property assessment placed him in the second highest quintile of Russia Township taxpayers at mid-century, and four of the children would later attend the preparatory department of Oberlin College—as the Institute was renamed in 1850—including one who went on to the Ladies Literary Course. The Camptons were an early Oberlin success story.⁴³

Occasionally African Americans came to Oberlin in multi-family groups. The foremost example in the 1840s was the migration of the Jones and Copeland families, along with the unmarried John Lane—in total more than fifteen people. Like the Camptons, whom they probably knew before embarking for Oberlin, they came from Raleigh, North Carolina, and over the next generation they would become important figures in Oberlin's emerging black community.⁴⁴

Allen Jones was a first-generation African American. His father, Charles, had been forcibly transported from Africa during the Revolutionary era, and Allen was born enslaved in 1794 in North Carolina. Trained as a blacksmith and gunsmith, he was often hired out by his master to perform work in Raleigh and the vicinity.[45] As a skilled urban craftsman, he enjoyed privileges denied the vast majority of enslaved people. Most notably, his marriage in 1821 to Temperance (Tempe) Josephson, also a slave, was registered under state law as if they were free.[46] According to family lore, because he was so strong and diligent, Jones found that he could complete his assigned work ahead of schedule and devoted his extra time to making money on his own account so he could purchase his freedom. He negotiated a price with his master, but when he had accumulated the requisite amount his master refused to grant Jones his liberty on the pretense that he had earned the funds on the master's time, not his own. Undaunted, Jones resumed the process of accumulation, and before he turned thirty-five he obtained his freedom.[47] In 1829 he purchased and emancipated his wife, their three children, and his father.[48]

During the 1830s, Tempe Jones gave birth to three more children, and Allen Jones prospered as the head of his own business. The 1840 federal census listed two adult slaves among the twelve members of his household, though whether he actually owned these slaves—one male and one female—or only leased their services on a temporary basis was not recorded. They may have been relatives whom Jones had acquired in order to emancipate them at a later date.[49]

Even a relatively affluent free person of color led a precarious existence in the slave state of North Carolina. In the spring of 1842, Allen Jones was arrested on forgery charges, but he was duly acquitted in court with the help of five defense attorneys.[50] Much more alarming was what happened the following October: he was "forcibly taken from his own house, in the dead of night, by a mob" and severely beaten.[51] The trigger for this attack remains uncertain. By one account, Jones had violated social norms by speaking at an antislavery convention in New York.[52] By another and more plausible account, he was targeted for supporting a controversial Quaker school for local children of color.[53] Whatever the immediate cause of the mob's furor—and notwithstanding a prompt public denunciation of the violence by members of Raleigh's white elite—Allen Jones decided to leave town soon after the attack.[54] In December he put up for sale at public auction his quite sizable estate, including a "good two-story wood Dwelling House" and neighboring blacksmith shop in Raleigh proper plus four acres of land "in the South eastern suburbs of the City" on which stood Jones's family residence—another "good two story Dwelling House"—and "two small Houses, with two rooms each."[55] In early 1843 Allen and Tempe Jones headed north with their six children.

Like Allen Jones, John Copeland was born into bondage in North Carolina. But unlike Jones, he was the mixed-race son of a white slaveholder. At age seven, in 1815, John Copeland gained his freedom upon the death of his owner-father, who manumitted John in his will. In his youth John took up carpentry as a trade, and in 1831 he married Delilah Evans, the free-born, light-complexioned daughter of African Americans Charles and Frances Evans of Hillsborough, North Carolina. Before the marriage Delilah had served as a favored nursemaid for the well-to-do Devereux family, even traveling with them to New England on at least one occasion.[56] During the 1830s John worked on constructing the new state capitol building in Raleigh, while Delilah gave birth to five children, one of whom died young. The couple also adopted a child, and the 1840 federal census for Raleigh listed a total of seven free persons of color in the Copeland household.[57] Another child was born in 1842, and the following year John and Delilah incorporated into their brood an orphaned boy while on their journey north.[58]

Less is known about John Lane's background. Born free in Fayetteville, North Carolina, around 1815, Lane as an adult made his living as a blacksmith.[59] But his name did not appear in the 1840 federal census for Raleigh and the vicinity, raising the possibility that he worked for and resided with Allen Jones, who was twenty years his senior. (Only heads of household were enumerated by name in 1840.) That would help explain why Lane migrated to Oberlin alongside the Joneses and the Copelands in 1843.

Traveling with three horse-drawn wagons, the Jones-Copeland-Lane contingent crossed from slave country into the free state of Ohio in the spring of 1843. After passing through Cincinnati, they headed for New Richmond, Indiana, a small community said to be friendly to people of color. There they attended an antislavery meeting where they met Amos Dresser, a graduate of the Oberlin Institute, former Lane Rebel, and active abolitionist. Dresser recommended that the contingent proceed to Oberlin if they were seeking a safe and prosperous place to live. Leaving the women and children behind in New Richmond, the three adult men set off as a scouting party. According to an account recorded nearly forty years later, "When within twenty miles of [Oberlin] they stopped at a tannery to inquire the way, and were told with oaths that there was no such place, that it had 'sank.' Mr. C[opeland] replied that he would go on and look into the chasm.'" When they reached Oberlin, the refugees from North Carolina "were much surprised ... to see two young men, one white and the other colored, walking arm in arm." Religious Oberlin residents, in turn, were surprised to see the newcomers "riding on Sunday," the Sabbath. Yet once they explained "that they were seeking a home for themselves and families," townspeople welcomed them with enthusiasm and arranged for temporary lodging in local homes. After a short period of reconnoitering, "Messrs. Copeland and Lane returned to New Richmond for the ... families, Mr. Jones sending word that he 'had found a paradise and was going to stay.'"[60]

Henry Johnson took a more circuitous route to Oberlin. Born into slavery in late eighteenth-century Virginia, Johnson was present at the Battle of New Orleans and may have been owned for a time by General (later President) Andrew Jackson.[61] During the 1820s and 1830s, Johnson resided in Kentucky, first in Frankfurt and then in Louisville. In the words of a press account published in 1882, around 1840 "he had a falling out with his master, who was about to flog him, and he concluded not to be flogged, as he had done nothing wrong." Eluding slave patrollers and their dogs, he escaped with a few clothes and some cash and took a stagecoach to Frankfurt, where he hid out with a friend while planning his journey north. After buying a horse, he made his way to the Ohio River. "At the river he sold his horse and crossed at Ripley"—a popular junction on the Underground Railroad. He then traversed the state of Ohio, and upon reaching Lake Erie "he paid two men $1.25 each to row him five miles to the Canada shore." He stayed in Canada through the ensuing winter, making his living by chopping wood. "Having heard of Oberlin, he came here in the spring."[62] His name first appeared on the Russia Township tax list in 1843 (he was assessed for one cow), and by 1850 he owned a modest lot in town.[63] Also by 1850 he had wed a white woman from Vermont—quite possibly Oberlin's first interracial marriage.[64]

The wealthiest African American to relocate to the Oberlin area during the 1840s was Thomas Jarvis, who arrived with his family in the middle of the decade. Born free in 1801 in the Tidewater region of Virginia, Thomas Jarvis was the second son of William Jarvis, a former slave whose master—

probably also his father—had provided for his manumission shortly before passing away in 1782. Under the terms of his master's will, William—referred to as a "Mulatto Boy" in legal papers—inherited his master's estate and was apprenticed at cabinet making in Williamsburg. In 1790 William successfully petitioned for release from his apprenticeship, and he subsequently turned to farming for his livelihood. By 1793 he had started a family and owned three slaves.[65]

Notwithstanding a general reduction in the legal rights and economic opportunities afforded free blacks in Virginia over the next three decades, William Jarvis continued to prosper. According to the federal census, in 1810 he owned seven slaves, and in 1820 he owned eleven.[66] Upon his death in 1825, he left an estate valued at $6,656. While his widow inherited $500, most of his land—two lots comprising 435 acres in all—went to his sons, Thomas and John. William's widow and sons also received one slave apiece, leaving the fate of his other bondpersons unknown.[67]

Thomas Jarvis followed in his father's footsteps as a successful farmer. The 1830 federal census listed him as the owner of five slaves, and the 1840 federal census recorded him as the owner of seven.[68] Early in the 1830s he married a woman named Nancy, and by the time they migrated to Oberlin in 1846 or 1847 they had nine, maybe ten children.[69] Precisely why they left Virginia remains unclear, as is the fate of Thomas Jarvis's slaves upon his departure. It is possible that they were relatives and that he freed them; it is also possible that they were unrelated to him and that he sold them.[70] Whatever the case, he arrived in Oberlin with a good deal of capital in hand. By 1849 he purchased a large tract of farmland in Russia Township, just northeast of Oberlin proper, and in 1850 he ranked among the top 10 percent of the township's taxpayers. Meanwhile, Nancy Jarvis died in 1848. Thomas proceeded to raise their many children on his own.[71]

Fewer African Americans migrated to Oberlin from the Lower South than from the Upper South for rather obvious reasons. The proportion of free blacks in the Lower South was smaller, the enforcement of caste distinctions in the Lower South was stricter, and the distance between the Lower South and northeast Ohio was greater. Yet some persons of color from the Lower South succeeded in making their way to Oberlin during the 1840s. Most notable among them were John and Margaret Watson, a married couple who "were held as slaves in the state of Louisiana" before "[t]hey determined to be free and came north." How they escaped bondage is unknown, but according to a posthumous account, when they reached Cincinnati "Mr. Watson left his wife... until he should find an asylum for them both, which he soon did in Oberlin."[72] The couple brought with them a young son, and all three family members were listed in the 1850 federal census as "mulattoes"—John aged thirty-two, Margaret aged thirty, and William aged eleven.[73] John worked early on as a brickmason, but in 1852 he opened a grocery and restaurant in the so-called commercial block, a sizable building on South Main Street that he and three white businessmen constructed.[74] He was a fervent abolitionist, and in 1858 both he and William were arrested for their roles in the Oberlin-Wellington Rescue of the fugitive John Price.[75] By 1860 the combined property assessments of John and Margaret Watson placed them among the highest quintile of taxpayers in Russia Township.[76]

In addition to the flow of African Americans to Oberlin from the South, there was a steady stream of people of color from free states where slavery had been abolished (or at least doomed to extinction by law) but where color prejudice and government-sanctioned racial discrimination remained strong. Among the more noteworthy examples of northern African Americans who migrated to Oberlin during the 1840s were Robert Van Rankin and his wife, Margaret (née Brown). Born in New York around 1799—the year that state adopted its gradual emancipation statute—they relocated to Ohio during the 1830s and were living in West Massillon, near Canton, in 1840. Soon thereafter they moved to Oberlin.[77] Robert's name first appeared on the Russia Township tax list in 1843, and the next year both he and Margaret were admitted to membership in the Congregational Church.[78] At mid-century they resided on North Main Street, near the center of town.[79] Although they were listed without occupations in the 1850 census, they apparently made their living by providing room and board to students and other young people of color. The census enumerated four males and seven females between the ages of five and twenty-four in the Van Rankins' household, each with a last name other than theirs. One of the lodgers was listed as "black" and the rest as "mulatto."[80]

Northerners of color who came during the 1840s to pursue college degrees at the Oberlin Institute played a major role in the life of the larger community. Of these, George B. Vashon, William Howard Day, Lucy A. Stanton, and John Mercer Langston deserve particular notice.[81]

George B. Vashon was the son of John B. Vashon, a highly respected leader of Pittsburgh's black population, veteran of the War of 1812, self-employed barber, friend of William Lloyd Garrison, and charter member of the American Anti-Slavery Society.[82] Upon his arrival in 1840, George Vashon entered the Institute at the collegiate level, and he went on to earn his bachelor's degree in 1844.[83] While living in Oberlin he helped introduce the practice of celebrating the First of August—the anniversary of emancipation in the British West Indies—as an alternative to honoring American independence on the fourth of July.[84] "Perhaps there has never been more interest felt, on any public occasion in this place, than at the celebration, by the colored people, on the first instant," rhapsodized the *Oberlin Evangelist* in the issue dated August 17, 1842. "The idea of the celebration originated with, and all the arrangements were made and executed by the colored people, with scarcely a suggestion from others." It was a full-day affair, with a meeting for prayer in the morning, followed in the afternoon by a general assembly where Vashon, then a college sophomore, presented one of four formal public addresses to an overflowing, racially mixed audience. The celebration closed with a "plain free dinner provided by the colored people" for 250 participants, both black and white. Observed the *Evangelist*, "If any one returned from this first celebration of the colored people, without feeling a stronger interest in their improvement and elevation, and a new determination not to cease his labors for the immediate and universal emancipation of the race, we envy not his head or his heart."[85]

Like George B. Vashon, William Howard Day was the northern-born son of a veteran of the War of 1812. His father, John Day, was a sailmaker by profession, while his mother, née Eliza Dixon, was an abolitionist who helped launch the African Methodist Episcopal Zion Church in New York City. When John Day died in 1829, Eliza Day was left to raise the couple's four children by herself. William was a precocious youngster, and his mother paid particular attention to his education. He attended school from the time he was four years old, and in the spring of 1834, at age nine, he joined with other students of color from across the city in founding the Garrison Literary Society, named in honor of abolitionist William Lloyd Garrison. A few months later New York's anti-abolitionist riots exposed Day's family to the violent wrath of white racism in the North. "We barricaded our windows," he remembered in old age, "we watched our arms [while] our neighbors heated water to give the mob a warm reception."[86]

In 1838, William Howard Day's intellectual potential came to the attention of J. P. Williston, an affluent white manufacturer and abolitionist from Northampton, Massachusetts, who, while visiting New York City, had occasion to observe Day's performance at a publicly staged examination. Williston approached Day's mother and offered to adopt the talented youth and educate him at his expense. Eliza Day agreed, and William spent the next five years residing with the Williston family in Northampton. While learning the printing trade on the side, he fixed his sights on pursuing a college degree upon his completion of secondary school. Williston supported Day in this ambition, but Williams College denied him admission after southern students protested the prospect of studying alongside a person of color. The Oberlin Institute was more welcoming. In the fall of 1843, Day entered as the lone African American among the fifty students entering the first year of the College Course.[87]

During his time at Oberlin, Day emerged as a leader within the town as well as the Institute. In 1844 he spoke at the First of August celebration and fervently decried American hypocrisy. "We, as Americans, are in far worse condition than the people of the West Indian Islands ever were," he declared. "Here, man exercises tyranny over his fellow man, debases the image of his Maker, unjustly tasks the sinews of his brother, and then, with his feet upon his neck, cries 'liberty.'"[88] In 1846, when "the colored citizens of Oberlin . . . assembled in mass meeting" to protest the death of white abolitionist Charles T. Torrey in a Maryland prison, Day headed the committee that drafted a series of resolutions that not only paid tribute to Torrey's martyrdom but also emphasized the human agency of the oppressed. "However discouraging the circumstances of our case may become, how many soever of us or others may fall," one resolve proclaimed, "we will not despond, but trusting to God, press forward in the full assurance that if 'hereditary bondmen would be free, themselves must strike the blow.'"[89]

Upon graduating with a bachelor's degree in the fall of 1847, Day decided to stay in the Oberlin area. Aligning himself first with the Liberty Party and then with the Free Soil Party, he continued to campaign against slavery.[90] In January 1849 he served as one of seven delegates from Lorain County to the Mass Convention of the Colored Citizens of Ohio, held in Columbus. (Other Lorain County delegates included Oberlinians John Lane and John Watson.) Among the most controversial topics debated at the convention was whether blacks should entertain emigration from the United States as an option in their struggle for freedom and equality. When a fellow delegate, as part of his argument in favor of emigration, alleged that "if you go to Oberlin, *there* you will find a colored school, brought into existence on account of prejudice even *there,*" Day immediately objected. "I deny it," he declared categorically.[91] The school at issue—known as the Liberty School—had in fact been established to serve adults of color, mainly ex-slaves, who lacked previous access to formal education. Contrary to the critic's implication, black youth were welcome in Oberlin's regular public schools as well as the Oberlin Institute.[92] To Day's mind, the town of Oberlin stood as proof that, notwithstanding the prevalence of slavery and racism elsewhere in the United States, Americans were capable of practicing equality without regard to color.

Yet in 1851 Day departed Oberlin for Cleveland. One reason was his desire to publish a newspaper expressly for black readers, an enterprise that was more likely to prosper in an urban setting. Another reason was his intention to marry Lucy Stanton, an Oberlin College alumna from Cleveland.[93] In 1850, at age nineteen, Stanton had become the first woman of color to earn the school's Ladies Literary Degree. (Unlike the bachelor's degree, the literary degree did not require the study of higher mathematics, Greek, or Latin.)[94]

The only child of Samuel and Mary Stanton, Lucy Stanton had grown up in relatively comfortable circumstances despite her father's death when she was two years old. After her father's passing, her mother married his business partner, John Brown, and gave birth to four more children. Brown was a prosperous African American barber, and the light-complexioned family resided in a largely white section of Cleveland. Yet Brown was strongly antislavery, and the family harbored fugitive slaves on their way to Canada and freedom. When Lucy was driven out of a neighborhood school because of her race, her stepfather paid for the construction of a school for Cleveland's children of color, including his own. The school prepared Lucy well for advanced study, and in 1846 she enrolled in the Ladies Literary Course.[95]

While at Oberlin, Lucy Stanton roomed with the former *Amistad* captive Sarah Margru Kinson and was elected president of the Ladies Literary Society.[96] At the school's commencement ceremony in the fall of 1850, Stanton made her mark on the wider community. In an eloquent speech titled "A Plea for the Oppressed," she denounced slavery as "the combination of all crime" and summoned women to advance the cause of emancipation by means particular to their gender. "Mother, sister, by thy own deep sorrow of heart; by the sympathy of thy woman's nature, plead for the downtrodden of thy own, of every land," she declared. "Instill the principles of love, of common brotherhood, in the nursery, in the social circle. Let these be the prayer of thy life."[97] At the close of her speech, John Keep rose from the audience to praise Stanton's performance, and in a departure from customary etiquette, the Oberlin crowd erupted in a "general, swelling burst of applause."[98]

No person of color who migrated to Oberlin during the 1840s would go on to greater fame in the nineteenth century than John Mercer Langston. The younger brother of Gideon and Charles Langston, the Institute's first African American students, John Mercer Langston followed their lead in making his way from Chillicothe to Oberlin in early March 1844. He was fourteen years old at the time, and he traveled with George Vashon, who had been his teacher in a Chillicothe grade school for students of color and was returning to Oberlin to complete his senior year.[99] In an autobiography published fifty years later, Langston recalled that the trip was especially challenging toward the end: "The last forty-eight miles of their journey, from Mansfield to Oberlin, were difficult by reason of the depth of the mud and the well-nigh impassable condition of the roads." The duo arrived at 1 A.M. on a Sunday, and "only after considerable knocking and calling" were they able to rouse Oberlin's lone hotelier and secure lodging for the remainder of the night.[100]

Langston's first Sabbath in Oberlin proved transformative. "At half-past ten o'clock," he remembered, "the chapel bell was tolled. The crowd which had hitherto appeared on the streets, and impressed the stranger as being large, seemed small now, as compared with the vast swelling company of students pressing to the great church" to hear Charles Grandison Finney "deliver one of his thrilling, matchless discourses." Interrupted by a single intermission, the service lasted for several hours and left Langston speechless. "Like all others who had been listening, at the close of the meeting he left the house so impressed that he moved away in silence," Langston wrote of himself in the third person. "Thus he commenced his life in Oberlin; and the impressions made upon his mind by the observations and experiences of his first Sabbath there, were so indelibly written in his thoughts and memory, that no lapse of time, or worldly care, has been able to efface them."[101]

During his first year at Oberlin, Langston resided in the household of George Whipple, professor of mathematics, along with a few other students at the Institute. Langston shared meals with his white host family and soon felt "wholly at home and at ease in his most agreeable surroundings." And he studied very hard. Like his older brothers before him, he enrolled initially in the Institute's preparatory department. On Whipple's recommendation, in 1845 he applied for—and was admitted to—the College Course.[102]

In his autobiography, Langston portrayed Oberlin during the 1840s as an interracial paradise, free of the harsh color prejudice common elsewhere in Ohio and throughout the United States. Other evidence, however, suggests that as a young man Langston found Oberlin less congenial and less thoroughly enlightened on racial matters than he remembered a half-century later. It was he who enraged William Howard Day at the Mass Convention of the Colored Citizens of Ohio in January 1849 by citing Oberlin's school for black adults as proof of racial "prejudice even *there*."[103]

At mid-century, persons of color comprised 9 percent of the more than two thousand people residing in Russia Township.[104] The manuscript federal census for 1850, supplemented by tax records for the same year, permits a comparison of the social profiles of the township's white residents on the one hand, and residents of color on the other, in regard to geographical origins, occupations, and wealth.[105]

Differences in the birthplaces of adults by race were striking. Whereas 72 percent of white adults had been born in New England or the mid-Atlantic states and only 2 percent had been born south of the Mason-Dixon line, the pattern was roughly the reverse for residents of color: 10 percent had been born in New England or the mid-Atlantic region while 74 percent had been born in the South. (The remainder of each group had been born in Ohio, other Midwestern states, or abroad. See chart 2.1.) Oberlin at mid-century represented an experiment in the integration not only of whites and blacks but also of northerners and southerners.[106]

The pattern of occupations among whites and blacks was also notably different. Two-thirds of the white township residents with recorded occupations were farmers or engaged in related agricultural pursuits, compared to about a quarter of the residents of color. While only 4 percent of employed white residents were laborers or sailors, 45 percent of employed residents of color pursued these comparatively low-skilled service occupations. More surprising, perhaps, is the relative proportion of each racial group engaged in artisanal trades: 17 percent of employed white residents compared to 31 percent of employed residents of color. Put another way, at a time when persons of color comprised only one in every fourteen members of the township's workforce overall, they accounted for an eighth of the local craftsmen.[107]

Chart 2.1. Birthplace of Adult Residents of Russia Township by Race, 1850

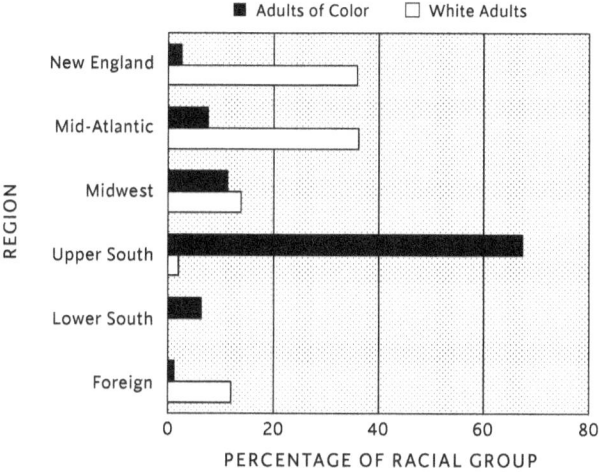

Source: Russia Township, Lorain County, Ohio, *Population Schedules of the Seventh Census of the United States, 1850* (National Archives Microfilm Publication M432), roll 705, pages 242A–266B, images 6–55.

A majority of both black and white households listed in the census owned real estate in 1850, and the difference in the proportion by race was rather modest: 57 percent of black households, compared to 69 percent of white households. Yet, according to the census, the average (mean) value of the real property possessed by black households was less than one-third of that owned by white households ($259 compared to $898).[108] Although African Americans fared better economically in Russia Township than their peers elsewhere in the United States, there existed a major disparity of wealth between white and black residents at mid-century.

Analysis of data from local tax records paints a similar but not identical picture of wealth inequality in Russia Township. Unlike the census, the tax assessment lists omitted people without any property. But tax lists did include valuations of personal estate, a kind of property not itemized in the 1850 census. Tax lists also counted property owners who did not actually reside in the town, while the census apparently omitted residents who were away in July 1850, when the census taker made his rounds. Taken together, these factors help to explain a significant discrepancy in the rosters of the two enumerations. Only about two-thirds of the households on each list could be found on the other. Neither source was comprehensive or totally reliable.[109]

While persons of color comprised 9 percent of household heads listed in the 1850 census for Russia Township, they accounted for only 4 percent of Russia Township taxpayers in that year. Moreover, taxpayers of color were considerably less likely than their white counterparts to own sufficient property to place in the top quintile of assessments and much more likely to own only enough property to place in the bottom quintile. Table 2.1 reveals that the pattern of wealth distribution among property-holders of color differed markedly from that among white property-holders at mid-century.[110]

Table 2.1. Russia Township Taxpayers by Assessment Quintile and Race, 1850

Property Assessment Quintile	White Taxpayers in Quintile	Taxpayers of Color in Quintile
5 (Highest)	20%	7%
4	21%	7%
3	20%	13%
2	20%	33%
1 (Lowest)	19%	40%
N	366	15

Source: Auditor's Duplicates for Oberlin and Russia Township, 1850, Lorain County Records Retention Center, Elyria, Ohio. The race of taxpayers was determined by record linkage with Patricia Holsworth, "Oberlin Genealogical Database," 2012, in the authors' possession.

Although a few early residents of color owned impressive amounts of property, African Americans as a whole were less affluent than their white peers in Russia Township. The explanation seems obvious: as ex-slaves and free people of color living in a deeply racist society, African Americans brought less property with them when they migrated to the community. Even if upon their arrival they enjoyed relatively equal opportunities to prosper, there was little time for them to "catch up" with whites by 1850.

Against the backdrop of rising sectional tensions over slavery, the imposition of a new, harsher fugitive slave law by the federal government, and an easing of Ohio's Black Laws, black migration to Russia Township accelerated markedly after 1850. Even more than before, during the 1850s Oberlin stood out as a safe space for people of color and a beacon of racial tolerance. By 1860, African Americans accounted for 15 percent of the population of Russia Township and 20 percent of the population of Oberlin proper.[111]

Several of the African Americans who settled in Oberlin in the 1850s had family ties to earlier migrants. Especially noteworthy were the free-born, light-complexioned brothers Henry and Wilson Bruce Evans, whose sister, Delilah, was married to John Copeland. The Copelands had migrated to Oberlin from Raleigh, North Carolina, with Allen Jones's family and John Lane in 1843. Eleven years later, the Evans brothers, their wives, and their children made a similar journey from Hillsborough, North Carolina, accompanied by various other free persons of color—an entourage of nineteen people in all.[112] In preparation for the expedition, Henry Evans enlisted the help of two white businessmen who assured the governor of North Carolina that the Evanses were "entitled to as much respect and regard as any Colored family in our State."[113]

The trip to Oberlin took about three months, and shortly after their arrival the Evans brothers opened a cabinetmaking establishment on East Mill Street.[114] Each brother was married to a daughter of Matthew Nathaniel Leary, a prominent free black saddler and harnessmaker in Fayetteville, North Carolina.[115] Henry Evans had wed Henrietta Leary in 1843, and Wilson Bruce Evans had married Sarah Jane Leary in 1853.[116] Lewis Sheridan Leary, Henrietta and Sarah Jane's younger brother, also made his way to Oberlin in the mid-1850s, perhaps as part of the same group migration.[117] Lewis had trained in their father's shop, and after his arrival in Oberlin he found employment with John H. Scott, another free man of color from Fayetteville who had learned saddlery and harnessmaking under the senior Leary's supervision.[118] The hometown connection figured as well in Lewis Sheridan Leary's choice of spouse. In 1858 he married a fellow native of Fayetteville: Mary Sampson Patterson, who had migrated to Oberlin with her parents, siblings, aunt, uncle, and cousins two years earlier.[119] Such family bonds undergirded the development of collective consciousness among Oberlin's burgeoning African American population. In 1859 Lewis Sheridan Leary died in the famous raid on Harpers Ferry organized by the revolutionary abolitionist John Brown.

A noteworthy proportion of African Americans who settled in Oberlin during the 1850s were former slaves whose transitions from bondage to freedom and journeys from South to North were actively assisted by their erstwhile white owners, who in some cases were also their fathers. Take, for example, the children of Stephen Wall, a prominent cotton planter in Rockingham, North Carolina. Between 1822 and 1843, Wall, who never married, fathered seven offspring by three different slave women under his dominion.[120] In 1838 he decided to emancipate and send north his children born to that date: Napoleon, Orindatus Simon Bolivar (O.S.B.), Caroline, Sarah, and Benjamin. Stephen Wall engaged his friend Richmond Love, a Mississippi slaveholder, to escort the youngsters from North Carolina to a new home in the Midwest. Love arranged for them to be placed with families in Harveysburg, Ohio, a racially tolerant Quaker community located about fifty miles northeast of Cincinnati. Wall supported his freed children financially until his death in 1845, when he bequeathed to each of them $1,000 plus a share of his Ohio land holdings. In his will he also provided for the emancipation and financial well-being of the two children whom he had fathered since 1838: "little John, and Albert."[121]

In 1850, Caroline and Sarah Wall made their way to Oberlin to enroll in the preparatory department of the newly renamed Oberlin College. The following year they entered the Ladies Literary Course. While Caroline would drop out and marry John Mercer Langston in 1854, Sarah received her degree in 1856. In the meantime, O.S.B. and Benjamin Wall followed their sisters to Oberlin in 1853.[122] O.S.B. promptly opened a boot and shoemaking establishment, and within two years he ranked in the middle quintile of Russia Township taxpayers.[123] Although Benjamin left town before the decade was out, by 1860 John and Albert had joined the Wall contingent in Oberlin.[124]

Like Stephen Wall, Dr. Stanislas D'Anglas was a white slaveholder who fathered a number of slave children and later arranged for them to journey north for a better life. Born in France in 1803, D'Anglas earned his medical degree in 1825 and immigrated to the United States ten years later. He arrived in New Orleans in March 1835 and soon established himself as a planter and slave owner in rural Natchitoches Parish, Louisiana.[125] From this position of power he initiated what would become an enduring sexual relationship with a black bondwoman named Diza. By 1840 Diza had given birth to two daughters: Mary Louisa and Belinda.[126] The 1840 census for Natchitoches Parish identified Stanislas D'Anglas as the head of a ten-person household, all of whose members except for him were enslaved.[127]

THE ARRIVAL OF AFRICAN AMERICANS

Over the next decade Stanislas and Diza had four more children.[128] More remarkably, in defiance of southern social norms, Stanislas emancipated Diza and their progeny and lived with them as a mixed-race nuclear family.[129] Yet he remained a major slaveholder. The slave schedules of the 1850 federal census listed him as the owner of eighteen bondpeople, ranging in age from two to sixty.[130]

Meanwhile, in 1849, with the help of a third party, Stanislas sent daughters Mary Louisa and Belinda to Oberlin, "supposing that they would at once be admitted" to the Institute. They were deemed unready, however, and attended local public schools instead. The 1850 census for Russia Township listed them as lodgers in the household of William Ingersoll, a prosperous white farmer.[131]

In 1853, Stanislas, Diza, and the remainder of their children, including a newborn, joined Mary Louisa and Belinda in Oberlin. Over the next few years the family continued to grow while Stanislas bought up valuable parcels of land in Oberlin and its environs. In 1855 he was assessed for more property than any other taxpayer in Russia Township.[132] He had little time to savor his elite standing in the community, however. Stanislas D'Anglas died on February 1, 1856.[133] In his will he affirmed that Diza was his wife, and he bequeathed to her for the remainder of her life "the use of a half of the real estate" that he owned, including "the house wherein" they had resided.[134] Formerly his slave, Diza upon Stanislas's death became one of America's wealthier black women.

Unlike Stephen Wall and Stanislas D'Anglas, slaveholder Maxwell Chambers acknowledged no slave children. He cited no ties of flesh and blood to explain his interest in manumission. Yet he ultimately freed more slaves than Wall and D'Anglas combined. His former bondpersons comprised the largest group of African Americans to migrate to Oberlin in the 1850s.

Born in Salisbury, North Carolina, in 1780, Chambers in his teens or early twenties moved with his uncle to Charleston, South Carolina, where he reputedly made his fortune.[135] Exactly how he acquired his wealth remains obscure, however. By one descendant's account, he developed a lucrative system for conveying information about overseas cotton prices to the hinterland faster than other Charleston merchants.[136] By another descendant's account, he was a profitable slave dealer who hid his participation in the noxious trade from public notice.[137] After his return to Salisbury in the 1820s, he was sufficiently rich to serve as a private banker for the community, and in 1836, at age fifty-six, he married Catherine B. Troy.[138] According to the federal census, in 1850 Chambers owned sixty-nine slaves, making him a large slaveholder by North Carolina standards.[139] Instead of operating a plantation, he seems to have hired out his slaves to work in the Salisbury (later Rowan) Cotton Factory, which he owned for a short time and subsequently sold to relatives.[140] In this respect, as in others, Chambers was an unusual slaveholder.

Most notably, he displayed an interest in African American emancipation as early as 1842, when he exchanged letters with John E. Patterson, a free North Carolinian of color who had recently visited Liberia, the controversial African colony founded by the American Colonization Society in the early 1820s. Patterson encouraged Chambers to emancipate his slaves and provide for their safe resettlement in freedom.[141] Chambers evidently took the proposal seriously, but he waited a dozen years to act.

In January 1854, Chambers drafted an extraordinary will announcing his intention to manumit and send to Ohio within a few months

> my woman Adeline and all her children, Marget and all her children and Garrison her husband, also Edwin, Isham, Hugh, and Chesley, brothers of Adeline and Marget, and to furnish them with a comfortable and plentiful outfit of good clothing and a full supply of provisions for the journey, (say three or four weeks,) also to hire a sober, steady person, with a waggon [sic] and team, to take them comfortably to their place of destination, and to furnish all, those over twelve years old with Sixty Dollars each, and those under that age with Forty Dollars each, in such money as will be current in Ohio.[142]

Chambers carried out this plan in May 1854, freeing eighteen bondpersons and arranging for their transportation "to the Town of *Oberlin* or its vicinity . . . under the care and protection of Moses Rymer."[143] Upon Chambers's death the following year, his will provided for the liberation of forty-eight more bondpersons on the same terms "as Adeline and her party."[144] In all, more than sixty African Americans came to Oberlin as a result of Chambers's benefaction. Not everyone stayed, but the 1860 census for Russia Township included thirty-three persons of color with the surname Chambers as well as at least five individuals with different last names who had once been owned by Maxwell Chambers.[145] The same census listed as an Oberlin resident John E. Patterson, the free African American who had urged Chambers to emancipate his slaves back in 1842. (John E. Patterson was also the father of Mary Sampson Patterson Leary, the widow of Harpers Ferry martyr Lewis Sheridan Leary.)[146]

The first generation of African Americans who settled in Oberlin and Russia Township came disproportionately from the Upper South, but otherwise varied among themselves in background. While many had been born enslaved, some had been born free. A few came with considerable property; others arrived impoverished but were able to prosper after settling in the community. A large percentage worked in service occupations and just got by. On the whole, in regard to opportunities for blacks, Oberlin compared favorably to other places in the free North, but at mid-century the town was neither a multiracial utopia nor a color-blind community. How Oberlin's experiment in racial integration operated "on the ground" is the focus of the next chapter.

3

AN EXPERIMENT IN RACIAL INTEGRATION

In his autobiography, published in 1894, John Mercer Langston remembered antebellum Oberlin as a place where residents abided by the Golden Rule in their day-to-day behavior. "[T]o the Oberlin community," he wrote, "belongs the distinguishing honor of being the first one on the face of the earth to realize in its teachings, its practices and its manners towards every human being, the high central Christian sentiment, 'that whatsoever ye would that men should do to you, do ye even so to them.'"[1] Especially notable in Langston's view was the absence of racial bigotry. "The treatment accorded colored people in Oberlin socially at this time was most remarkable," he recalled. "Every Sunday colored persons could be seen seated in conspicuous eligible places in the only church in the town, worshipping after the manner of those in whose midst they lived, and no one molested or disturbed them. Such persons were made welcome as equals in the best families . . . and thus were given the best social, as they were the highest educational advantages."[2] By this account, as the town's African American population grew in both absolute and relative terms between 1835 and 1860, Oberlinians fulfilled the founders' commitment to racial egalitarianism. In the language of a later era, antebellum Oberlin epitomized the radical ideal of "the beloved community."[3]

Or did it? As the town's richest, best educated, and most prominent African American resident in the 1850s, Langston almost certainly enjoyed more respect and more access to "the best families" within the community than ordinary persons of color. In a letter dated December 21, 1859, Zeruiah Porter Weed, a white graduate of the college who labored as a home missionary among Oberlin's poor, offered a very different picture of how race and racial attitudes operated in the community in the late antebellum era. "This place is by no means free from that spirit of prejudice which has kept free persons of color from rising to their proper places in Society," she wrote the secretary of the American Missionary Association. "[T]hough our Institution [the Congregational Church] and Union school are open for all who wish to attend, there are many here I am sorry to say who would keep the colored people out of them if they had the power," she elaborated. "Many of the colored people feel this so strongly that they keep themselves away from both school instruction and the means of grace."[4] According to Weed, a significant proportion of white Oberlinians looked down on local blacks, especially poor blacks, and effectively discouraged them from sharing in the religious and educational benefits that Langston would later celebrate in his autobiography. The Oberlin of Weed's account was no beloved community.

Yet even if antebellum Oberlinians failed to live by the Golden Rule and never achieved the level of interracial comity that Langston nostalgically portrayed, the town proved a safe haven for African Americans from 1835 forward. Indeed, the willingness of Oberlinians to harbor not only legally free persons of color but also fugitive slaves—freedom seekers who had escaped bondage illicitly—contributed greatly to the community's notoriety. In *Oberlin Unmasked*, a fiercely hostile exposé published in 1837, former student Delazon Smith declared, "To STEAL the *slaves* from their *masters*, and colonize them in Canada, is the *scheme* of which, if *Oberlin* is not the originator, she is most surely the *abettor*."[5] Four years later, the *Cleveland Advertiser* described Oberlin disparagingly as "the regular depot of all absconding slaves from the southwestern slave States."[6] Oberlinians made no effort to refute such charges. On the contrary, they took pride in their reputation as the friends and protectors of black people fleeing bondage.

Although most of the escaped slaves who made their way to Oberlin on what became known as the Underground Railroad proceeded onward to Canada, some stayed. In his autobiography, John Mercer Langston asserted that when he first came to Oberlin, in 1844, fugitives comprised a majority of the local African American population. They "remained there," he explained, "in the consciousness that they were safe against the capture of any slaveholder or his agent, any officer of the government or other."[7] Yet Langston may have exaggerated both the proportion of fugitives and the security felt by local residents of color. In February 1849 "a meeting of the colored citizens of Oberlin" thought it necessary to "urge all colored persons and their friends, to keep a sharp look-out for man-thieves and their abettors."[8]

The U.S. Congress's passage the following year of a new, more oppressive Fugitive Slave Law put freedom seekers at significantly greater risk. In April 1851, at the initiative of ex-slave John Watson, a gathering of Oberlinians, including both blacks and whites, adopted an explicit strategy of resistance. According to an account published a half-century later, "every man was called on to sign and pledge himself that [i]f any fugitive came to his home day or night, he would immediately take him in and secreet [sic] him to the best of his ability. And further, that if any one knew of any person trying to capture or carry off any fugitive, they would immediately inform the bell ringer, and he should first ring the fire, then the long toll, which would be a signal for everybody to rush to the corner."[9] This strategy would prove effective in September 1858, when it resulted in the famous Oberlin-Wellington Rescue of freedom seeker John Price. But by that time relatively few fugitives resided in Oberlin. In an address to "an Anti-Slavery meeting in the College Chapel" on January 1, 1859, the same John Watson reported that "the colored population of our town amounted to three hundred and forty-four, of whom twenty-eight were fugitives"—that is, about 8 percent of the total.[10] Overall, however, the town's population of color grew more than three times faster than its white population during the 1850s. In 1860 African Americans accounted for one-fifth of all Oberlin residents.[11]

Among Oberlin's greatest attractions for persons of color was the wide range of educational opportunities afforded them in the community, including access to integrated common schools. Such access was a rarity in the mid-nineteenth century, even in the North. Indeed, by providing for the education of white and black youth in the same public schools, Oberlinians for many years knowingly, though quietly, violated state law. In 1829, the Ohio legislature passed a statute mandating the establishment of tax-supported common schools across the state with the caveat that "nothing in this act . . . shall be construed as to permit black or mulatto persons to attend the schools hereby established."[12] Although this law was repealed two years later, the statute that replaced it specifically exempted from taxation "the property of blacks and mulattoes" because publicly financed schools were meant "for the instruction of white youth of every class and grade"—and, by implication, not for the education of youth of color.[13] The legislature reaffirmed this policy in 1838, and in 1842 the Ohio Supreme Court ruled that under state "law, white children, only, have the privileges of common schools."[14]

Yet in Oberlin students of color sat alongside white students in the town's original one-room schoolhouse. In his brief account of "Early School Days," published in 1899, Chellas S. Hopkins wrote that in the winter of 1842 his classmates included African Americans Thomas Janey and Patrick Minor. "A great boy was Pat," Hopkins recalled, "chuck full of fun. He could mimic anything or anyone. He used to make lots of fun for us boys."[15]

A circular published in the *Oberlin Evangelist* in 1844 noted that "all [the established schools in town] are open to people of color, from the district schools to the highest department of the institution [the Oberlin Institute]." Although the overseers of Oberlin's common schools never adopted a formal policy of racial integration, they found ways to provide children of color with tax-supported education.[16] Under state law, each school district was required to compile for referral to the county auditor an annual "enumeration . . . of all white youth in the district, between the ages of four and twenty-one years, not including any who are married."[17] Oberlin complied with this mandate, but in doing so it took full advantage of Ohio Supreme Court decisions that established a liberal standard for who qualified as white.[18] As the court explained in *Jeffries v. Ankeny* (1842), "all nearer white than black, or of the grade between the mulattoes and the whites, were entitled to enjoy every political and social privilege of the white citizen."[19] This capacious notion of whiteness allowed Oberlin school officials to act upon their principles by including the names of many light-complexioned African American children on lists of "white youth" submitted to the county auditor.[20]

Dark-complexioned African American children also attended Oberlin's common schools. According to an account published in 1847, although such children were not enumerated as "white youth," they nonetheless received "an equal share of the public money" and went to "the common schools the same as white children."[21] The most famous black student to attend an Oberlin common school during the antebellum era was Margru, also known as Sarah Kinson, who hailed from West Africa. Sold into slavery as a young child and transported across the Atlantic Ocean for resale in Cuba, Margru was aboard the slave ship *Amistad* when its human cargo seized control of the craft and inadvertently sailed into American territorial waters in the summer of 1839. After the *Amistad* was forced into port by a U.S. naval vessel, the fate of the stranded Africans became a cause célèbre. In March

1841 the U.S. Supreme Court ruled that they were entitled to their freedom. Sarah, as she by then called herself, sailed back to Africa ten months later, but in the summer of 1846, with the financial assistance of Lewis Tappan, she returned to the United States to pursue her education at Oberlin.[22]

Sarah began her studies at Oberlin in a common school taught by Lauretta Branch. In the fall of 1847, Branch offered a glowing assessment of Sarah's academic progress and intellectual potential:

> It is now about fourteen months since [Sarah] became a member of our school. She could then read and spell very well, but that was all. She commenced the study of Mental Arithmetic, Geography and writing, and found no difficulty in pursuing them. She always has her lesson and seldom fails in recitation. She had practiced writing but seven weeks when she wrote and read a very pretty composition. . . . Sarah is now studying Adam's Arithmetic, Grammar, Geography, and Mental Algebra, and is one of the best scholars in her class. Whatever study she undertakes she seems to find no difficulty in mastering it thoroughly—indeed, I have never had a more thorough and successful Scholar. She has gained the love and esteem of all her schoolmates.

Referencing the contemporary controversy over blacks' mental capacity, Branch added, "Often when I look upon her curly head and shining face lit up with the glow of intelligence and thought, I think 'Shame on the man who will say a Negro cannot learn.'"[23]

Under pressure from black activists and other abolitionists, the Ohio state legislature in 1848 passed a law "to provide for the establishment of Common Schools for the education of black and mulatto persons." Henceforth "property belonging to black or colored persons" was to "be taxed for school purposes" just like that "owned by white persons." The funds collected from property-holders of color would go to the education of students of color, and the new legislation explicitly allowed for—though it did not require—multiracial schools. In districts where "the children of black or colored persons are permitted to attend the common schools with the children of white persons," all collected taxes would be combined into a single "common school fund of the district."[24] As a result, Oberlin's school directors began to list "colored youth" as well as "white youth" in their annual enumerations, and they no longer had to worry about the possibility of state authorities challenging Oberlin's practice of racial integration at the common school level.[25]

As a private entity, the Oberlin Institute faced no legal obstacle to the admission of students of color so long as it retained its state charter. In the early 1840s anti-abolitionist Democrats in the Ohio legislature repeatedly sought to rescind that charter, but they failed.[26] By mid-century it was clear to partisans on all sides that the institution would endure, and in 1850 the Institute won legislative approval to retitle itself Oberlin College.[27]

Despite that name change, the school continued to operate a preparatory department, often simply called the prep, and that department accounted for over half the students who attended the institution before the Civil War. Of the 1,062 students listed in the catalogue for the 1855–1856 academic year, for example, 727 were enrolled in either the Preparatory or Ladies Preparatory Course, compared to 110 students in the College Course, 181 in the Ladies Literary Course, 24 in the Theological Course, and 20 in other courses of study.[28]

About a sixth of the students who attended the prep during the 1850s came from Oberlin or Russia Township. These local students—585 individuals in all—comprised a racially diverse group.[29] While the college made no mention of a student's race in its official records, linkage between the published catalogues and other sources reveals that approximately 6 percent were persons of color.[30] Although impressive evidence of black opportunity in antebellum Oberlin, this figure represented less than the proportion of African Americans in the local population as a whole. Not surprisingly, economic standing as well as race influenced the rate of participation. A majority of the local students of color who attended the prep during the 1850s belonged to a half-dozen relatively prosperous families: the Camptons, Copelands, D'Anglases, Jarvises, Joneses, and Pattersons. Moreover, the Joneses and Pattersons supplied all but one of the five African American students from Oberlin who went on to study at a more advanced level in either the College or the Ladies Literary Course.[31]

Oberlinians of color manifested their interest in the college's future when a controversy over the school's leadership broke out in early 1850. At issue was whether Asa Mahan should remain as president in the face of a concerted attempt by the college's faculty to remove him after fifteen years of service. "God does not appear to us to have given you that peculiar sort of wisdom & tact which is specially necessary in the President of a College to unite the Faculty in confiding & cheerful cooperation with him as their head & leader," the faculty tartly informed Mahan.[32] Mahan refused to resign, however, and townspeople rallied to his side in impressive numbers. Significantly, while African Americans joined in the campaign to retain Mahan, most of them did so by submitting their own petition rather than by signing the memorial that garnered the support of 280 whites.[33] Styling themselves "representatives of a downtrodden race," eighty-seven local residents of color addressed their separate petition directly to Mahan and beseeched him to stay on as president. "We have long looked upon you as being among our firmest and most able friends," they declared, "and believing the station you occupy to be a most favorable position for exerting a wide-spread and lasting influence for Humanity, we most earnestly desire and request that you may continue in your present field of great usefulness." In all, the petition's signers included members of over half the families of color residing in Russia Township at mid-century. That they chose to submit their own memorial suggests that they considered themselves a distinctive segment of the community with their own set of race-specific concerns and priorities.[34]

Oberlin College's commitment to racially integrated education set the school apart from most institutions of higher education in antebellum America. "Our doctrine is that *mind* and *heart*, not *color*, make the man, and the woman too," explained Professor Henry Cowles in response to an outsider's inquiry in 1851. He portrayed the college as a place where "colored and white students of the same sex" intermingled both inside and outside the classroom on a voluntary and mutually respectful basis.[35] Yet the college's commitment to integration did not include support for cultural diversity as that concept is understood today. The guiding assumption was that students of color would assimilate to the same social norms as white students and that white authority figures would enforce college rules in a color-blind manner. As James Harris Fairchild asserted in 1856 and reaffirmed in 1860, "Oberlin College was never designed to be a colored school; that is, to furnish facilities peculiarly adapted to the wants of the colored people; nor has there ever been an effort on the part of its managers, so to modify it as to meet these wants."[36]

An incident in July 1851 reveals how the college's avowedly race-neutral policy operated in practice. The affair began when two white female students from the college, accompanied by a young white female friend from the town, encountered two female students of color on a sidewalk built above

Oberlin's muddy streets to protect pedestrians from the muck below. Without enough room for the two groups to pass each other, neither side was willing to give way, and a contretemps ensued. While it is not clear whether she was pushed or simply lost her footing, one of the white students fell from the sidewalk and proceeded to hurl "vile epithets" at the two women of color. Brought before the college's Ladies Board—a disciplinary body composed of the wives of college faculty that enforced social and academic standards for female students—the students on both sides were ordered to write essays apologizing for their actions and words. Most likely the Ladies Board intended the penalty to be an even-handed punishment for all involved, but that was not how the board's action was received by the women of color. Refusing to back down or to express contrition, they enlisted the help of a third African American female student, who delivered an essay "said to be quite personal + giving an account of the whole affair" before her classmates. Although the composition has not survived, its author—Caroline Wall, the future wife of John Mercer Langston—clearly defied the expectations of the Ladies Board. Her resistance suggests that students of color embraced different conceptions of fairness and justice than those applied "impartially" by the white authorities who governed the college.[37]

Although Oberlin College declined, in James Harris Fairchild's previously cited words, "to furnish facilities peculiarly adapted to the wants of the colored people," the wider community recognized that illiterate former slaves had particular educational needs.[38] In 1842, residents established a "colored school . . . designed chiefly for adult persons who have been debarred in early life, by slavery or prejudice, from the advantages of education."[39] The students struggled to pay their teachers, however, and in 1844 an interracial Committee of Trust headed by Professor James A. Thome was formed to raise funds for the school's perpetuation. In making the case to potential donors, the committee observed, "The success of the separate schools [*sic*] for adults has been highly encouraging. . . . The scholars, some of them heads of families, are making good progress. They evince an interest in acquiring education even beyond the anticipations of the founders and conductors of the school."[40]

With the help of donations from both local supporters and abolitionists from afar, the Liberty School, as it became known, soon achieved financial stability, and it occupied its own building on North Main Street until fire laid waste to the wooden structure in 1860.[41] In March 1848, under the ironic title "Cannot Take Care of Themselves," both the *Liberator* and the *North Star* published a "letter from Oberlin" describing the enterprise in laudatory terms: "Mrs. D. is teaching a colored school of about forty scholars, almost every one of whom have *emancipated* themselves, and are now sustaining themselves here, paying their board, tuition, &c."[42] In his autobiography, John Mercer Langston recalled the Liberty schoolhouse, which doubled as an assembly space for African American residents, with deep affection. "Here was his Faneuil Hall in which the negro made his most eloquent and effective speeches against his enslavement," Langston wrote. "And no fugitive slave resident of Oberlin, attending such school or hearing such utterances, ever feared any successful assault upon his freedom."[43]

Leading white Oberlinians took pride in the educational accomplishments of the town's African Americans. In a historical account published in 1868, Edward Henry Fairchild—principal of the preparatory department as well as James's brother—observed of the students of color under his supervision: "there is no essential difference, other things being equal, between their standing and that of the white students. Some are among the best and some are among the poorest." More broadly, Fairchild portrayed the town of Oberlin as a community where blacks and whites got along easily. "Of our colored citizens," he wrote, "it is a pleasure to say that, in general, they are peaceable, orderly, industrious, and rapidly improving in cultivation and the comforts of life. They mingle freely with the white population in all the business relations of life, without the least danger of a 'war of the races,' or any other collision." Yet Fairchild acknowledged that a cultural gap existed between local whites and a significant segment of the town's black population. "Many of them, having recently come from slavery, retain, in great measure, the ignorance and peculiar habits of that institution," he reported with more than a trace of condescension. "A more intelligent, cultivated population would be desirable; but if asked to exchange them for an equal number of foreigners, of which we have none, we should beg to be excused."[44]

Apart from the college, the most important social institution in antebellum Oberlin was the Congregational Church, often called simply the Oberlin Church and later known as First Church.[45] Founded in 1834, the Congregational Church for two decades was the only formally constituted religious body in the community, and it was a major reason that white evangelical Christians from New England and upstate New York migrated to Oberlin during its early years. John Jay Shipherd served as the Congregational Church's first pastor. After he resigned for health reasons in 1836, the pulpit passed to Charles Grandison Finney.[46] In 1841, at Finney's urging, the congregation voted to construct a large brick building to accommodate the crowds of people who flocked from far and wide to hear him preach on Sundays.[47] When the new meetinghouse was completed in 1844, it stood as the most spacious auditorium in the American West.[48]

Before coming to Oberlin in 1835, Finney had entertained reservations about the wisdom of racially integrated religious assemblies.[49] But by the time he took over as pastor of the Congregational Church in 1837 its membership included blacks as well as whites, and throughout his long tenure in the pulpit—he did not step down until 1872—he welcomed all comers without regard to color.[50] A seating plan for the new meetinghouse, drafted in 1844, reveals that African American families rented pews next to white families on the building's main floor—a most unusual arrangement for the era.[51] Abolitionist Lucy Stone observed in 1849 that the Oberlin Church was the "one church [that she knew of] where the colored man was received in an equality with the white man."[52] Seven years later, the African American journalist William C. Nell wrote of his visit to Oberlin, "I was gratified to see equal participation of colored persons with white in church service. Not only were they seated promiscuously all over the house, . . . but even exercising their vocal gifts in the great choir. This latter sight is seldom witnessed publicly, unless at an anti-slavery gathering."[53]

Church membership records tell a somewhat different story, however. Although the records make no mention of race, linkage to other sources reveals that of the 1,401 individuals listed as church members at the start of 1857, approximately fifty—about 4 percent—were persons of color, and many of those were college students or alumni from out of town.[54] To be sure, some local African Americans, including John Mercer Langston, rented pews and attended services at the church even though they were not admitted to formal membership, which required evidence of conversion.[55] Still, at a time when people of color comprised an estimated 15–20 percent of Oberlin's total population, they appear to have been significantly underrepresented within the community's central religious institution.

In an article published in September 1853, the *Oberlin Evangelist* acknowledged that black and white townspeople tended to go separate ways on the Sabbath. "We never think or speak of these things but with pain," the paper reported. "We believe it to be almost universally the wish of the white people in our worshipping congregations to have their colored friends and neighbors meet with them. They are more than welcome. Many of them attend regularly. We wish they would *all* come."[56]

What accounts for the relatively low participation of local African Americans in the Congregational Church? The *Evangelist* quoted an explanation offered by an anonymous visitor: "There is as much natural prejudice among the blacks against the whites, as there is among the whites against the blacks." But the paper firmly disputed this assertion. "In our judgment this remark does the colored people injustice," the *Evangelist* declared, and it denied any moral equivalence between the racial prejudices of whites and blacks. The white man, the paper explained, "must hate and dislike the men he oppresses, in self-vindication. He must think meanly of the men he wrongs; else how could he justify himself?" According to the *Evangelist*, white prejudice was rooted in the class interest of slaveholders: "It is an aristocratic convenience to have a degraded *class,* and all the more convenient to have that class well defined by the color of the skin. If the class were to be defined by menial or moral worth, alas, some poor aristocrat might wake up on the wrong side of the line! Thus we trace the prejudice of the white man against the black primarily to slavery." By contrast, "the antipathy of the black against the white" was a defensive response to grievous oppression. "And so far as it results from a sense of wrong experienced," the *Evangelist* concluded, "we must always regard unprovoked infliction of wrong a greater crime than resentment under that infliction."[57]

Perhaps most striking about the *Evangelist*'s analysis of the dynamics of color prejudice is how modern, even postmodern, it sounds. At a time when American and European intellectuals were increasingly promoting "scientific" explanations of racial difference couched in biological terms and based on a premise of polygenesis, the *Evangelist* approached race as, in effect, a social construction shaped by the power dynamics of American society—in particular the institution of chattel slavery.[58] By this interpretation, color prejudice functioned as a cultural support for systemic exploitation, freeing whites from any sense of moral compunction for their abuse of fellow human beings. Especially noteworthy is the *Evangelist*'s explanation of why skin color proved a "convenient" marker for distinguishing members of the "degraded *class*" from those possessing privilege. Not only would a scheme of social categorization based on skill or character have been more complicated to maintain, it could have left "some poor aristocrat... on the wrong side of the line!"[59]

If black sensitivity to white bigotry was the main reason that, in the words of the *Evangelist,* "colored people ... usually prefer to attend religious meetings by themselves," other factors also played a part.[60] For one thing, most black Oberlinians came from the Upper South and had been raised in different religious traditions than the whites who migrated from the Northeast. Congregationalism—even Finney's enthusiastic version—was more text-based and rationalistic than the Methodist and Baptist faiths that predominated south of the Ohio River.[61]

Another factor was class. In a letter to the American Missionary Association dated April 2, 1861, Marcus Dale—Zeruiah Porter Weed's successor as the association's home missionary in Oberlin—observed, "There are two classes of colored people here. One class is made up of persons in pretty good circumstances. There is another class made up of persons who are ignorant and poor and they are said to be lazy and low. This latter class does not visit the large church."[62] Dale, who was African American, explained that he had approached "some of these people about two years ago & asked them why they did not come to church on sabbath." They replied "that they were very ignorant and could not understand the preaching of those that preached there." Although he then sought to reassure this group of poor blacks that "they might understand Mr. Finney though he was a very learned man," Dale still "could not persuade them to come out to the Oberlin church." Consequently, he began to preach to them himself "and held prayer meetings until they formed themselves into a wesleyan church and came under the wesleyan conference." Yet by Dale's account, his efforts to serve poor blacks in Oberlin drew criticism from a number of the town's more affluent African Americans. "Some of the colored people here who are in better circumstances than those with whom I have been labouring have remonstrated with me about going among such a low class," he wrote, "and they told me that if I did continue to go among them that I would not be much thought of."[63]

Data from the federal census lend credence to Dale's assertion that Oberlin's population of color was divided by an economic gulf in 1860. The 1860 census listed 429 residents of color in Oberlin proper, plus another sixty-five in the surrounding area of Russia Township, for a total of 494.[64] Although a small proportion were servants, students, laborers, or others living with white families, the vast majority (over seven-eighths) resided in one of the township's eighty-six households headed by African Americans. According to the census, these households collectively owned $114,002 in real and personal estate. The average (mean) property valuation for African American-headed households was $1,326—approximately one-third the average for white-headed households in Russia Township, but impressive nonetheless.[65] However, statistical analysis reveals stark differences among local African Americans in terms of wealth. Of the eighty-six households headed by a person of color, the ten wealthiest accounted for 60 percent of the total amount of property owned by African Americans in Russia Township in 1860. Most of the individuals who headed these elite households were already affluent at the time they settled in the community, including John Mercer Langston, Thomas Jarvis, John E. Patterson, Henry Evans, and O.S.B. Wall. Diza D'Anglas inherited a sizable estate from her late, white husband, who was rich before coming to Oberlin. John Watson, however, had made his fortune after settling in Oberlin in the early 1840s. A former slave, he achieved entrepreneurial success as a grocer, restauranteur, and co-owner of the commercial block erected on South Main Street. Watson was the third richest householder of color in Russia Township in 1860.[66]

In contrast to this wealthy elite, the poorer half of African American households accounted for less than 8 percent of the total amount of property owned by people of color. The gini coefficient of wealth inequality for households headed by persons of color registered .68 on a scale of 0 (total equality) to 1 (total inequality). By this standard statistical metric, it appears that African American residents were highly stratified economically.[67]

They were also differentiated by skin color. The federal census of 1860 distinguished between "blacks" and "mulattoes." Most likely the designations were made not by the individuals surveyed but by the census taker, who for Russia Township was Chauncey Wack, an openly racist, anti-abolitionist Democrat. Although Wack's perceptions were undoubtedly influenced by his general hostility to African Americans, it remains noteworthy that, according to his enumeration, "mulatto" heads of household outnumbered "black" heads of household in Russia Township by a ratio of more than 2 to 1. Even more striking is the reported wealth gap between households headed by "mulattoes" and those headed by "blacks." According to the census, all members of the wealthiest quintile of Russia Township's household heads of color were "mulattoes," while the average (mean) property assessment among "mulatto"-headed households was five times higher than the average among black-headed households. Likewise, "mulatto" household heads tended to pursue higher-status professional and artisanal occupations, while those listed as blacks were disproportionately represented among persons in service occupations. Whether skin color was an independent variable in shaping the pattern of inequality within Oberlin's African American population is unclear, however. On the one hand, it seems quite plausible that darker persons of color experienced greater economic and social discrimination than those who looked almost white. On the other hand, among those listed as mulattoes were the well-off children of wealthy slave owners, such as Thomas Jarvis, John Mercer Langston, and O.S.B. Wall. Their relative economic privilege almost certainly had more to do with the transfer of property from their fathers than with the disparate treatment of light-complexioned and dark-complexioned African Americans in mid-nineteenth-century Oberlin.[68]

One realm where the shade of a man's skin mattered a good deal was the polling place. From its inception as a state in 1803, Ohio granted the right of suffrage to "all white male inhabitants above the age of twenty-one years" who had lived in the state for at least one year and were subject to state or county taxes.[69] This wording appeared to exclude persons of color from access to the ballot, but in 1842 the Ohio Supreme Court ruled in *Jeffries v. Ankeny* that mixed-race individuals with over 50 percent white ancestry qualified as "white" for legal purposes.[70] By this decision, a significant share of Oberlin's African American men enjoyed the right to vote.

Critics charged that Oberlin went further than the law allowed. In October 1857 the rabidly racist *Cleveland Plain Dealer* reported that "scores of the blackest Africans that ever crossed the seas" cast ballots in Oberlin and that "[o]ver one hundred illegal votes were thus polled" in the latest contest.[71] A surviving poll list from two years before tells a different story, however. This rare document includes the names of the men from Oberlin and Russia Township who voted in the 1855 fall elections for governor, judges of the Ohio Supreme Court, state senator and representative from the area, as well as for other state- and county-level offices. Of the five hundred electors in all, twenty-four (5 percent) have been identified as men of color. Some, such as John Campton, John Copeland, Thomas Jarvis, John Lane, and John Watson, were longstanding township residents. Others, including Henry and Wilson Evans, Henry Patterson, and O.S.B. Wall, were recent arrivals. Most were mixed-race, light-complexioned individuals who met the statewide suffrage requirement as interpreted by the Ohio Supreme Court. Two, including John Craven Jones (a son of Allen Jones), had to sign affidavits attesting to their eligibility, most likely because of their dark hue. Taken together, the twenty-four electors of color represented an estimated one-third of all African American men of voting age residing in Russia Township at the time. While that was a substantial proportion, it was considerably lower than the estimated four-fifths of the township's adult white male population that cast ballots in the 1855 election. When it came to voting, blackness was a significant disability—even in abolitionist Oberlin.[72]

That fact did not stop John Mercer Langston from winning election as clerk of Russia Township in 1857.[73] Langston had previously held a similar post in nearby Brownhelm Township, where he had resided from 1854 to 1856, and he had longstanding ties to both Oberlin College and the broader Oberlin community. While he proudly identified as a man of color and worked tirelessly for African American advancement, he enjoyed broad support within Russia Township's predominantly white electorate, which chose him to replace a white incumbent.[74] Indeed, he may have stood in higher esteem among local whites than among local blacks. In his autobiography, Langston observed that for six years after he opened his law office in Oberlin in 1856, "The only class in the general population which did not supply him with patronage . . . were the colored people." He attributed this pattern to the racism embedded in the state's legal system. Oberlinians of color "could not understand what the result would be, should a black client appear before the court and jury represented by a colored lawyer."[75] There was probably another factor at work as well. As the free-born son of a well-to-do white Virginia planter, Langston enjoyed privileges of wealth and higher education denied the majority of Oberlin's African American residents. His experience of racial discrimination was qualitatively different from theirs, and they did not automatically feel a sense of shared, collective identity.

Nonetheless, evidence from a letter penned in 1853 suggests that an important social bond existed between Langston and less privileged Oberlinians of color. Employing racist terminology without apology, W. D. Patterson, a white student in the preparatory department, wrote his father about "a n—— that belonged to [an] old lady in the south" who, having fallen into debt, "advised her slave, this boy to run away so that her creditors could not get him." The boy had followed his mistress's advice and, by Patterson's account, had "been here 3 years at school" when "the other day the old lady[']s son came here with the boy[']s Father[,] who is free[,] to get the Boy." The mistress's son "promises to free the Boy in 4 years if he will come back and work for him," Patterson explained, while "the Boy[']s Father wants him to go." When the boy signaled that he would accede to their wishes, Oberlin's African American residents assembled to discuss the situation. By Patterson's account, Langston—whom Patterson characterized variously as a "half n——," "the smartest student in Oberlin," and "worth $30,000 or $40,000"— played a pivotal role in the proceedings. Langston protested the boy's decision to return to slavery, and other people of color joined him in opposition. According to Patterson, "the Father was there and I thought he would get mob[b]ed." Violence was avoided, however, and the meeting adjourned until the next evening for further debate. "It seems that a number of Slaves have written home to their masters that they were starving here and asked to be brought back," Patterson reported to his father. He added, however, that "the people here won[']t let them go back I don[']t think."[76]

Patterson's report that an unspecified "number of Slaves" who reached Oberlin wished to return to bondage comes as a shock. The government of Russia Township allocated public funds for the lodging of "transient paupers" in private households, and various local voluntary associations also provided fugitive slaves with financial assistance.[77] Yet an article published in the antislavery *Cleveland Herald* indicates that the episode described by W. D. Patterson was not an entirely isolated event. "Two old women, slaves, who some two years since were sent out of Virginia to prevent their sale for debt, had found their way to Oberlin," the *Herald* reported on February 26, 1853. "They had several times written their former master that they wished to return to him, and at length their request became so urgent that he visited Oberlin." As in the case described by Patterson, townspeople "determined that slaves *should not* return." Their erstwhile master "replied he had come at their own solicitation . . . and that he had no desire to take them back unless they desired to go." According to the *Herald*'s account, "Every argument was used to induce them to stay" but to no avail. The women chose to go back to Virginia.[78]

Incidents such as those described by W. D. Patterson and the *Cleveland Herald* serve as a reminder that the historical record is full of puzzles and surprises that defy easy explanation. The ideological evolution of Allen Jones provides further evidence that history sometimes unfolded in strange and seemingly inexplicable ways in antebellum Oberlin.

Jones was an iconoclast with an unusual background. Born into bondage in North Carolina in 1794, he succeeded by his mid-thirties in buying his freedom—and the freedom of his loved ones—through a great deal of hard work. After gaining his liberty and that of other family members in the late 1820s, he stayed in the Raleigh area and prospered as a blacksmith. He took a deep interest in black education and appears to have championed the larger cause of black rights. He and his wife named their sixth child Elias Toussaint in honor of the Haitian revolutionary leader Toussaint Louverture.[79] In late 1842, after suffering a violent assault at the hands of a white mob, Jones decided to move his family to a free state north of the Ohio River. Upon first setting eyes on Oberlin in early 1843, he reputedly pronounced it "a paradise."[80]

Soon after his arrival, Jones opened a blacksmith shop across North Main Street from the Congregational Church, then under construction.[81] He later relocated his operation to South Main Street, and although he never regained the level of wealth he had accumulated before leaving North Carolina, he proudly invested in the education of his several sons (but not his daughter) at Oberlin College, from which four graduated with bachelor's degrees.[82] According to family lore, when his oldest son "grew discouraged" and announced that he wished to drop out, Allen Jones "took him out into the back yard and showed him the chopping block and the sharp axe lying nearby, recited the tale of the trials and trouble he, the father, had undergone to bring the family where they might be educated, and then said, 'Now, James, you take your choice. You go back to college, or you lay your head on the chopping block, and I chop it off.'" The son duly returned to his studies.[83]

Initially Allen Jones embraced Oberlin's abolitionist ethos. In September 1848, along with other Oberlinians of color, he attended the National Convention of the Colored Freemen, held in Cleveland. Frederick Douglass served as the convention's president, and Jones was elected one of its four vice presidents. He also gave a brief address expounding on "the object of the Convention" and describing his life as a slave. According to William Howard Day's account, "He said he earned for his master $10,000 . . . and yet some people would say he was 'not able to take care of himself.'"[84] Eight years later, in August 1856, the *Cleveland Herald* described Allen Jones favorably as a "North Carolina emancipationist" and "Oberlin Character" fit "for the pen of Harriet Beecher Stowe." "He now owns a handsome property," the *Herald* reported, "and enjoys all the comforts of life and the luxury of freedom. His home is beautified with trees and flowers, and two of his six sons have graduated with College honors. Two others will at next Commencement, and his other sons and daughter are examples of industry and studiousness many of lighter skin might imitate with advantage."[85]

Despite this success, Allen Jones turned sharply against Oberlin orthodoxy. According to Denton J. Snider—an 1862 Oberlin College graduate who went on to become a popular lecturer and prolific author—Jones by the late 1850s "was a violent pro-slavery Democrat."[86] In an autobiography published in 1910, Snider, who was white, remembered Jones as "the mightiest negro individuality I have ever met."[87] Yet Snider found Jones's racial attitudes disconcerting:

> He had a very low opinion of his own race . . . and always with great contempt spoke of them, at least when I heard him, as n——s. He utterly refused to take part in the famous rescue case at Wellington. I went into his shop not long after and asked him: "Well, Mr. Jones, did you go along to Wellington to help rescue your colored brother?"
> Jones fired up. "No brudder o' mine."
> "Why, is not every colored man your brother?"
> "What, dose n——s? What are you talking about, man?"
> "And would you not help to free him of bondage?"
> "I say de n—— is not fit to be free."

Although Jones "was as black as any negro in Oberlin," Snider observed, "yet he had that grotesque inconsistency of the African damning the African because he is African. Jones, above all things in the world, wished to be a white man."[88]

Allen Jones's animus toward other persons of color is mystifying, especially since his racism appears to have developed after he resided in abolitionist Oberlin for over a decade. Perhaps the death of his wife in 1856 and the departure of a number of his sons for Canada shook his faith in the world and led him to abandon his earlier commitment to the collective advancement of people of color.[89] Perhaps Snider retrospectively misrepresented Jones's views on race, although other sources confirm Snider's description of Jones's partisan sympathies (he stood for election as justice of the peace under the Democratic banner in 1868).[90] Whatever the cause of Jones's apostasy, his renunciation of abolitionist principles reveals the limits of broad generalizations about how Oberlinians "saw race" in the antebellum era.[91]

Allen Jones was hardly the only contrarian in town. A convenient, though imperfect, measure of dissent from Oberlin's ideological orthodoxy in the 1850s was the number of local ballots cast for Democratic presidential candidates. The national Democratic Party stood for white supremacy and for compromise on the question of slavery's expansion—positions long at odds with the majority opinion in Oberlin. Yet in 1852, 95 out of a total of 455 ballots in Russia Township (21 percent) were cast for Franklin Pierce, the Democratic nominee.[92] Thereafter Democratic support declined, but it never disappeared. In the presidential election of 1856, Democratic candidate James Buchanan received 77 of 521 votes (15 percent) in Russia Township.[93] In 1860, Northern Democrat Stephen Douglas got 82 of 716 votes (11 percent) and John C. Breckinridge, a strongly proslavery Southern Democrat, received 21 votes (3 percent).[94]

Oberlin's most prominent and provocative Democrats were Lewis D. Boynton and Chauncey Wack. Like many other white Oberlinians of their generation, they originally hailed from New England. Boynton was born in Maine in 1802 and migrated to Russia Township with his wife, Ruth, and their children in the mid-1820s. Upon his arrival he purchased farmland, and he was well established in the township before the Oberlin colony's founding in 1833. How he responded to the newcomers, including the Lane Rebels, is not known, but in the mid-1830s he was almost certainly a supporter of the Whig Party: he and Ruth conferred the name Henry Clay on their seventh child, born in 1834.[95]

During the 1830s and early 1840s Boynton served in the state militia, rising to the rank of brigadier general—a largely honorific title since the militia never saw military action.[96] In 1840 he was one of the ten wealthiest householders in Russia Township.[97] After Ruth died that year, leaving him with eight children to raise on his own, he quickly remarried and subsequently fathered seven more children by his second wife.[98]

By the mid-1850s Boynton was a leader of the Democratic Party in Lorain County. At a party meeting in September 1857 he offered a resolution that made clear where he stood on the issues of slavery and race that so concerned his abolitionist neighbors: "*Resolved*, That 'Negro Equality,' 'Bleeding Kansas,' 'Horace Greely [*sic*],' and the [Salmon P.] Chase administration are the four greatest political humbugs of the age, and that it is the duty of democrats to see to it that at the coming election, this mongrel combination is routed, *horse, foot, and dragoon.*"[99] A month later, according to the *Plain*

Dealer, Boynton kept watch on election day and "challenged every darkey that dare show his wool" at the polls in Oberlin.[100]

Like Boynton, Chauncey Wack enjoyed playing the role of devil's advocate in a passionately pious community. Born in Bennington, Vermont, in 1815, Wack moved with his parents and many siblings to Carlisle Township in Lorain County in 1832. In 1840, at age twenty-four, he married Mary Ann Brown of nearby LaGrange, and they set up housekeeping in Russia Township.[101] Mary Ann gave birth to the first of their four children in 1841, and over the next several years Chauncey did some farming and practiced carpentry.[102] In 1845 he paid taxes on one horse and two cows but no real estate.[103] He subsequently purchased a parcel on South Main Street, and in 1852 he opened Oberlin's second hotel, conveniently located near the new depot of the Toledo, Norwalk, and Cleveland Railroad.[104]

Known variously as Russia House, Railroad House, Wack's Hotel, and Wack's Tavern, this establishment initially sought to distinguish itself by serving "spirituous liquors" in defiance of local custom. The "doubtful experiment" failed, however, and on December 23, 1852, Wack acknowledged defeat by hosting a grand "Temperance Festival." Under a banner proclaiming "Love, Purity, and Fidelity," he served an elaborate supper for more than eighty guests, and the Oberlin Glee Club supplied the evening's "soul-stirring" musical entertainment. Despite the absence of alcohol, participants offered a series of enthusiastic toasts. The chair for the occasion, fellow Democrat Edward F. Munson, raised his glass to *"Our Host—*Who has the Independence to be a temperance man without the aid of those who are continually proscribing him."[105]

If Wack retreated on the temperance issue—at least temporarily—he remained firm in his allegiance to the Democratic Party. In the fall election of 1856, when his neighbors voted more than five to one in favor of Republican John C. Frémont, Wack gloried in James Buchanan's national victory. "Through the energy of the friends of Constitutional Government," he crowed at a post-election celebration, "the enemies of the Union have met with the rebuke their impudence and infamy demanded."[106] In 1857 he and his wife went so far as to name their last child James Buchanan Wack.[107]

While Oberlin's small coterie of Democrats openly championed white supremacist ideas, other townspeople displayed symptoms of "colorphobia" in more subtle ways.[108] In his autobiography John Mercer Langston recounted what happened in 1856 when he, his wife, and their infant son moved into their newly constructed house on East College Street—in what Langston termed "the most desirable part of the village of Oberlin." The family had been residing in nearby Brownhelm Township and traveled to their new abode by horse-drawn wagon. "The horses were just turning . . . into East College Street," Langston recalled, "when a resident of this neighborhood, a white man of extremely doubtful Republican feelings and principles, always officious and meddlesome, addressing Mr. Langston, propounded the following interesting but vexatious questions, 'Are you coming to live among us aristocrats? Do you think you can maintain yourself among us?'" To Langston, the implication of the questions was clear: "Liberally and fairly interpreted these inquiries were intended to admonish the colored newcomers, the first of their class who had undertaken to purchase and locate a home in that particular section of the most noted Abolition town in America, that it would be necessary for them, according to this man's conception of their condition as to general society, to understand that they would find the usual social barriers erected against their advancement even there."[109]

Langston found his interrogator's comments deeply offensive, and they obviously still bothered him four decades later. Yet in his autobiography he was careful to distinguish this incident from the dominant response to his family's arrival on East College Street. The "nearest neighbors," he wrote, welcomed his family with "remarkable attentions and hospitable proffers," and henceforth the Langstons "spent the time of their residence there in happy and constant accord, good understanding and cordial neighborly treatment."[110]

Langston's anecdote raises the question of whether housing in antebellum Oberlin was racially segregated in practice, if not by law. Linkage of data from Oberlin's first city directory (published in 1859), the federal census of 1860, tax records, and an 1857 Oberlin map allows for an analysis of the geographical distribution of 278 households residing within the town's corporate limits in 1859–1860. Of these linked households, 236 (85 percent) were headed by whites and forty-two (15 percent) were headed by persons of color. When the town is divided into four sections along the axes of College and Main Streets, the northwest quadrant shows a marked racial imbalance, with whites comprising 96 percent of all household heads and blacks only 4 percent. The section with the highest proportion of black household heads (22 percent) was the southeast quadrant. In the other two quadrants the racial composition of household heads nearly matched that of the town

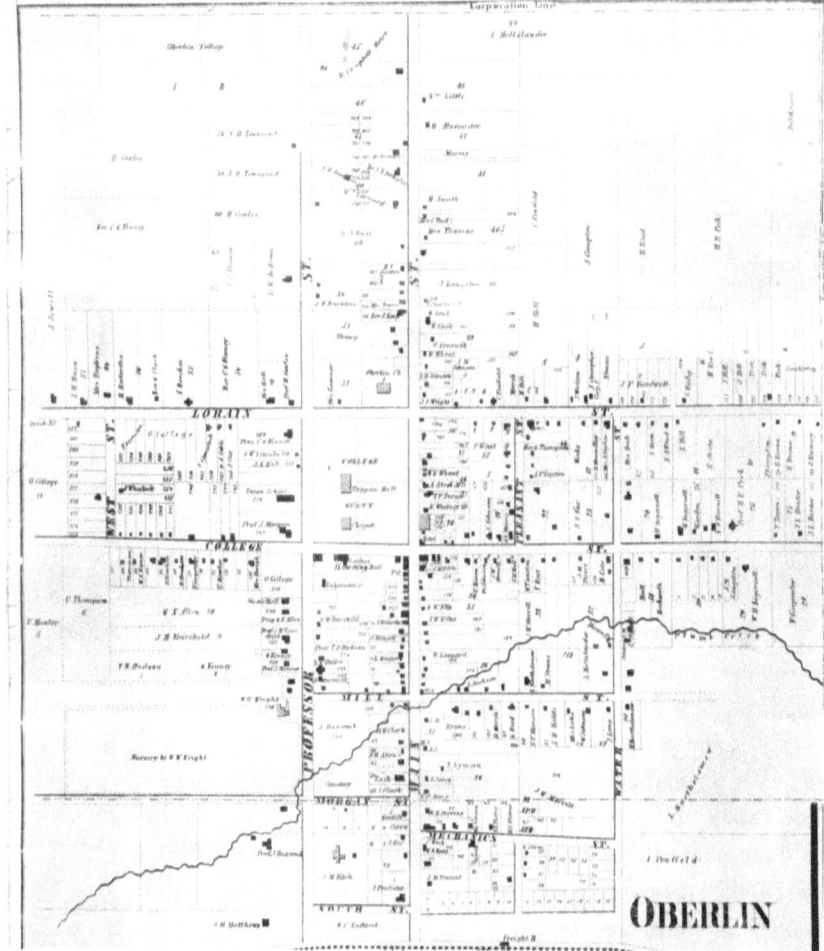

Map of Oberlin in *Atlas from the 1857 Map of Lorain Co. Ohio from Actual Surveys by John F. Geil*. Oberlin College Archives.

overall: 85 percent white and 15 percent black in the northeast; 84 percent white and 16 percent black in the southwest.[111]

Combining data from all four quadrants allows for calculation of the "index of dissimilarity," a commonly employed statistical measure of residential segregation between two mutually exclusive groups (for example, whites and persons of color) within a larger population. The index of dissimilarity can vary from 0 to 100, with 0 representing perfect integration and 100 representing total geographical separation between the two groups.[112] For Oberlin, the index of dissimilarity among linked household heads in 1860 was 18, which means that either 18 percent of white-headed households or 18 percent of black-headed households would have had to change quadrants for the town to have achieved perfect integration. In comparative context, this figure is impressively low: in 1860 the index of dissimilarity for whites and blacks in Boston was 61, while in Cincinnati it was 48, and in Philadelphia it was 47.[113] Yet there were at least a few distinct racial enclaves in antebellum Oberlin. Langston noted in his memoir that before his family's arrival in 1856, East College Street was uniformly white.[114] In 1859, Zeruiah Porter Weed referred to her efforts in "that part of Lorain St called 'Africa,'" and she added that "a still larger number of colored families" were concentrated "in the vicinity of the Depot."[115]

Perhaps the ultimate metric of the extent to which Oberlinians practiced racial egalitarianism in their daily lives was the frequency of interracial marriage in the community and residents' attitudes toward such unions. Although interracial marriage remained legal in Ohio until 1861, from the mid-1830s forward Oberlin's critics warned that social equality would lead to sex between blacks and whites and the speedy decline of American civilization.[116] In *Oberlin Unmasked*, for example, Delazon Smith suggested that student parties at the Oberlin Institute encouraged intimate relations between black men and white women. On such occasions, he wrote, "to cap the climax, the negro gentlemen accompany some of the 'discreet sisters' to their rooms. To what extent these intimacies were carried, I am unable to tell, and probably ever shall be, except the Lord . . . shall bring to light something more tangible."[117]

As late as 1862, Edward Henry Fairchild took pains to deny the charge still regularly made against Oberlin College that "our method of treating the colored people, granting them equal privileges with whites, allowing them to recite in the same classes, sit upon the same seats, and eat at the same tables, must result in amalgamation." "In the whole history of this Institution," he wrote,

> but one case has occurred. In this case a white young man chose for his bride a lady quite his superior in talent, education, and energy, in whom there was an "invisible admixture of African blood." Soon after, both were employed as teachers of a village school on the Ohio river. They had taught

with great acceptance for six months, when a rumor reached the village that some of the lady's ancestors were of African descent. At once the magnanimous people, indignant that their children should have been so long and so well instructed by a negro woman, and that they should have invited her to their tables and their parlors, promptly dismissed both from the school.

"This is the beginning and the end of amalgamation at this Institution," Fairchild concluded, "and such has been its punishment."[118]

Although the prospect of miscegenation among students at the college was a cause for consternation outside of Oberlin, marriages between blacks and whites failed to attract much notice within the town itself. For example, the self-emancipated slave Henry Johnson and his wife, Anna, a white woman from Vermont, resided in Oberlin without controversy from the 1840s until her death in 1867—with the exception of a two-year excursion that Johnson made to Haiti in the mid-1850s.[119] Likewise, when Jeremiah (Jerry) Fox, another self-emancipated slave, married Elizabeth Sullivan, a white woman from Ireland, in 1859, nobody objected—at least in public.[120]

Marriages between former slaveholders and women whom they had once owned comprised a distinct category of interracial relationships in Oberlin. Physician and planter Stanislas D'Anglas fathered several children by his bondwoman Diza in Louisiana before freeing her and their offspring in the 1840s. He formally acknowledged his paternity of the children before a notary public in New Orleans in 1853, and the family subsequently moved to Oberlin. In the will Stanislas wrote in 1854, he referred to Diza as his wife, and upon his death in 1856 her legal status as his widow went unchallenged.[121]

Less is known about Benjamin Franklin Adair and his wife, Charlotte. He was white and she was black. Circumstantial evidence suggests that she was the oldest of six slaves that he owned in Spring Creek, Arkansas, in 1850, and that the younger slaves were their children.[122] By 1860 the family had moved to Oberlin and Charlotte had given birth to three more children. Benjamin's occupation was listed as cotton gin builder in the 1860 census, and he ranked among the second highest quintile of Russia Township taxpayers that year.[123] The Adairs kept a low public profile.[124]

The one interracial relationship that generated a great deal of controversy in antebellum Oberlin was the unsanctified liaison between Malachi Warren and his erstwhile bondwoman Ellen. Born in Georgia in 1792, Malachi, like many ambitious white southerners of his generation, went west in search of economic opportunity. He settled in Lowndes County, Alabama, where he prospered as a cotton planter and as a slave trader. In the early 1830s, while doing business in Richmond, Virginia, he purchased Ellen and brought her back with him to Alabama. She was in her early teens at the time, and he exploited her for his sexual pleasure. In 1835 she gave birth to a daughter, Mary, and three sons followed over the next dozen years. In the late 1840s Malachi moved the family to Madison, Indiana, where Ellen gave birth to another daughter.[125] Apparently Malachi commuted back and forth to Alabama on a regular basis, and Ellen was listed as head of the Warren household in the 1850 federal census.[126] The following year Malachi legally manumitted Ellen and the children by signing an "Emancipation Deed" before a notary public in Indiana.[127]

Soon thereafter the family relocated to Oberlin. Malachi Warren never embraced the community's abolitionist ethos, however. He also never married Ellen. In 1853, Oberlin College ruled that Malachi and Ellen were unfit to board its students—even their own daughter, Mary—so long as "they sustain the relation to each other they do at present."[128] The Warrens departed for Salem, Ohio, in the mid-1850s, but by 1858 they were again living in Oberlin, on East Lorain Street—except for Mary, who got married and moved with her husband to Wisconsin.[129]

Malachi proudly displayed his southern sympathies, and when slave hunters came to Oberlin in the summer of 1858, he was happy to help them.[130] Oberlinians were outraged, and after Ellen gave birth to a new baby in February 1860, townspeople got their revenge. Malachi and Ellen Warren were indicted for the crime of "living and cohabiting in a state of fornication" and put on trial before a jury.[131] John Mercer Langston served as one of three prosecutors in the case, which concluded with the conviction of both defendants. Recognizing that Ellen was more a victim than a criminal, the court chose not to punish her for her transgression. It sentenced Malachi to a day in jail "on bread and water" and fined him $100 plus the cost of the trial.[132] The community through this process publicly shamed him. Although most antebellum Oberlinians viewed interracial marriage as morally acceptable, they could not tolerate a man and a woman having sexual intercourse outside of wedlock whatever the color of their skin.[133]

Oberlinians of color enjoyed a range of important benefits largely unavailable to African Americans elsewhere in the United States—including physical security, educational opportunity, and social respectability. But not all Oberlinians of color enjoyed equal access to those benefits. Those who possessed literacy, occupational skills, and a modicum of property fared much better than the town's black poor. Just as race mattered in Oberlin, so did class. Still, when the struggle against American slavery intensified in the 1850s, black and white Oberlinians came together and rallied in common cause against the Slave Power. The next chapter focuses on the racial dynamics of Oberlin abolitionism.

4

MEANS AND ENDS IN OBERLIN ABOLITIONISM

In establishing the Oberlin Anti-Slavery Society in June 1835, the organization's founders—all of them white—endorsed an array of strategies to achieve "the immediate emancipation of the whole colored race within the United States."[1] They would appeal to slaveholders' religious beliefs as well as to their "pecuniary interests," mobilize "public sentiment," and pray "for the Abolition of Slavery throughout the world." Pledging fealty to "the law of love," the founders promised to abide by the federal Constitution, and eschewed any resort to force or violence—including, specifically, the promotion of slave rebellions.[2] Yet on September 13, 1858, hundreds of Oberlinians, black as well as white, openly defied a federal law and intervened physically to rescue a freedom seeker who had been taken into custody by a government official. Fifteen months later townspeople packed the Congregational Church to honor two Oberlinians of color who had taken up arms and sacrificed their lives in devotion to John Brown's plan to incite a massive slave revolt across the South. Why did Oberlinians in the space of a generation forsake their faith in the efficacy of peaceful methods and embrace the use of coercive force to end human bondage in the United States? This chapter argues that the growing influence of African Americans—many of whom had experienced slavery directly—played a decisive role in the transformation of Oberlin abolitionism.[3]

Oberlin's early abolitionists believed in the superior power of moral suasion over other strategies because they possessed firm Christian faith in the God-given capacity of every human being to attain righteousness.[4] Oberlinians never shunned politics, however. In the fall of 1835 "sundry citizens of the township of Russia" petitioned the Ohio legislature to repeal the "acts of 1804 and 1807, regulating blacks and mulattoes, requiring a bond on their settlement in this State, &c."[5] Two years later over three hundred Oberlin women petitioned Congress in opposition to the prospective annexation of Texas, and by the early 1840s Oberlin men were deeply engaged in Liberty Party efforts to end slavery through the electoral process.[6] While William Lloyd Garrison urged abolitionists to withdraw from participation in all morally corrupt institutions, including governmental bodies, Oberlinians pursued a different course. Garrisonians Abby Kelley and Stephen Foster and later Frederick Douglass and Garrison himself spoke to large audiences in Oberlin in the mid-1840s, but their arguments for "come-outerism" gained little traction among local activists.[7]

On July 6, 1848, Oberlin's "Liberty Party men" gathered to decide whether they should take part in "the Free Territory Convention to be held in Buffalo" the following month. Under the terms of the Treaty of Guadalupe Hidalgo that had ended the Mexican-American War four months before, the United States acquired more than a half-million square miles of land previously owned by Mexico (not including Texas), and the question of slavery's status in the so-called Mexican Cession remained unresolved. When the Democratic and Whig Parties failed to address that question head-on at their presidential nominating conventions in the early summer, dissenters within their ranks raised the possibility of starting a new party dedicated to prohibiting slavery's expansion, as distinct from ending slavery entirely. The Liberty Party men who met in Oberlin on July 6 affirmed their willingness to support such an initiative so long as the new party's platform incorporated certain longstanding abolitionist objectives, including the elimination of slavery in Washington, D.C., the end of "the coast-wise slave trade," and "[t]he repeal of all laws in the nominally Free States which make any distinction among their people on account of their color." The Liberty Party men also insisted that the new party nominate only "the known and tried advocates of these measures."[8] Having thus articulated their bedrock concerns, Oberlin's Liberty Party supporters dispatched a delegation headed by Institute president Asa Mahan to Buffalo.[9]

Although the Free Soil Party that emerged from the Buffalo convention failed to endorse the principle of racial equality and nominated Martin Van Buren, an erstwhile doughface Democrat, for president, the Oberlin delegation—undoubtedly all white—heartily endorsed the convention's outcome. "Every man returned to his home with a joyful countenance, a glad heart, and a will fixed in its determination, to apply the torch of freedom . . . to light up the entire North into one universal conflagration," reported the *Oberlin Evangelist*.[10] "We hope much from this great movement, and shall hope all the more, according as we may see the hearts of its movers staying themselves in faith upon the Omnipotent Arm."[11]

A majority of Oberlin voters supported the Free Soil Party in the fall election. Van Buren garnered 179 of the 325 ballots cast for president in Russia Township (55 percent). Yet a significant minority of local electors stuck by the abolitionist Liberty Party and supported its nominee, Gerrit Smith, who received sixty-one votes (19 percent). The remaining township voters cast their ballots for one of the two major party candidates: Whig nominee Zachary Taylor (twenty-nine votes, 9 percent) and Lewis Cass, the Democratic candidate (fifty-six votes, 17 percent).[12] The national result was strikingly different: Zachary Taylor, a large-scale Louisiana slaveholder, won the presidency.

Although the election of 1848 failed to usher in a hoped-for political revolution across the North, Oberlin activists could take comfort in one important victory. They and fellow voters in Lorain County elected Norton S. Townshend, a trustee of the Oberlin Institute and a strong antislavery man, to the Ohio House of Representatives. Townshend ran on the Free Soil ticket, and he emerged as a political kingmaker when the legislature convened in December 1848. Initially neither Democrats nor Whigs possessed the majority of votes needed to organize the House, and consequently both sides lobbied the small number of Free Soilers for their support. Seizing this opportunity, Townshend struck an extraordinary deal with the notoriously racist Democrats. In exchange for his help in taking control of the House, they agreed to abrogate most of Ohio's racially discriminatory Black Laws and to elect Free Soiler Salmon P. Chase to the U.S. Senate.[13]

Yet even this progress was not enough for "the colored citizens of Oberlin" and a few white allies who met on February 12, 1849, to set forth a yet more radical agenda for full civil equality. The partial repeal of the Black Laws eliminated the 1804 statute requiring "all people of color [to] prove their freedom to a county clerk" and an 1807 law mandating "every colored immigrant to give security of $500.00 for good behavior and against becoming a pauper," as well as "another law of 1807 which excluded their testimony from all courts of justice, in cases where any white person is a party." But racial restrictions on jury service and suffrage remained in place. William Howard Day, Sabram Cox, and John Watson joined with others to assert the principle of "the 'Fathers of '76,' that taxation and representation ought to go together," questioning whether people of color should pay "any tax upon which representation is based" unless and until they gained the right to vote. More directly, the meeting "urge[d] the slave to leave immediately with his hoe on his shoulder, for a land of liberty" and advised "all colored persons and their friends, to keep a sharp look-out for men-thieves and their abettors, and to warn them that no person claimed to be a slave shall be taken from our midst without trouble."[14]

Significantly, these "colored citizens of Oberlin" affirmed a general preference for racial integration over separatist alternatives. They unreservedly attacked colonization as a "scheme opposed to our best interest," and they characterized as "reprehensible" any "attempt to establish Churches or Schools under the direction, and for the benefit of colored persons exclusively, where we can enter upon equal terms with the whites." Although they considered themselves a racially distinct constituency within the Oberlin community, they projected as their ultimate objective a fully inclusive and radically democratic social order.[15]

When townspeople gathered on February 21 for a daylong community celebration of the repeal of the Black Laws, congratulatory rhetoric masked African American dissatisfaction. In the morning, President Mahan preached "that Christianity contains in itself a sovereign remedy for all political and social evils." In the afternoon, "six speakers, all young gentlemen of color" addressed the question of "what our colored brethren can do for self-improvement by education and effort."[16] Nonetheless, after the event, Henry Cowles, the white editor of the *Oberlin Evangelist*, expressed disappointment that the African American orators failed to pay proper attention to "the gospel of Jesus Christ, as a grand relief for the wrongs of the oppressed." "We go for education with all our heart; but real virtue, such as gospel religion begets, is beyond comparison the first thing in value," Cowles asserted. "Therefore it is that we feel so strong a desire to see more done directly to promote pure religion and elevated morality as well as sound education among all the free people of color."[17]

Momentum toward black progress came to a decisive halt in 1850. The state constitutional convention that met that year refused to end the longstanding restriction on black suffrage.[18] More alarming, on September 18 the U.S. Congress adopted a new, more stringent fugitive slave law that put the lives of free blacks as well as escaped slaves residing in the North in unprecedented jeopardy. Part of a complex legislative package designed to reduce sectional tensions, the Fugitive Slave Act of 1850 provided material incentives for federal marshals, judges, and court-appointed commissioners to help slaveholders and their agents recover runaway slaves who sought refuge in the so-called free states. The act denied alleged fugitives the right to testify in their own behalf and threatened anyone who attempted to "obstruct, hinder, or prevent" the arrest of fugitive slaves or to help them escape after arrest with a sentence of up to six months in jail and a fine of up to $1,000. Also at increased risk were people of color who were legally free but lacked ready means of documenting their status.[19]

Oberlinians recoiled in horror at passage of the Fugitive Slave Act of 1850. Over the course of three days in early October townspeople held an extended public meeting to determine how best to respond to this "evidence that barbarism and oppression in our country have triumphed over the spirit of liberty and of progress." With Professor James Harris Fairchild serving as chair, participants adopted thirteen resolutions detailing their objections to the act and proclaiming their readiness to defy it. Whereas in 1835 the founders of the Oberlin Anti-Slavery Society promised to abide by the federal Constitution, the activists who assembled in October 1850 avowed their refusal to "pay the price" of "a union which brings us under the law of slavery, and enjoins upon us the loathsome work of slave-catching." Invoking the supreme authority of God, they justified their resistance to civil authority in terms of obedience to His higher law: "[W]hile we regard this law [the Fugitive Slave Act] as forbidding what God commands, and as commanding what God forbids—we will study to obey the law which transcends all human enactments, appealing in the language of the Apostle, even to those who have decreed this unrighteous decree, 'Whether it be right in the sight of God to hearken to you more than unto God, judge ye.'" From this reasoning flowed both a vague threat of secession and a more specific pledge to protect the "fugitive brother ... in our midst ... by all justifiable means in our power."[20]

The following spring townspeople gathered again to agree on a set of practical measures for shielding freedom seekers in defiance of the Fugitive Slave Act. According to an account published a half-century later by former Oberlin preparatory student John N. Beabout, the precipitating event was the difficulty a family of fugitives experienced in finding a place to stay in Oberlin while making their way toward Canada. In 1851 Beabout was a young man residing in Savannah, Ohio, a village located thirty-two miles south of Oberlin. One night in early April he and a friend transported a family of freedom seekers—"a man and wife and two small children"—from Savannah to Oberlin in a "large wagon." After stopping "at Rev. Mr. Clark's, north of Huntington," where "Mrs. Clark . . . put an excellent meal on the table," the party arrived in Oberlin about 4 in the morning. Beabout knew that local printer and bookseller James M. Fitch and his wife, Jane, were fervent abolitionists and might be willing to harbor the fugitives.[21] Indeed, their house included two rooms specially designed to hide freedom seekers.[22] Yet when Beabout and his party appeared at the Fitches' door, James M. Fitch turned them away. "We cannot possibly take you in, we are full," Fitch explained, "but go up to Darkey Watson's and he will take care of you."[23]

The ex-slave John Watson duly provided shelter for Beabout's party that night in April 1851. But Watson did more than that. The next evening he summoned Oberlinians "to the [college] chapel by the long toll of the bell" to discuss how to handle similar situations in the future. After "a committee was appointed" and reported its recommendations, everyone in attendance pledged to help "any fugitive [who] came to his house day or night," notwithstanding the Fugitive Slave Act of 1850. The attendees also promised that they "would immediately inform the bell ringer" upon learning of "any person trying to capture or carry off any fugitive."[24] For the next half-decade, this system of voluntary assistance and communal vigilance worked effectively. In 1856 James Harris Fairchild declared with pride, "No fugitive was ever taken here and returned to slavery; and this result has been secured without an instance of bloodshed or violence."[25]

Although Oberlinians increasingly questioned the authority of the federal government, they continued to believe in the efficacy of political action as a means to fight slavery and the Slave Power. On October 1, 1852, in his capacity as president of the Oberlin Young Men's Anti-Slavery Society—an organization composed mainly of students at the college—John Mercer Langston welcomed to town Senators Salmon P. Chase of Ohio and John P. Hale of New Hampshire to speak on behalf of the Free Democratic Party, the institutional successor to the Free Soil Party.[26] Hale had been nominated two months earlier to serve as the Free Democratic Party's candidate for president of the United States, and he addressed a large crowd at the Oberlin Church. Identifying himself with the plight of people of color, "he drew the contrast between the legal protection afforded under existing laws, to our *horses* and to our *daughters*." "Horses," he declared, "are protected by the [a]egis of the law: no affidavit gotten up in Kentucky can wrest them from their owner without due process; but our daughters have absolutely no legal protection, for a forged affidavit describing and supposed to identify their persons, entitles an irresponsible Commissioner to deliver them up on claim of a southern despot, and not the first element of justice—not the slightest admission of any human right—has place in the so-called *legal* transaction."[27] Hale's act of cross-racial identification and his powerful attack on the Fugitive Slave Act resonated with Oberlinians. In the presidential election that fall, voters in Russia Township cast 298 ballots for Hale (65 percent), 96 ballots for Whig candidate Winfield Scott (21 percent), and 62 for Democratic candidate Franklin Pierce (14 percent). While Pierce carried Ohio and the nation as a whole, Oberlin as usual stood proudly outside the mainstream.[28]

Supporters of the Compromise of 1850 hoped that it would quiet sectional debate over the future of slavery in the United States for at least another generation. Yet in January 1854 the controversy over slavery's expansion exploded again when Senator Stephen A. Douglas of Illinois introduced legislation to organize the remaining portion of the Louisiana Purchase—the area west and north of Missouri—into a federal territory with its own governor and legislature. Under the terms of the Missouri Compromise, adopted by Congress in 1820–1821, slavery had been banned from this region. But in 1854 southern congressmen demanded the abrogation of that ban as a condition for their support of Douglas's bill. Douglas acquiesced, and in its final form the Kansas-Nebraska bill divided the area into two parts and left the question of slavery's future to each territory's settlers to decide. Douglas defended this arrangement as consistent with the democratic principle of popular sovereignty, and despite heated opposition by antislavery northerners, the bill passed both houses of Congress. President Pierce signed it into law on May 30, 1854.[29]

"There can be no peace with the Slave Power," thundered the *Oberlin Evangelist* in response to the Kansas-Nebraska bill's success, and it prophesized that God would soon intervene to resolve the crisis. "Just how He will bring out the next forth-coming scenes of this drama, it behooves us not to determine," the *Evangelist* declared, "yet we know He will do all things well."

Anticipating the possibility of violence and perhaps even war, the paper added, "We may humbly ask Him to make our pathway quiet and peaceful, the remnant of our days; but let us not be surprised if we live to see the day when it will cost us something to have a conscience and to stand firmly for liberty and righteousness."[30]

On July 1, antislavery activists from throughout Lorain County assembled in Oberlin to choose delegates to attend a statewide "Convention of Freedom" to be held two weeks later in Columbus.[31] Out of this gathering would emerge the Ohio Republican Party dedicated to opposing "any further increase of slave territory or slave states in this Republican confederacy." "Many of the convention would have taken broader ground, opposing Slavery wherever the Free states have the pow[er] to do so," reported the *Evangelist*, "but it was thought wisest to adopt a platform on which the greatest strength could be rallied."[32]

On August 3, "the citizens of Oberlin" issued their own, more radical manifesto that implored "the people of the North [to] rally and combine their energies not only to prevent the spread of Slavery, but to crush the system itself." With faith in moral suasion's capacity to convert slaveholders long since lost, Oberlinians declared all compromises "null and void, as far as they require us to support slavery, or restrain us from doing any thing which just men may do for its overthrow." "Recent developments in Congress and in the country at large have proven that the contest between Slavery and Freedom, in the United States, is a war of extermination," the Oberlin Anti-Slavery Platform explained. "Either slavery must prevail throughout the land, or it must be entirely abolished."[33]

Three weeks later townspeople hosted the inaugural meeting of the Kansas Emigration Aid Association of Northern Ohio. The logic of popular sovereignty dictated that for Kansas to become a free-soil territory, antislavery men would have to outvote proslavery men in territorial elections. That prompted a movement across the North to promote migration to Kansas. The founders of the Kansas Emigration Aid Association of Northern Ohio pledged to "encourag[e] an Anti-slavery emigration to Kansas and [to provide] such aid to emigrants before their leaving and after their arrival as shall promote their success and prosperity." Significantly, however, all the men named to the association's twelve-man executive committee were white. Local African Americans were more concerned about threats to their rights and safety close to home.[34]

Throughout Ohio, antislavery politicians enjoyed unprecedented electoral success. In the fall elections of 1854, the fledgling Republican Party swept all of Ohio's congressional seats, and a year later Republicans gained control of the state government, including both houses of the legislature as well as the governorship.[35] In February 1856, newly elected state representative James Monroe, an Oberlin College professor and longstanding abolitionist, introduced a personal liberty bill designed to hinder enforcement of the Fugitive Slave Law. Under the bill's provisions, county courts and judges could issue writs of habeas corpus on behalf of alleged fugitives and direct sheriffs or coroners to remove the accused from federal custody in order to ensure compliance. Over the objections of Democrats and several conservative Republicans, the bill passed the General Assembly and became law on April 5, 1856.[36]

On July 4, 1856, Oberlinians demonstrated their opposition to "the state of things in Kansas" by raising the American flag only "half way up the staff, as a token of mourning," and by devoting the day "to fasting and prayer," rather than to fireworks and celebration. "[E]verything during the day wore the appearance of lamentation," observed a critic of the community's abolitionist stance, "and no one dare[d] speak in favor of the framers of the Declaration of Independence."[37]

In the presidential election of 1856, Russia Township voters favored John C. Frémont, the Republican nominee, over Democrat James Buchanan by a lopsided margin: 444 votes (85 percent) to 77 votes (15 percent). Though the statewide results were much closer, Ohio as a whole also went for Frémont. Nationwide, however, Buchanan, a Pennsylvanian with southern sympathies, prevailed.[38] He took office as president on March 4, 1857. Two days later Roger Taney, chief justice of the U.S. Supreme Court, proclaimed in the *Dred Scott* decision that under the federal Constitution blacks "had no rights that the white man was bound to respect."[39] To abolitionists—and increasingly to northerners in general—the Slave Power appeared stronger and more dangerous than ever before.

The *Oberlin Evangelist* adamantly denounced the Supreme Court's decision as "a disgrace to the Christianity, even the civilization, of the age."[40] Although, rather surprisingly, Oberlinians failed to hold a mass meeting in protest, the following month they signaled their disagreement with Chief Justice Taney's views on race by electing John Mercer Langston to the position of Russia Township clerk.[41] But the push for black rights stalled elsewhere in Ohio during 1857. In the fall elections, Democrats regained control of the state legislature, and in early 1858 they repealed James Monroe's habeas corpus statute. Once again persons of color in Ohio lacked meaningful legal recourse if they were accused of being fugitive slaves.[42]

Emboldened by this regressive change in Ohio law, slave hunters made their way to the Western Reserve in search of African Americans whom they could haul before federal commissioners for extradition to southern states under the prejudicial terms of the Fugitive Slave Act of 1850. During the summer of 1858, Oberlinians of color grew increasingly fearful that they would be kidnapped and dragged away, regardless of their legal status. Their anxiety was warranted. Three times in August slave hunters tried to capture local black families under the cover of darkness.[43] Although each attempt failed, Charles Langston—an older brother of John Mercer Langston—recalled several months later that when he visited Oberlin in early September everyone seemed nervous: "I found the country round about there, and the village itself, filled with alarming rumors as to the fact that slave-catchers, kidnappers, negro-stealers, were lying hidden and skulking about, waiting [for] some opportunity to get their bloody hands on some helpless creature to drag him back—or for the first time—into helpless and life-long bondage."[44] Six decades afterward, William Cochran still remembered vividly an exchange in late summer 1858 between his uncle and Augustus Chambers, a blacksmith of color who lived in Russia Township. Chambers pointedly asked Cochran's uncle, who was white, "[H]ow long are you going to let these man-stealers lie around Oberlin?" The uncle in turn counseled Chambers to "go into hiding for a few days" for his own protection. But Chambers indignantly rejected this advice and instead asserted his right to self-defense. "No, Sir!" he declared. "*I stay right here. And if any one of those men darkens my door, he is a dead man.*"[45]

Of special concern to local African Americans was the threat posed by Anson P. Dayton. Though a relative newcomer to the community, Dayton, a white attorney, had preceded John Mercer Langston as the clerk of Russia Township, and he knew Oberlin well. Evidently angered by his ouster as township clerk, Dayton had recently switched his political allegiance to the Democratic Party, for which he was rewarded by the Buchanan administration with an appointment to the post of U.S. deputy marshal for the Northern District of Ohio. Over the summer of 1858 Dayton began exercising his new powers with dangerous enthusiasm, actively searching for fugitive slaves to arrest in Oberlin and the vicinity.[46] In one instance he went so far as to contact the purported southern owner of African American James Smith, "a hard-working young stone cutter," prompting Smith in turn to thrash Dayton "[w]ith good hickory" for his act of treachery. On another occasion Dayton sought to apprehend the Wagoner family, who had been residing peacefully in Oberlin for the previous two years. Pretending to have a load of clothes for Mrs. Wagoner to wash, Dayton knocked on the family's door after midnight, hoping to gain easy entry. But a suspicious Mr. Wagoner yelled to his son to "hand me the gun" and "rushed to the door with a startling racket." Although Dayton retreated ingloriously, the Wagoners chose to leave Oberlin for Canada soon thereafter.[47]

On Monday, September 13, 1858, news reached Oberlin of an audacious kidnapping attempt undertaken in broad daylight. About 1 P.M., Ansel Lyman, a white college student and fervent abolitionist whose father owned a farm in the southern part of town, reported that while walking near Pittsfield at midday he had seen John Price, a young man of color, being whisked off against his will by three white strangers in a carriage heading toward Wellington.[48] A crowd promptly gathered in front of John Watson's grocery on South Main Street to decide on a course of action.[49] Keeping the pledge that he and fellow townspeople had made in 1851 to assist all freedom seekers in distress, Watson raced off to Wellington to rescue Price from the prospect of re-enslavement. Hundreds of other Oberlinians followed Watson's lead, many riding by horse and buggy but others going on foot. Whites and blacks occasionally traveled together, and a few women participated alongside the men. Several of the men, especially those of color, carried guns.[50]

When Watson arrived in Wellington, John Price and his captors were passing time at Wadsworth's Hotel, awaiting the arrival of a late afternoon train headed south toward Columbus—the first stop of a planned trip to restore Price to his purported owner in Kentucky. Soon a large, interracial throng surrounded the building, located on Wellington's town square, and loudly demanded Price's release. The men holding Price included Anderson Jennings, a Kentuckian who claimed legal authority to represent Price's owner, and Jacob K. Lowe, a Columbus-based U.S. deputy marshal for Ohio's Southern District, who carried with him a federal warrant for Price's arrest under the terms of the Fugitive Slave Act of 1850. At one point Jennings brought Price out on a balcony overlooking the assembled multitude, and Price publicly acknowledged that he had been a slave "and supposed he would have to go back" to his master.[51] But the crowd remained determined to save him from a return to bondage. Oberlinian John Anthony Copeland brandished a gun, prompting Jennings to retreat inside.[52] At another point Charles Langston sought unsuccessfully to negotiate Price's release, warning Lowe that otherwise the crowd "would have him anyway."[53] Ultimately it took force to rescue Price, although bloodshed was averted. As daylight turned to dusk, members of the crowd stormed the hotel, grabbed Price, and put him in a buggy that carried him safely back to Oberlin. He spent the night and the following few days hidden from sight in James Harris Fairchild's stately house on South Professor Street. What happened to Price afterward is undocumented. Presumably he made his way across Lake Erie and into Canada, perhaps guided by John Anthony Copeland, who himself would later take part in John Brown's raid on Harpers Ferry. In any event, John Price was never seen on the streets of Oberlin again.[54]

Most Oberlinians viewed Price's escape as a wonderful triumph for the community's abolitionist principles. Upon their return to Oberlin, the Rescuers were welcomed by impromptu rallies in front of the post office and the Palmer House, the hotel located at the corner of Main and College Streets.[55] The public celebration included speeches by Jacob R. Shipherd, nephew of Oberlin founder John Jay Shipherd, Charles Langston, and John Mercer Langston, who had been away on business when the rescue took place but returned in time to hail its success.[56] The evening's joyous mood was tinged with anger, however. Anson Dayton was denounced for his presumed role in Price's kidnapping, and "it was voted with deafening unanimity that whoever laid hands on a black man in this community, no matter what the color of authority, would do so at the peril of his life."[57]

Over the next few weeks townspeople debated the moral calculus of balancing ends and means in the pursuit of abolition and social justice. The *Oberlin Evangelist* defended the Oberlin-Wellington Rescue on the grounds that, although it may have violated the federal Fugitive Slave Act of 1850, it abided by "the *Higher Fugitive Law*" of "the fifth book of Moses: 'Thou shalt not deliver unto his master the servant which is escaped from his master unto thee; he shall dwell with thee even among you . . . in one of thy gates where it liketh him best: thou shalt not oppress him.'—Deut. xxiii: 15, 16." "The movement was doubtless very *imprudent*," the paper observed, "but there are higher virtues than that low prudence which men are wont to honor."[58]

According to the fiercely antiblack *Cleveland Plain Dealer*, Oberlin's post-Rescue debate had a distinctly racial dimension. On September 21 the *Plain Dealer* reported, "Last week Thursday a deputation of Africans waited upon the Deputy Marshal [Anson Dayton] and coolly requested him to leave town immediately!" There had already been local talk of tarring and feathering Dayton, and the delegation's "request" carried with it an implicit threat of physical harm if he failed to comply. Yet the *Plain Dealer* also noted that, fearing "things were being carried to [*sic*] far even for Oberlin," several of the community's "leading 'friends of freedom'" had circulated a "printed hand-bill" warning against a resort to "personal violence." "Tarring and feathering or burning the property of any man, however base he may be . . . cannot but seriously disturb good order, tarnish the fair name of the place in which it occurs, and in our opinion, should never be allowed," the handbill suppos- edly explained. Among the statement's reputed signers were several white Oberlinians with impeccable antislavery credentials—including James Harris Fairchild, James M. Fitch, James Monroe, Henry E. Peck, Ralph Plumb, and William D. Scrimgeour—but no persons of color. If the *Plain Dealer*'s report was accurate, while local African Americans were ready to take direct, physical action against Dayton, prominent whites recoiled at the prospect out of concern for maintaining social stability and protecting the town's public reputation.[59]

Anger at Dayton persisted throughout the fall.[60] In early November, after a federal grand jury was empaneled in Cleveland to bring charges against the individuals who rescued John Price, Dayton was assigned the task of serving subpoenas to several Oberlinians summoned to testify. According to the *Plain Dealer*, to deter him from fulfilling this duty, "a party of men . . . fired shots at [Dayton's house], shattering the windows and doing other damage" during the early morning hours on November 8.[61] The paper said nothing about the race of the assailants in this instance, but one month later it blamed a second attack on Dayton's residence squarely on "a party of negroes." "Mr. Dayton was absent at the time," the paper's "special Oberlin correspondent" reported. "Mrs. Dayton opened the door, the negroes rushed in, and proceeded to ransack the house in quest of Dayton, swearing they would have him, dead or alive."[62]

On December 6, 1858, the federal grand jury handed down indictments of thirty-seven men for their alleged complicity in the Oberlin-Wellington Rescue. Thirty-four were charged with direct participation in "rescuing a fugitive from service," while three were charged with "aiding, abetting and assisting to rescue a fugitive slave from service and labor." Twenty-two of the accused were from Oberlin or Russia Township; twelve from Wellington; one each from the nearby towns of Pittsfield and Penfield; and one—Charles Langston—was a resident of Columbus with longstanding ties to Oberlin. Some had played prominent parts in the Rescue, but the selection of others for prosecution was more surprising. From the time the grand jury announced its decision, critics contended that partisan politics influenced the pattern of indictments.[63]

Race also mattered. Fully half of the indicted Oberlinians were men of color. The *Plain Dealer* claimed that five were fugitive slaves, and it identified two by name: Thomas Gena and John Hartwell. Nothing is known about Hartwell's background, but "Thomas Gena" was most likely Thomas Janey, a free man of color born in Michigan. While at least three of the accused Oberlinians were born into bondage—Jeremiah (Jerry) Fox, O.S.B. Wall, and John Watson—none of these men appear to have been fugitive slaves at the time they were indicted.[64]

Significantly, the names of seven of the indicted African Americans appeared on the surviving poll list from October 1855: John Anthony Copeland, Jeremiah Fox, Henry Evans, Wilson Evans, O.S.B. Wall, David Watson, and John Watson. The fact that these men of color were politically active and almost certainly voted for Republicans made them especially attractive targets for a grand jury composed entirely of Democrats. A more surprising fact is how few of the indicted Oberlinians were longtime residents of the community. Only one of the accused whites and four of the accused men of color had lived in Oberlin or Russia Township when the federal census taker surveyed the local population in the summer of 1850. A majority of the indicted Rescuers had moved to the community over the previous eight years.[65]

Matthew Johnson, the U.S. marshal for the Northern District of Ohio, wasted no time in delivering arrest warrants. He traveled to Oberlin the day the indictments came down and promptly sought out Henry E. Peck, a professor of sacred rhetoric at Oberlin College and a well-known abolitionist. Peck offered Marshal Johnson no resistance. Indeed, he voluntarily helped Johnson locate several other accused Oberlinians. Although ultimately five of the indicted Oberlinians would evade arrest, the fifteen who were tracked down on December 7 agreed to cooperate with legal authorities.[66]

On December 8, fourteen Oberlinians showed up in federal court to enter pleas of not guilty before U.S. District Judge Hiram V. Willson. Through their attorneys, they asked the court to proceed to trial immediately—a request that caught the federal district attorney off guard. After brief negotiations, Judge Willson scheduled the trial for the spring term of 1859. He also released the accused Oberlinians on their own recognizance rather than requiring them to post bail. They returned home feeling confident and optimistic.[67]

Townspeople rallied to the cause of their indicted compatriots, staging two major demonstrations of support over the next several weeks. The first took place in the college chapel on the evening of January 1, 1859, under the auspices of the Oberlin Anti-Slavery Society—a different organization than its namesake founded in 1835. According to the *Oberlin Evangelist*, "This new association [was] composed principally or entirely of colored people" and dedicated to "a *practical* purpose which would, perhaps, be illustrated if another attempt to arrest fugitives should be made here about." Although the roster of speakers on January 1 included whites Henry E. Peck and Dr. Isaac Bigelow, African Americans predominated: Solomon Grimes, Lewis Sheridan Leary, William Rutledge, John Watson, and at least one of the Evans brothers. "It might have been expected that, as a result of recent occurrences here, there would have been much vituperation and bitterness," the *Evangelist* observed. "But such was not the case." In characteristic fashion, the paper assured its deeply religious and largely white audience, "The speakers recognized the fact that the help of those whose color subjects them to oppression is in God alone, and that it is by industry and the maintenance of good character that the free man of color is to accomplish most for his brethren in bonds."[68]

Ten days later, on the afternoon of Tuesday, January 11, a self-styled "Feast of the Felons" took place at the Palmer House, the town's most respectable hotel. Approximately sixty-five people attended, including fourteen of the indicted Oberlinians, nine of their wives, ten accused Wellingtonians, and two indicted men from Pittsfield and Penfield.[69] Reverend John Keep, who in 1835 had cast the deciding vote in favor of admitting blacks to the Oberlin Institute, offered an opening prayer, and Samuel Plumb, Esq., the brother of one of those indicted, presided over the proceedings. During the course of the afternoon, not only delicious dishes but also toasts that verged on speeches were served up for public consumption. In its laudatory coverage of the event, the *Cleveland Leader* observed, "The men in bonds were more closely knit together by the association, and the opposition to the execution of an unrighteous law is tenfold strengthened by the persecutions set on foot under it."⁷⁰

Yet the contrast between the meetings of January 1 and January 11 suggests the persistence of a racial cleavage in Oberlin. While the orators at the meeting of the Oberlin Anti-Slavery Society were mainly African Americans, of the dozen speakers at the Felons' Feast only John Mercer Langston was a person of color. Upon the feast's conclusion, the indicted men met privately to choose an executive committee to supervise preparations for the upcoming federal trial. Significantly, none of the five individuals selected for this responsibility was a person of color.⁷¹

Over time the experience of shared injustice helped to forge a greater sense of interracial solidarity among the accused. The first of the indicted men to go on trial was Simeon Bushnell, a twenty-nine-year-old white clerk, new father, and erstwhile student in the college's preparatory department who worked for printer James M. Fitch, his brother-in-law and fellow defendant. Bushnell's involvement in the Oberlin-Wellington Rescue was undeniable: he had driven the buggy that took John Price back to Oberlin after he was retrieved from Wadsworth's Hotel. Defense lawyers raised questions about the true identity of John Price, the legality of his capture and detainment, and the constitutionality of the Fugitive Slave Act, but they never challenged the basic facts of Bushnell's role in Price's escape. The trial lasted from April 5 through April 15. After brief deliberations, the jury, which at the insistence of the district attorney excluded anyone with antislavery sympathies, found Bushnell guilty as charged.⁷²

Although this verdict was expected, what happened next was not.⁷³ When the district attorney moved to try Charles Langston, Judge Willson announced that the same set of jurors that had just convicted Bushnell would hear Langston's case and those of the other defendants. Defense attorneys objected that this irregular procedure would gravely disadvantage their clients, and they signaled their intention to file a formal challenge when the court reconvened after a weekend break. At the prosecutor's urging, Willson responded by remanding the twenty defendants then in the courtroom to the custody of Matthew Johnson, the U.S. marshal, until the court reassembled. Although Johnson, in the words of the *Cleveland Leader*, "offered to let them go home, if they would give him their parole of honor that they would return on Monday morning," they unanimously refused. To draw attention to the court's unfairness and to rally public support for their cause, they went to jail.[74]

Because the federal government lacked its own holding facility in Cleveland, the defendants were transferred to the Cuyahoga County Jail, under the supervision of Sheriff David L. Wightman, a Republican sympathetic to the Rescuers. Over the weekend of April 16–17, "Hundreds of ladies and gentlemen of the highest standing called on the Oberlin prisoners," reported the *Cleveland Herald*. "On all sides they were greeted with assurances of sympathy and respect."[75]

Judge Willson reversed himself on April 18, agreeing to seat a new jury to hear Langston's case. But the Rescuers remained in custody in "Wightman's Castle," as the county jail was nicknamed. Most of the incarcerated men found life behind bars surprisingly comfortable, at least initially. Rather than being kept under lock and key, they were free to move about the jail and allowed access to the building's courtyard and rooftop for exercise. They found solace in song and prayer. Yet peace and tranquility were elusive. The building housed not only suspected criminals but also the mentally ill, whose "howlings and ravings" regularly disrupted the Rescuers' slumber.[76]

Federal authorities employed a divide-and-conquer strategy to try to break the defendants' spirit of solidarity and resistance. Over time, the charges against two men were dropped on technicalities, and the four incarcerated Wellingtonians were released on bail or their own recognizance. Of the twenty men remanded to the marshal's custody on April 15, only fourteen remained in jail a month later: eight whites and six persons of color, all of them residents of Oberlin except for Charles Langston, who remained closely connected to the town.[77]

Although the legal case against Langston was weaker than that against Bushnell, the verdict, returned on May 10, was the same: guilty. Before pronouncing sentence, Judge Willson—in keeping with standard practice—offered Langston a chance to address the court in his own behalf. Langston took full advantage of the opportunity and eloquently denounced the joint injustices of slavery and racism in the United States. "The colored man is oppressed by certain universal and deeply fixed *prejudices*," he declared. "And the prejudices which white people have against colored men, grow out of this fact: that we have, as a people, *consented* for two hundred years to be *slaves* of whites." Applying this general analysis of American racism to the specifics of his own case, Langston argued that deep-seated prejudice against people of color like himself had contaminated the entirety of the court's proceedings. "The jury came into the box with that feeling," he asserted. "The gentlemen who prosecuted me have that feeling, the Court itself has that feeling, and even the counsel who defended me have that feeling." As a result, Langston concluded, "I should not be subject to the pains and penalties of this oppressive law, when I have *not* been tried, either by a jury of my peers, or by a jury that were impartial."[78]

Langston's statement to the court was aimed primarily at a public audience reachable through the press. But to Langston's surprise, the judge reacted favorably to his remarks. "You have presented considerations to which I shall attach much weight," Willson said, and he sentenced Langston to twenty days in the Cuyahoga County Jail and a fine of $100—a significantly lighter punishment than the sixty days in jail and $600 fine Willson had imposed on Simeon Bushnell.[79]

The Rescuers' supporters staged a large, enthusiastic rally in downtown Cleveland on May 24, but the following week the defendants suffered a serious legal setback. An effort by defense attorneys to circumvent the U.S. District Court by appealing to the Ohio State Supreme Court for writs of habeas corpus failed when the latter body ruled against the Rescuers on May 30. Meanwhile, at the district attorney's request, Judge Willson had put off hearing future cases pertaining to the Oberlin-Wellington Rescue until the start of a new court term in early July. The Oberlin inmates could have posted bond and headed home for the duration, but for reasons of both principle and political effect, they chose to remain in custody.[80]

To fend off boredom, several prisoners pursued their trades, including printers Fitch and Bushnell, who determined to publish a newspaper.[81] The first and only issue of *The Rescuer* appeared on July 4, 1859. It included commentary on the Fugitive Slave Law, the federal judiciary, the handling of the Oberlin-Wellington Rescue cases, and the need for Ohio to stand up for its "State Rights" against the tyranny of a national government beholden to "the Slaveholding Power." In an article titled "A Few Words about Ourselves (The 'Rescue Company')," the inmates offered a collective profile of their geographical origins (three from North Carolina, four from New York, one each from Ohio, Louisiana, and South Carolina, three from England), their marital and family status (ten were married, with a total of thirty-seven children), their occupations (two printers, three upholsters and cabinetmakers, one shoemaker, one harness maker, one school teacher and student, one lawyer, one college professor and minister), and their religious affiliations (eight Congregationalists, one Methodist, one Episcopalian)—but not in terms of their physical appearance or racial ancestry. With newspapers from across the North following the case, they were determined to project a united front irrespective of color.[82]

On the afternoon of July 6, 1859, the months-long drama in the U.S. District Court for the Northern District of Ohio came to an abrupt end. In return for a promise by Lorain County authorities to drop kidnapping charges brought against the men involved in the seizure of John Price the previous September, the U.S. district attorney agreed to abandon any further prosecution of the indicted Rescuers. Judge Willson reluctantly acceded to the deal, and before nightfall twelve of the thirteen Oberlinians departed for home, leaving behind Simeon Bushnell, who remained in jail to finish his sentence.[83]

News of the Rescuers' release reached Oberlin before they did. When they arrived by train in the early evening, a jubilant crowd greeted them at the local depot. "A sea of heads could be seen extending for a long distance on both sides of the tracks," wrote James M. Fitch for the *Cleveland Leader*. "Youth and beauty vied with men of venerable age in their endeavors to catch a glimpse of these but recently contemptible, these reviled and abused men; and when they alighted from the cars, the heavens rang again with the united and prolonged huzzahs of nearly *three thousand* persons, who, though styled 'fanatics,' were not a whit behind the brightest ornaments of our country, in intelligence, purity, patriotism, and every excellence of which a nation should be proud."

James Monroe offered brief welcoming remarks, and then liberated Rescuers and townspeople paraded triumphantly up Main Street to the Congregational Church. "The vast building was in a moment crowded to its utmost capacity," reported Fitch. "It was a grand and cheering sight."[84]

From 8 P.M. until midnight, an array of orators addressed the assembled multitude, portraying the Oberlin-Wellington Rescue and subsequent federal prosecution as a redemptive episode in the holy struggle of good versus evil. John Keep opened with a short speech thanking the indicted men "for your wisdom and firmness in the rejection of all compromise between right and wrong."[85] Next spoke Ralph Plumb, the first of ten indicted men to address the gathering. He, too, emphasized the Rescuers' firm resolve: "Fellow-citizens, it gives me great pleasure to assure you that the band of Rescuers... stand before you to-night, with yourselves breathing the free air once more of free Oberlin, without having in the least degree compromised themselves or you."[86]

Henry E. Peck followed. After recalling the death of his mother when he was a boy and the more recent loss of his firstborn child, Peck observed that the Oberlin-Wellington Rescue had opened a new stage in his life, "a state of special consciousness" prompted by the sacrifice required of him and his compatriots in jail.[87] James M. Fitch echoed Peck's sentiments. He, too, recollected the loss of family members before adding, "I see to-night that I am not friendless." "Never since I became a lover of truth have my hopes risen so high, and my confidence in her speedy triumph been so great," he said.[88]

John Watson, the first orator of color to address the gathering, offered a decidedly less celebratory perspective. Highlighting the divergent experiences of blacks and whites, he remarked, "[W]hen I heard Mr. Fitch and Prof. Peck speak about the death of their mothers, brothers, children and friends, my own mind was led to the contrast between the separation of mothers and children by death, and that unspeakably more awful separation at the Auction-block." Watson reminded his listeners that blacks in the North as well as the South faced distinctive dangers because of their race. "[E]ven here in Oberlin have we wolves in sheep's clothing," he maintained. "They come to us with fawning fingers and smiling lips, while in their hearts they are plotting the most piratical and inhuman atrocities, and plotting them against us, their next-door neighbors, who never lifted a finger to harm them or theirs, and never would." He decried Oberlin's tolerance of "these traitors" and argued that "if emphatic leave of absence had been given these men long ago, we should have been saved all the trials of the last year." After leveling this tough criticism at his fellow townspeople, however, Watson closed his speech on a more conciliatory and optimistic note. "I rest in this confidence," he said, "that ... whatever you may have done in the past, henceforth you will show oppression *no quarter*."[89]

After Watson, eleven more men gave speeches, including African Americans John H. Scott and Henry Evans. Nobody repeated Watson's harsh criticism of Oberlin. Instead, the remaining speakers lavished praise on the community for its steadfast opposition to slavery and for its firm support of the Rescuers and their quest for justice. As midnight approached, the audience passed a resolution praising the erstwhile inmates "who, rather than give the least countenance to the Fugitive Slave Act, have lain eighty-four days in Cleveland jail." "To our faithful friends," the townspeople avowed, "we express our warmest gratitude and our unqualified commendation for the firmness, the wisdom, and the fidelity with which they have maintained our common cause."[90]

The success of the Oberlin-Wellington Rescue and the failure of federal authorities to isolate and humiliate Oberlin in the Rescue's aftermath appeared to vindicate the *Oberlin Evangelist*'s contention that God would support the righteous when they defied civil statutes in service to His Higher Law. The liberation of John Price also confirmed the efficacy of direct action in the struggle against slavery, an approach long advocated by Oberlinians of color. Yet, while the Rescuers employed force in reclaiming Price, they stopped short of physically injuring, much less killing, the "man-stealers" from whom they wrested him. Although several of the Rescuers carried guns with them to Wellington, no one ever fired a shot. The Oberlin-Wellington Rescue is properly classified as a radical yet nonviolent form of collective, extralegal intervention.[91]

The famous raid led by John Brown on the federal armory in Harpers Ferry, Virginia, on October 16, 1859, was qualitatively different. By design, it shed blood. In attacking the armory, Brown hoped to instigate a slave insurrection in the surrounding countryside, induce widespread panic, and foment a large-scale war over slavery. Although as a military exercise the raid ended in miserable failure, it served Brown's larger purpose by frightening slaveholders throughout the South and by inspiring abolitionists and other antislavery advocates to accept violence as a morally justified means to rid the nation of the vile sin of human bondage.[92]

News of the Harpers Ferry raid hit Oberlin especially hard because two African Americans from the town took part in the attack: John Anthony Copeland (also known as John Copeland Jr.) and Lewis Sheridan Leary. Aged twenty-five and twenty-four, respectively, they were friends and relatives. (Leary, although a year younger, was Copeland's uncle.) Born free, Copeland had migrated to Oberlin from Raleigh, North Carolina, with his parents and siblings in 1843. Also born free, Leary had fled Fayetteville, North Carolina, in 1856 after beating a slaveholder for whipping his bondman. In 1858 Leary married North Carolina-born Oberlinian Mary Sampson Patterson, and the next year she gave birth to a daughter. Both Copeland and Leary were skilled artisans: Copeland practiced carpentry, while Leary worked as a harness and saddle maker. Both men participated in the Oberlin-Wellington Rescue, although only Copeland was indicted for his role in that event—and he successfully evaded arrest and trial.[93]

When U.S. Marines led by Robert E. Lee overwhelmed John Brown and his followers on the morning of October 18, Leary was killed in the maelstrom of battle while Copeland was among five raiders captured alive by federal forces, including John Brown himself.[94] Once the identities of Leary and Copeland became known, Democratic newspapers in northeast Ohio and elsewhere tied the raid to Oberlin's alleged extremism, unnerving some of the community's white leaders. Henry Cowles took to the pages of the *Oberlin Evangelist* to dissociate Oberlinians from Brown's attack on Harpers Ferry as much as possible. "We have no fellowship with bloody violence," Cowles insisted. "We deplore it when used even against slave-holders." Significantly, however, he drew a racial distinction among local residents. "The attempts made to implicate our white fellow-citizens of Oberlin, in this movement at Harper's Ferry, are utterly without foundation in truth," he wrote confidently. Concerning the role of black townspeople he seemed less certain. "Two colored men, sometimes resident here, were with Brown in this tragedy," he acknowledged. "[H]ow they came there we know not; but we do know that such violence meets and has ever met among our citizens with decided reprobation."[95] To a twenty-first-century ear, Cowles's attempt to exonerate "our white fellow-citizens of Oberlin" while admitting the complicity of "two colored men, sometimes resident here" sounds plainly racist. The phrase "sometimes resident here" was also disingenuous, since John Anthony Copeland had lived in Oberlin for more than fifteen years and Lewis Sheridan Leary for the last three.

Yet a sense of racial solidarity undoubtedly factored into the decisions of Copeland and Leary to enlist in John Brown's project.[96] Moreover, they acted with the foreknowledge of Oberlin's most prominent African American, John Mercer Langston. In his autobiography, Langston described how John Brown Jr. sought him out in Oberlin before the raid on Harpers Ferry and outlined his father's plan. "My father is John Brown of Ossawatomie, who proposes to strike at an early day, a blow which shall shake and destroy American slavery itself," the junior John Brown explained to Langston as the two men walked from Langston's law office to his home at midday. "For this purpose we need, and I seek to secure, men of nerve and courage." According to Langston's recollection, after lunch he and the younger John

Brown retired to the parlor, where Brown elaborated on his father's plan, and Langston, though skeptical of its chances for success, agreed to introduce Brown to potential volunteers. "In this connection, the names of Sheridan Leary and John Copeland . . . come quickly and unbidden to the memory," Langston wrote in 1894, "and their heroic and manly decision to die, if need be, with John Brown as their leader, challenges the admiration of those who witnessed their conduct and heard their words."[97]

In the immediate aftermath of the raid on Harpers Ferry, John Mercer Langston said nothing about his involvement in the enterprise, but his brother Charles openly praised Brown for his courage and moral righteousness.[98] In a statement published in the *Cleveland Plain Dealer*, Charles Langston argued that Brown's actions were consistent with both "Biblical principles" and the ideals of the American Revolution. "Did not he obey God by resisting tyrants?" Langston asked rhetorically. "Did he not in all things show his implicit faith in the equality of all men? and their unalienable right to life and liberty."[99]

James A. Thome, a white Lane Rebel who had enrolled in the Oberlin Institute in 1835 and later served on the school's faculty, also championed John Brown. While Henry Cowles sought to distance Oberlin from the raid on Harpers Ferry, in the same issue of the *Evangelist* Thome wrote boldly: "*God's hand is in this transaction,* and his people should *see it,* should discern this sign of the times, and should *give the nation warning.* They should fearlessly proclaim in the ears of the panic-stricken south the natural right inherent in the slaves to rise against their oppressors and achieve their liberties by sword and torch. . . . The affair at Harper's Ferry is but a signal fire, it is a tongue of flame darted up at that point to forewarn the South of the coming outburst that shall pour red hot lava into every master's dwelling." "We apprehend," Thome concluded, "that at a higher tribunal the denouncers of John Brown may be adjudged traitors and madmen."[100]

In the weeks that elapsed between Brown's October 18 capture, his conviction on November 2, and his December 2 execution, white Oberlinians came increasingly to admire his courage, to applaud his righteous purpose, and to respect his choice of means. On the day of his hanging, the bell of the Congregational Church rang for an hour, and that evening townspeople gathered for prayer and lectures in the college chapel. Among those who spoke were James Harris Fairchild, James M. Fitch, John Keep, Henry E. Peck, Ralph Plumb, Samuel Plumb, and Uriah Thompson—all white men of local distinction. According to the *Oberlin Students' Monthly*, the highlight of the occasion was Peck's address: "His summer incarceration has given him a rich experience from which to draw, when about to speak for the downtrodden, or recount the deeds of the martyrs of Liberty."[101]

In the end, the execution of John Anthony Copeland, one of Oberlin's own, had the most profound impact on the community, provoking greater white appreciation of black bravery and commitment than ever before. In the weeks preceding his death on December 16, Copeland penned a series of letters to his family and friends, and much of their content soon became public. In his first letter, dated November 26 and published on December 12, he assured his parents that he was at peace with himself and with God. "If die I must," he wrote, "I shall try to meet my fate as a man who can suffer in the glorious cause in which I have been engaged, without a groan, and meet my Maker in heaven as a christian man who through the saving grace of God has made his peace with Him."[102]

In a letter to his brother dated December 10 and published on the day he died, Copeland drew a direct parallel between the fight against slavery and the American Revolution against British tyranny. "I am so soon to stand and suffer death for doing what George Washington, the so-called father of this great but slavery-cursed country, was made a hero for doing," he asserted. "Washington entered the field to fight for the freedom of the American people—not for the white man alone, but for both black and white." Copeland also highlighted the sacrifices made by men of color in fighting and winning the War of Independence. "The blood of black men flowed as freely as that of white men," he insisted. "Yes, the *very first* blood that was spilt was that of a negro. It was the blood of that heroic man, (though black he was,) Cyrus [*sic*] Attucks. And some of the very last blood shed was that of black men. To the truth of this, history, though prejudiced, is compelled to attest."[103]

Copeland's correspondence both reflected and shaped the radical vision of Oberlin's black abolitionists. A final letter, drafted on the morning of his execution and published posthumously, reaffirmed his sense of moral purpose and his faith in God. "It is not the mere act of having to meet death that causes me regret (if I should express regret), but that such an unjust institution should exist as that which requires my life, and not only my life, but that of those to whom my life bears but the relative value of Zero to that which is infinite," he wrote his family. "I beg of you one and all, not to grieve for me, but to thank God that He has spared me to make my peace with Him."[104]

On the evening of December 16, after the news of Copeland's death reached Oberlin, townspeople gathered at the college chapel to express "sympathy for the bereaved parents and friends, and indignation against the cruel oppression that is so fast driving good men mad." While Mayor A. N. Beecher chaired the meeting and James Monroe offered an address, most of the speakers were men of color: John Watson, John Mercer Langston, and James H. Muse, an African American student at the college. Before the meeting adjourned, James M. Fitch moved that a committee be appointed "to erect a monument in the Cemetery, in memory of Leary and Copeland, our martyred fellow-citizens." Langston seconded the motion, which evidently passed without debate.[105]

Desperate to prevent the desecration of their son's body and wishing to provide him a proper burial, Copeland's parents the next day asked James Monroe to journey to Virginia to retrieve the corpse. John Copeland Sr. had previously sent inquiries to the state's governor about the prospect of recovering his son's body. The governor had responded that, as a free person of color, the father could not legally enter Virginia but that government authorities would turn the body over to the family's designated agent so long as he was white. At John and Delilah Copeland's personal request, Monroe reluctantly agreed to undertake this assignment.[106]

To the dismay of the Copelands and the wider Oberlin community, Monroe failed in his mission. By the time he reached Virginia, custody of the corpse had been transferred to the Winchester Medical College. Although the college's president and faculty agreed to turn it over to Monroe, the school's students claimed it as their own for dissection purposes and successfully secreted it away. Monroe returned to Oberlin empty handed on December 24.[107]

The next day Oberlinians again assembled to honor John Anthony Copeland's life and to mourn his death. On "short notice," an estimated three thousand people flocked to the Oberlin Church to listen to Henry E. Peck's funeral sermon venerating Copeland and to hear James Monroe's narrative of his unsuccessful attempt to retrieve the young martyr's body. In the course of his story Monroe mentioned that while at the Winchester Medical College he had encountered the corpse of Shields Green, another African American hanged for his role in the Harpers Ferry raid. Monroe thought he recognized Green as a fellow Oberlinian. Although Monroe was almost certainly mistaken, when the local committee appointed to erect a monument memorializing Leary and Copeland issued a public circular describing the project, they added Green to the list of intended honorees.[108]

Aimed at potential donors outside the Oberlin community, the circular was framed as a paean to black masculinity. The purpose of the proposed monument, it announced, was "To Commemorate the Manly Virtues of those Noble Representatives of the Colored Race of the Nineteenth Century, John A. Copeland, Lewis Leary and Shields Green, who, for the Cause of Freedom, laid down their lives at Harper's Ferry and Charlestown, Va., October 17, and December 16, 1859."

While the circular noted that those who attended Copeland's funeral service in Oberlin had already donated $175 toward erection of the monument, it argued that the project was more than just a local enterprise of transitory significance. At issue was the reputation of black Americans for generations to come: "The more money we raise the more noble the monument we rear to the memory—not of a man only—*but of a race.*"[109]

Appended to the circular were the names of eleven Oberlinians who comprised the monument committee. The committee's composition was notable for its racial balance. Six members were white: A. N. Beecher, James M. Fitch, William E. Kellogg, George Kinney, James Monroe, and Samuel Plumb. Five members were persons of color: Sabram Cox, Henry Evans, Solomon Grimes, John Mercer Langston, and John Watson. Compared to the demographic profile of the town as a whole, blacks were overrepresented. Equally important, the monument project represented an interracial commitment to ending slavery by force of arms if necessary. By courageous example, Oberlin's African American activists had persuaded local white abolitionists that methods of moral suasion and political mobilization were no longer adequate. Even the Rescuers' strategy of collective civil disobedience and nonviolent direct action appeared insufficient to the task at hand. The Slave Power's mounting influence threatened freedom throughout the nation. By 1860, white as well as black Oberlinians were primed to fight a civil war for emancipation and the equal rights of all men regardless of color.[110]

❧ 5 ❧

FIGHTING FOR EQUAL RIGHTS IN
THE CIVIL WAR ERA

Although many Oberlinians would have preferred a Republican nominee with stronger antislavery credentials, the town voted overwhelmingly for Abraham Lincoln in the presidential election of 1860.[1] In the tension-filled months that followed his victory, while seven states of the Deep South issued declarations of secession and formed the Confederate States of America, Oberlinians, with few exceptions, stood firmly opposed to any new compromise with the Slave Power, even for the sake of preserving peace and restoring national unity. At a public meeting on February 4, 1861, townspeople "solemnly protest[ed] against any concession to slavery, or to the demands made by its abettors in any form whatsoever, and especially against making such concessions at the behest of traitors in arms against the Union."[2] Lincoln took office one month later. In his inaugural address he denounced secession as contrary to democratic principles, yet he also pledged not to initiate a military conflict. Confederate officials proved less reticent. On the evening of April 12, Confederate forces fired on U.S. troops stationed at Fort Sumter in Charleston harbor. The fort surrendered the next day, and President Lincoln promptly asked for volunteers to take up arms, suppress the rebellion, and save the Union. America's bloodiest war had begun.

Reports of the Confederate attack and Lincoln's response electrified Oberlin. "Oberlin is excited above measure, especially the *Negro population*," a student in the preparatory department wrote home on April 14.[3] "WAR! and volunteers are the only topics of conversation or thought," wrote another student six days later. "Since the news of the attack and capture of Fort Sumter reached here, an excitement has prevailed which has daily been increasing until it is now truly alarming."[4]

The outbreak of the Civil War opened a new era in Oberlin's pursuit of racial equality. From the onset of hostilities—long before Lincoln issued either the preliminary or final version of the Emancipation Proclamation—Oberlinians, unlike most northerners, regarded the war's main objective to be the complete abolition of slavery throughout the United States, not restoration of the Union "as it was" prior to secession. Even after the gruesome military conflict came to a close in 1865 and the Thirteenth Amendment officially ended slavery nationwide, Oberlinians continued to fight for black rights, especially the equal right of black men to vote. In 1870 townspeople held a daylong celebration to mark the ratification of the Fifteenth Amendment to the U.S. Constitution. With color-blind male suffrage formally achieved, Oberlinians rejoiced in the belief that the community's bold commitment to racial egalitarianism—first articulated in 1835—had been duly fulfilled.

"Treason and Rebellion are in League against the Government," proclaimed Mayor Samuel Hendry on April 16, 1861, and he asked "all the people of Oberlin and its vicinity to meet in the First Church" the following evening. As requested, two thousand "earnest men and thoughtful women" turned out to "enquire for duty in this eventful hour of our country's peril" and to establish a "Vigilance Committee, 'to take such action as circumstances may demand.'" Chaired by the mayor, the gathering on April 17 was both bipartisan and biracial. Longstanding Democrat Lewis D. Boynton was one of four men selected to serve as a vice president for the occasion, while African American activist John Mercer Langston was named one of the meeting's three secretaries. The seven-man Vigilance Committee included O.S.B. Wall, Langston's brother-in-law and onetime defendant in the Oberlin-Wellington Rescue case. Although the meeting stopped short of calling for enlistments, it "pledg[ed] to aid in every needed way the Government in maintaining itself against the rebels." The evening closed with "spirit-stirring" renditions of "The Marseillaise" and "The Star-Spangled Banner" sung by Oberlin's Musical Union, accompanied by the Citizen's Brass Band. Rarely had the community appeared so united.[5]

Two days later, students at the college took the lead in mobilizing for military service. On the evening of April 19 they met with members of the faculty at the college chapel and resolved to form an Oberlin company of volunteers. The next day Professor James Monroe returned from his duties as state senator in Columbus with the requisite enlistment forms, and young men started signing up. Townspeople raised a subscription of $4,000 for the company's support, and within thirty-six hours the roster exceeded the standard limit of one hundred men per company. The volunteers duly elected theology student and tutor Giles W. Shurtleff as their captain and took as their nickname "The Monroe Rifles," in the professor's honor. A week later they would become known officially as Company C in the Seventh Regiment of the Ohio Volunteer Infantry.[6] "A nobler lot of fellows never trod college halls," declared the *Lorain County News*, the recently established weekly local newspaper, "and their comrades from other walks of life are true as steel."[7]

Before the Monroe Rifles left town to train at Camp Taylor in Cleveland, they helped to suppress an insurrection of sorts in Oberlin itself. On April 24, Malachi Warren "was brought before the Mayor on the charge—preferred against him by his son 'Jim'—of abusing his family."[8] Malachi Warren, it may be recalled, had migrated to Oberlin in the early 1850s, accompanied by his former slave Ellen and their six children. Despite his decision to settle in a community renowned for its abolitionist sentiments, he himself did not oppose slavery in principle, and he quickly gained notoriety in Oberlin for his southern sympathies as well as for his disregard of the local moral code. As Mayor Hendry considered the case against Malachi Warren inside the town hall on April 24, a hostile crowd formed outside the building and prepared to take matters into its own hands.[9] Jim Warren urged the crowd to lynch his father and even supplied several feet of rope to facilitate the hanging. At that point members of the Monroe Rifles intervened. "We formed into a line, marched to the besieged building and deployed around it," recalled veteran James M. Guinn decades afterward. "A number of Indian clubs from the College gymnasium had been put into sacks and hauled down to the town hall. . . . With these ponderous shillalahs . . . ready to strike, we stood off the mob while old Warren, carrying the stars and stripes, was escorted . . . down the back stairs, placed in a buggy and rapidly driven out of town."[10] Chastened by the experience, Warren two weeks later left Ellen and the children behind in Oberlin and headed south to Alabama, where he died in 1862.[11] His exile demonstrated that the advent of war had placed new limits on Oberlin's tolerance of ideological dissent.

Although Oberlin College had long defied mainstream American norms by admitting women and blacks to study alongside white males, membership in the Monroe Rifles was strictly limited by gender and race. When President

Lincoln called on loyal states to raise troops to suppress the rebellion, only white men were legally welcome to serve in the Ohio militia. Oberlin women who wanted to help the Union cause promptly formed their own organization, the Florence Nightingale Association, "for preparing woolen hose and underclothing for the volunteers" and, more generally, "for contributing comfort to those who enlisted."[12] In doing so, they accepted the time-honored assumption that soldiering was a masculine activity for which women were physically and temperamentally unfit. At a meeting of the Ladies Literary Society held a few months later, members posed for debate whether "ladies should organize themselves into Military Companies and drill."[13] Yet nothing came of the idea, and Oberlinians never seriously challenged the prohibition against female military service throughout the Civil War.

The ban on African American men stirred much more controversy. At the war's inception, blacks from Oberlin and elsewhere in Ohio petitioned state officials for permission to enlist but were summarily rebuffed.[14] Although a handful of Oberlinians of color managed to join Union forces by passing as white, darker-complexioned African Americans lacked that option.[15] But as the war raged on and white enlistments flagged, the idea of recruiting black soldiers attracted new attention. At a public gathering on July 6, 1862, and again at a "war meeting" ten days later, Oberlinians endorsed the formation and training "of a company of colored men in this place, with the intention of its forming part of a regiment, or if possible a brigade of colored men in Ohio, that they may be in readiness to offer their services . . . as soon as the way is opened."[16] John Mercer Langston subsequently met in person with Governor David Tod and asked for his blessing to recruit volunteers of color throughout the state.[17] Tod refused, however, offering an explicitly racist rationale for his decision. "Had the people elected a colored Lieutenant Governor," he reportedly told Langston, "I would not have taken my seat, and I cannot ask the noble men from Ohio who are in the field to do what I would not do myself."[18]

While Langston devoted most of his energy in the early years of the war to advancing the cause of black rights at the state and national levels, he found time in February 1862 to defend a female student of color at Oberlin College against charges that she had deliberately poisoned two other female students, both of them white. The case of Mary Edmonia Lewis is sometimes cited as damning evidence of white racism in wartime Oberlin, but Langston framed it in different terms in his 1894 autobiography.[19] By his account, Lewis and her accusers were close friends who roomed with the same family and "held conversations in free and frank manner upon every conceivable subject of interest to them, confiding to each other even their most important, special and sacred personal affairs."[20] On one winter's morning, Lewis served her white friends warm beverages of her own concoction. A little more than an hour later, both became seriously ill during a sleigh ride with male companions to Birmingham, Ohio, the hometown of one of the women. Arriving at her parents' house, the woman "declared to them that she had been poisoned, naming the person who had done it, and saying that she herself must die." Doctors confirmed the diagnosis, and when the news reached Oberlin, Lewis was "charged with the grave crime of poisoning her associates and friends."[21]

The two white female students remained bedridden for several days, during which time public opinion in Oberlin turned increasingly against Lewis. Yet she had not been formally arrested, and she continued to move freely about the town. One night a group of vigilantes meted out their own vicious sense of justice. According to Langston, "as she was passing out of the back door of the house in which she still roomed, she was seized by unknown persons, carried out into the field lying in the rear, and after being severely beaten, with her clothes and jewelry torn from her person and scattered here and there, she was left in a dark, obscure place to die." Fortunately, when her absence was noticed, her housemates mobilized, "bells were tolled," and a "search with lanterns" was initiated. After being located, Lewis was brought back to her room, where she recuperated over the next few weeks.[22]

By the time the trial—actually a judicial hearing—took place in late February, Lewis's accusers had returned to good health, and Lewis, though still unable to walk unassisted, was also on the mend. "The community," Langston recalled, "was about equally divided upon the question of innocence or guilt." "Many were prejudiced against the accused on account of her color," he observed, but the role of race and racism was surprisingly complex. According to Langston, "The major part of the colored people themselves, largely because of her easy and rather unusual social relations to the whites, were ready and did pronounce her guilty in advance."[23]

Langston mounted a successful defense in court. Facing off against a team of experienced prosecutors, he pointed out that the state had failed to supply any physical evidence that a crime had been committed. Without question, the white young women had taken sick, but that fact by itself did not prove that they had been poisoned. Nobody had thought to collect "any portion of the contents of the stomach or bowels" for forensic analysis, and now it was too late. Langston's logic prevailed. All charges against Lewis were dropped, and she "was carried in the arms of her excited associates and fellow-students from the court room . . . to her home, fully vindicated in her character and name."[24]

Of all the predominantly white communities in the United States in 1862, probably only in Oberlin could a woman of color represented by a lawyer of color have received such a fair legal hearing. Lewis's nighttime assailants were never identified or punished, however, and a year later she exited Oberlin under a cloud of suspicion for the alleged theft of art supplies.[25] Although racial prejudice likely played a part in this outcome, in subsequent years the local press tracked her rise to international prominence as a sculptor with evident pride.[26]

From the Civil War's inception, Oberlin abolitionists insisted that the conflict's real cause was slavery, not secession, and that only the elimination of human bondage throughout the country could redeem American democracy. Oberlinians raised this argument repeatedly during the spring and summer of 1862. On April 24, townspeople gathered at the college chapel to celebrate the emancipation of bondpersons in Washington, D.C., by an act of Congress. Henry Evans, an African American cabinetmaker who three-and-a half years earlier had been indicted for his role in the Oberlin-Wellington Rescue, was chosen chair, and a mix of white and black speakers offered short addresses. The meeting then adopted a series of resolutions, including one that hailed "the beginning of a change which shall rapidly eliminate slavery from our whole land, and that so regarding it, we look upon it as second in importance to no other which ever occurred in the history of Freedom."[27]

Ten weeks later, as part of the town's Independence Day celebration, Oberlinians filled "the great Church . . . to its utmost capacity" and unanimously endorsed another set of resolves heralding the growth of abolitionist sentiment. "Our people are generally beginning to see and acknowledge that slavery is the only interest opposed to our government, and to demand that this sole cause of rebellion shall be opposed in all legitimate ways, even to its utter annihilation," one resolution declared. "We believe that the wisest and most benevolent disposition to be made of rebels is to rid them speedily of their slaves, their property, and if need be their lives."[28]

On July 29, townspeople assembled at the college chapel to call upon

President Lincoln to make abolition the Union's central war aim. Attending "at a great risk to his health," Charles Grandison Finney argued that while Lincoln's "policy ... may have been right and wise at the beginning of the war," it was no longer morally adequate. The Union would be better off losing the war than winning it without "liberating the slave." The meeting as a whole adopted a forceful resolve drafted by Henry Cowles, John Mercer Langston, and Edward Henry Fairchild. Characterizing "the present war as a Divine rebuke for the national sin of oppressing the slave," the resolve "entreat[ed] our President, without delay, to proclaim universal emancipation, and to enforce the same to the full extent of his executive ability."[29]

Although Lincoln bided his time, on September 22 he issued a preliminary Emancipation Proclamation announcing that "on the first day of January in the year of our Lord, one thousand eight hundred and sixty-three, all persons held as slaves within any State, or designated part of a State, the people whereof shall then be in rebellion against the United States shall be then, thenceforward, and forever free." Delighted Oberlinians forgave the president his hesitation in embracing abolition. "From the beginning of the war we have hoped that slavery was to perish before its close," the *Lorain County News* declared. "We hail [the proclamation] as an important means to a great end: we hail it as an event which comes at the right time: we hail it as the Providential sign that freedom is soon to be the lot of all."[30]

On January 1, 1863, Oberlin residents flocked to First Church for a "Jubilee Meeting" while they awaited word that Lincoln had delivered on the promise he had made the previous September. The daylong program opened with a sermon by Charles Grandison Finney. "It was a masterly effort," reported the *Lorain County News*. "Every heart beat in unison with the speaker when he declared that the efforts of the humane should never cease until the emancipated had been rewarded for all their toil by being put in possession of so much of the soil of the South, which for ages they had moistened by their blood and tears, as would be necessary for their support."[31] In the afternoon and evening, Oberlinians of color as well as prominent whites addressed the assembly. According to the *News*, "The great speech of the day ... was the speech of Esq. Langston," who demanded that the federal government allow black troops to fight in the Union Army. "[W]e can't whip the rebels without the help of the negro," he declared. "God has ordained it, and you must call the negro to your aid or perish." Before adjourning, the meeting established the Freedmen's Relief Association of Oberlin "to aid in affording to the freedmen of this country such relief as their wants, physical, mental and moral, may seem to demand." A mixed-race board of officers, including the ex-slave Sabram Cox, was appointed to lead this new organization.[32]

Only one thing was missing from the Jubilee meeting: word from Washington that Lincoln had actually issued the final Emancipation Proclamation. That information eventually arrived by train the following evening, and it prompted a fresh celebration at the college chapel. "[W]ithout previous understanding or announcement, almost as if by magic," reported the *Lorain County News*, "a large audience gathered to hear the words of freedom read." John Mercer Langston did the honors, reading the text of the final Proclamation aloud twice, once with "the audience seated" and again with everyone standing in joy. Public festivities continued well into the night. To cap the occasion, "The colored people formed in procession and marched to the residence of Mr. Langston." Observed the *News*: "Never did we see an extempore demonstration on the part of the people so pleasant and appropriate."[33]

In the final Emancipation Proclamation, President Lincoln invited newly freed southern slaves to join "the armed service of the United States to garrison forts, positions, stations, and other places, and to man vessels of all sorts in said service."[34] With varying degrees of enthusiasm, Unionist governors soon decided that if blacks from the South could fight the rebels, so could blacks from the North. Massachusetts governor John A. Andrew, a long-standing abolitionist, took the lead, and John Mercer Langston promptly signed on as lead recruiter of men of color in Ohio and other western states for the 54th Massachusetts Volunteer Regiment. His brother Charles Langston and his brother-in-law O.S.B. Wall joined him in the effort.[35] By early April, the *Lorain County News* reported, "fourteen of [Oberlin's] colored citizens enrolled themselves in the black regiment . . . forming near Boston"—including "[t]hree . . . fugitives, and three emancipated slaves." Before leaving town, most were "presented with four dollars in money and a Testament [Bible]" supplied by local supporters. "The party," observed the *News*, "numbers among its names some of our most industrious and respected colored townsmen," and as they went off to war they carried with them "the God speed and good wishes of all our people."[36]

That was only the beginning. Over the next two years, black Oberlinians enlisted in several other "colored" units, including the 127th Ohio Volunteer Infantry—later renamed the 5th U.S. Colored Troops—commanded by Giles

Shurtleff, former captain of the Monroe Rifles. By war's end, an estimated sixty African Americans with Oberlin associations—including sojourning students as well as long-term residents—had served in Union forces.[37]

Notwithstanding the initial prohibition on black enlistments, Oberlin's white-headed households and black-headed households contributed soldiers to the Union cause in similar proportions over the course of the Civil War. Of the 542 white-headed households enumerated in the 1860 census for Russia Township, 115 (21 percent) sent at least one household member off to military service. By comparison, 21 of the 86 black-headed households (24 percent) supplied at least one individual to Union forces. All the local men who served were volunteers, not draftees, and most were in their teens or twenties when they enlisted. Yet blacks who enlisted were on average six years older than their white counterparts, and a much higher proportion of blacks than whites were age thirty or higher: 44 percent compared to 9 percent. Conversely, a much larger proportion of whites than blacks were identified as students in the 1860 census: 42 percent compared to 14 percent. Undoubtedly, the economic impact of sending soldiers off to war was greater for black households than for white households in Oberlin and Russia Township.[38]

Both white and black Oberlinians saw extensive military action during the Civil War—in famous battles such as Antietam, Chancellorsville, Fort Wagner, and Gettysburg, as well as in numerous comparatively obscure skirmishes. They fought bravely and paid a steep price for their valor.[39] According to one analysis, Company C suffered a higher rate of casualties than any other company in the 7th Ohio Volunteer Infantry Regiment, which in turn "stood second in battle losses among Ohio's 198 infantry regiments." Over the course of four years, "Out of 151 enrolled [in Company C] 28 were killed or died of wounds, five died from other causes; 68 were wounded; 40 were taken prisoner."[40] A separate analysis reveals that the death toll among Oberlin's African American soldiers was approximately 20 percent, with marginally more succumbing to disease than to injuries inflicted on the battlefield.[41] For Oberlinians, the Civil War was a particularly deadly affair.

Throughout the gruesome military conflict, townspeople held fast by their commitment to the intertwined goals of Union victory and the abolition of slavery. They also continued to affirm the principle of racial equality that had set the community apart from dominant opinion in American society for three decades. In August 1862, after Henry Palmer, keeper of the college-owned hotel in the center of town, barred "gentlemen from his table, for no social fault save that they belong to the oppressed race of this country," his fellow citizens publicly denounced his behavior "as in flagrant violation of the principles held and avowed by the founders, patrons, and present authorities of the College . . . and as an outrage upon the principles and usages of a true Christian civilization."[42] Thus shamed, Palmer reversed himself. In August 1864, Oberlinians inaugurated a new, multiracial cemetery that had been under development for three years. Significantly, its planning committee included Henry Evans, and from the cemetery's opening the graves of blacks and whites lay side by side, a highly unusual burial pattern in mid-nineteenth-century America.[43]

In March 1865, as the Confederate war effort neared collapse, Oberlinians proudly heralded the path-breaking appointment of a local African American to serve as a commissioned officer in Union forces. On March 16 they held "a well attended meeting . . . in the Chapel" to witness the ceremonial "presentation of a sword to Capt. O.S.B. Wall of the U.S. A[rmy]." After an opening prayer, Sabram Cox introduced Professor Henry E. Peck, who, in presenting the sword, recalled Wall's role in the Oberlin-Wellington Rescue. Peck observed that seven years earlier "the Capt. and himself had been imprisoned for aiding a fugitive slave to escape by the same government which was now doing honor to the Captain." In accepting the gift, Wall thanked "his friends" not only for their personal generosity to him but, more importantly, for "showing their appreciation of the . . . great principle of the equality of all men by this government in deed as well as word." John Mercer Langston, Wall's brother-in-law, closed the occasion with an address highlighting "the advancement of the colored man in this country" in recent months. According to Langston, American progress toward a racially egalitarian social order was accelerating in the face of slavery's imminent demise.[44]

The abolition of slavery did not mean the end of racism, however, and as the war drew to a close a number of Oberlinians foresaw daunting challenges ahead. In an article announcing William Lloyd Garrison's plan to cease publication of the *Liberator* at the end of the calendar year, the *Lorain County News* declared, "Mr. Garrison, we trust, will live to see the generation after him, as heartily engaged in the work of combating the prejudice which is to be overcome against the colored race, as he and his coadjutors engaged in that of removing their chains." Presciently, the paper added, "The contest to come . . . will be scarcely less severe, or protracted than that which is past."[45]

On the evening of April 3, a "volcano of jubilation broke forth" in Oberlin upon confirmation of reports that Union forces had taken Richmond, Virginia, the capital of the Confederacy. Observed the *Lorain County News*: "The old six-pounder was brought out on Tappan Square, and belched forth, a large bonfire blazed up, rockets shot towards the heavens, a balloon ascension was greeted by a score of voices singing 'John Brown's body,' drums beat, and speeches by the citizens and students occupied a late hour of the night."[46] Six days later Robert E. Lee surrendered his remaining troops to Ulysses S. Grant at Appomattox Court House, Virginia. The military conflict was over, and the Union stood triumphant.

"In accordance with Gov. [John] Brough's Proclamation," Friday, April 14, was "set apart . . . as a day of Thanksgiving and Prayer" in Oberlin as elsewhere across Ohio. The college canceled classes, and townspeople and students alike crowded local churches to hear sermons in the morning and take part in prayer meetings in the afternoon. A more raucous celebration followed after dark, complete with another bonfire on Tappan Square, the illumination of college buildings, and a grand parade.[47] But the festive spirit did not endure. "Early on the following day" Oberlinians received the devastating news of President Lincoln's assassination. "The sudden transition from overflowing joy, and praise and gratitude to God, to the overwhelming grief which the terrible tidings brought upon us, was too much for the great heart of the people to bear," reported the *Lorain County News*, "and all sunk beneath it like a crushed reed."[48] Feelings of sadness mixed with anger and led to calls for righteous retribution. In a daylong sermon on Sunday, April 16, Charles Grandison Finney spoke out firmly "in favor of hanging rebel leaders."[49]

During the summer of 1865, Oberlinians launched an ambitious campaign for black suffrage. Local African Americans had long demanded equal voting rights regardless of color, and James Monroe had raised the issue in the Ohio legislature in the 1850s. Yet at the conclusion of the Civil War suffrage in Ohio was still restricted to adult white men—interpreted by the state's Supreme Court to include men of color with predominantly white ancestry. In the early months of Andrew Johnson's presidency, as political conflicts developed over federal Reconstruction policy, the debate over black suffrage extended to the national level. Radical Republican congressmen argued that the enfranchisement of freedmen in the ex-Confederate states was essential to the transformation of the southern social order, while President Johnson, Democrats, and many conservative Republicans adamantly disagreed.[50] In this context, Oberlinians rallied to make their position clear.

On the rainy afternoon of Wednesday, July 19, "a large audience filled the 'Big Church'" to hear speeches and pass resolutions on the subject of "Negro Suffrage."[51] A month before, a core group of local abolitionists, including John Mercer Langston, Edward Henry Fairchild, and Samuel Plumb, had gathered in the college chapel to discuss the issue "under the auspices of the Oberlin Equal Rights League"—the local affiliate of the National Equal Rights League, an African American organization founded the previous fall and headed by Langston.[52] On July 19 a broader swath of Oberlinians joined the conversation about black suffrage. John Keep—now commonly referred to as "Father Keep"—called the meeting to order, and James Harris Fairchild took the chair. After Judge Bellamy Storer of Cincinnati gave an opening address, the Committee on Declarations and Resolutions recommended the election of state legislators "who will erase from the constitution of this State the word 'white.'" Members of the audience gave their unanimous approval, and the committee then presented a wide-ranging critique of President Johnson's Reconstruction policies, which it deemed insufficiently supportive of the ex-slaves and unduly lenient toward the defeated rebels. "Above all, let the colored race be brought up under the protection of our national government to a status of safety, self-support, and progress," the committee proclaimed. "Make them equal before the law to the white race. *Give them the elective franchise on the same terms as white men.*"[53]

Following the Committee's presentation, Father Keep offered a motion to the same effect:

Resolved, That we demand equal suffrage, not simply because, like the negro's musket, it is now needed to save the freshly imperilled nation, but because Justice, whose eyes are bandaged so that she may never know the difference between the white man and the black, holds an even scale in her hand, wherewith she weighs the right of one citizen by the exact weight of every other.[54]

Audience members endorsed Keep's motion without dissent, and the meeting closed with a peroration by John Mercer Langston. Oberlin's most prominent African American affirmed that the interests of northern and southern people of color were one, and he refuted claims that blacks lacked the intellect and moral character required to vote responsibly. "In answer to the weak charges of ignorance and degradation, he told some home-truths and pulverized the opponents," reported the *Cleveland Leader*.[55]

Yet within a few days word reached Oberlin that Jacob Dolson Cox, the Republican candidate for governor running on a Union ticket, did not share the town's enthusiasm for black suffrage. This news came as a shock because Cox was an Oberlin College graduate, the husband of Charles Grandison Finney's daughter Helen, and a person with impeccable antislavery credentials. He had joined the Republican Party at its inception, and in 1859, while residing in Warren, Ohio, he had won election to the state senate. In short order, Cox, James Garfield, and Oberlin's James Monroe became known as that chamber's "radical triumvirate." After the Confederate attack on Fort Sumter in April 1861, Cox enlisted in the Union war effort, and over the next four years he demonstrated impressive prowess as a military leader, rising to the rank of major general.[56] Although he had not resided in Oberlin since 1851, local activists considered him one of their own.

Cox, however, harbored serious doubts about whether whites and blacks could live together harmoniously in postwar America. In a letter to his former classmate John M. Ellis, who was now a professor at the college, Cox warned that black enfranchisement would lead to a race war in the South.[57] Ellis immediately relayed Cox's opinions to members of the Oberlin community, and on the evening of July 23 the town's "colored citizens" gathered to formulate a collective response. After listening to impassioned remarks by John Mercer Langston, the meeting appointed a committee to "wait upon [Cox] and ascertain [his] views on the subject" of black voting rights.[58]

The next day, white allies Edward Henry Fairchild and Samuel Plumb dispatched a letter to Cox asking him to clarify his position on black suffrage, both as it applied to the Ohio state constitution and as it applied to the former rebel states. In Oberlin, Fairchild and Plumb asserted, "there is but one opinion on this subject, and we were never more in earnest on any political question." "We believe that the distinction made by our Constitution between white and colored people was made in the interest of slavery," they explained. "And we believe that to re-construct the Southern States and admit them with Constitutions excluding colored men from the polls would give the country and the negro into the power of the very men who have sought and still desire to ruin the one and enslave the other." The moral as well as political fate of the country was at stake. Were the United States to pursue such a path, Fairchild and Plumb warned, "a terrible retribution will await us."[59]

Cox responded to Fairchild and Plumb promptly and publicly. In a letter dated July 25 and subsequently published in newspapers across Ohio, he bridled at the suggestion that he should be held to any political test other than allegiance to the platform adopted at the Union Party's convention in June. While that platform called for the complete and irrevocable elimination of slavery throughout the United States, it was notably silent on the question of black suffrage. Cox suggested that his Oberlin interrogators were out of line, and he called for party unity.[60]

Even as he made that appeal, however, Cox put forth his own, highly idiosyncratic plan for Reconstruction. At its foundation was Cox's firm conviction that racial integration in the postwar South was neither feasible nor desirable. "Never between Norman and Saxon, nor between Gaul and Frank was there a more conscious hatred, or an antagonism more likely to prove inveterate, than between black and white on our Southern soil," he wrote. Extension of the franchise to the freedmen would only exacerbate this situation. "The struggle for supremacy would be direct and immediate," he insisted, "and I see no hope whatsoever that the weaker race would not be reduced to hopeless subjection, or utterly destroyed."[61]

To Cox the best—perhaps the only—prospective alternative to this grim scenario was "a *peaceable separation of the races on the soil where they now are.*"[62] More specifically, he proposed that the federal government set aside "contiguous territory in South Carolina, Georgia, Alabama, and Florida" for settlement by "freedmen in a dependency of the Union analogous to the Western territories." Though less fully self-governing than a state, this domestic black colony would offer former slaves many significant benefits. "Give them schools, laws facilitating the acquirement of homesteads to be paid for by their own labor, full and exclusive political privileges," Cox advised. "There need be no coercive collection of the colored race in the designated region," he asserted, since "the majority are there now, and the reward of political power would draw thither the remainder."[63]

Cox's letter provoked a good deal of controversy in Oberlin. The *Lorain County News* faulted Cox for ignoring the question of black suffrage in Ohio, and it raised concerns about his plan for Reconstruction in the former Confederacy. "We have no doubt that Gen. Cox greatly exaggerates the antagonism between the two races in the South," the paper declared. Moreover, even "if the theory advocated by him be a good and practical one," there remained the issue of "whether, in the meantime, the blacks who have fought so bravely, and in various ways served the Union cause . . . may not be allowed to participate in the re-organization of the States."[64]

Much harsher were criticisms lodged by William P. Michener and John Mercer Langston. A former student in the preparatory department of the college, Michener had returned to Oberlin after serving three years in the Union Army, the last as a white officer commanding a black regiment.[65] Characterizing "the question as to granting the right of suffrage to the colored man" as "*the* question of the hour," he argued in a letter to the *News* that Cox's failure to endorse black suffrage disqualified him for the governorship.[66] Langston agreed. In a speech at the college chapel on August 15, he denounced Cox "as one who would 'eat his anti-slavery antecedents to catch the popular vote.'" "He could not vote for [Cox]," Langston declared, "and believed that those who did would turn their backs on the great principles of the Republican platform."[67]

Support for Cox's position on the suffrage question came from a surprising quarter, however: Ralph Plumb, Samuel Plumb's younger brother and one of the men indicted in 1858 for his role in the Oberlin-Wellington Rescue. During the Civil War, Ralph Plumb had served as quartermaster at Camp Dennison, near Cincinnati, where he remained stationed in August 1865. Although he regarded Cox's plan for racial separation as a "Utopian impracticality," he also viewed black enfranchisement as politically infeasible. "If the Union party adopt the affirmative on the question of negro suffrage now, and appeal to the people on that platform," he predicted, "the first result would be their defeat at the North." Ralph Plumb was prepared to compromise the principle of racial equality for the sake of securing electoral victory.[68]

Cox made his case to Oberlinians in person when he came to town for the college's commencement festivities in late August. It was a momentous occasion. Union victory and the concomitant demise of slavery had vindicated Oberlin's commitment to abolitionist principles after decades of ostracism. Among those who attended commencement in 1865 were Theodore Dwight Weld and ten other Lane Rebels who had helped set the college and the community on a radical course three decades earlier. Yet nobody suggested that Oberlin's mission was complete, and during commencement week there was much talk about the importance of obtaining black suffrage. In a speech at First Church, Weld "declare[d] that he must be stone blind who did not see that black people must vote in this country—by all the advancing spirit of the age—by the principles of true democracy and Christianity—by our own constitutional guarantee of a Republican form of government in every state." Likewise, at a "Festival . . . given in the Ladies' Hall in honor of the returned colored soldiers," three distinguished black orators—William Still of Philadelphia, Alexander Crummell of Liberia, and Oberlin's own John Mercer Langston—"declared the right of the colored men to vote, as they have historically fought."[69] Charles Grandison Finney agreed. In his baccalaureate "sermon to the Graduating Classes" he "urged the duty of extending equal suffrage to the colored people, North and South, as a plain dictate of common justice, of public safety, and of religious obligation."[70]

Despite his public dissent on the suffrage question, Jacob Dolson Cox received an enthusiastic welcome when he spoke to an interracial audience at First Church on August 21. Edward Henry Fairchild, a champion of equal suffrage, chaired the meeting and introduced Cox on this occasion. Cox, in turn, sought to highlight his Oberlin ties and areas of ideological agreement with his listeners.[71] In regard to suffrage, he remarked, "We perhaps agree on the fundamental right, but differ as to mode." "In principle," he elaborated, "I am inclined to give it to all—to Chinese—to all coming from abroad, but when I look at their idolatries and peculiarities, it is wise to ask whether we should not confine this principle of democracy." By Cox's reasoning, although universal suffrage was the ideal, in practice the vote should be restricted to those who could exercise it safely and responsibly. Context mattered, and Cox claimed empirical expertise on conditions in the former Confederate states: "I have said that among the whites and blacks in the South, as they are situated *there*, not elsewhere, . . . there is an antagonism, and my decision comes from actual observation." "The colored people themselves," he assured his audience, "say they would rather live apart than with those who had been their oppressors."[72]

Upon finishing his speech, Cox "took his seat to a storm of applause." Not everyone in the audience was satisfied, however. According to a press report, "Mr. Hale, a negro, raised in his seat and asked permission to ask Gen. Cox a question." Hale then pressed Cox to make clear "if he is elected Governor of Ohio, [whether] he will be in favor of bestowing upon the colored men of this State—saying nothing about what he would do for those in the South— the right of suffrage."[73] Cox responded carefully. "[H]e understood the colored people of Oberlin, and elsewhere, took the position that their interests should not be separated from those of their brethren in the South," he said, and he endorsed that position. "But if in the course of events the rights and interests of the colored people of the State should become an independent question," he added, "it would be found that his views and actions would be such as to satisfy all classes." In short, while Cox would not take the lead in advocating the enfranchisement of black Ohioans, he would not block such a move if it gained support among the populace at large.[74]

Cox's performance on August 21 succeeded in pleasing almost everyone. As he left First Church, persons of color joined whites in seeking to shake his hand and offer congratulations. The *Cleveland Leader* remarked, "His earnestness, his frankness, and the deep feeling manifested by him in his references, seemed to effect a corresponding manner in his audience, and all were favorably impressed."[75] "Even those who could not agree with the General's theories of reconstruction," opined the *Lorain County News*, "must have been satisfied of his honesty and real fidelity to antislavery conviction, of his pre-eminent fitness to be the leader of the great Union party of Ohio."[76] At least one observer dissented from this glowing assessment, however: Sallie Holley, Oberlin Class of 1851, and a longstanding Garrisonian abolitionist. By her account, Cox offered merely "a weak and lame defence of his position." "His speech was in the interest of the White Unionists of the South, not of the loyal black people there," she wrote in disgust. "And yet Oberlin will vote for him!"[77]

Oberlin did indeed vote for Jacob Dolson Cox in 1865, and it did so by a large margin: 469 to 81. Yet the *Lorain County News* noted that Cox ran "some forty votes behind his ticket" and attributed this lag to the reluctance of "radical Republicans" and "our colored friends" to cast their ballots for him.[78] Statewide, the race was significantly closer than in Oberlin, but Cox still won comfortably: 54 to 46 percent.[79] Upon reflection, the *Lorain County News*—now edited and published by J.B.T. Marsh, an Oberlin College graduate, abolitionist, and war veteran—declared the outcome "most gratifying," but the paper also expressed regret that the Republican Party had ducked the suffrage issue. "Who believes that if we had boldly taken [a] stand in favor of equal suffrage we should have been defeated?" the *News* asked rhetorically.[80]

On January 24, 1866, a few weeks into the fifty-seventh session of the Ohio legislature, Washington Wallace (W. W.) Boynton, the newly elected representative from Lorain County, introduced a resolution to amend the state constitution by omitting the word "white" from the specification of who was entitled to vote in Ohio elections.[81] As might be expected, W. W. Boynton was a staunch Republican. More surprisingly, he was also a son of Lewis D. Boynton, the prominent Russia Township Democrat, and an older brother of Shakespeare Boynton, the young man who on September 13, 1858, lured John Price into a trap laid by slave hunters—the incident that gave rise to the Oberlin-Wellington Rescue.[82]

Following standard procedures, W. W. Boynton's resolution was referred to the House Judiciary Committee, where it languished for the next several months. In the meantime Oberlinians focused much of their attention on worrisome developments in the South and the deepening conflict between Congress and President Johnson over federal Reconstruction policy. On March 2, 1866, a mass meeting convened at the college chapel to express support for congressional Republicans in their refusal to seat representatives from former Confederate states that failed to provide "full protection to the freedmen in the exercise of all rights and privileges which we claim for ourselves."[83] On April 10, townspeople gathered again at the chapel, this time to herald the congressional Republicans' success in overriding Johnson's veto of the civil rights bill. "[W]e are profoundly impressed by the danger which threatened our beloved country from the rash, unwarranted and ruinous course of our chief magistrate," the meeting declared. "[W]e regard the passage of the Civil Rights Bill over the President's veto, as a triumph of civil liberty scarcely inferior to any in the annals of history, and the harbinger of a brighter era in our political life."[84]

When it came to gathering information about conditions in the ex-Confederate states, Oberlinians had trustworthy sources to draw on: local residents and former college students who went south to work in freedmen's schools and otherwise help people of color make the transition from bondage to freedom. On January 24, 1866, the *Lorain County News* published the names of thirty-four "teachers from Oberlin, who are now in the Freedmen's work under the auspices of the American Missionary Association." They comprised mostly women but also men, mostly whites but also blacks. They were stationed in places ranging from Natchez and Meridian, Mississippi, to Atlanta and Macon, Georgia, and Nashville, Tennessee. "We look upon this list with some thing of an added glory in Oberlin, its faith and its works," the *News* commented. "We feel as if it were true to its long time professions of regard for the oppressed."[85]

Many of the reports from the South were disheartening. In early March the *News* told its readers, "Rev. John Vetter of this place, Chaplain of the 5th U.S. Colored Cavalry[,] is on duty in the Freedmen's Bureau in Arkansas. His testimony to the unvarying hatred and persecution of union men, black and white, accords with the general current of intelligence from the south."[86] Later in the month, the *News* reported that theology student J. C. Cannon "has been teaching during the winter, in the employ of the Freedmen's Bureau, in Louisiana. He writes the opinion that social and moral reconstruction is fully as much needed there as the political article."[87]

Reverend John P. Bardwell, a longtime resident of Oberlin who headed south in February 1866, wrote home intermittently about his experiences as an organizer and supervisor of American Missionary Association schools in Mississippi.[88] In early May the *Lorain County News* reported that "while sitting in the law office of a leading citizen, he was assailed by a former slave holder—backed and encouraged by a mob—dragged out of his chair, beaten with a heavy cane and his life directly threatened." Reflecting on this episode, Bardwell wrote, "The effort to educate colored children stirs to its lowest depth the wrath of the old slaveholder. I have good reason to believe that if a vote of the community were taken in this case the great mass would say 'served him right.'"[89] The situation quickly grew worse: "Three days after the assault on Mr. B[ardwell], the agent of the Freedmen's Bureau who had done Mr. B. the simple kindness to aid him in washing his bruises . . . was deliberately shot down in the street in broad day."[90]

The bloody race riot in New Orleans on July 30 provided further evidence of southern white intransigence. A "late resident of Oberlin" dispatched an eyewitness account of the riot's horrific brutality:

> At first the fight was confined to the street between the police and colored people, but soon shots were exchanged with those inside the buildings. Then we began to see the wounded and others trying to make their escape. One negro was running for his life, a policeman was after him with a revolver, he fired, and the negro fell on his face, but not being satisfied with shooting him down, the excited mob stoned him and beat him with clubs after he was dead. . . . Another man came staggering along so covered with blood that we could not tell whether he was black or white. A man caught and held him while another knocked him in the head with a club. Then came Michael Hahn, ex-governor of Louisiana, and although he was a crip-

ple, and held the emblem of surrender in his hand, he was shot through the head, struck with a club and stabbed with a knife.[91]

Jacob Dolson Cox's worst fears of racial warfare in the post-emancipation South appeared to be coming true.

As the fall election approached, a deepening sense of crisis impelled Oberlin activists to mobilize on behalf of Republican candidates running on the Union ticket and in support of the proposed Fourteenth Amendment, which would guarantee civil rights regardless of race and promote equal suffrage nationwide, albeit indirectly.[92] In mid-September a group of college students formed a "young men's Union League" to rally prospective Republican voters and distribute campaign literature.[93] The high point of the campaign in Oberlin was Benjamin Butler's speech to an enthusiastic crowd at First Church on September 29. Butler, once a Democrat but now a Republican war hero, argued that blacks should be allowed to vote on the same terms as whites. "Let there be no differences on account of color, said the speaker," the *News* reported with approval. But it also pointed out that equal suffrage did not mean the same thing as universal suffrage. From the paper's perspective, voting restrictions based on factors other than color—such as education or gender—might be acceptable. "The main issue now," however, was ending racial discrimination. "If we can turn the position in which this mean and unchristian prejudice against color has entrenched itself, the battle will be won," the *News* declared, "and all else that ought to follow it will be easily gained."[94]

Russia Township voted for the Republican ticket in 1866 by 715 to 79—a margin of 636 votes, notably greater than the already hefty margin of 388 votes the year before.[95] The rest of Ohio and the North as a whole also went heavily for anti-Johnson candidates in Congressional contests. The *News* observed proudly, "It is a noble comment on the manliness and intelligence of the loyal North that all [the president's] bribery of patronage, this haste for peace, this lust for office, could not swerve the friends of a free and purified Union from their convictions and their conscientious purpose."[96]

In the aftermath of this sweeping Republican victory, Oberlin activists mounted a new effort to secure black voting rights in Ohio. They formed an Impartial Suffrage Committee and called on "leading citizens throughout the State" to join the "movement, thus aiming to secure united, general and efficient action throughout our commonwealth."[97] Serving as the committee's secretary, Giles Shurtleff, now a professor at Oberlin College, dispatched letters to former Governor William Dennison and to Congressmen James Garfield and Robert Schenck, among others, asking for their support. John Mercer Langston took to "the field as lecturer and agent" to promote the cause. As momentum in favor of black enfranchisement began to build, state legislators again turned their attention to the suffrage question in January 1867.[98]

The Republican-dominated legislature took three months to agree upon a proposed amendment that would strike the word "white" from the state constitution. After it passed by the requisite three-fifths majorities in both chambers, however, the amendment still needed to be ratified by the electorate at large in order to take effect.[99] "The friends of Equal Rights have their summer's work laid out before them," the *Lorain County News* informed its readers on April 10. "It is hand to hand work that is to be done. Let Republicans remember that we want *lay labor* now more than ever—personal effort with friends and neighbors."[100]

The campaign for ratification of the equal suffrage amendment got off to a promising start. Unlike in 1865, Republicans endorsed "impartial manhood suffrage" as a core element of the platform adopted by the party's state convention at Columbus on June 19.[101] In the place of Jacob Dolson Cox, who declined to run for re-election, Republicans nominated Rutherford B. Hayes as their candidate for governor. "Gen. Hayes is a standard bearer about whom the party can heartily rally," the *Lorain County News* declared. "His war record is excellent, his Radicalism unimpeachable, and his fitness for the position beyond all question." Yet the paper warned that even if the Republican ticket proved triumphant in the fall election, ratification of the equal suffrage amendment was not assured. "The conservatism of Southern Ohio, hide bound in its prejudices, will be hard to overcome," the *News* explained, "and there is every argument in this aspect of the case why the Reserve counties should lend every energy to poll the fullest possible vote for the Amendment."[102]

The Ohio State Convention of Colored Men gathered in Columbus two weeks after the Republicans. Participants elected Oberlinian John Watson president of the convention and passed a series of resolutions expressing support for the equal suffrage amendment.[103] "The noble position held by the Union men of Ohio in the war to suppress the slaveholders' rebellion, . . . their grand and unselfish devotion to right principles at all times," the convention declared, "gives us cause to confidently hope that they will meet the issue now presented, of equal suffrage, in the same magnanimous spirit, and will sweep from our Constitution all clauses making distinctions on account of color."[104]

Over the summer Oberlinians mobilized in multiple ways at the local level. In late June the Oberlin Equal Rights League "passed a resolution 'heartily endorsing' the Republican state ticket."[105] In early July the Union Campaign Club—a reincarnation of the previous fall's young men's Union League—"fully endorse[d] the issues as presented by the Republican Convention, and [went] into the stirring work of the campaign with hearty good will."[106] In early August the Union caucus elected an interracial delegation to represent Oberlin at the upcoming county convention in Elyria, which in turn selected candidates to complete the Republican ticket for the fall election.[107]

Campaign activity intensified in the fall. On the evening of September 20, John Mercer Langston reported to the Oberlin Equal Rights League on his recent travels throughout the state on behalf of the equal suffrage amendment and the Republican ticket. According to the *Lorain County News*, "he made a rousing speech, telling his friends in his frank way that they must hope to secure their rights through the Republican party only, and must therefore make every effort to poll their full vote in the coming election."[108]

Oberlin's Republican campaign culminated on the afternoon of September 30, when gubernatorial candidate Rutherford B. Hayes came to town for a "Grand Rally" at First Church. The Campaign Club went all out to publicize the event, and the guest speakers "were greeted by an overflowing house." "In the gallery faces rose tier above tier," the *News* reported, "and below seats were filled so that many were obliged to stand." By the paper's account, the rally's most memorable moment occurred when the band played "a patriotic air" and "two six year old urchins, one white and the other colored, clambered upon the stand and listened, with eyes and ears agog to the entrancing music. The cheers of the audience, who saw in the act an illustration of the issues of the day[,] were joined in by the unconscious causes of the tumult, and the applause grew to a perfect roar."[109]

On October 10 the voters of Russia Township cast their ballots overwhelmingly in favor of Hayes for governor (737 to 78) and in favor of ratification of the equal suffrage amendment (729 to 92).[110] The statewide results were decidedly more mixed, however. While Hayes won the gubernatorial contest by a narrow margin, Ohio voters soundly rejected the equal suffrage amendment. Moreover, Democrats gained majorities in both houses of the state legislature.[111] Consequently the movement for racial equality in Ohio suffered a major setback in the 1867 election. Posing the question "What does it Signify?" the *Lorain County News* answered with righteous dismay: "[T]he election signifies . . . that the masses of the people are not educated quite up to the Golden Rule—not up to the declaration of Independence—they have not yet dared to be just."[112]

When black male enfranchisement finally came to Ohio in the spring of 1870, it arrived by a circuitous route. In 1868 the Democratic majority in the state legislature passed a statute designed to reduce the proportion of people of color eligible to vote by banning men with a "visual admixture" of black ancestry from casting ballots. Although state courts soon struck down the statute as incompatible with the judicial interpretation of what "white" meant in the state constitution, dark-complexioned African Americans still faced legal obstacles to voting, even in Oberlin.[113] The *Lorain County News* reported that during the fall elections of 1869 "the irrepressible Chauncey Wack, as usual, stood by the polls all day . . . to challenge any man whose face seemed a shade too dark for an intelligent view of his country's good."[114] Yet events at the national level moved in a more progressive direction. A Republican-dominated Congress passed the Fifteenth Amendment to the federal Constitution in February 1869, and one year later it was ratified by three-fourths of the state legislatures—including that of Ohio, which had reverted to Republican control.[115] The amendment declared, "The right of citizens of the United States to vote shall not be denied or abridged by the United States or by any State on account of race, color, or previous condition of servitude." It took effect on March 30, 1870.

On Wednesday, April 6, Oberlinians celebrated the amendment's adoption with a day of reflection and festivities.[116] Five years after the Union triumph in the Civil War, local activists had good reason to believe that the chief goals of the abolitionist movement were now largely attained: not only was slavery destroyed, but by Constitutional mandate people of color would henceforth possess the same civil and political rights as whites, at least according to the law. Although nobody doubted that color prejudice persisted, the progress toward social justice since Oberlinians had initially committed themselves to racial egalitarianism in 1835 appeared truly extraordinary.

The community celebration on April 6 was a racially integrated affair, as reflected in the choice of officers for the occasion. African American Rescuer John Watson served as president, two men of color (Garrison Chambers and

John Thomas) and two white men (Andrew Edwards and Hiram Pease) served as vice presidents, a white man (Reverend J. B. Sackett) served as chaplain, and a man of color (William T. Henderson) served as secretary. "The exercises of the day were inaugurated with a national salute at sunrise," the *Lorain County News* reported, "and the thunder echoing on the clear morning air told us, not that independence was declared, but that independence was attained."[117] In the afternoon, townspeople gathered in First Church for a "thanksgiving meeting." According to the *News*, "While the trials of the past hightened [*sic*] the joy of the present, still the spirit which pervaded every heart appeared to find expression in 'Not unto us, O Lord, not unto us, but unto thy name give glory.'" The thanksgiving meeting lasted "several hours" and was followed by "a salute of 29 guns . . . in honor of the states which had ratified the Amendment."[118] Then came a break for supper.

At 7:30 P.M. the festivities resumed at First Church, which "was filled to its utmost capacity, and many were obliged to stand during the evening." Six speakers—five of them white and one of them a man of color—offered public remarks. Oberlin College professor Judson Smith led off, hailing "the triumph of . . . the cause of humanity and the cause of God." "We might well stand on the shore of the Red Sea through which we had passed," he said, and "'sing unto the Lord, for He hath triumphed gloriously.'" After William C. French, rector of Oberlin's Episcopal Church, read "a poem . . . by a colored boy in an Episcopal Mission school at Philadelphia," Professor John M. Ellis recalled the Oberlin-Wellington Rescue and "spoke of the marvelous changes of the few last years." Implying that the abolitionists' work was complete, he declared, "The door of progress was now opened before the colored citizen, and it was for him to prove by his own efforts and developments that the Amendment is a blessing." Storrs S. Calkins, principal of the local business institute, celebrated the fact that "for the first time in our history he could, with entire consistency, address such an audience as 'fellow citizens of the United States.'" Calkins noted, however, that major challenges lay ahead. Democrats, he warned, "would try to flatter, and secure the vote of the colored man. He hoped the colored voter would remember who had been his friends and stand for the country's safety."[119]

The sole African American to speak at First Church that evening was Robert J. Robinson, a barber, preacher, and entrepreneur from Wellington, whose daughter was a student at Oberlin College.[120] "All were white now,"

Robinson proclaimed provocatively. "No American citizen would be stopped at the polls and asked if his mother was black—if his father was not of dark color—and if his father and mother were married!" But Robinson also argued that "this was not the time to put off the armor." He advised his listeners, "Work on, and having raised the slave to citizenship raise the citizen to the highest type of manhood."[121]

The evening's final orator was James Monroe, the former Oberlin College professor, abolitionist, and Republican politician who had recently returned from seven years of service as American consul in Rio de Janeiro.[122] Like Robinson, Monroe argued that the struggle for freedom and justice was far from over. "We had met the enemy's skirmish line, and had triumphed," he said, "but the heavy warfare was yet to come." Still, he exuded Christian faith and hope. "He spoke of the great moral needs of the country, and expressed his conviction that the Grace of God would eradicate the evils which afflicted us," reported the *Lorain County News*. "He fully sustained his reputation, evincing the thoughtfulness of a scholar and the heart of a philanthropist." After Monroe finished his speech, Oberlinians filed out of First Church to enjoy a splendid display of nighttime fireworks on Tappan Square.[123]

Notably absent from Oberlin's daylong celebration on April 6, 1870, was John Mercer Langston. For many years Langston had been the preeminent "bridge" figure in Oberlin, moving comfortably in both black and white circles and facilitating interracial collaboration within the community. Although he still owned a house in town and visited the community periodically, he had relocated to Washington, D.C., where he served as dean of the law school at Howard University and focused his political energies on developments at the national level.[124] Henry E. Peck had been another bridge figure in Oberlin during the 1850s and early 1860s, but he left town in 1865 to serve as American consul to Haiti. He died there two years later.[125] Also absent at the April 6 celebration was Father John Keep, who had passed away two months earlier, at age eighty-eight. On the eve of his funeral "the colored people of Oberlin" gathered to pay special tribute to his memory. "[I]n the death of Father Keep," they declared, "the colored people of Oberlin do deeply mourn the loss of a true Christian advocate of freedom, one who was ever valiant in battle for the cause of the oppressed."[126] The torch of leadership in Oberlin was passing to a new generation that would face daunting challenges to the egalitarian promise of the Civil War amendments.

THE TOWN CENTER OVER TIME

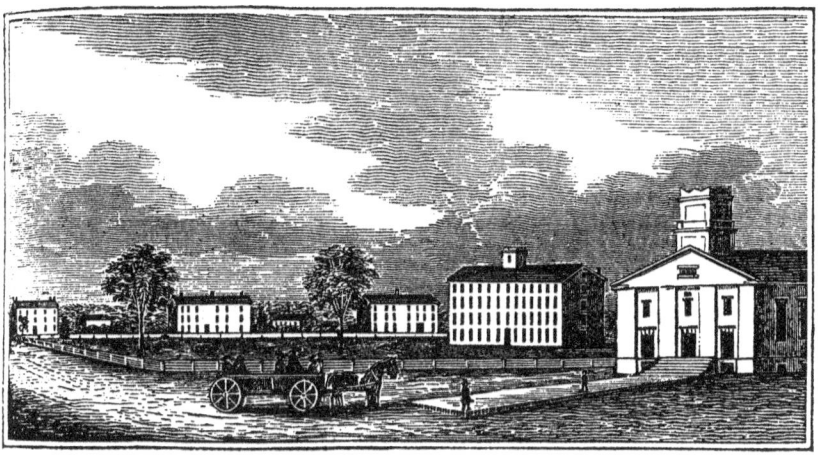

Oberlin Collegiate Institute buildings and the Congregational Church. Wood engraving based on a drawing by Henry Howe, 1846. Oberlin College Archives.

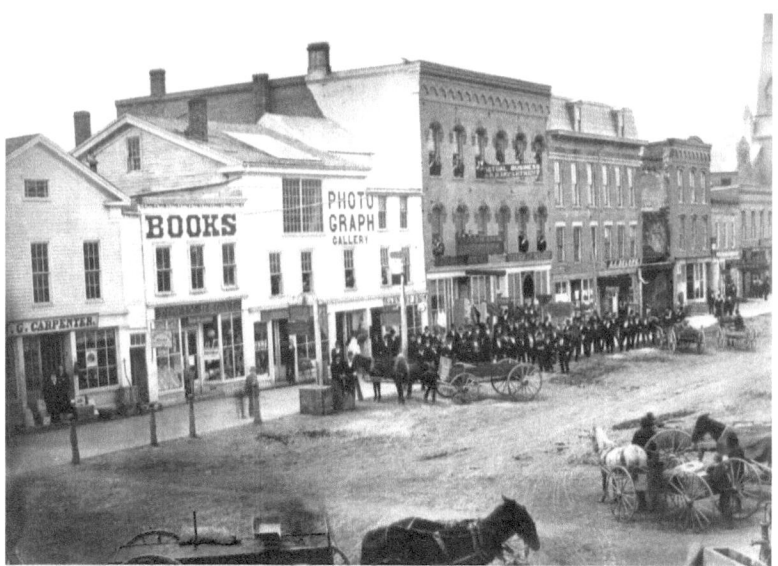

West College Street from North Main Street, 1876. Oberlin College Archives.

North Main Street from West College Street, 1903. Oberlin College Archives.

Postcard of College Street looking west from Pleasant Street, circa 1920.
Oberlin Heritage Center/O.H.I.O. Oberlin, Ohio.

ABOLITIONIST OBERLIN

Program of the First of August Celebration, 1846. Oberlin College Archives.

Charles Grandison Finney, 1850.
Oberlin College Archives.

John Mercer Langston, 1853.
Oberlin College Archives.

James Harris Fairchild, John Morgan, and James Monroe, 1857.
Oberlin College Archives.

Oberlin-Wellington Rescuers at the Cuyahoga County Jail, April 1859. From left to right: Jacob R. Shipherd, O.S.B. Wall, Loring Wadsworth, David Watson, Wilson Bruce Evans, Eli Boise, Ralph Plumb, Henry Evans, Simeon Bushnell, John H. Scott, Matthew Gillett, Charles Langston, Ansel W. Lyman, James Bartlett, William E. Lincoln, Richard Winsor, John Watson, James M. Fitch, Henry E. Peck, and Daniel Williams. Oberlin College Archives.

Notice of a celebration to welcome back the Rescuers upon their release, July 6, 1859. Oberlin College Archives.

John Anthony Copeland, circa 1859.
Boyd B. Stutler Collection,
West Virginia State Archives.

Giles Waldo Shurtleff, 1861.
Oberlin College Archives.

THE LATE NINETEENTH AND EARLY TWENTIETH CENTURIES

John H. Scott and his family, circa 1875.
Oberlin College Archives.

Henry Lee, circa 1890. From William H. Rogers, *Senator John P. Green, and Sketches of Prominent Men of Ohio* (Washington, D.C.: Arena Publishing, 1893).

Elias Toussaint Jones, 1859. Oberlin College Archives.

Blanche Virginia Harris, 1860.
Oberlin College Archives.

Advertisement by George M. Glenn, 1903.
Oberlin College Archives.

Third grade class on the steps of the Union School, early 1900s.
Oberlin Heritage Center/O.H.I.O. Oberlin, Ohio.

Mary Church Terrell, between 1880 and 1900.
Library of Congress. LC-USZ62-54722.

Henry Churchill King, 1917,
Oberlin College Archives.

❦ 6 ❦

THE POSTWAR PURSUIT OF BLACK
POLITICAL POWER

In the wake of the passage of the Fifteenth Amendment, Oberlin's men of color firmly staked their claim to full participation in the town's vibrant political arena. Political equality appeared as the fulfillment of full citizenship, promising power, prosperity, and self-determination. As the fiercely Republican *Lorain County News* enthusiastically opined in 1870, the black man "has thrown aside his chrysalis, and spread his burnished wings. . . . He has power; he has influence; he is the State; in politics and in society an integer."[1] Neither white nor black Oberlinians could know that the next decades would bring not greater opportunity but increased economic inequality between the races, creating challenges to the fulfillment of the promise of political power. Nor could Oberlinians envision the creation of a "color line" that would impinge, first nationally and then locally, to limit African American possibilities.

Although Republicans presumed their right to the partisan allegiance of much of the community, both black and white, divisions within the Republican Party over the priority to be accorded issues of race precipitated consternation for African Americans, in Oberlin as in the state of Ohio and the nation. Black residents pondered their political loyalty; contemplating how best to pursue equality, they considered whether individual action or consolidated racial efforts most effectively improved black lives. They deliberated about whether integrated institutions or race-based organizations were preferable, and they reflected on the relationship between politics, civil rights, and economic progress. Above all, members of the black population debated the Republican Party's claim to black loyalty on the basis of its historical legacy, a discussion that was incomprehensible to most of their white Oberlin allies, for whom Republican loyalty was an unquestioned allegiance.[2]

More clearly than in the period before the Civil War, Oberlin's black politics in the era of Reconstruction took place in two racially distinct settings: an integrated world of partisan politics where African Americans frequently differed with their white counterparts about the urgency of racial concerns, and a distinctive African American arena focused on the continued struggle for racial justice in the local as well as the larger regional and national political arena. Moreover, within the black community, debates over self-definition, autonomy, and integration were intrinsic to the ongoing dialogue about the direction of African American life, increasingly developing into a racially distinct culture within black churches and voluntary organizations.

This chapter focuses on the concerns and conversations of Oberlin's black men seeking to mobilize political power on behalf of African American interests both within and outside Oberlin after the attainment of "equal suffrage." It explores the interplay between politics and Oberlin's black cultural institutions, particularly its African American churches, and concludes with Oberlin's semi-centennial celebration in 1883. African Americans reached the peak of their influence on local political affairs during this period. Yet, just as they achieved recognition and the ability to exert electoral power, Oberlin's leading men of color found their advance slowed by distinctly local circumstances that not only blocked further community progress but also effectively distracted them from participating at the state level in the tumultuous jockeying for partisan power. Although Oberlin was, by national standards, late to succumb to the disenchantment of the post-Reconstruction years, even in Oberlin the vibrant optimism of the Union victory would prove unsustainable.

At the heart of Oberlin's local electoral structure was its nominally Republican caucus, a meeting open to all of the town's men, regardless of race, as evidenced when it put forward the name of self-emancipated Sabram Cox for councilman in April 1865.[3] A flexible and inclusive organization, the caucus regularly gathered the week before spring elections. After discussion, those present voted for nominees. A committee then ordered the resulting slate printed and distributed to voters, who took the "ticket" with them to the polling place. Highly motivated voters might literally "scratch" or "split" their tickets to alter their preferences, but the caucus candidates almost always prevailed. Most years the ticket faced little opposition. In 1867, for example, the *Lorain County News* reported that the election "was attended with the least excitement imaginable. . . . [T]here was not only no rival ticket but hardly any 'scratching.'"[4] Still, periodically, the *News* printed complaints about the caucus system. In 1875, for example, the paper grumbled that the caucus "is very loosely organized." "By this looseness," it observed, "a great many citizens are induced to stay at home," allowing rowdy "boys" to "cause . . . much inconsiderate action" in public spaces.[5] Nonetheless, the community cherished the tradition, and it outlasted the nineteenth century.[6]

Sabram Cox, who served one two-year term, was among the small but significant number of African Americans who did well in Oberlin elections. "The colored people now have one [township] trustee, one constable, the street commissioner, and one constable who is also deputy marshal," the *Oberlin News*—the journalistic successor to the *Lorain County News*—reported matter of factly in 1879, when Cox became street commissioner, the only man of color to hold this office in the state of Ohio.[7] A dependable Republican loyalist, he had entered the party during its antebellum years when he was well-known for his antislavery activism. Respected by his peers, the hard-working Cox was sent by his colleagues to party conventions at the county level and served at public events in which the Republican Party honored its historic commitment to African American rights. Cox seemed to exemplify the progress of the race. While he made his living by manual labor as a drayman and street worker, Cox's daughter attended Fisk University and sang with its renowned Jubilee Singers. Cox's success demonstrated that, at least in these postwar years, the local party looked out for its faithful—irrespective of race.[8]

Party loyalty was an important part of success for Cox and for other black candidates. In 1868, contrarian and maverick Allen Jones, the patriarch of a prominent African American family who had sent all his sons to Oberlin College in the antebellum years, ran as a Democratic candidate for justice of the peace. He lost. For all his prominence, Jones never served in elective office.[9] In contrast, the caucus provided an important entry point into local politics for Republicans of color. With caucus backing, townspeople regularly elected black men to the town council. Each year between 1870 and 1883, an African American occupied one seat out of six on this local representative body. In these moments, Oberlin seemed to celebrate its multiracial polity.[10]

As the predominantly white town council incorporated African Ameri can members, so too black activists in Reconstruction Oberlin reached out to enlist white allies. An 1872 petition to Congress asking for passage of Charles Sumner's civil rights bill received signatures from a large number of both black and white Oberlinians.[11] Together they applauded its provisions to end segregation in public accommodations, extending the equality provided in the now ratified Fourteenth and Fifteenth Amendments. They also worked together in 1872 to re-elect President Ulysses S. Grant. In this complicated election, white Republicans in Oberlin toed the party line, denouncing what they saw as Charles Sumner's treachery in abandoning Grant for Horace Greeley, the candidate tapped jointly by "Liberal Republicans" and Democrats, asserting that only true Republicans could defeat the rising tide of violence against African Americans in the South.[12]

With occasional exceptions, Oberlinians of color agreed. Carefully balancing their loyalty to Sumner with the political demands of the moment, Oberlin's people of color gathered in August 1872 at "one of the most enthusiastic meetings ever held." Although their proclamation unanimously praised Sumner's "life long devotion . . . to the cause of human freedom," they nonetheless pledged their "allegiance to the Republican party" in the upcoming election.[13] In town for a visit, John Mercer Langston, who had worked with Sumner to write the civil rights bill, joined in supporting the Republican ticket and spoke enthusiastically for Grant. Former slave and Union Army veteran Jerry Fox, "one of the most wide-awake Grant men in Oberlin," was said to drill a "company of 'wide-awakes'" numbering over thirty.[14] But press reports of the local celebration after the 1872 election made no mention of African American participation, even though the Grant bonfire "blazing upon the Park" reminded the *Lorain County News* "of the bonfires there after the first anti-slavery victories, twelve or fifteen years ago."[15]

Oberlin's men of color continued to care deeply about the politics swirling around Sumner's civil rights bill, which they hoped would provide protections against the attacks on freed people by white southerners. Like other people of color throughout the state of Ohio, they were distressed by Republican inaction, and they sought the political autonomy to pursue their own goals.[16] Following the 1872 election, some pondered working outside the Republican Party to better secure their interests. After a statewide convention that expressed black dissatisfaction with the organization, in September 1873 a number of prominent African Americans called for a meeting "of the colored voters of the 14th District of the State" to discuss "questions of various unjust discriminations"; "manly self respect compels us," they wrote, to "consider... matters vital to the full enjoyment of our rights and liberties."[17] The resulting meeting, however, deadlocked and adjourned without passing any resolutions.[18] In November, another local gathering of people of color to elect delegates to a national convention to be held in Washington also adjourned without accomplishing its purposes, due, the local paper reported, to the "rowdyism" of a group of boys.[19]

The prime mover behind both the September and November meetings was Henry Lee, a controversial African American activist who for more than half a century goaded and bedeviled his fellow Oberlinians, both black and white. Engaging in quarrels over politics, churches, and various business dealings, he preferred conflict to compromise and repeatedly took his concerns to the courts and beyond. In contrast to Sabram Cox, with whom he frequently clashed, Lee practiced a fluid politics that foregrounded the struggle for racial equality and collective black autonomy, even as his profoundly eccentric actions often left him standing alone. Lee was combative, aggressive, and unstinting, and he always chose black rights over partisan loyalty. Born a slave in 1836 in Virginia, he escaped in 1858, making his way north by the Underground Railroad to Syracuse, where he worked and attended school until abolitionist friends sent him to Oberlin. After taking classes at the public school and then in the preparatory department of the college, Lee reached freshman status in 1865.[20] In February of that year, with the Civil War still in progress, he wrote from Harpers Ferry to the *Lorain County News* that he had returned to Virginia for the second time in six weeks to rescue family members from slavery. He reported having set free a sister and three of her children on an earlier mission. Now he hoped to bring back three more sisters, a brother, and two of their children: "I know not what will be my fate, but this I do know: that I wish to bestow upon my friends the blessings of a free civilization."[21]

Lee compiled an impressive record as a fighter for racial justice and equality, but with it he gained a reputation for confrontation. In the fall of 1864 he had attended the National Black Convention in Syracuse, where he tangled with John Mercer Langston, his sponsor for the gathering, charging him with negotiating an agreement to make Philadelphia the headquarters for the newly founded Equal Rights League in exchange for election as its first president.[22] In September 1865 Lee insisted that his first-class railroad ticket be honored on a trip from Wheeling, West Virginia, back to Oberlin.

Only the intervention of former Oberlin College president Asa Mahan, who fortuitously found himself in the same railroad car, saved Lee from forcible ejection by the train's conductor.[23] Four years later, returning from a trip to Indianapolis on behalf of the Freedman's Union Educational Society, Lee again refused a conductor's command that he relinquish the first-class seat to which his ticket entitled him for a place in the smoker. This time Lee was beaten unconscious and left on the platform. He remained undaunted, however. He brought a legal suit against the railway and ultimately received an award of $2,600 after more than two years of litigation.[24]

Lee eventually reconciled himself to John Mercer Langston's National Equal Rights League, which defined its objectives as "the achievement of civil and political equality, through the instrumentality of those agencies which the colored people themselves are able to wield in changing public opinion, namely, the newspaper, the lecture, the petition, and the appeal to judicial tribunals."[25] In 1867 the Oberlin branch was said to include over one hundred people.[26] Through the league, Langston maintained his prominent role in Oberlin's black community, and Lee, at least at that moment, accepted his leadership.[27]

In December 1869 Lee joined with Langston in attending the National Colored Labor Union in Washington, D.C., where Langston rallied the participants in support of the Republican Party, and Lee's Committee on Resolutions offered effusive praise of Langston and others "for their cooperative labors in the establishment and good government of hundreds of schools in the Southern States, whereby thousands of men women and children have been and are now being taught the rudiments of an English education."[28] In March 1872, Henry Lee, with the title "Rev." preceding his name, urged African Americans in Cleveland to push forward with their claim to the full rights of citizenship, including office holding.[29] Later that same year, at a Cleveland celebration of the Fifteenth Amendment, Lee stood as the day's orator, rejoicing in the achievements of freedom and citizenship, and, in the moment, praising the Republican Party for its "brilliant record" except for "one single spot": "the failure to pass Mr. Sumner's Supplementary Civil Rights Bill."[30]

Lee pushed himself forward, a provocative figure in both the partisan and personal arenas. In April 1873 the brother whom Lee had rescued in 1865 sued him, claiming that Lee had failed to pay him for his labor the previous year. Lee lost the case and was soon embroiled in yet another confrontation when an Oberlinian of color shot at Lee several times after Lee roughed him up over a delinquent debt. Lee miraculously escaped unharmed, while his assailant went to jail.[31]

Despite these clashes, Lee continued to build his reputation as a leader of "the colored people of Northern Ohio."[32] In January 1874 he sought to secure his local standing by reporting on his work as Oberlin's self-appointed representative to the meeting of the Colored Men's National Council held in late 1873 in Washington, D.C. Influenced by the Cincinnati black activist Peter H. Clark, that gathering called for African Americans to declare their independence from the Republican Party, a position opposed by many other black leaders, including—at least at that moment—John Mercer Langston.[33] When Lee tried to give an account of the Washington conclave to an audience of "colored citizens" in Oberlin, he brought the controversy home. Republican loyalist Sabram Cox, joined by the more independently minded John H. Scott and Oberlin College student Robert B. Bagby, retroactively challenged Lee's right to represent Oberlin at the National Council's deliberations and moved to prevent him from making his report. But they were not able to rally the Oberlin audience to their side. On the contrary, their efforts to silence Lee prompted an outcry from those wanted to hear the report, generating a contretemps that in turn provoked a visit by the town marshal. Upon the marshal's arrival, Cox and Bagby departed, Scott quieted down, and Lee proceeded to read his report without further interruption. It was duly accepted by the audience, and Lee was tendered a vote of thanks by those who remained.[34]

But the matter did not rest there. Editorial commentary offered by the *Oberlin News* in the wake of the event infuriated both factions. Chiding "Our Colored Brethren" for the "characteristic disturbances" that seemed the "inevitable consequence that so unfailingly attends upon every occasion where our colored people convene for deliberation," the paper's white editors argued that such behavior was "destroying what influence the colored people might otherwise possess." With paternalistic condescension, the editors told black Oberlinians, "The colored citizens and residents of Oberlin have access to peculiar advantages that are of priceless worth to you. . . . There should be no discordant purposes nor hostile measure among you to divide your strength and destroy your influence." By this logic, internecine disputes among blacks undermined their claims to equality and lent credence to the arguments of their racist opponents. "Your political enemies who forged the chains for your race and would return you to the doom of slavery," the editors warned, "witness your failures in any department of life with malicious delight and charge them against you and your friends as evidence of their pet theory that the colored man is incapable of taking care of himself, or of taking any part in any species of government."[35]

Infuriated by such criticism, Andrew Jackson, Wilson Bruce Evans, and Cornelius J. Burnett—three of Oberlin's most widely respected persons of color—responded in a letter to the editors that the newspaper's coverage of the meeting had misrepresented what happened, and they charged the editors with doing "great injustice to almost the entire colored population of this place." Of the five hundred persons who had gathered to hear Lee's report, only three had acted badly. Jackson, Evans, and Burnett closed their letter by calling upon the editors to acknowledge and respect black self-determination: "We recognize the fact that we must make our own history, let that history be good or bad, and we ask in the name of justice that when it is written it may reflect upon itself."[36]

Sabram Cox, Henry Lee's harshest critic, sent his own letter to the *News*, insisting that "as colored citizens, we had a *right* to go to this colored citizens' mass meeting, and in a parliamentary way offer our protest." By his account, the dissidents were merely asking "in a perfectly legitimate and orderly manner" if Lee's report "should be heard." Contrary to the editors' opinion, local African Americans needed no instruction on how to conduct themselves. Cox believed that debate within the black community was legitimate, and he resented any intervention by whites.[37]

A few months later, on March 13, 1874, "the colored people" of Oberlin gathered to "mourn the loss of a true and faithful friend," Charles Sumner.[38] While white Oberlinians did not attend the assembly, the local paper urged passage of Sumner's long-stalled civil rights bill. Referring to plans to eliminate the provision requiring integrated schools, the paper insisted: "There should be no facilities made by the government from which the colored youth should be excluded."[39] This cross-racial show of support for Sumner's goals belied ongoing differences among African American residents, however. Planning for a May 1874 anniversary celebration of the Fifteenth Amendment revealed fragmentation. On the same day that the *News* celebrated that "There is no other place in America where any event of interest to the colored citizens could be so fittingly celebrated as in Oberlin," the *Cleveland Herald* reported that disputes among blacks had forced the event to be rescheduled for Cleveland.⁴⁰ In the end, two festivals took place, one event in Cleveland and the other in Oberlin.

At the Cleveland event, Henry Lee took the stage at Garrett Hall alongside John Patterson Green, a young man of color born in North Carolina who had been briefly apprenticed to Oberlin harness maker John H. Scott before moving to Cleveland. After the Civil War, Green began his career as a lawyer in South Carolina, but he had recently returned to Cleveland, where in 1872 he was elected justice of the peace, the first man of color to be chosen by Cleveland voters for any position. Green was at the start of a political career that would take him to both houses of the Ohio legislature and eventually earn him a federal appointment. While a leader on race matters, he was a loyal Republican and emphasized that he relied on whites as well as blacks to gain elective office. In this respect, he seemed a curious ally for Henry Lee.⁴¹

In contrast to the short evening program in Cleveland, the Oberlin celebration was a daylong gala. Riding "on a gray charger," African American carriage maker Andrew Jackson served as grand marshal of a morning parade that featured "a wagon with thirty-seven colored girls dressed in white representing the States, and another the Goddess of Liberty."⁴² Banners along the procession route proclaimed, "We want civil rights," "Sumner's last words—'Take care of my Civil Right's [sic] bill,'" and more, including "Oberlin foremost in the battle for freedom." In the afternoon, Sabram Cox sat as president on the dais at First Church, surrounded by white leaders, including Oberlin College president James Harris Fairchild, as well as influential men of color, among them shoe manufacturer Alfred J. Dyer, local Methodist minister Matthew Goosland, and William T. Henderson, then on Oberlin's town council.⁴³

John Mercer Langston, now the acting president of Howard University, took pride of place as speaker of the day. He proclaimed his "heart full of gratitude" to Oberlin for welcoming him thirty years ago when, he exaggerated, as a "poor and a colored boy, I found no obstruction against me in your hotel, in your institution of learning, in your family circle." Langston concluded with a plea for passage of Sumner's civil rights bill, which he had assisted the senator in drafting.⁴⁴ According to Langston, the legislation would secure to "the colored citizen" the rights and privileges "so indispensable to rational and useful enjoyment of life, that without them citizenship itself loses much of its value, and liberty seems little more than a name." In its editorial marking the occasion, the *Oberlin News* agreed, asserting,

"There is no equality before the law when social customs are permitted to abridge the rights of any."[45]

In the months that followed these celebrations, black and white Oberlinians came together in shared concern over the erosion of the rights of freed people in the South and the failure of the Republican-controlled Congress to pass the civil rights bill.[46] In October, the *News* framed the challenge in partisan terms: "Will the Republican party . . . timidly stand by . . . when such vital issues are at stake?" Noting the massacres taking place in the South, the paper warned that unless the federal government upheld black rights, "The colored man . . . will be murdered . . . and such a reign of terror as our country has never experienced will prevail."[47]

As the year came to a close, reports that Indiana was implementing separate schools for African Americans and that New Orleans had ejected black students from public educational facilities raised fears in Oberlin that the civil rights bill might be revised "to omit the mixed school provisions and require only that equal educational facilities shall be provided for both races."[48] In late December a "large and enthusiastic meeting of colored citizens" assembled to protest the version of the bill recently reported to the U.S. House of Representatives by the Judiciary Committee. Black Oberlinians rejected "any and all legislation whose tendency is to legalize, evade, or admit of unjust discrimination toward any of its citizens."[49] They sent a memorial to James Monroe, now their congressman, who introduced it to the House on January 6, 1875.[50] The *News* followed the bill's progress with interest, asserting: "Let Congress promptly settle the question of citizenship, and make it understood that all men, and not white Democrats only, are citizens under the Constitution, and will be protected in the exercise of their rights."[51]

When it finally passed in weakened form, the Civil Rights Act of 1875 set out legal prohibitions on discrimination in public accommodations and transportation, but it failed to foreclose the possibilities of racial separation in public schools or in cemeteries, two institutions that Oberlin had proudly integrated. Yet Joseph H. Battle, the new editor of the *Oberlin News* who, despite his Oberlin College education, would prove among its most conservative proprietors, reacted with restraint.[52] The paper covered the horrors of the Vicksburg Massacre and the spread of violence in Louisiana, but it overlooked the removal of integrated education from the legislation. Instead the *News* reproached African Americans for their dissatisfaction with the law, rebuffing their calls for what Battle branded "extra and peculiar rights" beyond those secured in the recently passed statute. "The reasonable and thoughtful colored man, as well as his political friends[,] can ask simply and only that he be treated in all respects as equally as a citizen with his white neighbors," the *News* declared. "He cannot claim that his dress, or lack of culture, or bad habits shall be over looked because he is colored."[53] This new attitude suggested a growing concern with standards of social respectability as well as the editor's contempt for the culture of the black poor, an early sign of Oberlin's retreat from a commitment to social as well as legal equality.

Oberlin's people of color reacted to passage of the Civil Rights Act of 1875 with mixed feelings. John Mercer Langston, now based in Washington, faulted the Republicans for not passing a stronger law. In a speech delivered in Cleveland and reported in full in the *Oberlin News,* he observed that people of color had "peculiar relations with, and obligations to the Republican party," but he cautioned that "to be governed by mere gratitude . . . in determining one's political course of action, might prove pernicious." He hinted ominously, "Should the Republican party ever prove false . . . to the highest good of the republic, influenced by corrupt leaders or erroneous doctrine, the duty of the colored voter to abandon and leave it would be as imperative and obligatory as that of his other fellow-citizen." And he spoke directly to the freed people of the South, counseling them to exercise political leverage in their own collective interest: "If you are to become the subject of barter among political parties, my advice to you is to become a party to the sale yourselves. You can make better terms with your former masters than can the old-time Abolitionists, for if they make the sale, you gain nothing by it in the way of political power; but if you, yourselves, enter into the combination, you can reasonably hope to secure some share of the political power and influence for yourselves and your posterity."[54] In this way, Langston suggested limits to partisan loyalty, endorsed African American autonomy, and imagined a politics in which black votes mattered.

As the 1876 elections approached, African Americans in Oberlin, as throughout the state and the country, debated what they owed to the party of Lincoln. Three local men of color—carriage maker John Cowan and college students Robert C. Henderson and Benjamin A. Imes—organized a meeting on March 29 to "take into consideration the propriety of electing and sending a delegate to the National Colored Convention to be held in Nashville" the following month to discuss black political options. As they deliberated about whether to participate in the Nashville convention, Oberlinians of color heard speeches that "deplored the condition of the colored people in the South [and] censured the Administration for the position it held relative to the outrages committed upon the colored people in some Southern states."[55] In response, the attendees on March 29 issued a "demand" to Republicans: "[I]f they would longer secure our votes," they must provide "equal protection in all the rights and privileges which under the Constitution all men enjoy."[56]

The next order of business was to choose a delegate to attend the Nashville convention. The irascible Henry Lee vied with Reverend George W. Hatton for the honor. Newly settled as the pastor of Oberlin's Second Methodist Episcopal Church—Lee's own congregation—Hatton was a seasoned politician who had once been nominated for city council in Washington, D.C., and had stumped for Horace Greeley in 1872.[57] Yet the March 29 meeting opted for neither Lee nor Hatton, selecting instead John Craven Jones. The youngest son of Allen Jones, John Craven Jones was born free in North Carolina, raised in Oberlin, and graduated from Oberlin College in 1856 before he moved to British Columbia, Canada, where he taught school. Recently returned to his hometown, he regarded political independence as his birthright.[58]

Upon his arrival at the Nashville convention, Jones encountered some familiar figures, including John Mercer Langston and the convention's presiding officer, Philadelphia-born Mifflin Wistar Gibbs. In the late 1850s, John Craven Jones and his brothers Elias and William Jones had met Gibbs when they all resided in British Columbia. The Jones brothers evidently introduced Gibbs to Maria Alexander, who had grown up in Oberlin and attended Oberlin College with them. Married in the United States in 1859, Mifflin and Maria settled together in British Columbia, where they soon produced six children.[59] Around 1870, Maria Alexander Gibbs returned to Oberlin, where she raised their offspring while the adventurous Mifflin made his way to Reconstruction Florida, where his brother served as secretary of state, and then to Little Rock, Arkansas, to practice law and gain election to the bench. Gibbs's career ultimately peaked in 1897, when President William McKinley appointed him U.S. consul to Madagascar.[60] Gibbs was a political person, and he knew the rewards that party loyalty could now bestow. But he also knew the limits of Republican support for southern blacks.

At the Nashville gathering, Louisiana's P.B.S. Pinchback argued that blacks should assert their political independence. Currently serving as governor, Pinchback had been named by the state legislature to the U.S. Senate, but that predominantly Republican chamber refused to acknowledge his disputed election. Now, a disappointed Pinchback sought to ensure that people of color "would never again vote for the Republican ticket in solid column as heretofore." C. S. Smith, a member the Alabama state legislature, went even further when he "advised that the blacks no longer remain in the Republican party."[61] In the end, however, the Nashville convention pulled back from a full break and instead voted to "endorse and reaffirm our devotion and adherence to the National Republican party and its principles" despite having "just reasons for complaint against those members who have proved recreant to the trusts committed to their keeping." In an early use of a key term, the majority of convention delegates attacked "the increasing efforts of the enemies of our race to establish what is known as the *color line*" and asked "all good men . . . in their sovereign capacity to strengthen the arm of the law and protect all citizens against mobs, assassination and violence."[62] The convention warily navigated between anger that "the party in power since the war has not given us protection" and recognition that "the history of the Democratic party has not given us ground for hope."[63]

Black and white Oberlinians followed news of the Nashville convention closely, but with different reactions. The *Oberlin News* responded to John Craven Jones's participation in the meeting with criticism of any suggestion that African Americans should secede from the Republican Party. "Such a threat coming from an Oberlin colored man is certainly astounding," editor Battle fumed, and he posed a rhetorical question: "[T]o whom does the colored race owe the enactment of the 13, 14, and 15th amendments?" He continued: "After the Republican party has for ten years made the colored man's rights the one great ultimatum of its policy, after it has passed a civil rights bill which fairly thrust the colored man into the very face of his relentless foe with safety, after such thankless endeavor, it is downright base ingratitude to turn upon it with a threat."[64]

Yet local African American supporters of the Nashville convention stood their ground. "It would be as you say, base ingratitude, to assume an attitude of disrespect for [the Republican Party's] great principles and the worthy men who stand by the same," they explained, "but when the spirit of partisanship imposes the obligation that, right or wrong, we must vow allegiance, we are disposed to question the authority."[65]

Political maverick John H. Scott, who had spent time in jail for his role in the Oberlin-Wellington Rescue, fiercely defended the principle of black autonomy. During the Civil War he had served in the 5th U.S. Colored Troops, and in 1865 he had participated in the founding meeting of the Ohio branch of the National Equal Rights League. All four of his daughters attended Oberlin College, and one of them would soon take John Craven Jones as her second husband. While frequently at odds with Oberlin's gadfly Henry Lee, Scott commanded attention as a respected local leader. So it was significant when, in a letter to the *New York Witness* published in late April 1876, he charged that Rutherford B. Hayes, a frontrunner for the Republican presidential nomination, owed his election as Ohio governor to "colored votes" and yet had "taken no steps to put an end to the wholesale massacre of colored people in the Southern States." Scott concluded, "We will support the party which protects us in our lately acquired rights."[66]

Joseph H. Battle responded caustically in the pages of the *Oberlin News*: "It seems to be the theory of the writer that since the Nation has freed the negro, and legislated for his complete enfranchisement, it must officiate as his big brother and prevent the other boys from knocking ships [*sic*] from his shoulder." Calling any thoughts of alliance with the Democrats "stupid" and efforts to start an independent party "folly," Battle ignored the rising tide of racial violence in the South and the persistent structures of racial inequality, commanding: "Vote with the Republican party and make secure the principles for which the war was waged."[67]

With glee, Battle published resolutions of an Ohio African American convention held in Columbus on April 19 that disavowed the actions of the Nashville convention. The editor underscored the final Columbus resolution expressing "pity for any colored man" endorsing the Nashville gathering, and charging such people with undermining "the respect of public opinion for the intelligence and judgment of colored voters."[68] In addition, the same issue of the *Oberlin News* included a letter from "A Colored Voter" that challenged Scott's position. While noting that "Colored men should be Republicans from principle and not from a sense of gratitude," the letter's anonymous author maintained "that the colored voters, not only of this community, but of the whole country, will testify their appreciation of the Republican party, and their continued fealty to it in their election this fall."[69]

Continuing the exchange, Scott retorted with anger, "I am indignant ... when right in the face of the general government, controlled entirely by Republicans, over fifty thousand black men, to say nothing of the Union white men, since 1865, have been shot, hanged, and otherwise murdered." Renewing his criticism of Hayes, he argued that a "speech or letter" from the Ohio governor to President Grant would demonstrate that the White House "had at least one eye—the Buckeye—on her yet." Less playfully, he stormed, "Are we, the colored men, simply voters, or are we American citizens? If simply party voters, then we must as servants of that party submit to the party lash; but if we are American citizens the sooner we, as such, act out the full-fledged American the better it will be for us and for the country we saved with our blood. . . . If our liberties rest only on the perpetuity of the Republican party, or any other political organization, the sooner we know it the better."[70] For Scott, full citizenship meant the right to free choice in the exercise of the franchise, not simply the opportunity to endorse Republicans.

Scott's skepticism of Hayes and the Republican Party notwithstanding, after the Ohio governor received the party's presidential nomination in mid-June, with William A. Wheeler as his running mate, Oberlinians of color organized the town's first Hayes and Wheeler club.[71] Sabram Cox called the club's inaugural meeting to order, and Reverend George W. Hatton served as chair. Among those in attendance were Oberlin College student Arthur Langston, John Mercer Langston's son, and John Craven Jones, Oberlin's delegate to the Nashville convention. When asked to address the gathering about the wisdom of staying within the Republican fold, Jones called it "eminently appropriate" and praised the party's 1876 platform for addressing the need to protect the rights of black southerners. Reporting that "the meeting was a very cordial one," with "no division of sentiment in regard to supporting the Hayes and Wheeler ticket," the *Oberlin News* sheepishly acknowledged, "A good many feel very deeply the apparent neglect of the Republican party in providing for the protection of the Republican voters in the Southern States."[72]

Two months later, in August, the *Oberlin News* announced the formation of another Hayes and Wheeler club.[73] Although the call had invited "every man" to attend, the officers elected were all white and there is no evidence of African American membership.[74] Indeed, over time local black engagement in the presidential campaign receded. The newspaper's coverage of Oberlin's massive celebration of what Ohioans believed to be Hayes's victory on November 4, 1876, lacked any mention of African American participation.[75]

As Oberlinians watched the protracted negotiations that eventually brought Hayes to the presidency, even local whites began to raise questions about whether the Republicans had done enough to secure black voting rights and provide for "equal protection."[76] In March 1877 the Oberlin caucus for local elections reflected partisan disarray. Supported by Henry Lee, longtime Democrat Chauncey Wack won a spot on the nominally Republican caucus ticket and, with it, election to the town council. To make things yet more complicated, Lee rallied enough support to defeat the bid of fellow African American and Republican loyalist Sabram Cox for re-election as street commissioner.[77] With doubts about Republican dedication to the defense of the exercise of black suffrage, party allegiances gave way to the politics of personality.

The municipal election was a harbinger of difficult times for Ohio Republicans, who had long assumed that they could rely on the loyal support of black voters.[78] Throughout the spring and summer of 1877, party leaders reached out to people of color in nervous anticipation of fall elections for the Ohio state legislature. In Cincinnati, the party put forward George Washington Williams, a black Baptist minister and sometime newspaper man; in Cleveland, Republicans tapped John Patterson Green for legislative office. They also attended to African American patronage and enlisted prominent black orators.[79] Nonetheless, in April, the *Oberlin News* observed, "The colored people of Oberlin have become quite anxious over 'Hayes' Policy' because [it is] not understood." Yet the paper had little to offer blacks except advice that "they should accept Hayes' past career as a guarantee that . . . as a conscientious cool headed patriotic American he will seek to settle the color question."[80] In August, and again in September, the *News* made frankly partisan appeals.[81] Although in October Russia Township went for the Republican gubernatorial candidate by 574 votes to 149, both the turnout and the margin were significantly lower than in the previous gubernatorial election, when Hayes had carried the township by 850 to 140 votes.[82] Statewide, Republicans took a drubbing. They lost control of both houses of the Ohio legislature and every major elected state office except auditor and secretary of state. The failure of the Republican Party to rally African American support was one of the key factors in its defeat.[83] Ohioans of color understood and rejected Hayes's policy of sectional reconciliation at the expense of black rights; they recognized their betrayal in the so-called Compromise of 1877.[84]

In the face of Republican desertion of the cause of black rights at the national level, people of color in Oberlin worked to preserve and advance their local standing. In their efforts to salvage remaining fragments of public influence, some of Oberlin's African American leaders began to construct a strategy based on respect for their achievements and their demonstrable propriety. These black activists dominated the evening of January 1, 1878, when members of Oberlin's African American community staged a celebration commemorating the fifteenth anniversary of the Emancipation Proclamation at the Second Methodist Episcopal Church on South Water Street. While the audience included "gentlemen and ladies of all shades and complexion, [including] many of the white people," the celebration was created and managed by black people for black people. Amid portraits of Lincoln, Greeley, Sumner, Seward, Frederick Douglass, and even Rutherford B. Hayes, Henry Lee acted as chair and master of ceremonies, while Moses Fleetwood Walker, an Oberlin College student who would later become the first African American to play in the Major Leagues, served as secretary. Lewis Clark, known locally as the model for George Harris in *Uncle Tom's Cabin*, gave "an urgent appeal to the colored people to lead honorable lives," and Oberlin College student Solomon Glenn Watkins, who would go on to a career as a teacher and civil rights advocate in Topeka, Kansas, declared he "looked forward to a bright future."[85]

Henry Lee's old ally John Patterson Green presented the evening's central oration. Still a justice of the peace in Cleveland, in four years Green would become the second person of color elected to the Ohio General Assembly.[86] Although he remained a loyal Republican, in his speech Green lamented that "in many sections of this fair land, the colored American is a proscribed man, subject to the caprice of uncertain rulers and existing under such a condition of political and social ostracism, as forcibly recalls to his mind his former state of servitude." He noted that even in Ohio, remnants of the Black Laws still constricted "the sacred natural rights known to man," including "the right of marriage," referring to the ban on interracial unions in effect since 1861.[87]

But Green's message was, above all, a call for black initiative. Identifying "the social equality of the colored citizen" as "the last great problem" confronting African Americans, he argued that its solution "does not depend altogether upon either the repeal of laws unfavorable or the enactment of laws favorable." "[N]o amount of legislation can itself . . . elevate us one jot or tittle on the scale of social being," he explained. "[T]o a very great extent . . . 'every man is the architect of his own fortune;' and if we but do our whole duty earnestly and reasonably, not even oppressive laws can keep us at the bottom; but true merit will assert itself, and be known and honored of men."[88] Although Green also called for "the use of the ballot and a unity of action," his emphasis on black self-help had distinctly conservative implications. As the *Oberlin News* concluded, people of color would need to "learn to stand alone, to maintain their rights, to keep their own political consciences, to be their own leaders, to direct their own destinies."[89] It was a mixed message at best: in their pursuit of full equality, African Americans would necessarily become free and independent agents because they could not count on white support.

The venue for the 1878 Emancipation Day celebration was, itself, a sign of the quest for black autonomy in Oberlin. The Second Methodist Episcopal Church was the first black religious institution formed in Oberlin, and it had not always enjoyed wide acceptance among whites.[90] In 1867, when the question of separate black churches had first been broached in town, the local newspaper mused, "We cannot see why our colored friends should seek . . . to keep up class distinctions that have so long been a proper cause for complaints against their enemies."[91] Later, in retrospect and somewhat wistfully, James Harris Fairchild reminisced, "The colored church came into existence not because the colored people were not welcomed to all the other churches, or because a separate organization was desired by those who had been most favored with education and culture, but because considerable numbers of them felt more at home with a style of service and instruction more like that with which they had been familiar."[92] Fairchild failed to note the absence of black ministers in Oberlin's predominantly white churches.

The process of institutional differentiation was rooted in antebellum practices but took material shape after 1870, when Oberlin's Methodists began building their own house of worship. Like the preceding Oberlin congregations that had gathered in First Church, its offshoot Second Church, and the Episcopal Church, the original Methodist Episcopal congregation was an interracial assembly. White Methodists worshipped alongside black Methodists, a population to which African American organizer Marcus Dale had preached a decade earlier.[93] But plans for the integrated Methodist church literally fell to pieces when its scaffolding gave way during construction in 1871, sending fragments of masonry—and workers—down to its unfinished foundation. After the accident the races pulled apart, and by the time the building was finally completed in 1873, black Methodists had departed for the separate ministry of Matthew Goosland, a former slave from Virginia who had purchased his freedom and migrated to Oberlin on the eve of the Civil War.[94]

Soon after the building disaster of 1871, black Methodists purchased a small structure, which they replaced in 1877 with a larger building on Water (later renamed Park) Street in the heart of Oberlin's southeast quadrant. Yet from its inception Second Methodist Episcopal was part of the interracial Lexington Methodist Conference, not the African Methodist Episcopal (A.M.E.) Church headquartered in Philadelphia. In 1882 the Oberlin congregation would adopt a new name: Rust Methodist Episcopal Church, in honor of the white educator and abolitionist Richard Rust, who served as secretary of the Freedmen's Aid Society.[95]

Founder Matthew Goosland left his position as pastor soon after the new congregation was established, but he and his wife continued to live in Oberlin while he accepted assignments to preach for Methodists of color elsewhere.[96] His successor was a female pastor, Mrs. Elizabeth Carr, who in 1876 made way for George W. Hatton, Henry Lee's political rival.[97] The conflict between Lee and Hatton had repercussions for Second Methodist Episcopal Church, which became yet another site for confrontations personal and political. With matters of religion and politics inextricably intertwined, leaders moved between their civic and religious mantles. And nobody rivaled Henry Lee in this fusion of sacred and secular, personal and political.

Apparently warned by his congregation about the contentious Lee, Hatton moved quickly to expel Lee from the church as a "chronic disturber." Lee charged in return that Hatton had assaulted him while trying to eject him from the building.[98] Although Lee's charges against Hatton were dismissed, trouble soon burst forth again when new accusations against Hatton's conduct surfaced, prompting an investigation by Elder W. C. Echols under the auspices of the Lexington Methodist Conference. Echols, a black preacher based in Indianapolis, found Hatton guilty of five counts of lying and suspended him.[99] By Christmas 1876, Reverend Hatton was "absent" from the Second Methodist Episcopal Church holiday gathering to which Henry Lee provided the welcome. Yet Hatton appears to have remained in Oberlin until at least 1878, gathering around him a new congregation that became the nucleus of a short-lived African Methodist Episcopal Church.[100]

Though he outlasted Hatton at Second Methodist, Henry Lee continued to generate controversy within the congregation. In 1878 his fellow congregants determined to replace Lee as superintendent of the church's Sabbath school. Once again, the result was a physical struggle for control of the church building. This time, Second Methodist reached out to the wider

Oberlin community for a solution. With the permission of the congregation, local pastors, all white, constituted themselves an arbitration committee, which proceeded to recommend that Lee "withdraw from all official and personal connection with the church and with its meeting."[101] Although not a victory for Lee, for African American autonomy, or for black unity, this outcome apparently restored peace in the church.

The cantankerous Lee engaged in new secular as well as religious conflicts. In the so-called Omnibus War that began in October 1878, Lee challenged town regulations that placed limits on the number of livery drivers permitted to solicit customers at the railway station at any one time. The contest took on a racial edge since Lee was the only black livery proprietor in Oberlin. In its various permutations, the dispute lasted more than a decade and encompassed numerous arrests of Lee for assorted infractions, including trespassing, larceny, and lack of appropriate licensing. Lee boldly—and bodily—defied the town's efforts to regulate commerce at the train depot through passage of local ordinances and eventually with physical barricades.[102] To advance his cause, Lee sought to mobilize local African Americans, who repeatedly submitted petitions to the town council on his behalf.[103] Whether praised or scorned, Lee wielded economic and social power among the town's people of color.

As contests for power persisted within Oberlin's African American community, people of color also continued to seek ways to influence electoral politics. In the fall of 1878, John Patterson Green again returned to Oberlin to rally black support for the Republican Party. This time he met opposition from some notable residents of color who were intrigued by the possibilities for alliance with the Greenback Party. Cincinnati African American educator and politician Peter H. Clark, the prime mover behind earlier efforts to undercut the loyalty of Ohio's people of color to the Republican Party, now sought recruits for a movement to restrain capitalism while empowering workers through a modification of the money supply.[104] John H. Scott, to whom Green had once been apprenticed, now declared himself a Greenbacker, as did John Craven Jones. In a familiar refrain, Jones asserted that people of color "had not been well used by the Republicans of Oberlin."[105] When the *Oberlin News* charged Jones with ingratitude, a writer under the pseudonym "Voter" pushed back against Republican demands for black allegiance "on the ground of obligation." "I wish to say that it is about as weak and childish to say 'because we freed you'—as to answer back 'we freed ourselves,'" observed "Voter." He accepted the notion of a "debt of gratitude," but not the concept of "perpetual obligation."[106]

When election results for state and local offices were tallied in the fall of 1878, the *News* fairly crowed that "the majority of colored voters in Oberlin came around right at last."[107] But what was their reward for supporting the Republican Party? In the Republican victory parade following the election, African Americans were viewed as a source of amusement, not as serious political allies. "About a dozen [young African American men] dressed to represent a minstrel troup [*sic*] of both sexes, were mounted upon two wagons," the *News* reported. "A banjo and bones furnished the instrumental music. Songs were sung, jokes and speeches got off for the entertainment of the crowd, the performance tending to ridicule the greenbackers."[108]

While minstrelsy occupied a distinctive place in nineteenth-century American culture, this performance suggests that support for the Republican Party left Oberlin's people of color in, at best, an ambiguous position. White Republicans depended on, and wooed, African Americans' votes, which they believed they deserved as the party of emancipation and black suffrage. Yet white Republicans also happily laughed at caricatures of black behavior. Was the pageant directed by white people who sought to consolidate the local racial order? What did black participants gain from such self-mockery?

Whatever its explicit purposes, the performance did not signal the acquiescence of all of Oberlin's people of color to the town's emergent racial hierarchy. In January 1879 an attentive audience filled the fledgling A.M.E. Church on East Lorain Street to listen to an address by the Reverend T. H. Jackson, a former member of the board of Wilberforce University, founded in 1856 as the first private black university in the United States. After recounting the history of the A.M.E.'s separation from the mainstream Methodist Episcopal Church, Jackson asserted that the rationale for a black church persisted beyond emancipation. As evidence of the tenacity of color prejudice, Jackson cited the absence of appointment of any African American to a professorship at Oberlin College. The persistence of racial barriers, Jackson argued, meant people of color needed their own organizations that they operated by and for themselves, not simply as a "colored branch" attached to a predominantly white institution.[109] This was a pointed attack on Second Methodist, which had remained within a larger predominantly white regional Methodist conference.

And members of Second Methodist responded: the next month, they hosted a lecture by Reverend Marshall W. Taylor, the recently appointed presiding elder of the Lexington District. Born into slavery and Methodism, Taylor had the unusual experience of attending school and achieving literacy before emancipation, and then advancing from school teaching through Methodist ordination to receipt of his Doctor of Divinity degree. Throughout his career, Taylor rejected racially separate organizations. Speaking in Oberlin in February 1879, he went even further, asserting that "nearly everything that has been done for the colored race has been done by the whites." According to the *Oberlin News*, "He urged his hearers to mix up with the whites and do away with caste. He said that if the whites were taken away in six weeks there would not be a colored man in Oberlin. They would be found stiff and stark in the roads in every direction." As the newspaper pointed out, this was a curious position to advocate at Second Methodist, a church "composed exclusively of colored members."[110]

In the fall of 1880, black and white Oberlinians supported the candidacy of another Ohio Republican for president, James Garfield. Formed in August, the local Republican club included as a vice president A.M.E. Church member William T. Henderson, who had recently served four years as a township trustee. An early September rally featured African American Benjamin Imes, now an Oberlin College graduate and seminary student.[111] Later that month, the Republican club's "Grand Meeting" brought more than eight hundred people to the college chapel to hear two Ohio notables: Alphonso Taft, the father of future President William Howard Taft, and George Washington Williams, the first man of color to serve in the Ohio General Assembly. Williams "made one of the most telling speeches of the campaign," in which he urged black Oberlinians to vote the Republican ticket. The *Oberlin News* followed up with an attack on the racism of Democratic vice presidential candidate William H. English, citing as evidence his pronouncements that "the negro is now and has been in all ages but one degree removed from the beasts of the field" and that "the free negro, as a general thing, is unfit to govern himself."[112] In this election cycle, Republican courtship of African Americans proved successful. Still, some Oberlinians of color resisted the Republican cause; John Wall and John H. Scott remained Greenbackers.[113] Overall, the electoral tally in Oberlin was 836 votes for the Republican ticket, 127 for the Democratic ticket, 33 for the Greenback Party, and 17 for Prohibition.[114]

The following March, three Oberlinians of color participated in the inaugural festivities in Washington, D.C.: barber Alexander Wynn, his wife, Cornelia Dyer Wynn, and James Cowan, a carriage maker and wheelwright who had arrived in Oberlin three decades earlier as part of the Chambers group. The local newspaper did not report any white Oberlinians in attendance.[115] It seemed a moment of particular political significance for Oberlin's African American citizenry. Six months later, at the memorial service that brought together members of local churches to mourn the death of President Garfield, the minister and congregation of Second Methodist Episcopal participated fully in the ceremony.[116]

But 1880 would be the last presidential election in which Republican Oberlin would focus with intensity on the contest for African American rights. While subsequent statewide contests would manifest significant contests between Republicans and Democrats for black votes, Oberlin's politics would spin into a distinctly different orbit, ruled by the ascendant issue of temperance, whose pull would both cut across racial lines and undercut the politics of race. At this moment, black votes mattered, in Oberlin and in Ohio more broadly. Despite the courtship of African American electoral support that would propel legislative progress on school integration and other civil rights at the state level, the new Oberlin priority would instead undermine social equality.[117]

While Gilded Age Oberlin boasted several integrated institutions, including the public schools, the cemetery, and at least one of two baseball teams, other signs pointed to an emergent color line. Oberlin in the late nineteenth century fielded racially segregated fire companies, distinguished not only by the color of their members but also by the quality of their equipment. While the white "Hook and Ladder" company bragged about its steam-driven equipment and regularly competed in county contests for best performance, "Engine Company No. 2" enlisted thirty African American men who worked a basic hand pump.[118] Likewise, Oberlin was home to two cornet bands, one predominantly or all white and the other all black. The latter was formed when the original band retired its old instruments, returning them to town authorities when it purchased new ones. The used instruments were redistributed upon request to "a number of young colored men," who had to raise money for their repair in order to make them playable.[119]

White Oberlinians responded haltingly as color prejudice increasingly constricted black opportunities across the nation. In the spring of 1879, "ladies" of First Church sent "two barrels of clothing" to help African American migrants fleeing the violent South for Kansas; the *Oberlin News*—no longer edited by the conservative Joseph H. Battle—considered this response inadequate to the threat.[120] Over time, however, local whites increasingly viewed racism as an irrevocable fact of American life, not as a sin to be resisted and eradicated. When, in the fall of 1882, a young man of color sued the Oberlin Telegraph Company for refusing to admit him to its telegraphy school, the company's proprietor, M. C. Peterson, defended the action on the grounds that "it would be of no use" for the would-be student "to learn the business, as he could not get a situation." Indeed, Peterson claimed that he had made a distinctly honorable decision since it would have been "a fraud to take the young man's money, under the circumstances, just as much as to accept the money of a dead man." Yet the plaintiff won in court, and the *Cleveland Herald* headlined its report on the case "No Color Line in Oberlin."[121]

As the community's semi-centennial anniversary approached, troubling reports by students suggested an abandonment of "Oberlin principles" at the college. In particular, some students criticized the advent of racially segregated seating in the Ladies Hall dining room, including the formation of a "colored table." In its report on the controversy, the *Oberlin News* lamented that the "interference comes from without" and was generated by "extremists."[122] But if the newspaper resented what it saw as outsiders' meddling, James Harris Fairchild, the college's president, and Adelia Field Johnston, its formidable dean of women, acted swiftly to remedy the situation. Johnston, who had charge of Ladies Hall, decided to reserve for herself one seat at each table, to be assigned as she wished—the implication being that she would engineer integrated dining.[123]

The controversy continued to simmer over the winter of 1882-1883. In February the *Oberlin Review*—the student newspaper—reported that the president and the dean of women found their efforts to desegregate dining "unwillingly complied with." The *Review* carefully distinguished between "Oberlin [C]ollege as an institution, and the students, as individuals." It charged that an increasingly wealthy student body had brought "class prejudice which gives rise to the color line," and insisted that "The students, and the students alone, can eradicate the evil."[124]

The next month, a group of alumni of color published an article in the *Review* expressing dismay over the news of deteriorating race relations at the college but suggesting, in contrast to the *Review*, that "poor whites" were more likely than "the refined woman or man" to promulgate a color line.

They pointed to changes in the town as well the college as a cause of the increase in racial discrimination. "Twenty years ago a respectable negro student could find board at any private boarding house in town," they observed. "Can he now?" Presuming the negative answer, they continued: "This is the fault of the students and citizens." At the same time, they scolded the faculty for abdicating their moral responsibilities. "It is true that the faculty cannot change each student's heart," the alumni wrote, "but they can demand that this principle of the Institution shall be carried out in the Ladies Hall at least."[125]

Now pastoring in Memphis, Oberlin College graduate Benjamin Imes also joined the debate in the pages of the *Review*. Suggesting that "the romance of anti-slavery has died away," he urged the college to recommit itself to eliminating "even the beginning of a so-called color line." "Those of us who in other places are confronted by the demon of race-hatred," he declared, "can by no means afford to lose faith in Oberlin, a name to us as significant as 'Marathon' to the Greek."[126] The next year Professor Giles Shurtleff, who had commanded black troops during the Civil War, echoed the sentiments of African American alumni when he publicly chided white students for not welcoming students of color into "the Christian and cultured homes of the community." Clearly Shurtleff worried about a hardening color line that threatened what he cherished as Oberlin's historic commitment to equality.[127]

Oberlin's heritage was much on display during the 1883 Jubilee celebration, which featured a reunion honoring the abolitionist students whose idealism had established the college's reputation for radical racial egalitarianism. But the Jubilee program did not include any discussion of the current state of race relations in either Oberlin or the United States as a whole. Significantly, the town's original planning committee included no person of color, and its public celebration in April included no speaker of color. Likewise, no person of color spoke from a public platform during the college's commemoration in July, and since the college employed no black faculty or administrators, only whites had been involved in the event's planning.[128]

The four-day Jubilee celebration at the college honored multiple dimensions of the school's heritage. Speeches memorialized Oberlin's pioneering initiatives in the education of women, the decisive role of the Lane Rebels in the abolitionist movement, the heroic sacrifices made by Oberlin soldiers during the Civil War, and the moral work of Oberlin missionaries on behalf of Native Americans and freedpeople. Yet in the sole address devoted to looking ahead, Professor Judson Smith, an Oberlin graduate, characterized the school's mission mainly in academic terms. "Oberlin College was founded to promote culture, science and art, to raise up Christian scholars for all the growing needs of the great West and the wide world," he explained. Indeed, he asserted, "If there had been no slavery in the land, she would have been planted, and she would have taken root, just as she has done."[129] He confidently proclaimed that Oberlin's "first, its great, its unchanging aim is culture."[130] He predicted that "she will cultivate in her halls, as of old, the spirit of universal brotherhood, the love of liberty, a sacred animosity toward every social prejudice and prescriptive wrong," but he closed his address with a plea for material, not moral, support, asking listeners to provide the financial resources needed for "new departments of instruction."[131] While the college proudly enshrined its antislavery past, it failed to engage in the continuing struggle for racial equality. The priorities of the college, like those of the town, shifted with the times.

⁋ 7 ⁋

RACE AND OPPORTUNITY IN THE
LATE NINETEENTH CENTURY

On January 1, 1863, John Keep presented what he called his "New Year's Gift" to Oberlin's people of color. Speaking at First Church to a large, racially mixed audience awaiting news of President Lincoln's promised Emancipation Proclamation, Keep read aloud from an article that had appeared the previous week in the *Springfield Republican*. The article confidently predicted that the end of slavery would lead to the diminution of color prejudice nationwide—in the North as well as in the South. With earnest optimism, Keep told his listeners, "The next half century is to be one of unprecedented activity and progress among the colored People of this country and talent and industry will gain their just rewards, without respect to race or complexion." Blacks would enjoy opportunities for social improvement and economic mobility on par with whites. "Let no smart colored boy lay aside his books, then, with the idea that he can never be anything better than a barber or boot-black or waiter," Keep declared. "He may become a lawyer, a preacher, an educator, and win his way to fortune and distinction at the same time that he does invaluable service to his race."[1]

Father Keep's optimism was well justified. The achievements of Thomas Jarvis, John Mercer Langston, O.S.B. Wall, John Watson, and other prosperous Oberlinians of color demonstrated that blacks possessed the intelligence, talent, and determination to succeed in a society devoid of "colorphobia." By Keep's logic, with slavery destroyed, the misbegotten idea of white supremacy that it embodied would surely give way to the more enlightened and truly Christian recognition that everyone shared a common humanity. Indeed, as the Civil War progressed, an increasing proportion of white northerners had come to accept the basic principle that all men, regardless of race, were created equal. And once the social barriers erected on a foundation of racial prejudice fell, blacks would join whites in reaping the just rewards of a democratic society that prized—and paid for—free people's hard work.

But in the wake of the Emancipation Proclamation and subsequent Union victory, Keep's inspirational vision went unrealized. Although African Americans in general enjoyed greater freedom after the Civil War, color prejudice persisted, and so did economic inequality rooted in different collective racial experiences—in Oberlin as elsewhere in the postbellum United States. Indeed, by various quantitative measures Oberlin was a notably less egalitarian community at the close of the nineteenth century than it had been when Keep presented his gift to "the Colored People of Oberlin" on January 1, 1863.[2] The subject of how and why Oberlin grew more racially stratified in the decades following emancipation deserves careful study.

The general contours of Oberlin's demographic and economic transformation in the late nineteenth century are easy to identify. According to the federal census, the town's total population doubled between 1860 and 1890 (rising from 2,115 to 4,376) and then declined modestly (to 4,082) over the next decade. In the meantime, the proportion of people of color in Oberlin's population rose slightly between 1860 and 1880 (from 20 percent to 21 percent) but then dropped markedly over the next decade and remained at the same level in 1900 (16 percent). For African Americans, Oberlin apparently lost some of its attraction in the last two decades of the nineteenth century. (See table 7.1)

More striking is the pattern of racial difference revealed by analyzing Oberlin's tax lists at five-year intervals between 1865 and 1900. Had Father Keep's projection of expanding opportunities for people of color been realized in Oberlin, the average wealth of blacks and whites should have tended to converge over time. Yet tax lists indicate that the gap between the average real estate assessments of white and black households persisted, even widened, across the late nineteenth century. While there were noticeable fluctuations in the interim, in 1900 the mean real estate assessment of black taxpaying households was only 37 percent of that of white taxpaying households, compared to 67 percent in 1865 (see chart 7.1). Likewise, in 1900 the median real estate assessment of black taxpaying households was

Table 7.1. Population of Oberlin, with Breakdown by Race, 1860–1900

Census Year	Total Population	White Population	% White	Population of Color	% of Color
1860	2,115	1,693	80%	422	20%
1870	2,888	2,276	79%	612	21%
1880	3,242	2,552	79%	690	21%
1890	4,376	3,688	84%	688	16%
1900	4,082	3,443	84%	639	16%

Sources: U.S. Census Office, *Population of the United States in 1860; Compiled from the Original Returns of the Eighth Census* (Washington, D.C.: Government Printing Office, 1864), 386; U.S. Census Office, *Ninth Census of the United States; Statistics of the Population of the United States* (Washington, D.C.: Government Printing Office, 1872), 234; U.S. Census Office, *Statistics of the Population of the United States at the Tenth Census* (Washington, D.C.: Government Printing Office, 1883), 292; U.S. Census Office, *Compendium of the Eleventh Census of the United States: 1890, Part 1: Population* (Washington, D.C.: Government Printing Office, 1892), 323; U.S. Census Office, *Twelfth Census of the United States Taken in the Year 1900, vol. 1, Population, Part 1* (Washington, D.C.: U.S. Census Office, 1901), 313.

39 percent of that of white taxpaying households, compared to 50 percent in 1865 (see chart 7.2.). Charts 7.1 and 7.2 offer powerful evidence that the economic standing of Oberlin's people of color, examined collectively, failed to improve relative to the economic standing of white Oberlinians in the three and a half decades following emancipation and the end of the Civil War.

Related to the failure of Oberlinians of color to "catch up" with local whites financially was an enduring difference in the distribution of black and white men's occupations. In his speech on January 1, 1863, Father Keep prophesized that over time men of color would increasingly make their living as professionals rather than in menial pursuits. On this point, Keep proved sadly mistaken in regard to Oberlin. As charts 7.3 and 7.4—taken together—illustrate, the proportion of black men employed in the professions declined from 4 percent to 3 percent between 1870 and 1900, while the proportion in service jobs rose from 44 percent in 1870 to 55 percent in 1900. Although the proportion of white men in service jobs also rose during this period (from 10 percent in 1870 to 16 percent in 1900), at the close of the nineteenth century white men in Oberlin were over eight times more likely to be in commercial

Chart 7.1. Mean Real Estate Assessments by Race of Oberlin Taxpaying Households, 1865–1900

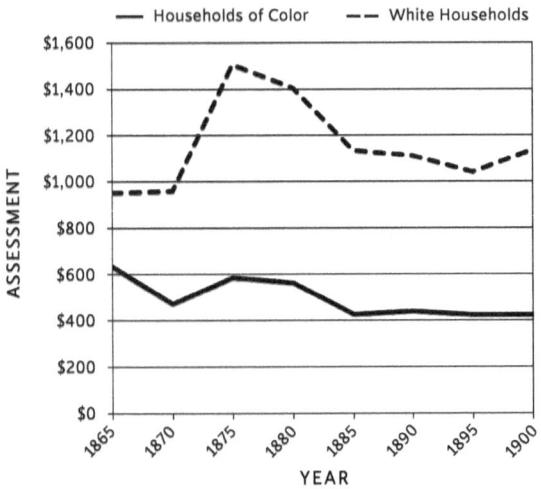

Sources: Auditor's Duplicates for Oberlin and Russia Township, 1865, 1870, 1875, 1880, 1885, 1890, 1895, 1900, Lorain County Records Retention Center, Elyria, Ohio.

Chart 7.2. Median Real Estate Assessments by Race of Oberlin Taxpaying Households, 1865–1900

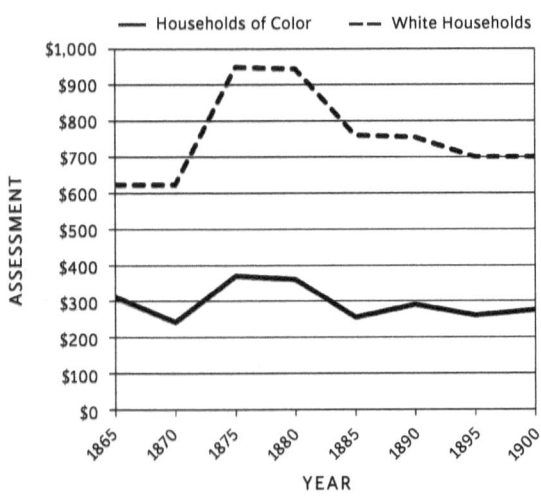

Sources: Auditor's Duplicates for Oberlin and Russia Township, 1865, 1870, 1875, 1880, 1885, 1890, 1895, 1900, Lorain County Records Retention Center, Elyria, Ohio.

Chart 7.3. Occupational Distribution of Oberlin Men by Race, 1870

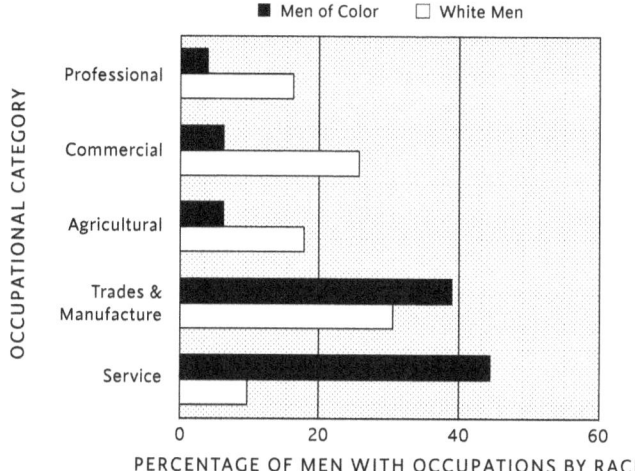

Source: Oberlin, Lorain County, Ohio, *Population Schedules of the Ninth Census of the United States, 1870* (National Archives Microfilm Publication M593), roll 1235, pages 628A–664A.

Chart 7.4. Occupational Distribution of Oberlin Men by Race, 1900

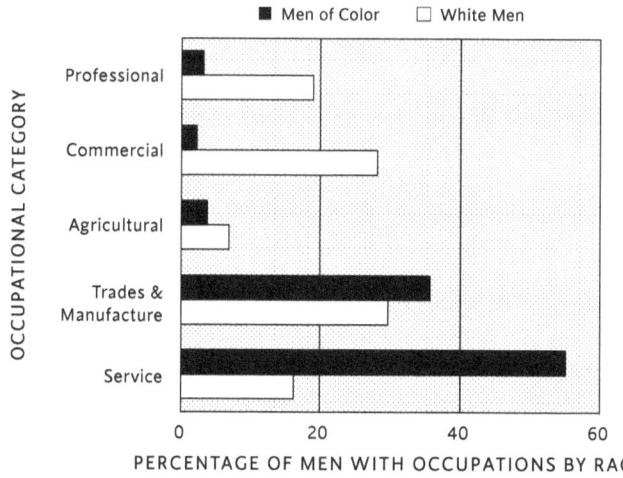

Source: Enumeration Districts 90–91, Russia Township, Lorain County, Ohio, *Population Schedules of the Twelfth Census of the United States, 1900* (National Archives Microfilm Publication T623), roll 1294, pages 218A–258B.

or professional occupations than black men. Black men held their own in the artisanal trades and small-scale manufactures, but they did not achieve occupational parity with whites in the wake of the Civil War.[3]

Why did John Keep's vision of an increasingly egalitarian, color-blind society fail to materialize in late nineteenth-century Oberlin? National developments, most notably the federal government's retreat from progressive Reconstruction policies and the Republican Party's desertion of black people in the wake of a resurgence of white racism in both the North and the South, played a major part in shaping Oberlin's postwar course.[4] So too did the decisions of local black residents. Many of the town's most accomplished African Americans and their children—the sort of people whom W.E.B. Du Bois would later call "the Talented Tenth"—chose to depart from Oberlin in the years after the Civil War.[5] For them, Father Keep's prediction was, in a sense, borne out: the Civil War opened up new opportunities outside of Oberlin for persons of color with education, ambition, and professional skills. With their exodus, the social structure of the black population in Oberlin was transformed. While a new elite of color emerged in Oberlin to take the place of those who left, postwar African American leaders lacked the prestige, wealth, and influence of their antebellum counterparts.

No individual's departure was more significant than that of John Mercer Langston. Although Langston remained on the Oberlin School Board until 1871, in the late 1860s he resided for part of the year in Washington, D.C. In 1868 he joined the faculty of Howard University, where he subsequently served as dean of the law department, vice president, and acting president. For many years he continued to visit Oberlin on an occasional basis, but he sold the family home on East College Street in 1872.[6] From 1877 to 1885 he served as the U.S. minister to Haiti, and in 1890–91 he served in Congress as a representative from Virginia.[7] While John Mercer and Caroline Langston sent some of their children back to their alma mater for higher education, in their later years Oberlin became, for them, a place to have been *from*—but not a place where they could continue to rise.[8]

The Langstons were the most prominent Oberlin family of color to relocate to Washington after the Civil War, but they were hardly alone. Various relatives and members of their extended social network did likewise. Caroline Langston's brother O.S.B. Wall, his wife, Amanda, and their children settled in the nation's capital in the late 1860s. Commissioned shortly before the war's end as a captain in the Union Army, O.S.B. Wall was posted to

Charleston, South Carolina, in the spring of 1865. With the advent of Reconstruction, he was assigned to the local office of the Freedmen's Bureau, seeking to help former slaves exercise their rights and to resolve economic disputes between blacks and whites in an increasingly hostile environment. Upon joining her husband in the fall of 1865, Amanda Wall taught in a local freedpeople's school sponsored by the American Missionary Association. The Walls remained in Charleston for two years before moving to Washington in early 1867. There O.S.B. took up a new position with the Freedmen's Bureau while Amanda taught classes in the family's sizable domicile. In 1869 the city's newly elected Republican mayor named O.S.B. a police magistrate and President Ulysses S. Grant appointed him a justice of the peace. The following year Wall began legal studies at Howard, where his brother-in-law was dean of the law department. After surviving an assassination attempt in June 1871, Wall won election to the District of Columbia's House of Delegates in November. A majority of his constituents were white. Like the Langstons, the Walls gained widespread recognition and respect in postwar Washington as upstanding citizens of color.[9]

Although they continued to own property in Oberlin, Henry and Henrietta Evans joined the Langstons and Walls in Washington for extended periods of time in the 1870s and were recorded as residing there in the 1880 federal census.[10] Henry and his brother, Wilson Bruce Evans, had jointly operated a cabinetmaking and undertaking establishment in Oberlin, and both were among the indicted Rescuers held in the Cuyahoga County Jail while awaiting trial in 1859. Henry and Henrietta Evans believed deeply in the importance of education and sent five of their children to Oberlin College.[11] An equal number of the children ultimately became teachers in Washington's schools: Sarah (born 1849), Delilah (born 1853), Anna (born 1855), Lewis Sheridan (born 1859), and Wilson (born 1866). In 1879 Anna married Daniel Murray, assistant to the Librarian of Congress, who would go on to assemble the incomparable collection of African American pamphlets that today bears his name.[12]

Washington also attracted two of the daughters of Maria Alexander Gibbs, a longtime Oberlin resident whose ambitious, peripatetic lawyer and diplomat husband, Mifflin Wistar Gibbs, bought the Langston house on East College Street before heading off to pursue his political ambitions in Florida, Arkansas, and then Madagascar as the U.S. consul.[13] Ida, the elder Gibbs daughter, pioneered a path in the District of Columbia, teaching in the schools, sometimes living with Oberlin college classmate Mary Church Terrell, and ultimately marrying her father's secretary and successor in the foreign service. Her younger sister, Harriet Althea Gibbs, the first African American woman to earn a bachelor of music degree at Oberlin College, also moved to Washington, where she founded the Washington Conservatory of Music, which was committed to the professional education of musicians of color. She eventually married Napoleon Bonaparte Marshall, who subsequently served as attaché to the Haitian legation. Ida and Mary's Oberlin classmate, activist, educator, and scholar Anna Julia Cooper, eventually lived near the sisters in the prestigious and newly integrated LeDroit Park. Cooper, who also taught in the D.C. schools, eventually earned a doctorate from the Sorbonne.[14]

Oberlin-born and -trained African Americans were critical to the development of high-quality public education for people of color in post–Civil War Washington. Five of the six children of Henry Patterson, a prosperous brickmason who had arrived in Oberlin in the mid-1850s, came to the district beginning in the late 1860s. Katharine, a former Oberlin Conservatory student, kept house for her brother and three sisters, all teachers. The best known among them, Mary Jane Patterson, had become the first woman of color in the United States to earn the bachelor's degree when she graduated from Oberlin in 1862. After teaching in Ohio, in Norfolk, Virginia, and at the Institute for Colored Youth in Philadelphia—under the supervision of Oberlin College alumna Fanny Jackson Coppin—Mary Jane Patterson pursued a long teaching career at Washington's M Street School, where she also briefly served as principal.[15]

Oberlin offspring also found employment in federal government offices located in Washington: John Berry worked in the Census Bureau, the Pension Bureau, and the Treasury; William Jackson served for a time in the War Department; Stephen Wall, O.S.B. and Amanda Wall's son, worked in the Government Printing Office.[16]

Some prominent Oberlinians of color migrated much farther geographically. In 1869 Mary Patterson Leary, the widow of Harpers Ferry martyr Lewis Sheridan Leary, wed Oberlin-Wellington Rescuer Charles Langston. Langston had relocated to Leavenworth, Kansas, early in the Civil War and was deeply engaged in that state's postwar fight over black suffrage. In anticipation of his marriage to Mary Leary, he bought a 125-acre farm in rural

Douglas County, Kansas, in 1868. There the newlyweds set up housekeeping in "a comfortable residence" and proceeded to have two children together: Nathaniel Turner Langston, named for the leader of the 1831 slave rebellion in Virginia, and Caroline Mercer Langston, named for Charles's brother and his wife. The household also included Louise Leary, Mary's daughter by her first husband, and Dessalines Langston, a foster son named after the revolutionary Haitian hero. In 1888 the family moved to nearby Lawrence, where Charles died almost penniless in 1892. Mary lived until 1915.[17] In her later years she helped raise her grandson, the future poet Langston Hughes, whom as a baby she wrapped in the bloodstained shawl worn by Lewis Sheridan Leary when he was slain at Harpers Ferry.[18] Hughes in his autobiography remembered his grandmother as an admirably "proud woman" who "sat in her rocker and read the Bible or held me on her lap and told me long, beautiful stories about people who wanted to make the Negroes free."[19]

About a dozen years after the Civil War's conclusion, Oberlin-raised Frank Adair returned to Arkansas, his state of birth, to practice law. The son of slaveholder Benjamin Franklin Adair and his slave Charlotte, Frank—formally Benjamin Franklin Adair Jr.—had arrived in Oberlin as a young boy in the late 1850s along with his father, mother, and siblings. His parents lived together as husband and wife, and they were accorded social respect by other members of the community. In the early 1870s Frank Adair attended the preparatory department of Oberlin College. Where he studied law remains unknown, as does the precise date of his migration back to Arkansas. In September 1879 he married Docia Wright, a woman of color, in Lee County on the Mississippi River, and a few months later she gave birth to a son. In 1880 the family resided in the tiny town of Cotton Plant, Woodruff County, and Frank was listed as a lawyer in the federal census. Within a few years the Adairs moved to Pulaski County, and Frank opened a law office in Little Rock. He was subsequently elected the county's prosecuting attorney, and in 1891, running as a Democrat (an unusual party affiliation for a candidate of color), he won a seat in the lower house of the Arkansas state legislature. Yet his political career proved short-lived. He served only one term and died under mysterious circumstances—he may have been assassinated—in 1902.[20]

Other children of color who moved away from Oberlin included Joseph Wiley, who went to Dallas, Texas, where he became a lawyer and his sister taught school.[21] Edward Wynn, son of Leonidas and Lucy, built a career in music, first in the East and then in Seattle.[22] Carriage maker Andrew Jackson's son George established himself as a pharmacist in Memphis, Tennessee.[23] Arthur Mitchell became a postal clerk in Chicago, where he was living when he secretly married Ida de France, also of Oberlin.[24]

Above all, Oberlin—both town and college—launched large numbers of African American educators, sending forth teachers, principals, and school founders throughout the country in the decades following the Civil War.[25] For example, William Montgomery Jackson, who had for a time worked in Washington, became a professor at the Frankfort, Kentucky, Normal School, while his brother, John Charles Fremont Jackson, was a teacher and principal in Princeton, Indiana, in Ripley, Ohio, and in Chattanooga, Tennessee.[26] Another Jackson brother—and a Jackson sister—taught in Birmingham, Alabama.[27] Joseph Russell grew up in his uncle's Oberlin home, and after graduation he became a teacher in Virginia, where he also served as a deacon, Sunday school superintendent, and secretary of a local Republican club.[28] The daughters of barber Cornelius Burnett taught in Arkansas, Maryland, and Minnesota. After marrying real estate developer William H. Talbert of Buffalo, Burnett's daughter Mary hosted W.E.B. Du Bois on the eve of the first Niagara Movement meeting in 1905 and subsequently became a founding member of the NAACP in 1909.[29] Ednah Jane Mason taught in Canada as well as Kentucky.[30] Mary A. Campton taught in Atlanta, while Lizzie and Alice Simms taught in Kentucky, as did Samantha Tuck.[31] Henry Lee's daughters, Lillie and Lizzie, taught in North and South Carolina.[32] Alice Alexander Davis joined Sarah Jane Evans Inborden at the Brick School in North Carolina.[33]

Such outmigration begs explanation. Why did these well-situated African Americans leave Oberlin? Many of the best educated felt a responsibility to teach other African Americans in order to promote racial uplift, and they were attracted by opportunities at new schools for students of color that sprang up throughout the United States. Yet they also left town because Oberlin itself did not offer employment to teachers of color. "Some 400 or 500 of college students are enabled to pay their expenses here in college by teaching in the preparatory department, but . . . no colored student has this privilege," a local critic charged in the *New National Era*, an African American newspaper, in 1871. "The faculty say that it is *inexpedient* for colored students to teach at present, as the college can't bear the pressure."[34] In response, Oberlin College president James Harris Fairchild wrote that the total number of college-level and theological students teaching in the prep was actually only thirty to forty at any given time, but he acknowledged that none was currently a person of color. Selection for the positions was highly competitive, he explained, and the handful of eligible African American students simply did not rise to the top. After observing that "in 1866 we did employ Miss Fanny M. Jackson, now a distinguished teacher in the Colored High School of Philadelphia," he insisted, "Nothing could have pleased us more from that day to this than to have colored pupils who could follow in her footsteps."[35] Meanwhile, throughout the nineteenth century all the teachers in the town's public school system were white, as were all members of the college faculty.

Although the families of the "Talented Tenth" increasingly left town in the decades following the Civil War, families of color on the whole were more likely to stay in Oberlin than their white counterparts during this period.[36] Meanwhile, new families of color came to settle in Oberlin, usually migrating from the same geographic region as their predecessors in the antebellum era: the Upper South. To be more precise, of the 102 adults of color enumerated in the 1870 census who had not been listed in Oberlin in 1860, 73 percent had been born in the Upper South, 16 percent had been born in the Midwest, 4 percent in the Lower South, 3 percent in the mid-Atlantic region, 2 percent in New England, and 2 percent abroad. But these "newcomers" of color were considerably less well off economically than "persisters" of color who had resided in town for at least ten years. Calculations using 1870 census data reveal that the mean combined value of real and personal estate owned by adult black newcomers (including women) was $424—barely half the comparable figure of $857 for adult blacks who had resided in Oberlin for a decade or more.[37] Alongside the departure of the "Talented Tenth," the influx of relatively poor persons of color from outside Oberlin helps to explain why the average property holdings of residents of color failed to rise vis-à-vis the average property holdings of white townspeople in the aftermath of the Civil War.

Did the postbellum influx also "darken" Oberlin's African American population? According to the census, the proportion of Oberlinians of color listed as "mulatto" dropped from 68 percent in the 1870 census to 35 percent in the 1880 enumeration, while the proportion listed as "black" rose from 32 percent to 65 percent.[38] Whether this shift actually reflected a dramatic change in the complexion of Oberlin's African American population within a span of just ten years is hard to know, however. The apparent trend may have been simply an artifact of different individuals serving as census takers, since the distinction between "mulatto" and "black" was largely in the eye of the beholder.

In contrast to those of the earlier era, white migrants to Oberlin in the postbellum period did not move to the community because of its abolitionist reputation, nor did they necessarily come from crucibles of progressive racial ideals. After the war, white newcomers increasingly came from other places in the Midwest (especially Ohio) rather than from New England and New York. The proportion of adult white residents who had been born in New England or the mid-Atlantic states dropped from 58 percent in 1860 to 42 percent in 1880, while the proportion born in the Midwest rose from 29 percent in 1860 to 47 percent in 1880. Also noteworthy, ongoing population turnover meant that only about one in eight residents of Oberlin in 1880 had been living in the community at the time of the Oberlin-Wellington Rescue. Demographic dynamics help to explain why Oberlin's collective memory of the founders' commitment to racial egalitarianism began to fade.[39]

Data from local tax lists allow for close examination of the property holdings of Oberlinians in the postwar era. Although less comprehensive than census records since they omitted residents without taxable property—an estimated 15 percent of household heads in 1870—the tax lists were compiled more frequently and, unlike the census, consistently included valuations of real estate, the predominant source of household wealth. By combining the real estate assessments of married couples, ranking the assessments of households in hierarchical order, and dividing that ranking into fifths, one can determine which households belonged to each of the five quintiles of taxpaying units for any given year and, through linkage to another source, identify the race of the household head. Using this process, the distribution of real property holdings by race was calculated at five-year intervals across the period 1865–1890.[40]

The results are striking. White households were spread rather evenly across the assessment quintiles throughout this quarter-century—with the partial exception of the lowest quintile, where they were somewhat underrepresented. By contrast, households of color were heavily concentrated at the bottom of the property-holding hierarchy and underrepresented at the top. Indeed, after the Civil War the share of black-headed households that were comparatively affluent by community standards actually shrank. Whereas in 1865, 21 percent of black-headed households were listed with real estate assessments in the top two quintiles, by 1870 the proportion had dropped to 14 percent, and between 1875 and 1885 it hovered at 11 percent; it stood at less than 10 percent in 1890.[41] Meanwhile, throughout the period about half the black-headed households were located in the poorest assessment quintile. (See table 7.2.)

Table 7.2. Distribution of Taxpaying Oberlin Households across Real Estate Assessment Quintiles, Sorted by Race of Household Head, 1865–1890

Assessment Quintile	1865 white	1865 of color	1870 white	1870 of color	1875 white	1875 of color
5 (Highest)	21%	7%	22%	8%	23%	5%
4	21%	14%	22%	6%	23%	6%
3	21%	7%	21%	12%	22%	8%
2	20%	23%	20%	20%	18%	30%
1 (Lowest)	16%	49%	14%	55%	14%	51%
N	333	47	404	66	517	100

Assessment Quintile	1880 white	1880 of color	1885 white	1885 of color	1890 white	1890 of color
5 (Highest)	23%	5%	23%	5%	23%	4%
4	23%	6%	23%	6%	22%	5%
3	22%	9%	22%	10%	21%	12%
2	18%	33%	18%	29%	18%	30%
1 (Lowest)	15%	47%	14%	50%	15%	48%
N	560	106	619	118	665	113

Sources: Auditor's Duplicates for Oberlin and Russia Township, 1865, 1870, 1875, 1880, 1885, 1890, Lorain County Records Retention Center, Elyria, Ohio. The race of household heads was determined by record linkage with Patricia Holsworth, "Oberlin Genealogical Database," 2012, in the authors' possession.

Yet the founding generation's commitment to ameliorating racial inequality might still have been realized if Oberlinians of color who started off poor could rise over time. Abraham Lincoln, among others, framed the egalitarian ideal in terms of social mobility, not the distribution of wealth per se: "The prudent, penniless beginner . . . labors for wages awhile, saves a surplus with which to buy tools or land for himself; then labors on his own account another while, and at length hires another new beginner to help him. This is the just, and generous, and prosperous system, which opens the way to all—gives hope to all, and consequent energy, and progress, and improvement of condition to all."[42] Was Lincoln's version of the American Dream an accurate description of reality in postwar Oberlin? And was it accessible to African Americans in particular?

Although no Oberlinian of color ascended all the way from rags to riches (understood as great wealth) in the late nineteenth century, several made their way from poverty into the middle ranks of the town's economic hierarchy. Among those whose stories are most inspiring were George and William F. Robinson, brothers born into slavery who fled bondage as young men and arrived in Oberlin in 1855. In a memoir originally delivered orally and preserved in typescript by his descendants, William Robinson—the younger brother by five years—recounted how he and George acquired not only freedom but a modicum of property in their adopted community.[43]

William began his narrative with the story of his mother as a young girl being taken by her master from Virginia to Mason County, Kentucky, where he subsequently hired her out to the Runyon family in the small town of Mayslick. While serving as the Runyons' cook, she was impregnated by James Runyon, "a grown son" living with his parents. William was the product of this rape. Soon after his birth in 1832, his "father left Kentucky for the east."[44]

When William was six and George was eleven, they were "sent to the home of Simon Lettrell," the "very cruel" master of their mother and themselves. After Lettrell (or Luttrell, as the name was commonly spelled in public records) died in the fall of 1839, the brothers were separated from each other as well as from their mother. William "was sent up in Fleming Co[unty]," where for the next seven years he performed household and farm labor for "Patsy Summers, whose six children were all grown." After he broke his leg and took ill, however, his "young master"—Lucien Luttrell, the son of Simon—retrieved William and put him to work caring "for his children at night" and tending the family's sizable garden during the day.[45]

While living in Lucien Luttrell's household, William—like the young Frederick Douglass—learned to read with the help of his "mistress . . . on the sly" and white "children willing to tell me the letters." With Mrs. Luttrell's encouragement, he also earned small amounts of money by processing hempseed and selling produce he was allowed to raise for himself. After moving out of the Luttrell residence into "a log cabin alone," however, William learned from his niece that his "master said I knew too much, and he had better sell me or he would lose me." William acted preemptively. "At the age of 23," he recounted, "I decided to seek my freedom."[46]

William enlisted his brother George, his uncle Barnard, and Armstead White—a slave whose wife and children had earlier escaped to Canada—to join him in fleeing Kentucky. Taking advantage of the laxness of surveillance procedures on a Sunday, they walked from Mayslick to Maysville, and then, upon paying a boatman $25 per person, they took a skiff across the Ohio River to Ripley, Ohio. White headed to Canada, while the others set out for Oberlin. Over the next two weeks they "traveled all night and hid in the daytime," pursued by slave catchers but helped by "[g]uides who were always on hand at every station of the under-ground railroad until we were . . . near New London." From there they "took the train" to Grafton and "up to Oberlin, arriving late in the afternoon of a June day in 1855."[47]

Once in Oberlin, William, George, and Barnard were immediately offered work "splitting rails at $1.00 per hundred and fifty cents per cord to cut up 700 rails." They subsequently found similar jobs "with no trouble," and within "about three months" they had accumulated enough to put a down payment on "a home on East Lorain Street." In the meantime, William seized the opportunity to enhance his education. He learned to write under the tutelage of Dr. James F. Siddall and took classes at the Liberty School taught by ex-slave and college student Fanny Jackson. He later "attended the Public Schools for a short time," finding the instructor "Miss Mary Monroe and several in the class . . . very kind and helpful."[48]

William and George stayed in Oberlin despite the danger posed by slave hunters under the Fugitive Slave Act of 1850. Exactly when the brothers began using the surname Robinson is unknown, but they were enumerated under that name in the 1860 federal census. (Barnard was omitted.) The occupation of each brother was designated "laborer" in the census, and George, as household head, was listed as owning $600 in real estate and $100 in personal estate. Residing with the brothers in 1860 was Sarah Baker, a washerwoman of color whom William identified in his memoir as "my uncle's sister-in-law." She cooked and "kept house until her son came from Canada and bought her a home out in the country."[49]

In December 1864, William wed Nora Jane Nowell, a free-born, mixed-race woman from Virginia who had migrated to Oberlin with her widowed mother and three brothers. The following June, George married Amanda Scott, a woman of color who had been born in Kentucky. The two couples "for several years . . . lived in the same house, but in separate apartments."[50] Conditions soon grew crowded on William and Nora Jane's side, as they welcomed five children during their first nine years of marriage.[51] In 1873 William "purchased one acre of land on N. Main St. from Theodore Keep and built a house," which his growing family promptly occupied.[52] George and Amanda continued to reside on East Lorain Street for the rest of their lives.[53]

The Robinsons prospered in Oberlin, but they never grew rich. From 1870 until his death in 1890, George was usually identified in public records as a farmer, though the 1880 census gave his occupation as "teaming" and the 1887 city directory listed him as a laborer. When he passed away at the age of sixty-two, he owned enough real estate to rank in the second quintile of the tax list. Thereafter Amanda was able to keep the house and live on her own by doing "laundry work." She died in 1913 at the age of seventy.[54]

How William accumulated enough funds to buy the land on North Main Street and construct a new family residence in 1873 is not fully clear. In the 1870 census he was listed as a day laborer, and in the 1880 census he was listed as a common laborer. In the latter census, Nora Jane was listed as a washerwoman, but that, too, was a low-paid occupation. Yet the couple continued to have more children until the total reached ten, four of whom would go on to earn degrees from Oberlin College. After Theodore Keep died in 1889, his widow sold William "twelve more acres" of land, "on which [he] raised fruit and vegetables for market."[55] During the 1890s William was listed as a gardener in the city directory, and he was identified likewise in the 1900 census. According to the 1900 assessment list, by then he owned enough real estate to rank in the middle quintile of Oberlin taxpayers.[56] Nora Jane passed away in 1906, but William lived for another twenty years, dying on June 21, 1928, at the impressive age of ninety-six.[57] In marking his passing, the *Oberlin News* observed that he was not only "industrious and careful in his dealings," but also "a man of strict honesty and . . . well respected by his neighbors."[58]

Another African American who climbed partway up the economic ladder in late nineteenth-century Oberlin was George M. Glenn. Born in 1829 in

Monroe County, Virginia, Glenn was probably the son—and originally the property—of slaveholder James Glenn.[59] By 1850 George was residing in Chillicothe, Ohio, where the census taker listed him as a free black man boarding with a local family of color and making his living as a barber.[60] In 1855, at age twenty-six, he wed Augusta Louisa König, a seventeen-year-old white woman who had emigrated with her family from Germany to Defiance, Ohio, in 1849.[61] (Although quite rare, interracial marriages were legal in antebellum Ohio.[62]) George and Augusta Glenn were recorded in the 1860 census as residents of Marion Township in Allen County, Ohio. Living with the couple were their two small children, ages two and three, and Augusta's eleven-year-old sister. Interestingly, the census taker in 1860 made no mention of the race of any members of the Glenn household.[63]

According to a newspaper account published long afterward, George M. and Augusta Glenn relocated to Oberlin in 1866 "for the sake of the educational advantages" available in the town to their children, who numbered five by then and would ultimately total ten.[64] During his early years in Oberlin, George worked as a drayman while Augusta kept house. Then, in the fall of 1873, George "resumed the razor and shears" by opening up a barbershop on College Place. It proved a popular establishment, and over time he gained the sobriquet "the college barber."[65] The *Oberlin Tribune* noted in its 1916 obituary of George M. Glenn, "For many years Mr. Glenn knew every Oberlin student by name and his shop in those days was the leading one in town."[66] Yet he continued to do hauling work on the side into his early sixties. An advertisement for his barbershop in 1891 included the following notice: "Draying done to order. Moving Pianos a specialty."[67]

George M. Glenn enjoyed the friendship and respect of a broad swath of Oberlinians. He joined First Church in 1870, served as a constable in 1872–1873, and won election to a two-year term on the town council in 1882. He and Augusta also launched their offspring on successful careers.[68] Most notably, Charles H. Glenn, their oldest child, trained as a carpenter and over time became a well-regarded architect and building contractor in partnership with Frederick Copeland, younger brother of Harpers Ferry martyr John Anthony Copeland. "The firm [of Glenn and Copeland] has been doing some of the best work in Oberlin for several years," the *Oberlin News* reported in 1896.[69] A number of the attractive and spacious houses they built toward the end of the nineteenth century remain standing in Oberlin today.

The career of William Madison Mitchell offers further evidence that, despite a persistent pattern of racial inequality, a visible minority of African Americans were able to rise from poverty to "financial independence" and social respectability in late nineteenth-century Oberlin. According to an account published after his death, "Mr. Mitchell was born in 1842, in Milton, N.C., of free parents but harassed by all the limitations of slavery." At a time when public authorities often bound out "children of the free poor" to "employers of cheap labor," William's family lived in the forest to avoid detection. In his early teens William took a job in a "tobacco factory and worked there for long hours and little pay without any opportunity for attending school." The onset of the Civil War presented new possibilities: "[K]nowing little of the true cause and purpose of the war, he hired himself to a Confederate officer to act as his hostler." Over the course of the military conflict, William "was twice captured by the opposing forces, was imprisoned with his officer and was at the siege of Baltimore and at Gettysburg." Influenced while in captivity by the views of Northern soldiers, he came to favor Union victory, and at the war's conclusion he settled in southern Ohio.[70]

On August 16, 1866, William Madison Mitchell married Missouri Ann Mason in Gallipolis, Ohio. Like the groom, the bride, who went variously as Ann and as Caroline, was a person of color who had been born free in a slave state. They were approximately the same age, yet she was considerably better educated than William, who remained illiterate when they wed. Her family had migrated from Virginia to Ohio in the 1850s, and she had subsequently studied at a "small school conducted by Mrs. Adelia Field Johnston," an Oberlin College graduate who had witnessed the Oberlin-Wellington Rescue and who would serve as the institution's dean of women from 1870 to 1900. In 1867, perhaps inspired by Mrs. Johnston's example, the Mitchells moved to Oberlin with their infant son, Walter.[71]

Once in Oberlin, William Madison Mitchell supported himself and his growing family by painting houses. Within ten years he had earned enough to build a house of his own on North Main Street, and in 1880 he was ranked in the second quintile of Oberlin taxpayers. By then Ann had given birth to five surviving children.[72] She died the next year shortly after delivering another. Left to raise the children alone, William found solace in his Christian faith and emotional support among the predominantly white members of First Church, who demonstrated their "confidence in his uprightness and devotion by electing him a deacon for as many terms as he was willing to serve." In 1894 he wed a fellow congregant of color: Edith Campton, the North Carolina-born widow of John R. Campton. This second marriage for each partner proved long and durable.[73]

Like those of many other craftsmen, William Madison Mitchell's income fluctuated with the business cycle. The family's economic situation was further complicated by "several serious accidents" that he suffered on the job—two of them life-threatening. Edith helped out by turning their home into a popular "boarding house for young colored college girls." Gradually, through hard work and perseverance, William Madison Mitchell was able to grow his business, becoming eventually "a contractor of painting, etc., taking large jobs and employing a crew of workers." His reputation for quality was such that in flush times "some of the most substantial and particular residents of the town . . . would wait months to obtain his services."[74]

In 1914, at the age of seventy-two, William Madison Mitchell was hit by an automobile while biking to work. "He never fully recovered from this accident," and two years later he fell off his bike and seriously reinjured himself. He spent the remainder of his life as an invalid, passing away at the house on North Main Street on September 18, 1919. Edith died four years later.[75]

The life stories of George and William Robinson, George Glenn, and William Madison Mitchell demonstrate that the economic order of postwar Oberlin was fluid, rather than rigidly fixed. But as the extensive historical literature on social and economic mobility has demonstrated, case studies of a few well-documented individuals are not necessarily representative of general patterns.[76] To gain a fuller picture of the relationship between race and economic mobility in Oberlin during the late nineteenth century, a roster was compiled of taxpaying individuals and married couples that initially appeared in the bottom quintile of the 1865, 1870, 1875, and 1880 listings of real estate assessments. The trajectories of the taxpayers on this roster—216 in all—were then traced at five-year intervals from their first appearance on a tax list for up to twenty years, with the quintile of assessment used as a metric of economic mobility.[77]

Significantly, taxpayers of color who began in the lowest quintile of real estate assessments were twice as likely as lowest-quintile white taxpayers to remain on the Oberlin tax rolls ten years later. On the assumption that most people dropped off the tax lists because they left town in search of greater opportunities elsewhere, the higher rate of decadal persistence for taxpayers of color—61 percent—suggests that Oberlin appeared a comparatively better place to live and work to poor blacks than it did to poor whites. Whites could expect to find a range of economic opportunities in other towns that would be denied to people of color.[78]

Yet while poor African Americans were more likely than poor whites to stay in Oberlin, they were less likely to ascend the economic ladder across the course of a decade. Two-thirds of persisters of color who started in the lowest quintile of the tax list remained at that level ten years later. By contrast, over half of the white persisters moved up at least one quintile, and nearly a quarter reached one of the top two quintiles.[79] (See table 7.3.)

Table 7.3. Mobility Out of the Lowest Real Estate Assessment Quintile after Ten Years, Sorted by Race (1865, 1870, 1875, 1880 Cohorts Combined)

Race of Taxpayer	Number of Persisters	Real Estate Assessment Quintile after Ten Years				
		1 (Lowest)	2	3	4	5 (Highest)
of color	39	67%	23%	8%	3%	0%
white	47	47%	19%	11%	15%	9%

Sources: Auditor's Duplicates for Oberlin and Russia Township, 1865, 1870, 1875, 1880, 1885, 1890, Lorain County Records Retention Center, Elyria, Ohio. The race of household heads was determined by record linkage with Patricia Holsworth, "Oberlin Genealogical Database," 2012, in the authors' possession.

For African Americans who persisted longer, the odds of rising improved. Of the taxpayers of color who stayed in Oberlin for two decades, 42 percent advanced at least one quintile, 13 percent rose two or three quintiles, and 3 percent ascended from the lowest to the highest quintile. Still, white taxpayers who persisted twenty years fared even better. Fifty-nine percent rose at least one quintile, 27 percent rose two or three quintiles, and 17 percent reached the highest quintile. The racial gap in upward economic mobility was narrower for twenty-year persisters than it was for those who stayed in Oberlin only a single decade, but it remained considerable.[80] (See table 7.4.)

Notwithstanding the ability of some African Americans to advance economically over the course of the late nineteenth century, in 1900 people of color comprised a smaller proportion of the top quintile of Oberlin taxpayers than they had in 1860—2 percent compared to 5 percent. At the same time, their share of the lowest quintile of taxpayers had more than doubled and stood at 35 percent in 1900.[81] Overall, the association of wealth with whiteness and of poverty with blackness was much stronger at the close of the nineteenth century than it had been on the eve of the Civil War. (Compare charts 7.5 and 7.6.)

Table 7.4. Mobility Out of the Lowest Real Estate Assessment Quintile after Twenty Years, Sorted by Race (1865, 1870, 1875, 1880 Cohorts Combined)

Race of Taxpayer	Number of Persisters	Real Estate Assessment Quintile after Twenty Years				
		1 (Lowest)	2	3	4	5 (Highest)
of color	31	58%	26%	10%	3%	3%
white	29	41%	14%	24%	3%	17%

Sources: Auditor's Duplicates for Oberlin and Russia Township, 1865, 1870, 1875, 1880, 1885, 1890, Lorain County Records Retention Center, Elyria, Ohio. The race of household heads was determined by record linkage with Patricia Holsworth, "Oberlin Genealogical Database," 2012, in the authors' possession.

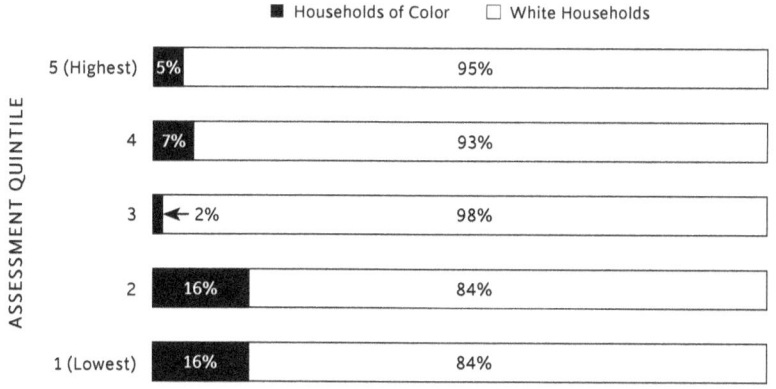

Chart 7.5. Racial Composition of Real Estate Assessment Quintiles, 1860

Sources: Auditor's Duplicates for Oberlin and Russia Township, 1860, Lorain County Records Retention Center, Elyria, Ohio. The race of household heads was determined by record linkage with Patricia Holsworth, "Oberlin Genealogical Database," 2012, in the authors' possession.

Chart 7.6. Racial Composition of Real Estate Assessment Quintiles, 1900

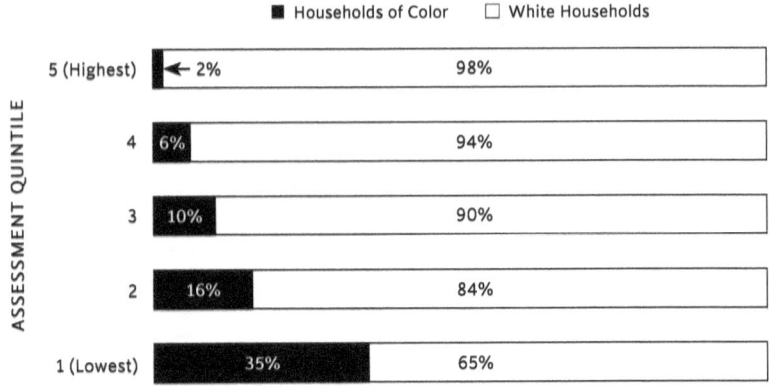

RACIAL COMPOSITION OF ASSESSMENT QUINTILE

Sources: Auditor's Duplicates for Oberlin and Russia Township, 1900, Lorain County Records Retention Center, Elyria, Ohio. The race of household heads was determined by record linkage with Patricia Holsworth, "Oberlin Genealogical Database," 2012, in the authors' possession.

In a parallel development, the town's residential geography grew more racially segregated in the late nineteenth century. In 1860 the index of dissimilarity—a standard measure of segregation—was 18 on a scale of 0 to 100. In 1900 the index of dissimilarity was 40, more than twice as high. A telling sign of this transformation was the increased concentration of the town's population of color in the southeast quadrant. Whereas in 1860, 43 percent of local households headed by an African American resided in that quadrant, 57 percent did so in 1900. In a converse yet complementary trend, the proportion of white-headed households living in the town's two western quadrants rose from 44 percent in 1860 to 57 percent in 1900.[82]

A pattern of racial separation was also evident at the street level at the end of the nineteenth century. According to the federal census of 1900, fully one-quarter of Oberlin's white-headed households resided on streets with no black-headed household, mostly on the west side of town (for example, Elm, Forest, Morgan, North and South Cedar, South Professor, and Union Streets). Another quarter of white-headed households lived on streets with just one household headed by a person of color. Even on streets with a relatively balanced racial mix (such as East Lorain, Groveland, North Water, and Spring Streets), black- and white-headed families tended to cluster on different blocks. With the possible exception of South Main and South Pleasant Streets, the town lacked truly integrated neighborhoods.[83]

In his keynote address to the first annual meeting of the Associated Charities of Oberlin, in November 1889, William Goodell Frost, a professor of Greek at the college, commented with evident regret on the changing social geography of the town. "[T]here are streets in Oberlin which do not know how other streets live," he told his predominantly white, well-heeled audience. "If you reflect you will realize that you have almost no poor neighbors. The poor families live in the obsc[u]re parts of the town. We do not meet them in our ordinary routine of business. . . . [T]hey are strangers to us."[84] To an extent that would have dismayed Father Keep, Oberlin at the close of the nineteenth century was a town increasingly riven by differences of race and class.

Compared to other American communities, however, Oberlin remained a safe haven for African Americans. During the 1890s, the lynching of blacks spread across the South as a terroristic counterpart to the Jim Crow statutes adopted by state legislatures with the federal government's acquiescence.[85] Racist aggression also increased in the North, where a growing number of "sundown towns" effectively prevented people of color from residing among whites.[86] A scholarly compilation of "antiblack collective violence in the Lower Midwest" identifies twenty-five separate incidents between 1885 and 1900, including an attempted lynching in 1894 in Washington Court House, a small town in southwest Ohio where African Americans had previously been welcome.[87] Although Oberlin after the Civil War retreated from its earlier commitment to radical racial egalitarianism, white Oberlinians did not publicly repudiate that commitment, nor did they seek to force people of color from the community. Instead, white Oberlinians increasingly ignored the "race question" and turned their attention to the issue of temperance. The consequent neglect of African American concerns was not malicious, but neither was it benign. The impact of the temperance movement on racial dynamics in late nineteenth-century Oberlin is the focus of the next chapter.

8

TEMPERANCE, GENDER, AND THE RACIALIZATION OF RESPECTABILITY

A feeble fire bell at midnight on March 6, 1882, announced the largest conflagration that Oberlin had ever witnessed. In two hours, a raging blaze spread from the rear of the Tuttle and Farr Meat Market westward along East College Street and then headed south down Main Street, consuming nine buildings in the core of Oberlin's business district. Among the enterprises destroyed were a photography studio, the new telephone exchange, Bacon's omnibus office, Carter and Wood's hardware store, two barbershops, and two drugstores—including one that had been the site of recent confrontations between temperance activists and local toughs hired by the owner to protect his establishment from protesters.[1] Overall damages were estimated at $37,000, equivalent to nearly $1 million today.[2] In the fire's aftermath, Oberlin's anti-alcohol activists recoiled in horror at the destruction that they feared their aggressive tactics had unleashed. Drawn to "the unpleasant conclusion" that "an incendiary" had set the blaze, the Oberlin Temperance Alliance joined with the town council to offer a reward of $1,000 "for information that will lead to the detection and conviction of the guilty party or parties."[3] Thereafter, leading temperance men would shun direct action and pursue more narrowly political strategies to achieve their goals while they sought to divert temperance women's energies to more traditional maternalistic benevolence. In conjunction with the deterioration of the economic status of Oberlin's people of color, these shifts would produce significant, if unintended, consequences for race relations in late nineteenth-century Oberlin.

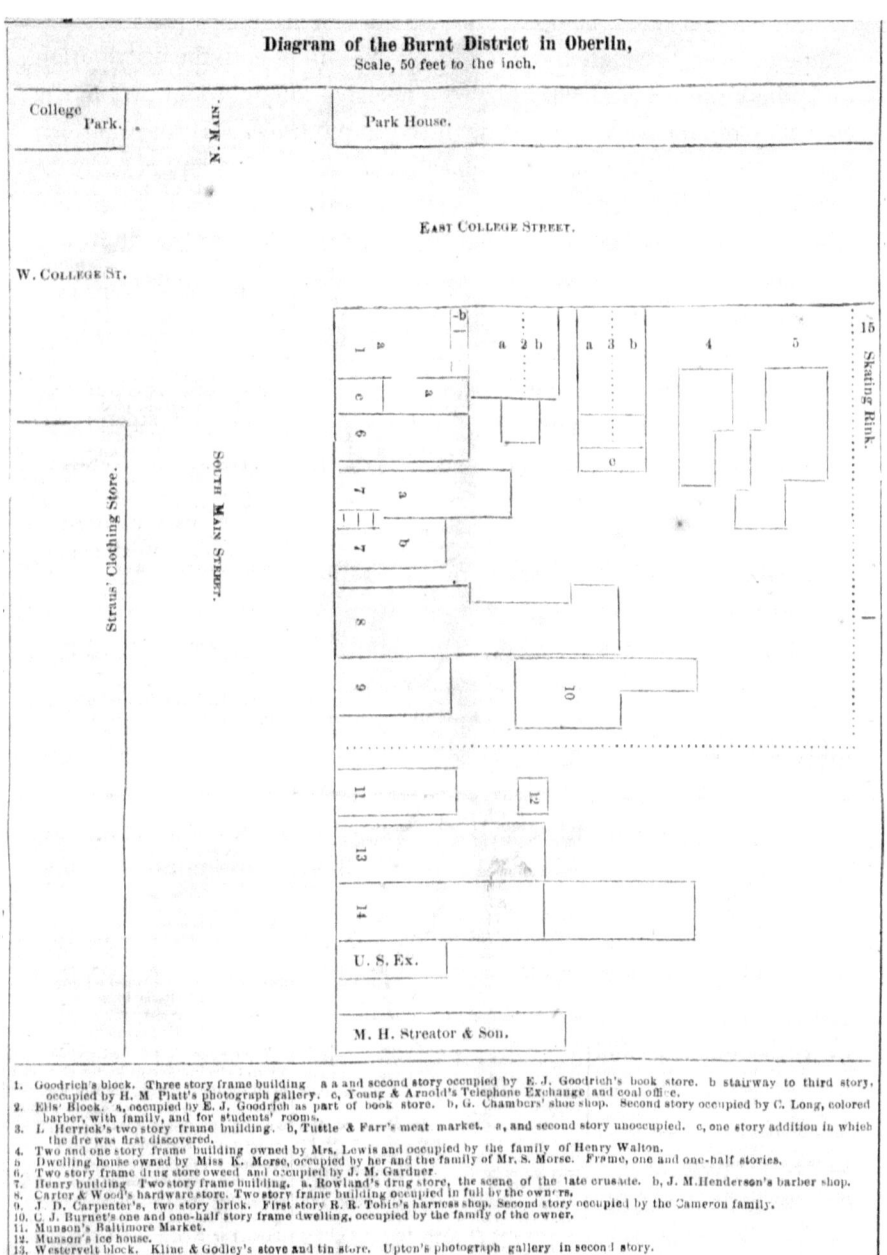

1. Goodrich's block. Three story frame building a a and second story occupied by E. J. Goodrich's book store. b stairway to third story, occupied by H. M Platt's photograph gallery. c, Young & Arnold's Telephone Exchange and coal office.
2. Ellis Block. a, occupied by E. J. Goodrich as part of book store. b, G. Chambers' shoe shop. Second story occupied by C. Long, colored barber, with family, and for students' rooms.
3. L. Herrick's two story frame building. b, Tuttle & Farr's meat market. a, and second story unoccupied. c, one story addition in which the fire was first discovered.
4. Two and one story frame building owned by Mrs. Lewis and occupied by the family of Henry Walton.
5. Dwelling house owned by Miss K. Morse, occupied by her and the family of Mr. S. Morse. Frame, one and one-half stories.
6. Two story frame drug store owned and occupied by J. M. Gardner.
7. Henry building Two story frame building. a. Rowland's drug store, the scene of the late crusade. b, J. M. Henderson's barber shop.
8. Carter & Wood's hardware store. Two story frame building occupied in full by the owners.
9. J. D. Carpenter's, two story brick. First story R. R. Tobin's harness shop. Second story occupied by the Cameron family.
10. C. J. Burnet's one and one-half story frame dwelling, occupied by the family of the owner.
11. Munson's Baltimore Market.
12. Munson's ice house.
13. Westervelt block. Kline & Godley's stove and tin store. Upton's photograph gallery in second story.
14. Skating rink.
Dotted lines—Limits of burnt district.

"Diagram of the Burnt District in Oberlin," published in *Oberlin Weekly News*, March 17, 1882. Oberlin College Libraries.

This chapter tells a complex story about how seemingly color-blind—although clearly gendered—efforts to rid Oberlin of both the distribution and consumption of alcohol played a decisive role in undermining the collective reputation and standing of the community's African American population. From its inception, Oberlin had professed temperance principles, and for decades most local residents—male and female, black and white—responded vigorously when alcohol threatened to invade its dry precincts. After the "Great Fire," however, Oberlin's Temperance Alliance channeled pro-temperance energies away from the public confrontations largely driven by women. And, although some people of color participated in the anti-alcohol movement, the new emphasis on achieving temperance through politics displaced the previously preeminent political issue of racial equality. Meanwhile, female temperance activists fell back on an ideology of gendered benevolence that had long justified their public participation in reform, which they now melded with a commitment to "scientific charity," emphasizing the need for rigorous discrimination between the worthy and unworthy poor in combating social ills. Identifying intemperance as the primary cause of poverty and poverty as a marker of personal inferiority, they conflated economic class and social respectability in a town where people of color disproportionately occupied the lowest echelons of wealth and income. By this process, Oberlin's temperance women—financially secure and overwhelmingly white—participated actively, albeit inadvertently, in the deepening stigmatization of people of color. In the latter decades of the nineteenth century, temperance activism in Oberlin undermined the community's commitment to racial equality.

Temperance had long been an Oberlin cause. Even before they committed themselves to the ideal of racial egalitarianism, Oberlinians had embraced temperance as a moral virtue. The founding covenant included a pledge by the colonists to "deny ourselves all strong and unnecessary drinks, even tea and coffee," and, as James Harris Fairchild later remembered, they had largely kept their word, at least so far as alcohol was concerned, throughout the antebellum era.[4] After the Civil War, a renewed fear of drunkenness emerged with the return of demobilized troops. In 1865 a "Vigilance Committee" chaired by college professor and veteran commander of black troops Giles Shurtleff investigated the sale of spirits at two local drugstores and the "small ale saloon kept by Samuel Munson." Shurtleff and his colleagues persuaded the druggists "to sell [alcohol] only for medicinal and mechanical purposes," but Munson, son of the antebellum Democratic postmaster, resisted, insisting he ran a "legitimate business, and has no respect for the sentiments that prevail generally in this community." Munson remained a determined enemy of Oberlin's temperance forces for the rest of his life.[5] The 1865 accord between the druggists and Oberlin's temperance leaders soon collapsed.

When new efforts to prohibit the sale and consumption of alcohol ramped up, people of color often found themselves targeted as sources of the problem. In 1869 the local newspaper reported on "a whiskey hole" in a grocery near the train depot, blaming "a colored family" that sold drink by the pint from their residence.[6] Mapping out "not only the beer, tobacco and billiard room up town, but the doggery at the bottom of the hill, and the groggery near the depot," the paper subsequently described an emergent geography of respectability, with the most dishonorable establishments located in the neighborhoods most heavily populated by blacks.[7] Moreover, the "doggery at the bottom of the hill," with its suggestion of a venue fit for less than fully human pursuits, was run by African American William O. Jenkins, whose alcohol sales would trouble Oberlin for a quarter-century.[8]

Yet Oberlin's people of color could be found on both sides of the temperance controversy. At its founding in 1870, the Oberlin Temperance League—the community's first formally organized anti-alcohol association—included at least seven African Americans among a membership totaling just over one hundred men: abolitionist and harness maker John H. Scott, grocer and builder John E. Patterson, wealthy farmer Thomas Jarvis, shoemaker A. J. Dyer, respected barber Cornelius J. Burnett, carpenter John Campton, and undertaker Henry Evans.[9] Although they comprised a smaller proportion of the league's membership than blacks did in the town's population as a whole, these African Americans joined hands with their white counterparts to affirm that "the welfare of the community is greatly endangered by the increasing sale and use of intoxicating drinks among us."[10]

Temperance activists characteristically began their reform efforts with persuasion, escalating to legal remedies only when their arguments failed to secure the voluntary closure of establishments that dispensed liquor.[11] In fact, the laws to which they had recourse were limited. Although a state statute known as the Adair Law allowed injured parties to sue liquor sellers for damages, this time-consuming and awkward procedure was a blunt instrument for the relief of women and children endangered by intoxicated men. Local ordinances banning the sale of alcohol, including one passed by the Oberlin town council in 1869, proved difficult to enforce in court.[12] After Samuel Munson was arrested in February 1870 for violating Oberlin's ordinance, he successfully sued the mayor for "false imprisonment" and was awarded $25 in compensation.[13] Yet the courts left intact state regulations against sales to minors and local penalties for public drunkenness. Throughout the 1870s and into the 1880s, Oberlin's temperance men deployed these imperfect tools even as they pushed unsuccessfully for stronger legal measures.[14]

Oberlin's temperance men respected the rule of law. When the front window of Albert Nichols's saloon was found smashed in 1875, temperance activists met with him to "utterly and unqualifiedly [sic] condemn all measures of violence."[15] Yet they savored their victory over what they called "the first open bar in Oberlin" when, "by purely legitimate and orderly means, by persuasion and moral influence, and concentrated public sentiment, with God's blessing," they closed Nichols's establishment by buying him out.[16] Still, local leaders knew the triumph was at best unstable. To suppress the sale and consumption of alcohol on a continuing basis, they encouraged Oberlin women to exert their moral influence on the community.

Excluded from the electorate, women did not make the laws, and they stood aside from legal enforcement. But, as James Harris Fairchild explained in 1870, "Women have a work to do in this matter which is more pressing than that of voting. . . . The customs of social life are in their keeping. It is for them to say whether the cup shall be pressed to their neighbor's lips."[17] Many Oberlin women took up this challenge. To keep those around them safe and sober, they personally and directly confronted community members they saw as at fault or at risk. In their passion to prevail, these temperance women invaded drinkers' haunts, confronted sinners, and tested the limits of civility. Theirs was a "militant maternalism."

Especially concerned about the moral character and behavior of young men, particularly college students separated from their own mothers, Oberlin's temperance women drew a bright line between good (abstinence) and evil (intoxication). The saloon could "lure young men from home, and start them on the downward career, that more frequently than otherwise, ends in a drunkard's grave," female temperance advocates warned.[18] As "mothers whose sons are in danger," they also demanded action against druggists who sold alcohol in the guise of medicine.[19] Although little was said about racial identification, the motherly advocates were overwhelmingly white, as were the young men they intended to protect. Women's temperance in Oberlin mobilized along lines of race.

Women's organized anti-alcohol labors began in earnest in 1874. On March 20 of that year an "immense gathering" of two thousand men and women assembled at Oberlin's First Church to hear Pastor James Brand exhort listeners to embrace "radical temperance reform for the present and prevention for the future."[20] The meeting elected James Harris Fairchild president of the Oberlin Temperance Alliance—the reorganized and renamed men's anti-alcohol association—with the ministers of the established white churches serving as vice presidents. In addition, ten people, all white and all male, comprised the executive committee.[21] These men uniformly believed that women's efforts were essential to their new organizational strategy. Theology professor Hiram Mead publicly praised Oberlin women who, inspired by the successful crusade launched three months earlier in Hillsboro, Ohio, by health reformer and educator Dio Lewis, had already embraced militant anti-alcohol strategies that relied not "on Legislation but upon God" and direct action.[22]

Dio Lewis had told the women of Hillsboro about how, when he was small, "My father had forgotten everything but drink," leaving his five small children to the solo care of his mother, who became "general provider, cook, housekeeper and nurse. In addition to all this she was the victim of abuse and violence."[23] To protect her home and family, Mother Lewis enlisted her female neighbors to visit the town's saloonkeepers and successfully persuaded them to cease selling liquor. Lewis applauded his mother's valiant action, and, according to one young listener, urged, "Ladies, you might do the same thing."[24] And they did. On Christmas Eve 1873, under the leadership of Mrs. Eliza Thompson, daughter of a former Ohio governor and wife of a highly respected local judge, seventy women arose from prayer in the local Presbyterian church to invade a nearby saloon. After convincing the proprietor to close, they continued their religiously inspired efforts at the town's remaining saloons. By the time Dio Lewis left town, Hillsboro was dry, and a powerful social movement was born. In the next two months, women in over 250 Ohio communities mobilized to shut down the saloons in their towns.[25]

Inspired by Lewis's temperance crusade, over one hundred Oberlin women—overwhelmingly but not exclusively white—came together in early

March 1874 to form the Oberlin Ladies Temperance League. They chose as their leader Marianne Parker Dascomb, who had arrived in Oberlin forty years before, when her husband, Dr. James Dascomb, was hired to teach chemistry at the fledgling Oberlin Institute. Trained at the Ipswich Academy, then among the most advanced institutions open to women, Mrs. Dascomb served as the principal of Oberlin's female department for nearly three decades. Although adamantly opposed to woman suffrage, she supported women's participation in a host of social causes during the antebellum era, especially moral reform, antislavery, and female education. She now seized upon the opportunity for temperance work, pronouncing "the way is open for us to do much that public sentiment would never have sustained us in doing before."[26]

Members of the Oberlin Ladies Temperance League undertook a program of self-education that fueled their fierce commitment to the elimination of alcohol. They discussed the case of "a cultured and successful physician, who became the victim of an appetite for strong drink stimulated by his mother's use of *brandy* in her *pies*."[27] They decried the amount of liquor inserted in chocolate cordial candies, demanding such confections be removed from sale in Oberlin lest they inflame the appetite and intoxicate the consumer.[28] They fussed over the amount of cider that could be used in apple butter without stimulating in children a dangerous taste for alcohol.[29] For members of the Ladies Temperance League, a "one drop" rule held. Although the organization's name spoke to moderation, their collective discussions pointed toward zealous, even fanatical, enforcement of absolute abstinence.

And they acted on their beliefs. Convinced of their divinely ordained mission and unconstrained by the need to please an electoral constituency, Oberlin's female temperance reformers enjoyed greater freedom to chart their own path than the men with whom they collaborated. In their first local effort, members of the Ladies Temperance League circulated a temperance pledge throughout the town, systematically collecting signatures and keeping a list of all who would not sign. They would do what they could to withhold the cup from their neighbors' lips.[30]

They visited Oberlin's saloonkeepers, first William O. Jenkins at his "doggery" and then the druggist Henry Avery, who, they recorded, "seems ... to have no fear of God nor regard for man in his unholy dealing out his liquid poison."[31] And they fearlessly traveled beyond Oberlin's municipal boundaries to nearby communities. During a trip to neighboring Kipton, Oberlin women drew the local bartender, his wife, and mother to their temperance meeting. To the singing of "Must Jesus Bear the Cross Alone?" a delegation of female activists departed by train to visit saloons in nearby Black River.[32] During a subsequent Black River visit, "a lawyer, who expressed his want of sympathy with the woman's movement, because it interfered with the transaction of a *legal business,* was so ably *answered* that he only contributed to the interest and success of the movement."[33] But, lest they become too self-satisfied, Mrs. Dascomb "warn[ed] the ladies against the temptation that Sat[an] might present to them, arousing their pride in the work as being one of their own doing—suggesting that we think of and call it—not as is so universally done 'The Woman's Movement,' but as God's especial movement."[34]

Religion was central to the mission and organizational structure of the Ladies Temperance League. The association's vice presidents were the white wives of Oberlin's white pastors.[35] Meetings began and ended with prayer, and prayer was viewed as *the* essential weapon in the fight against alcohol. Upon hearing rumors of a saloon soon to be opened in town, "it was thought much prayer ought to be offered that the design of the wicked might be thwarted."[36] When the establishment opened nonetheless, league members offered "several prayers . . . that it might not succeed."[37] In an interesting conflation of religion and democracy, they prayed on election day for the defeat of a state constitutional amendment that included a licensing provision.[38]

For both male and female temperance activists, the object became the total annihilation of the sin of imbibing alcohol. Like antebellum abolitionists who decried the sin of chattel slavery, temperance reformers denounced intoxication as both a moral evil and an aggressive political threat. And the movements to end slavery and intemperance were frequently compared. According to Dio Lewis, the activism surrounding prohibition was "the most signal event of the age, next after the great uprising against American slavery, and it seeks the overthrow of a vastly greater evil than did the latter. The bondmen of the South might be the Lord's freemen, but the rum power makes its every victim the devil's slave."[39] Speaking in Oberlin, General W. H. Gibson, a Civil War hero, proclaimed, "[T]wo serpents were sent to prey upon the life of this Republic—slavery and intemperance." He predicted that the extinction of intemperance would require "the same heroic purpose exhibited in the former contest."[40]

Such rhetoric obscured the struggle for racial justice that persisted beyond emancipation. Moreover, the analogy between slavery and intemperance was imperfect. After chattel slavery was "killed dead," freedpeople felt no desire to return to their former condition, while the victims of drink, temperance activists warned, could never escape the urge to imbibe again.[41] In addition, the Oberlin evangelicals, who condemned human bondage, did not look upon enslaved people as responsible for their own enslavement, instead identifying slave owners and slave traders as the sinners. But while fervent temperance activists frequently held those who sold alcohol as particularly responsible for the evils of drink, they also viewed drunkards themselves as sinners who lacked the will to convert and leave their wicked ways behind. Abolitionists felt deep compassion for the enslaved, but temperance men and women all too often lacked empathy for those addicted to alcohol.

Whereas a common commitment to abolitionism had fostered cross-racial alliances in antebellum and Civil War Oberlin, temperance activism proved more problematic in its effect on local race relations. On the one hand, in the postwar era leading white men sought out their African American counterparts to create alliances with which to navigate partisan elections. On the other hand, Oberlin women—white as well as black—remained outside the political sphere and instead grounded their activism in their religious identities and communities—spaces that became increasingly segregated with the founding of black churches in the 1870s. Hence Oberlin's white-dominated Ladies Temperance League barely took note of the black temperance revival that took place in Oberlin during the summer of 1874.[42] On the evenings of June 10 and June 15, African Americans gathered en masse to hear Reverend Amanda Smith—a woman of color, former slave, and arguably the era's best known female preacher in the United States—lend her voice to the campaign against alcohol. With visible support from local black leaders Matthew Goosland, Henry Lee, John H. Scott, and Sabram Cox, Reverend Smith urged her female listeners, in particular, to pray "for the right" and to take "a bold and firm stand on the side of temperance."[43] Those female listeners were almost exclusively women of color.

Anti-alcohol efforts failed to create cross-racial alliances among women. In 1880 the Ladies Temperance League decided that "the colored people of our own village [are in] need of missionary labor," yet league members were unsure how to proceed since they knew few African Americans as friends or colleagues.[44] They asked the white pastors of Oberlin about the wisdom of hiring an agent for their purpose but failed to consult the town's black ministers.[45] Visitors to the fledgling African Methodist Episcopal congregation reported, "[T]hey did not seem to need help in the school but ... good work might be done by getting the mothers together for a mothers meeting."⁴⁶ Two years later, however, league members expressed disappointment in an African American mothers' meeting they observed, and the organization abandoned any focused effort to connect across lines of race.⁴⁷ The Ladies Temperance League remained an overwhelmingly white organization, distant from all but a handful of women of color whose families had longstanding ties to the old Congregational Church.

In August 1881 the campaign against alcohol, by men and women, took on new intensity when Ohio passed a law requiring businesses to purchase licenses to sell beer. The first battle in what became known as the "Oberlin Temperance War" commenced when temperance activists employed disruptive tactics against Oberlin establishments that had bought such permits. Male and, more commonly, female "crusaders" systematically visited places where beer was now being openly sold and prayed over drinkers as they sought their conversions, thus interfering with commercial operations. Three of the businesses targeted were located on the perimeter of the town's heavily African American southeast quadrant: a "grocery store" operated on South Main Street by William Sheldon, a saloon near the railway station run by Alfred M. Talley, and John H. Broadwell's Forest House.⁴⁸

Temperance women charged that Sheldon's grocery attracted "drunken men ... late at night."⁴⁹ Their male temperance allies agreed, alleging that Sheldon spiked his cider with "disorderly alcohol."⁵⁰ For his part, Talley had taken over a longstanding nuisance that housed billiard tables, which temperance advocates viewed as invitations to gamble, an immoral activity they tied to inevitable inebriation.⁵¹ In addition Talley possessed an unsavory reputation; a white man married to a woman of color, he had allegedly been a slave driver before the Civil War.⁵² As for Broadwell, by selling alcohol at a tavern near the railroad station, he maintained the sordid tradition begun by Chauncey Wack, the Democratic gadfly who helped slave hunters track down freedom seeker John Price in 1858. Besides these three proprietors, temperance activists also targeted Thad Rowland, who had bought out Avery's drugstore near the center of town, where he sold tobacco as well as alcohol and had reportedly installed a billiard table.⁵³

Oberlin's temperance activists were ambitious; they sought to shut down all three of the recently opened saloons and to monitor carefully the sale of intoxicants at all of the town's drugstores—not just Rowland's but also J. M.

Gardner's and the Harmon and Beecher partnership. Originally activists had been willing to allow druggists to sell alcohol for medicinal and mechanical purposes, but in August 1881 Oberlin's temperance movement took a radical turn when, at the urging of Mary A. Keep, the Temperance Alliance embraced a policy opposing *all* sales of alcohol whatsoever within the town.[54] Subsequent crusading by temperance advocates secured Talley's agreement to close his saloon, although his pledge would prove short-lived. Sheldon and Broadwell also expressed a willingness to cooperate, though their actions, too, would soon belie their words. Most surprising was Rowland's agreement to a total ban on the sale of intoxicants. He made it conditional upon all his fellow druggists accepting the same embargo, and when they did so on September 3, Oberlin officially became fully "dry."[55]

But not for long. Druggist E. N. Beecher was forced to apologize when he was found to have sold a bottle of Hostetter's Bitters, a concoction that was more than 44 percent alcohol.[56] Sheldon was discovered drunk and selling liquor in October, and Talley's "club" reopened in December.[57] More worrisome was news that Thad Rowland had sold his establishment to Frank Bronson of neighboring Elyria, who declared that he was not bound by the pledge to cease the sale of alcohol since he had not signed it.[58] Temperance leaders rightfully suspected that the arrangement was a subterfuge and that Rowland still controlled the enterprise. When Giles Shurtleff, E. J. Goodrich, and Levi Whitney visited Bronson in early January 1882 and pleaded with him to stop dispensing alcohol, Bronson remained intransigent.[59]

At the mass meeting that soon followed, an angry Shurtleff drew a dire picture of the effect that Bronson's liquor sales were having in Oberlin: "Farms mortgaged . . . children in distress, and families in want," he grimly asserted, adding, "Some have recently left, confirmed drunkards." He compared Bronson to the "pirate wreckers who give false lights on the shore during a storm, in order to lure vessels into the rocks," and he expressed special outrage that the drugstore "held out to boys, who are here away from home and parental influence, the temptation to drink and gamble."[60] Other equally passionate speeches followed. Reverend James Brand warned, "God defeats every such effort to oppose the spirit of temperance." James Monroe asked the audience directly, "Are your young men safe in Oberlin?" Professor Judson Smith declared, "This is warfare." Methodist pastor A. D. Knapp ominously hinted, "A community has a right to defend itself. In cases of necessity it may resort to extraordinary measures."[61]

If the rhetoric was relentless, so were the subsequent visits by teams of men and women who descended upon Bronson's business every hour it was open. Modifying previous "crusading" tactics, these temperance activists promised to reason with Bronson, not to stay and pray. Nonetheless, Bronson charged that he was threatened by a "mob." The visitors might not openly pray, but they were not silent. Women "conversed with loungers and distributed religious and temperance literature," effectively "thinning out [Bronson's] customers."[62] The prospect of violence loomed. When Bronson burned red pepper in his stove to chase away "crusaders," a melee broke out and a window was shattered to let in fresh air.[63] During other "crusader" visits, Bronson reputedly "laid hands on one lady and pushed her out the door," while an elderly man was also treated roughly.[64]

Insisting that he had a right to defend himself, Bronson hired as his protectors the notorious "Durham boys," who—according to his opponents— "were glad to assist him in insulting his temperance visitors."[65] The Durhams were members of an Oberlin family of color long viewed as disgraceful by the town's "respectable" citizens. Sixteen-year-old Butler Durham was described as "a regular bull-dog ... ready to pound any man that came across his path."[66] When constable Frank Stone had sought to arrest Butler in May 1881, Butler's brother Tom had tried to shield him and was grazed by a bullet fired by Stone. In response, Samuel Durham, Butler and Tom's father, shot Stone, who lingered for a month before succumbing to his injury.[67] Not surprisingly, most Oberlinians sought to steer clear of the Durhams.

Bronson's decision to hire the Durham brothers escalated a tense situation and complicated the Oberlin Temperance War's racial dynamics. When local authorities asked for volunteers to serve as deputy marshals to help keep the peace by sitting outside Bronson's drugstore, black temperance advocates Henry Lee and John H. Scott were among those who swiftly answered the call.[68] Yet on February 20, 1882, the *Cleveland Leader* published an article charging that "the negroes of Oberlin and the renegade whites" supported the sale of alcohol at Bronson's establishment. Outraged by this "deliberate falsehood and slander," an Oberlinian writing under the pen name "JUSTICE" fired back that the *Leader*'s anonymous author was "a great deal worse than Southern Ku Klux or White Leaguers, who will on some occasions take life, but never stigmatize your honor, character and fair name." Although JUSTICE acknowledged "that there are some few colored people who get their drink at the 'historic' drug store," he insisted that in Oberlin a "majority of the colored people are good temperance men and women . . . and would like to see this evil wiped out of the community."[69]

Students at Oberlin College were also on edge. Dan F. Bradley, a member of the college's senior class and editor of the student newspaper, invoked Oberlin's heritage of civil disobedience in denouncing Bronson's drugstore. "In Anti-slavery times, Oberlin tackled the United States and downed it, and now Bronson must be driven out," Bradley proclaimed.[70] Likewise, in an open letter to the druggist, members of the freshman class insisted that laws supporting Bronson's business "have no authority over decent men or in good society." "Your zeal for Law . . . seems dressed in a suit of gray," they charged, comparing Bronson to Confederate rebels in the Civil War.[71] In fact, college students had already taken direct action against alcohol. Previously, they had physically dismantled a potential saloon on the outskirts of town before its scheduled opening. Then, on another occasion, the windows of an established saloon were mysteriously broken and the kegs of liquor moved to the street, where their contents were tapped into the gutters.[72] On the temperance question, as on the antislavery question in earlier times, Oberlin College students were prepared to obey a higher law.

With such violent excitement in the air, Giles Shurtleff in early 1882 concluded that "the enthusiasm had reached as high a pitch as was useful," and, in an effort to contain the potentially ominous passions, the Oberlin Temperance Alliance began to explore a new legal strategy for shutting down Bronson's establishment without provoking violence. Shurtleff personally financed undercover "detective work" to gather evidence against the drugstore, and the alliance raised funds to bring a court case against Bronson.[73] Students and townspeople eagerly subscribed to a fund "for the vigorous prosecution of the temperance work in this village," and the Oberlin Temperance Alliance examined laws that might permit them to close Bronson's establishment.[74] But the *Cleveland Leader* had already prophesized a more radical outcome. At the end of February it published a special supplement entitled *The Whole Story: History of the Oberlin Temperance War*. The twenty-page, double-columned document fervently supported the anti-alcohol crusaders. Its tenth and final chapter carried the heading "Exit of Rowland From Oberlin—Universal Joy." Under this heading, the *Leader* portentously announced: "This chapter will be published as an appendix at an early date."[75]

Amid these heightened tensions, Oberlin's great fire ignited on March 6,

1882. When the smoke cleared, pressing questions came into focus. Who were the arsonists who had taken the law into their own hands to rid the town of Bronson's drugstore? Why had the "first responder" to the scene, a man of color, been discouraged by the fire chief from using buckets of water to douse what then seemed only a small fire?[76] Was the offer of a reward for information about the fire's origins evidence of temperance reformers' remorse?

Although answers proved elusive, the Oberlin Temperance Alliance subsequently moved away from the direct action of "crusading." Going forward, its members shifted their energies to focus almost exclusively on electoral work. In so doing, they accelerated a process already in motion that would consign African American concerns about racial discrimination to a secondary place in Oberlin politics. In addition, as the men of the alliance sought greater power at the polls, they forced their unenfranchised female associates into a clearly subordinate position within the local temperance movement. No longer at the center of action on temperance, women charted their own, independent direction, which ultimately led them to "scientific charity," with its distinctly racial implications.

This new phase opened decisively on March 27, 1882, when the Ohio legislature passed the Metcalf bill, named for George P. Metcalf—Oberlin's representative to the Ohio General Assembly—which granted incorporated municipalities "having within their limits a college or university . . . the power to provide by ordinance against the evils resulting from the sale of intoxicating liquor within the corporation limits."[77] Many celebrated the expanded authority to banish liquor from Oberlin's sacred soil. But not every Oberlin anti-alcohol activist joined in the jubilation, and although the divisions were primarily among white prohibitionists, they had profound repercussions for Oberlin's people of color.

Divisions within the local temperance movement increasingly separated supporters of the upstart Prohibition Party, who insisted on a total ban on alcohol in all its forms and in all places, from steadfast Republicans, who were prepared to compromise on temperance legislation in order to maintain harmony with "wets" in their party with the hope of eventually luring them into the temperance fold. Prohibitionists did not trust Republicans' willingness to embrace partial and gradual means of restricting the sale of liquor, including "high license," which required payment of a tax or license fee heavy enough to discourage most would-be sellers; they also disliked the "local option," which allowed individual communities to proscribe the sale of alcohol without banishing its distribution in neighboring towns, to which sinners might easily resort. Prohibition purists believed, in the words of local activist Croydon Tambling, that "God has forsaken the National Republican party."⁷⁸ As a variety of local option, the Metcalf law offended the moral absolutism of Oberlin's most ardent prohibitionists.

But loyal Republicans like James Monroe argued that rational temperance men should enlist with the Republican Party in order to move "the great mass of Republican voters . . . into active sympathy with the Temperance work." He charged that the unrealistic demands and feeble party apparatus of the Prohibitionists precluded their success, while the Republican Party remained "a great temple dedicated to patriotism and liberty." Invoking the party's antislavery heritage, Monroe declared, "Its walls are hung with broken chains and manacles from the freed limbs of millions of emancipated slaves. Do not leave such a temple! . . . The mothers and wives and daughters of men freed from the bondage of drink will soon bring, with glad tears, their disenthralled fathers and husbands and sons to join the happy assembly."⁷⁹ A longtime political champion of racial egalitarianism, Monroe rhetorically joined together freedom from drink and freedom from slavery.

While the Republicans used analogies, the Prohibition Party had its own, more direct, take on race. Its supporters charged that intemperance represented a "fearful peril to the colored population" and was a central cause of Reconstruction's failure.⁸⁰ Some men of color found this analysis persuasive, and the national Prohibition Party conventions always included a small number of black delegates. Locally, John H. Scott, Wilson Bruce Evans, and Henry Lee all embraced the party, which had the advantage of allowing them, at the same time, to demonstrate their political independence from the Republicans.⁸¹

In the fall of 1883, a constitutional amendment to prohibit the sale of alcohol throughout Ohio appeared on the state ballot. Although voters supporting prohibition prevailed numerically by a resounding margin of 323,189 to 240,975, because passage of a state constitutional amendment required the support of more than half of all *qualified* voters—not merely those who actually cast ballots—the measure failed.⁸² At the same time, Prohibition Party candidates drew votes away from Republicans running for state offices, so in 1884 Democrats swept to power in Ohio, winning the governorship and control of both houses of the General Assembly despite their longstanding opposition to temperance legislation.⁸³

For much of the 1880s, Ohio's Democrats profited from the Prohibitionists' political strength; they also benefited from a segment of African American voters alienated from the Republicans. At the state level, Democrats promised to reward support from people of color by backing civil rights legislation and school integration. Yet it took most of the decade, and a contested election that ultimately seated a new Republican majority in the state legislature in 1886, to finally accomplish these goals, including repeal of Ohio's twenty-five-year-old prohibition on interracial marriage.[84] Ironically, however, in Oberlin, once the epicenter of agitation for racial equality, the statewide contests over civil rights were eclipsed by the battle over alcohol.

In this complicated political environment, Oberlin's dry Republicans gradually came to recognize the need for collaboration with Prohibitionists across party lines, at both the local and state levels. Finally, in March 1893 Oberlinians from the two parties came together to create a new temperance organization: the Ohio Anti-Liquor League. Soon renamed the Ohio Anti-Saloon League, the new organization "unite[d] the churches and all the temperance people in an effort to awaken and interest and secure wise action destroying the open saloon and securing individual total abstinence."[85] Officially nonpartisan, it provided a fresh opportunity for Republicans to demonstrate their temperance credentials while they enlisted Prohibitionist support on a sustained, institutional basis.

To signal the Anti-Saloon League's partisan inclusiveness, ardent Prohibitionist Azariah Smith Root, the Oberlin College librarian, sat on the platform alongside Republican hero Giles Shurtleff at the new organization's first public meeting.[86] However, if the Anti-Saloon League brought together members of different political parties, in other respects it was exclusionary. Whereas the Oberlin Temperance Alliance included prominent black as well as white men in its original roster, there were no African Americans among the Anti-Saloon League's founding leadership, though some may have enlisted as members at large. (Unfortunately, no membership list survives.)[87] Nor were there any women in leadership positions. Oberlin's female temperance activists continued to fight the scourge of alcohol through their own gender-segregated—and white-dominated—organizations, and they plotted an independent political course.

But the women, too, had problematic politics to navigate. Oberlin's temperance women had participated in the 1874 Cleveland convention that founded the Woman's Christian Temperance Union (WCTU), but they insisted on their local autonomy.⁸⁸ In so doing, they permitted themselves latitude with respect to the two most fraught and intertwined issues: race and partisan politics. The Oberlin Ladies Temperance League ignored the recommendation of the National WCTU in 1882 that local unions establish separate units within each neighborhood church, a plan that might have promoted outreach to black churchwomen but would also have reinscribed racial segregation since Oberlin's congregations were arranged largely along racial lines.⁸⁹ But the league's action probably was not motivated by a concern for integration. As it had before the temperance war, in the years that followed, the organization included a handful of well-to-do women of color, most notably Congregational Church members Maria Alexander Gibbs and Eliza Colwell Evans, sister-in-law of Henry and Wilson Bruce Evans. But it still did not reach out to the large number of African American women who participated enthusiastically in the lives of the black churches. With their standing in First Church and their unimpeachable respectability, Mrs. Gibbs and Mrs. Evans were, for most purposes, treated as white.

With impressive racial insensitivity, early in 1884 the organization offered to send ten teachers to Oberlin's African American Rust Church to instruct the congregation in temperance. Rust Church did not respond.⁹⁰ Later that year, word reached Oberlin that Frances E. W. Harper—a renowned African American author, equal rights activist, and national organizer of "colored sections" for the WCTU—"desired to come here and work among the colored people." League members had no difficulty in arranging for Harper to give a lecture at First Church, but by their own account, they were uncertain whether the town's "colored people were interested" in hearing her. To try to build an audience for the event, they contacted a black minister, visited an African American Sabbath school, and did "what they could to speak to the colored people."⁹¹ While the turnout for Harper's talk proved satisfactory, league members expressed disappointment afterward that the event did not result in the formation of a local temperance organization "for colored sisters."⁹² They also spoke about their desire to do uplift work "among our colored people."⁹³ In the minds of Oberlin's white temperance women, racial encounters took place largely between patrons and clients, not between equals.

The temperance women demonstrated a similar gracelessness in their approach to politics. When, in 1880, the National WCTU embraced woman suffrage—"the ballot for protection of her home"—Oberlin's affiliate remained silent. Two years later, Oberlinian Lucy Thompson returned from the state WCTU convention enthusiastically reporting "three words summed up the whole: Agitate, Educate, Legislate," but she did not mention Frances Willard's declaration of alliance with the Prohibition Party.[94] Many of Oberlin's temperance women continued to think conservatively about partisan political engagement, seeing their public role, if any, as reinforcing actions calculated to strengthen home-based maternal morality. They supported legislative interventions, but they did not necessarily embrace a direct role for women in lawmaking, which many thought would be accomplished better by men who could translate women's passions into legislative initiatives. Moreover, strident embrace of suffrage or of party politics threatened to split their local union. The National WCTU stand—first, on woman suffrage, and second, on party affiliation—endangered relationships with male temperance allies in Oberlin, who, themselves, stood divided on the question of female enfranchisement and for the most part remained loyal to the Republican Party.

Oberlin's temperance women undertook their first, cautious foray into the electoral arena in October 1883, when they mobilized on behalf of a proposed prohibition amendment to the state constitution. They did not push for the vote for themselves, or for any particular party. Rather, on election day they took shifts sitting at the polls in the "Hook and Ladder room" at the town hall, which they festooned "in a very tasteful style with carpets, curtains, banners, mottos, mirrors, and pictures." Perhaps in competition with the free meals characteristically offered by saloons, the women set up "an attractive lunch table," supplied food, and even provided ballots for the convenience of the all-male electorate.[95] Domesticating the site of the election, they brought to it their maternal concern.

Although local temperance men generally welcomed female support for the prohibition amendment, many did not endorse women's direct participation in the voting process. Prohibition Party leader William Goodell Frost, for example, found the notion of political women deeply distasteful and adamantly opposed woman suffrage.[96] His colleague Croydon Tambling was hardly more enthusiastic.[97] Yet Prohibitionist Azariah Smith Root spoke out publicly in favor women's right to vote. Republican temperance men were similarly split over the woman suffrage question. As the *Oberlin News* observed, "woman suffragists are not all Prohibitionists, neither all Prohibitionists woman suffragists."[98]

Some local temperance women who supported Frances Willard's positions pressed their quest for the right to vote so that they might use their political power to effect the total prohibition of alcohol. In the spring of 1887, now openly identifying itself as the Oberlin Woman's Christian Temperance Union, this group organized a "sham" election to demonstrate their capacity to cast ballots as responsible citizens and make known their party preferences. Forty women participated, and when the results were tallied, votes for the Prohibition Party outnumbered those for the Republican, thirty-two to eight.[99] Oberlin women "voted" again in the fall of 1887, and in both the spring and fall of 1888.[100] In all these contests, the Prohibition Party prevailed overwhelmingly among female participants.[101]

Oberlin women with Republican sympathies worried about the WCTU's alliance with the Prohibitionist Party, and in 1888 they split from the organization's local chapter to form "a new organization ... which can unite all women interested in temperance reform, whatever may be their party sympathies."[102] Members of this self-styled Non-Partisan Woman's Christian Temperance Union (NPWCTU) expressed regret at the "unhappy divisions of the late years, which have so crippled the efforts of the union," and they made overtures to supporters of the regular WCTU to engage in joint meetings.[103] But the institutional split endured for many years.[104]

Significantly, neither of Oberlin's female temperance organizations took a position on the controversy that broke out at the WCTU's national convention in Cleveland in November 1894, when African American activist Ida B. Wells demanded that Frances Willard explicitly renounce lynching and recant her remarks about how, inflamed by liquor, southern black men sexually attacked white women.[105] Willard had special ties to Oberlin: as a young child, she had lived in the town for a half-dozen years while her parents pursued their educations at the college, and she liked to cite this pedigree as proof of her racial enlightenment.[106] But when Wells challenged Willard on this score, Oberlin's temperance women chose not to involve themselves in the dispute. Nonetheless, in May 1895 the *Oberlin News* published a lengthy defense of Willard signed by, among others, the recently deceased black abolitionist Frederick Douglass.[107] Six months later "several Loyal White Ribboners" (as members of the WCTU styled themselves) complained to the paper that Wells "refused to be convinced" by the Union's "Christian sympathy" for "the negro."[108] By remaining mute during this controversy, Oberlin's female temperance organizations signaled a lack of engagement in the ongoing struggle waged by people of color.

In March 1885, Oberlin's white temperance women again demonstrated insensitivity to racial politics. Under the terms of a new state statute, women for the first time could participate in the election of Ohio local school board members—both as voters and as candidates. Even for social conservatives, voting on matters pertaining to the education of children transgressed no gender boundaries, but instead empowered women to act more effectively on their maternal concerns. At a "mass meeting of the women of Oberlin" called to identify a female candidate, the participants chose as their nominee Oberlin-born and Oberlin-educated Alice Mead Swing, a thirty-nine-year-old white mother of three whose late father had been among the founders of the Oberlin Temperance Alliance and whose widowed mother was then serving as the tenth president of Mount Holyoke College.[109] While Swing was undoubtedly well qualified for a seat on the Oberlin School Board, her supporters ignored the racial dimension of the forthcoming contest. Already standing for the position was African American barber William T. Henderson, who had come forward "as a representative of the colored people" of the Oberlin community. In the wake of Swing's nomination, Henderson withdrew his candidacy, and Swing easily won the March election.[110] Swing's victory represented a political milestone for Oberlin women, but it came at the expense of the town's African American residents.

Women's activism in late nineteenth-century Oberlin often had racial implications, even when it lacked a consciously racial focus, with no arena more significant than mobilizations for benevolence. Stimulated by conversations with her housekeeper, a young woman who had been born a slave in Washington, D.C., Mary Burton Shurtleff in 1878 helped to found the Oberlin Freed Woman's Aid Society, associated with First Church.[111] After interest in this society waned, it merged with the Home Missionary Society in 1882 to become the Ladies Aid Society of First Church. Under this organizational rubric, women provided "help irrespective of race, place or previous condition: sending supplies to colored people in the South, to Mission Indians in the West, ... to the Bohemian Mission in Cleveland, and to the needy in our town and church." Their efforts connected them to Christian activists around the world as they prepared "outfits for missionaries to China, Japan, Africa, and the Isles of the sea ... [and] carpets for missionaries in Turkey." In 1891, the Ladies Aid Society boasted a membership of 150.[112] Discussing the plight of people of color in Hannibal, Missouri, and distressed by news of lynchings in Memphis, they projected their concerns about racial inequality outward. Oberlin was not their primary focus for action.[113] Although they declared—perhaps apologetically—that "the poor in our own community have to some extent been remembered," they ignored the racial divide that was reflected in the town's enduring economic disparities.[114]

One prominent female reformer, however, focused her attention on local needs: Julia Finney Monroe, a daughter of Reverend Charles Grandison Finney and wife of Oberlin College professor and Republican politician James Monroe. In 1888, drawing on her experience in the local WCTU and the Ladies Aid Society, Monroe sent inquiries to the Associated Charities of Boston, the Brooklyn Bureau of Charities, and other big-city organizations asking for information about "scientific charity." A recent innovation in the systematic administration of private relief, scientific charity advocated coordination among benevolent groups to prevent "double-dipping" by those who applied for assistance, and championed work-based relief to prepare the poor for self-reliance.[115] Impressed by what she learned from her inquiries, Monroe—with the financial help of other elite local women—reshaped the humble Oberlin Citizens Aid Society into a "scientific" enterprise, complete with a new, urban-sounding name: the Associated Charities of Oberlin.[116]

The core of the new organization was its "Friendly Visitors" program, which enlisted at its inception forty-eight women volunteers, all members of the town's white Protestant churches. Friendly Visitors physically entered clients' homes "not only to relieve but *improve*."[117] The Associated Charities provided its clients with physical locations for gendered work: a wood yard for men and a laundry room for women, both offering wages below "the price usually paid" in the belief that this arrangement would incentivize—and thereby speed the transition to—self-reliance.[118] After two years, Monroe boasted, "perhaps *one half* of the *indiscriminate* alms giving of the town has stopped."[119] Applying a version of her evangelical father's belief that individuals could and should find their own salvation, she sought to eliminate "the expectation that, when want pinches . . . the benevolence that has helped in the past will do so in the future. Is it not the proper answer in such cases, 'If any will not work neither shall he eat'?"[120] Monroe's Associated Charities ensured that work, and with it redemption, was available to all—that is, all who were willing to allow the well-meaning white women to judge and direct their lives.

Race shaped the work of Associated Charities most obviously in the composition of its board, which soon reached across lines of gender but remained all white, as was its agent, Reverend Richard Hicks.[121] Although Associated Charities claimed to "represent all the Christian denominations of the town," the churches it cited as affiliates did not include the black congregations.[122] Yet the laundry room and wood yard were both located in neighborhoods with high concentrations of African Americans. Perhaps race also shaped the group's instructional strategy. In order to turn the minds of the female clients from "petty thoughts or gossip," they heard, while working, readings from "ancient parables or modern tales—in such volumes as the New Testament or Uncle Tom's Cabin," the latter considered black literature by the end of the century.[123]

With little reflection, the white members of the organization intruded in black lives. When George Dyer, an African American widower, lay terminally ill, the all-white board took charge of arrangements for his children, including assessing the appropriateness of a family that sought to adopt Dyer's son Willie.[124] In another case, the board arranged for their white agent to become the guardian of the wayward African American McConico boys.[125] Likewise, the board unilaterally removed the black "little Hudnell girl four year of age" from "a disordered [and] an immoral" home.[126] There is no indication that board members ever questioned their fitness to make such decisions, nor evidence of consultations with neighbors, families, or any people of color. Yet in the spring of 1892, when considering a "plan of securing a person to work as a city missionary among the colored people," board members admitted that "the question was not one properly belonging to the society" because they lacked sufficient familiarity with the African American community.[127]

Significantly, this demurral took place at the same moment that a fledgling black Baptist congregation was developing plans to build a new church in the heart of Oberlin's southeast quadrant, the neighborhood where people of color increasingly resided. The church initiative proved surprisingly divisive. Reminiscent of the debate over the founding of Second Methodist Episcopal Church (later renamed Rust Methodist Episcopal Church), the controversy began when an Oberlin College student objected that such a church would "draw the color line [that] savors so much of the Southern prejudice which is so opposed in principle."[128] The pastor of the town's white Baptist church, Reverend C. J. Rose, responded that, on the contrary, a black Baptist church would perform "much needed work." Mary J. Blake, the African American superintendent of the congregation's Sunday school, agreed, arguing that the church would enhance people's "moral welfare."[129]

Into this fray stepped Reverend Daniel Webster Shaw, who only recently had been lured away from his pastorate at Rust Methodist Episcopal to serve as minister of an African American Congregational church in Cleveland. Born in Louisiana to a free black mother and white father, Shaw studied theology at Oberlin College and in 1888 married the daughter of a prominent local family.[130] During his three years at Rust, he galvanized the congregation, instituting a literary society that offered public performances of Shakespeare, organizing a young people's society, using his own musical talents to promote large choral presentations, and forming an unabashedly Republican men's political club.[131] Now he bluntly charged that "Oberlin's white churches are not doing nor can they do the Christian work which ought to be done among the colored people as a mass." Shaw argued that "the colored people can do more for God and humanity in their own churches than in white churches," and he pushed hard against what he saw as white Oberlin's inexcusable inaction in the face of racial inequality. Criticizing the college in particular, he declared, "on every hand, Oberlin is pressed with the question 'What are you doing for your colored people?' The question is spoken louder and louder every year. . . . At present Oberlin makes an apology for existing circumstances among her colored people. She cannot answer. . . . She looks into space, puts her index finger to her lips, and observes—silence."[132] For Shaw, as for the white Baptist minister C. J. Rose, the construction of another church for people of color would be "placing this people upon a moral equality with the best elements of the place."[133] With these endorsements, the work to build Mount Zion Baptist Church in Oberlin went forward and Reverend B. B. Hill assumed its pastorate.[134]

Two years later, when Reverend H. M. Tenney, pastor of the Second Congregational Church, raised the alarm that "one hundred men and women, not all black or white" were "debauching the innocent" in Oberlin, Reverend Hill joined with other pastors and leading local officials in sponsoring a "Law and Order" meeting to address the crisis.[135] Yet Hill's analysis diverged significantly from those of his peers. Rust pastor R. L. Dickinson read from I Corinthians 5, the biblical chapter on fornication and sexual immorality, and Reverend Tenney lectured the meeting about "the apparent increasing laxity on the part of the people and the increasing energy on the part of evil doers." Police justice Alfred Fauver expressed himself "astonished at the amount of crime in Oberlin," while the pastor of the First Methodist Church argued for "a higher standard of public sentiment in favor of enforcement of the law." Most ominously, Reverend James Brand of First Church declared, "The argument to be used with a mob is not religious appeals but cannon."[136]

In the midst of these pronouncements, Reverend Hill struck a different note. Reflecting on his two years in town, he affirmed, "Oberlin is better than many places, but not as good in some respects as it ought to be." He observed that "certain portions [of the town] are neglected in the matter of sidewalks, waterworks and light," concluding, "if we want people to respect law we must show them we have respect for them."[137] Hill made a valid point. When stone sidewalks were laid in 1893, all-white residential streets on the west side— such as Elm and Forest—were included, but Groveland, Mechanic, South Pleasant, and South Water Street in the southeast quadrant were not.[138] Oberlin's 1894 sewer project, and even its 1902 expansion, concentrated on Oberlin's west side, leaving much of the southeast quadrant untouched.[139] Hill argued that equal services would promote a sense of justice among Oberlin's diverse citizenry.

Doubtless, Hill also knew that Oberlin's African Americans were overrepresented in local arrest records, a purported gauge of the town's "evil doers." According to the census, blacks comprised approximately one-sixth of Oberlin's total population in the 1890s. Yet in January 1895 the *Oberlin News* reported that forty-three of the ninety-five people arrested in Oberlin the year before—45 percent—were people of color. Although arrests for liquor violations were distributed proportionally by race, 63 percent of those arrested for the crime of "disturbance" were African American, suggesting that the arrest *rate* for blacks for that particular offense was roughly four times as high as the rate for whites.[140] Moreover, the numbers reported by the *News* were part of a larger trend. Between 1887 and 1897, the Oberlin Mayor's Court logged almost seven hundred arrests. Record linkage reveals that at least one-third of the liquor violations were charged to persons of color, as were minimally just under half of the bookings for assault, drunkenness, and disorder.[141] Yet these figures should not be taken at face value as proof of black social pathology since in Oberlin, as elsewhere, white prejudice and differential policing doubtlessly contributed to the pattern of black criminalization.[142] Still, when Reverend Brand of First Church spoke of deploying cannon against "the mob," the people he had in mind were disproportionately African Americans.

Julia Finney Monroe and her female allies turned to education rather than criminalization or violence as their preferred method of social control, at least for those they thought still capable of salvation. As a local female temperance leader tartly remarked, "[O]ur aim should be not to save the drunkard but to save the youth by building up character and Christian principle."[143] In 1896 the Associated Charities joined with the WCTU and other groups to form the Mutual Benefit Association and create what would soon become Oberlin's own settlement house. Through a gift from Medora Eliza Wack Peck, the do-gooder daughter of the now deceased Democrat and provocateur Chauncey Wack, the Mutual Benefit Association came to own the Centennial Building on South Main Street, which had previously housed William Jenkins's infamous doggery. As one local resident commented, "The old Centennial building was for years a menace to the peace and good order of the village. Now it is a blessing to the town and a promoter of all that is good and uplifting."[144]

The racial implications of establishing an outpost of the Associated Charities in the Centennial Building were clear. As soon as possible, the "enterprising women" of the Mutual Benefit Association installed a kindergarten, which, they earnestly declared, performed the "most important work" by teaching "the little ones . . . self-control and self-discipline." While the Centennial kindergarten was the third such school established since the founding of the Oberlin Kindergarten Association in 1894, it was the only one located in Oberlin's increasingly African American southeast quadrant.

Previously kindergarten classes had been held at Rust Church, and African American councilman Charles H. Glenn had been known for transporting children there.[145] But Rust stopped offering classes when the Mutual Benefit Association inaugurated its kindergarten in the Centennial Building. Members of the association boasted that the new setting was far superior: "This bright, sunny room is a great improvement over the Rust church, which was quite unsuited to the needs of Kindergarten work." At Rust, daily attendance had averaged twenty-three youngsters, two-thirds of them black. At the new location, fifty-three students attended, half of them children of color and "most of them a new element not before reached." The leaders of the Kindergarten Association expressed interest in opening another school "somewhere near Rust," commenting, "The improvement in the thoughts, conversations, habits and lives of the children after attending kindergarten is usually so marked that this community cannot afford to be without the influence of a kindergarten in that district."[146] Yet no Oberlin children from "that district" or any other in Oberlin would ever see a teacher of color. As the Kindergarten Association evolved into the Oberlin Kindergarten Training School—eventually certifying 711 teachers between 1894 and 1923—only 6 graduates, or less than 1 percent, would be women of color, and none of them ever taught in Oberlin.[147]

Kindergartens were designed to instill proper values in children at a very young age, when personal character was thought to be especially malleable. Kindergarten instruction took on great social significance in late nineteenth-century Oberlin as local leaders increasingly lost faith in their ability to shape the character and behavior of adults, either through religion or education. And while a large proportion of white Oberlinians still believed in racial equality in principle, in practice they increasingly associated blackness with poverty, drunkenness, and crime. The local newspaper they read during the 1890s was chock full of stories of illicit mayhem featuring a handful of infamous families of color.[148] In other ways, too, the press promoted an image of blacks as socially disreputable and morally irresponsible. Although the U.S. Supreme Court's *Plessy v. Ferguson* ruling in 1896 received no coverage in the *Oberlin News,* readers found on its pages disparaging articles with titles like "The Colored Brother: Not a Good Tenant for the Southern Landlord," which sympathized with white property-owners and their complaints about the supposed laziness of black workers. "Like his African ancestors," the *News* reported, "the American negro is miserable without jollifications and feasting," now carried on, it suggested, under the guise of church revival meetings.[149] Racial insults abounded. The disparaging term "n——" appeared with some frequency, and brief "filler" articles were often published in dialect as a mode of entertainment.[150] Evidently the newspaper's editor assumed that white Oberlinians were happy to laugh at the expense of their black neighbors.

A speech at the annual meeting of the Oberlin Temperance Alliance in January 1898 exemplified the tightening connection between blackness, drink, and disorder in the minds of whites. Gilbert Raynor, a white Oberlin College graduate who served as district secretary of the Ohio Anti-Saloon League, shocked his audience at First Church when he testified that he had obtained two bottles of liquor in Oberlin, on a Sunday, in the brief time between a YMCA meeting that he led in the late afternoon and the evening meeting at which he then stood.[151] Raynor went on to identify seven "gambling hells" operated by "Negroes," and he charged that "the colored people of Oberlin were the ones who bought liquor and patronized the beer wagon."

Raynor's allegations outraged longtime African American leader and prohibitionist John H. Scott. In a letter to the *Cleveland Gazette*, a black newspaper, Scott wrote, "I protest against all the colored people being classed together, so that when one does something wrong, all are blamed.... There are low whites as well as low colored people who drink, and there is a big majority of colored people who do not drink at all."[152] Scott's complaint could not erase the fact that in Oberlin color was increasingly a marker of social disorder tied in the "white imaginary" to the sins of drink and the drunkard.

However, white Oberlinians were seemingly oblivious to their role in promoting racist stereotypes. In June 1898, Rust Church pastor J. E. Wood objected that a presentation at the Oberlin Academy (formerly the college's preparatory department) entitled "The Negro in the South" ridiculed people of color as "ignorant and superstitious." Frances Hosford, an 1891 Oberlin College graduate then teaching at the institution, responded obtusely, "The Southern negro is undeniably and happily picturesque.... [B]efore the raciness has quite vanished, shall we find fault with those who try to catch and preserve it in literary forms?"[153] For Hosford, who would later write histories of Oberlin College's commitment to women's education, the impact of racial burlesque was a question about folklore, not a problem in the struggle for social justice.

By the end of 1898, when retired missionary Delavan Leonard published *The Story of Oberlin* to great applause, the stigmatization of blackness within the community was largely complete. Whereas Oberlin's antebellum abolitionists had denounced color prejudice and affirmed the principle of racial equality in opposition to reigning assumptions of white supremacy, Leonard expressed open contempt for the character and culture of most people of color residing in Oberlin. He divided the town's African American population "into three classes." "A considerable portion are intelligent, industrious, well-to-do, thoroughly respectable and in every way good citizens," he acknowledged. "A few are superior as blacksmiths, builders, etc." Yet, in Leonard's view, Oberlin's respectable persons of color were exceptions to the norm. "[T]o these are joined a considerably larger number of the unlettered, who are good-natured and well meaning and harmless, but only semi-industrious and seriously lacking forethought, ambition, and energy, content therefore to live from hand to mouth," Leonard wrote with racist condescension. "Then there is an over-large fraction composed of the shiftless and worthless, shading off into the vicious and criminal.... [T]heir craving is for animal indulgence, and being given to drink, petty thieving and related offences, are well known in the courtroom and the county jail."[154]

Leonard offered no comparable analysis of Oberlin's white population. Most likely he believed that some white townspeople were unambitious, shiftless, and worthless—but only a small minority. For Leonard the default assumption was that whiteness represented respectability and virtue, just as blackness represented depravity and vice. At the close of the nineteenth century, in Oberlin—as elsewhere in America—dark skin was a marker of indolence, intemperance, and social pathology. Respectability had been racialized. In the decades following abolition, Oberlin's color line had hardened and the effects of racial prejudice had become ever more insidious.

9

UTOPIA FORSAKEN

Shortly before noon on May 31, 1899, Henry Lee died from injuries sustained the previous day when a small building he was trying to move onto his property toppled over and crushed his sixty-three-year-old body. With his demise, Oberlin lost its last great militant voice for radical racial egalitarianism.[1] After Lee's death, African American leaders backed off from the confrontations that had characterized Lee's fight for rights, instead trying to leverage their own respectability in efforts to pursue racial justice both locally and nationally. At the same time, Oberlin's color line continued to harden. In the opening decades of the twentieth century the local economy stagnated, and the economic insecurity of most of Oberlin's people of color deepened. Concurrently, their erstwhile white allies no longer stepped up to denounce the brazen disregard for black rights that spread northward in the wake of the U.S. Supreme Court's affirmation of racial segregation in *Plessy v. Ferguson*. With the racialization of respectability and the growing stigmatization of blackness, white Oberlinians even lost their belief in the power of education to create a racially egalitarian social order, once a key component of Oberlin's utopian vision.

Throughout his life, Henry Lee agitated unremittingly for black rights and racial justice. Six months before his death he served as secretary to a meeting of "Colored Citizens" in Oberlin that protested the "frequent and brutal murder of colored citizens ... in North and South Carolina" and demanded the punishment of those guilty of this "high-handed barbarity." Citing "Negro bravery" in the Civil War and the more recent Spanish-American conflict, the meeting condemned the United States for failing to protect black citizens on their return from service, and specifically indicted the Republican Party for its inaction. Lee subsequently appealed to foreign rulers for "aid and protection for the colored people of the United States against Mob violence."[2]

Lee had never been conventionally "upright." He embroiled Oberlin's black Methodist church in controversy, resulting in his physical ejection from its building and expulsion from the congregation.[3] He quarreled endlessly with municipal officials about his livery service.[4] He was accused of beating his wife.[5] He was unapologetically confrontational, tirelessly pursuing his own interests—in church, at the railroad station, in the "eating room" he opened during the 1883 Jubilee of the college, and at his fancifully named "Consolation Skatorial Toboggaganonal [sic] Park"—and he refused to be cowed by influential enemies.[6]

Lee fought tirelessly for black education. While he had not been able to pursue his own studies much beyond the preparatory department at Oberlin, he pressed for the interests of others. Two of his Oberlin College-educated daughters became notable educators in the South, and Lee raised money for the Freedman's Western Education Society, the outfit that sponsored them.[7] More provocatively, in 1892 he criticized the Oberlin College Board of Trustees for allegedly mishandling a bequest made twenty-five years earlier for the purpose of providing free tuition to needy students of color. "We respectfully demand justice, equity and fairness in behalf of the poor, weak and defenceless colored student," he told the trustees. "And we believe that every consideration of honor demands with us, that this great College accord to him his full meed [sic] of impartial and exact justice."[8] Nor was the college Lee's only local institutional target. In 1894, he called on the Oberlin School Board to remove from use Charles F. King's *Picturesque Geographical Reader* "because of sentences in it which tend to lower respect for the Afro-American."[9]

Lee demanded respect for himself and his race, but he refused to abide by the mainstream norms of respectability. At his funeral he was remembered as "a man of a good deal of natural ability . . . [who] took great interest in defending the rights of his race." Yet mourners agreed that he possessed a difficult personality. With regard to Lee's "faults," the officiating cleric "advised all to have charity."[10] In Lee's mind, human rights were inherent in personhood, not dependent on the performance of social roles according to a particular code of proper behavior. But he lived—and died—at a moment when most of Oberlin's prominent African Americans took a different approach. In the wake of the racialization of respectability that accompanied the ascendance of the temperance movement in late nineteenth-century Oberlin, they sought to reclaim respectability for themselves and to use their respectability as a lever by which to raise the status of others of their race. For proof of the success of their strategy in the postwar era, they could point to the presence of a black man on the elected town council during all but three years between 1870 and 1897.

In marked contrast to Henry Lee, the Oberlinians of color who served as councilmen in the late nineteenth century satisfied whites' expectations of social respectability. They were recognized and praised for their hard work, economic success, moral character, and social decency. William T. Henderson, who sat on the town council between 1872 and 1876, distinguished himself as a steady and "highly esteemed" barber with a shop on East College Street for over fifty years. A longstanding member of First Church, Henderson also served as a superintendent in the fledgling Mount Zion congregation.[11] The next black man to sit on the council was Arthur Wellington Mitchell, a painter and paperhanger who had arrived in Oberlin before the Civil War and, like Henderson, worshipped at First Church. His daughter later married John Patterson Green, the highly influential African American politician and office holder from Cleveland.[12] After Mitchell came Andrew Jackson, a skilled carriage maker who argued against Henry Lee's position that black people should desert the Republican Party.[13] George Mathewson Glenn followed Jackson onto the council. Known as "the college barber," he was called by a friend and patron "the most perfect gentleman he had ever had the pleasure of knowing."[14]

William Madison Mitchell, Glenn's successor in the council's black seat, was one of the few Prohibition Party members to win election in Oberlin. Born to free parents in antebellum North Carolina, he was a deacon at First Church and a "true soldier of God, standing up in the face of all misfortunes and opposition." He painted houses for a living and demonstrated that the virtuous would be rewarded for hard work.[15] The next African American councilman was Charles H. Glenn, George's son, who served three terms, beginning in 1891 and ending in 1897. The younger Glenn was the gifted designer and builder of many of the elegant houses on the rapidly developing west side of town. When he decided not to stand for a fourth council election in 1897, he urged the Republican caucus to name his business partner, Frederick Copeland, to succeed him. The nomination went instead to Thomas Nixon Carver.[16]

An economics professor at Oberlin, Carver had completed his Ph.D. at Cornell before arriving in Oberlin in 1894; he took up a temporary appointment that was eventually extended, resigning in 1902 to move to Harvard. In the spring of his first year at Oberlin, Carver wrote to a friend at Trinity College in North Carolina—later renamed Duke University—declining the friend's offer "to send us a N.C. negro boy" and revealing his view of race in Oberlin. "Oberlin has too many negroes now and if we were to be the means of adding to their number we should lose our position sure [sic]," he declared. Noting that Oberlin been a stop on the Underground Railroad, he asserted that the town "became, in later days, a negro paradise." Yet Carver decried the current situation. "Oberlin now has her nemesis in the form of a considerable negro population," he reported. "There are some good ones, but there are a lot of shiftless vagabonds among them."[17] Carver's nomination was a clear insult to Oberlin's black population.

When voters ratified the caucus's selections in April 1897, the town council became all white for only the fourth year since 1870.[18] It remained all white for a decade, until 1908, when the African American carpenter Thomas Bows won election. Called "a true Christian gentleman," Bows was a devoted member of Mount Zion Church, where he served for many years as chair of the Deacon's Board.[19] After Bows completed his second term in 1912, however, the tradition of a black seat on town council came to an end. Oberlin did not elect another African American councilman until 1957.[20] The whitening of local government after an extended period of black representation was stunning evidence of Oberlin's retreat from racial integration in the early twentieth century.

Gradually, yet inexorably, the stigmatization of blackness deepened. In 1903, in one of a series of essays published in the *Oberlin News* under the title "A Legacy From President Fairchild," retired missionary and author Delavan Leonard reflected on how he had learned to navigate race relations in Oberlin. Upon settling in the town in the 1890s, he wrote, "I had noticed that though almost no color prejudice was discernable, and not a few ex-slaves or their children were held generally in high esteem, yet at a certain point an impassable line had been drawn between white and black." He asked his friends what would happen if, as "a reputable citizen, in good standing for respectability and intelligence," he were to "invit[e] fifty or a hundred neighbors to spend a social evening" with him and include "among them . . . a half-dozen or so colored" people. "[W]hat would my white guests say?" he inquired. He was told in response that, although none would say so to his face, "everyone of them would be certain to think, What's the matter with Leonard? He must have a soft spot in his head somewhere, or else he is cranky."[21] Well-situated white Oberlinians no longer felt comfortable sharing private space and socializing with persons of color as equals.

In the face of this hardening of Oberlin's color line, leading African Americans doubled down on their strategy of respectability. Part of this effort involved strengthening local black institutions. By the beginning of the twentieth century, both Rust and Mount Zion Churches boasted distinguished congregations with choirs and children's programs, Bible study, civics clubs, and women's groups. The more recently established Mount Zion Church hosted an Emancipation Day celebration to greet the new century, featuring speakers on "The Religious, Moral and Intellectual Improvement of the Colored People Since the Civil War" and "The Negro as an American Citizen."[22] Rust sponsored special sessions on "Child Training," temperance, character, and manhood.[23] Religious orators stressed that education would overcome ignorance, thereby putting an end to the "race problem."[24] Strikingly, after President William McKinley was felled by an assassin's bullet in September 1901, Rust pastor R. P. Robinson underscored black respectability by announcing from the pulpit, "While we colored people confess our sins, we can praise God that there is not an anarchist or socialist among us."[25]

In addition to black churches, Oberlinians of color supported secular race-based organizations. In the first decade of the twentieth century they formed black literary societies, including one in 1904 that crossed the town-gown divide.[26] In 1908 black freemasonry came to Oberlin with the founding of Central Star Lodge #73, accompanied by the female Order of the Eastern Star the next year.[27] In all these endeavors, African Americans connected with each other to reinforce their social standing and promote their collective interest. By exemplifying irreproachable respectability, leading black Oberlinians hoped to insulate themselves and protect other persons of color from the rising tide of white racism.

The founding of an African American chapter of the Woman's Christian Temperance Union in Oberlin in 1906 held distinctive promise for people of color seeking social respectability. For decades, local white women had sought to promote the organization of women in the black community. Formed as a result of visits to Oberlin by Mrs. Katie Ramey, an activist in Cleveland's all-black Lucy Thurman Union, the "Twentieth Century Union" brought into the fold "sixty enthusiastic members" under the leadership of the "efficient president, Mrs. B. V. Jones."[28] Oberlin's white female temperance activists warmly welcomed the new organization. "[T]hough we can claim no credit for it, it is a cause of great gratification to us," they declared. "[W]e regard it as a valuable ally."[29]

The "efficient" President Blanche Virginia Harris Brooks Jones epitomized black respectability in early twentieth-century Oberlin. Born in Monroe, Michigan, in 1847, Blanche was the fourth child and second daughter of freeborn parents who, in the 1850s, moved to Oberlin with their six children. At least four of the siblings attended Oberlin College, including Blanche, who received a diploma from the Literary Course in 1860. Soon after graduation Blanche became one the first teachers sent by the American Missionary Association to educate freedpeople in the South. Posted initially to Norfolk, Virginia, then to Natchez, Mississippi, and subsequently to Henderson, North Carolina, she finally settled in Knoxville, Tennessee, where she married fellow teacher William Lafayette Brooks in 1871.[30] The following year she returned to her parents' home in Oberlin to give birth to her only child, Maude Rebecca, but she soon rejoined her husband and resumed her work. After William died in 1887, Blanche stayed on in Knoxville, where she was promoted to school principal. In *Noted Negro Women*, the pioneering biographical compendium for outstanding women of color published in 1893, Monroe Alpheus Majors praised Blanche's "natural endowment of taste, judgment, firmness and decision of character, softened and modified by a sweetness of temperament," and he commended her especially for her five years of service as president of Knoxville's WCTU.[31] Yet the same year that Majors's book appeared, Blanche left Knoxville for Oberlin, where Maude enrolled in the conservatory and Blanche married a childhood acquaintance, the distinguished Elias Toussaint Jones.

The sixth of the seven children born to Allen and Temperance (Tempe) Jones, Elias had arrived from North Carolina in Oberlin with his family in 1843 at about age ten. Like Blanche, he attended the college, receiving his bachelor's degree in 1859. Shortly thereafter, with some of his brothers and other young men of color, Elias left his widowered and cantankerous father for adventure in the goldfields of California, later moving on to western Canada, where mining produced for him a tidy fortune that made possible his retirement to Oberlin in 1891. He returned to the family home on South Main Street, where he lived with his sister. Blanche joined them there upon her marriage to Elias in 1893. Except for a two-year hiatus between 1903 and 1905 that she spent with her daughter and son-in-law, who were educators in Henderson, North Carolina, Blanche and Elias resided together in Oberlin for the next quarter-century.[32]

After returning to Oberlin in 1893, Blanche rejoined First Church, in which she had grown up, and immersed herself in the work of predominantly white benevolent organizations. She took charge of the sewing school operated by the Mutual Benefit Association in conjunction with the work of the Charitable Organization Society in the Centennial Building, and then joined the board of the Kindergarten Association.[33] She also joined the Oberlin WCTU, where she testified to "a steady advance in the Purity department, and made a strong plea for reform on the subject of divorce."[34] Nominated by a fellow African American at the Republican caucus, she ran unsuccessfully for the Oberlin School Board in 1899. The next year, she ran and lost again, this time nominated on the "Independent People's Ticket."[35] In 1903, while she was preparing to leave for North Carolina to assist with her new grandchild, members of the Mutual Benefit Association noted that for nine years "she has been a most faithful and enthusiastic work[er] in conjunction with the Centennial." They concluded their tribute: "The society feels that her place will be hard to fill."[36]

Her colleagues were right. As a comfortable, well-educated woman of color long connected to Oberlin, Jones was uniquely positioned to work in both the black and white communities; no other woman of her generation achieved such prominence on both sides of the racial divide. Especially after her return from the South in 1905, Blanche Harris Brooks Jones focused on improving the situation of African Americans in Oberlin and beyond. Her efforts on behalf of the WCTU targeted behavior that compromised propriety while it also threatened women, children, and household stability. Yet in 1908 she and Elias deployed their reputations in a more aggressive fashion when they chose to help welcome the Niagara Movement, a forerunner to the NAACP, to Oberlin for its annual meeting, endorsing W.E.B. Du Bois and the movement's militant approach to the "race problem." Reacting against deteriorating race relations, Oberlin's most proper and prominent couple of color sought to reclaim Oberlin's radical heritage, casting their lot with the feisty and confrontational upstart civil rights organization. Blanche's name topped the roster of the Local Arrangements Committee.[37]

The Niagara Movement had emerged from an informal meeting in 1905 at the Buffalo, New York, home of Mary Burnett Talbert, the Oberlin-born daughter of barber Cornelius J. Burnett. When Du Bois sent out a call "for organized determination and aggressive action on the part of men who believe in Negro freedom and growth," some three dozen people came together, officially convening across the national boundary, at Fort Erie in Canada. Incorporated in 1906, the Niagara Movement met that year in Harpers Ferry, and the next year in Boston. Du Bois's assertive attitude permeated the organization, which, he wrote, "eternally protests." As he explained, "We will not be satisfied to take one jot or tittle less than our full manhood rights. We claim for ourselves every single right that belongs to a freeborn American, political, civil, and social; and until we get these rights we will never cease to protest and assail the ears of America."[38]

The 1908 meeting occasioned Du Bois's first visit to Oberlin. Booker T. Washington, Du Bois's famous rival in the debate over African American strategy, had already appeared in the town twice, applauded by audiences who embraced his less confrontational approach to racial advancement.[39] In 1897, two years after the Atlanta Compromise speech that brought him to national attention, Washington spoke in Oberlin on "The Negro Problem in the Black Belt of the South," calling for practical education to improve the "industrial condition" of people of color. In regard to the "social question," he counseled, "Friction will disappear as the Negro learns to produce the things the white man wants."[40] Returning in 1904, while his son was a student at the college, Washington lectured at First Church under the auspices of the YMCA. Praised by the local press for his "humorous illustrations, those in dialect told in an inimitable way," he "spoke of the colored man's gratitude to Oberlin" while gently affirming that African Americans "had some rights in this country—rights as men and citizens." After his lecture at First Church, Washington spoke separately to the black congregation of Rust Church. During his visit, college president Henry Churchill King entertained Washington at his home.[41] King's hospitality demonstrated a modicum of courage since U.S. president Theodore Roosevelt had endured harsh criticism when he had hosted Washington for lunch at the White House three years earlier.[42] But King would prove an unreliable ally on race.

The Niagara delegates who convened in Oberlin at the end of August 1908 assembled against the backdrop of violent antiblack riots that had ripped through Springfield, Illinois, less than two weeks before. The delegates spent their first day receiving reports from state secretaries of the organization and from the "Women's Circles," as well as updates about a protest against the Pullman Company for its support of Jim Crow railroad cars. A mass meeting the following evening attracted an audience of about seven hundred to Warner Hall on the Oberlin College campus. Du Bois introduced the town mayor, "who extended cordial words of welcome." Cleveland author and lawyer Charles W. Chesnutt, whose family ties to Oberlin spanned more than a half-century, offered the evening's main oration, focusing on the problem of the color line. The third and last day, September 2, the delegates elected officers and, after considerable debate, endorsed a closing declaration.[43]

The radicalism of that declaration took local residents by surprise. The delegates' advice on how persons of color should respond to the prospect of mob violence was especially provocative: "Obey the law, defend no crime, conceal no criminal, seek no quarrel; but arm yourselves, and when the mob invades your home, shoot to kill."[44] Republican Oberlin was also shocked by the meeting's advice that voters should "leave no stone unturned to defeat William H. Taft," the Republican candidate for president, and "establish next November the principle of Negro independence in voting."[45] The local Taft club promptly invited black Chicagoan Hale G. Parker, an 1873 graduate of the college, to speak in Oberlin against the Niagara Movement's position. Invoking the memory of the Oberlin-Wellington Rescue, Parker denounced "the insult" leveled against "proud historic Oberlin" by a "handful of malcontents so plainly insensible to the spirit of this place." "If Mr. Bryan [the Democratic nominee] is elected," he predicted, "the confederacy will at once be back in the saddle in the city of Washington, and the negro in the north will feel the shock of southern civilization insidiously creeping into the life of every city and village situated near [the] Mason and Dixon Line." Parker viewed the Niagara Movement's strategy as wrongheaded, counterproductive, and dangerous. "This doctrine of punishment urged by the Niagara movement will cost the negro his best friends in both parties," he warned. "It will turn him back twenty-five years in the scale of human progress."[46]

Less than two months after the Niagara Movement stirred such controversy in Oberlin, Booker T. Washington visited the community for a third time, offering a more conciliatory vision of race relations that was well received. Addressing a "very large audience" at the college's recently completed Finney Chapel, he spoke primarily about his own life and the history of the

Tuskegee Normal and Industrial Institute, where "ignorant colored boys and girls [who arrive] with no appreciation of the value of their lives, leave as trained industrial leaders, teachers, or ministers."[47] A white commentator applauded Washington's "good advice to his race" and praised his sense of humor. "He is a good talker," the commentator noted, "and a fine entertainer."[48] Washington avoided divisive topics during this trip, which turned out to be his last to Oberlin before his death in 1915.[49]

Some prominent Oberlinians of color preferred Washington's approach to that of Du Bois. In the early fall of 1908 a number of black men assembled "for the purpose of uplifting their own people to a higher degree of citizenship." Styling themselves the Colored Law and Order League, they emphasized the need to comply with duly constituted legal authorities and to behave according to established norms of propriety. They expressed particular concern about newcomers to the town who, they believed, propagated mayhem and drunken disorder, especially on the streetcars that connected dry Oberlin to alcohol-sodden Elyria. The recent arrivals, they charged, "have not lived here long enough to know that such unlawful conduct is not countenanced or tolerated in Oberlin by either colored or white people."[50]

The founders of the Colored Law and Order League included William H. Glenn, brother of the recently deceased former councilman Charles Glenn; Edward Wellington Mitchell, the son of former city councilman Arthur Wellington Mitchell; the octogenarian John H. Scott; teamster Julius Burton; Thomas Bows, the carpenter who would become the last man of color to serve on the town council for nearly half a century; and Henson Tuck, who had served on the Niagara Movement's Local Arrangements Committee. They framed their call to action in terms of racial solidarity: "Being negroes, we must stand or fall together, unless we come out plainly and clearly for morality, purity, honor, and industry." Yet their sense of racial fellowship had limits. "[I]f the evil can not be stopped," they warned, "it is then best to rid the town of both the evil and the evil-doer."[51]

The male organizers of Oberlin's Colored Law and Order League asked local black women to help in the "work of reformation." These genteel matrons of color had already embraced a strategy of "lifting as we climb," as the slogan of the National Association of Colored Women's Clubs (NACWC) proclaimed. Established in 1896, the NACWC brought together the many societies that African American women joined for sociability and social action, particularly in support of woman suffrage and against lynching. Emphasizing the role of women as wives, mothers, and volunteers, the NACWC targeted for membership comparatively affluent black women seeking to enhance the social standing of both their communities and themselves.[52]

In Oberlin, many respectable women of color embraced the club movement. As early as 1905, Cordelia Quinn Fisher, daughter of one of Oberlin's richest men of color, had joined with friends to form the Women's Progressive Club.[53] Focusing on self-education and community improvement, they discussed a wide range of topics at their meetings, including woman suffrage, the role of women in Oberlin's history, the "aims and ideals" of the Oberlin public schools, and "Degeneracy and Poverty: Disease in the Guilty, the Innocent and the Next Generation."[54] Among the club's more notable members was Margaret Sallee Barnes, who proved a powerful organizer. The local unit's president in 1912, she became the vice president of the Ohio Federation of Colored Women's Clubs the following year and brought the statewide meeting to Oberlin.[55]

Alongside the Women's Progressive Club arose the Oberlin Mutual Improvement Club. Founded in 1913, the Mutual Improvement Club initially focused on aspects of gendered domesticity, such as "the influences of flowers in the home." Yet in short order members turned their attention to more controversial issues, including education and the "social condition of the Negro."[56] In 1916, the Women's Progressive Club and the Oberlin Mutual Improvement Club joined forces as the Oberlin Council of Colored Women. The new organization targeted youthful bad behavior, school absences and tardiness, unsightly rubbish, and poor health conditions.[57] By means of "cooperation and social uplift," Oberlin's respectable women of color sought to use their social status within the black population to promote better living standards for African Americans throughout the town.[58]

But respectability proved a weak weapon against the hardening of Oberlin's color line. Evolving attitudes left even the most cultivated and self-consciously proper African Americans in Oberlin without local white support in the face of racial discrimination. In the summer of 1908 over one thousand Oberlinians, both black and white, bought tickets for an excursion to Cedar Point, "a fine outing place" with bathing lagoons, a dance pavilion, and theatrical amusements located on a breezy peninsula in Lake Erie. Although an article about the trip in the *Oberlin News* carried the headline "Lively Time Enjoyed By All," participants' experiences actually varied greatly by race. The newspaper's praise for the prompt excursion trains, the breezes, the beach, and the merry-go-round almost crowded out a separate short notice that defensively reported: "Oberlin colored people feel aggrieved because they were allowed no privileges at Cedar Point last Thursday. They were not permitted to bathe or get into the hotel, or on the dancing floor, as the color line was closely drawn." The paper commented, "If the facts are as they are stated to us they have every reason to resent the treatment they received." But the *News* exonerated white Oberlinians from any responsibility for the discrimination experienced by their counterparts of color. "It is a rule at Cedar Point that colored people are not allowed bathing privileges or to enter the dancing pavilion, and the matter was beyond the power of the local committee to secure these privileges for the colored people," the paper explained.[59] Notably absent was the interracial radicalism that marked the Oberlin-Wellington Rescue. Whereas a half-century earlier black and white Oberlinians had protested together against an unjust law targeting people of color, now white townspeople accepted the color line drawn by a private amusement park as an unalterable social fact. Rather than mobilize as allies for equal rights, they acquiesced in the practice of racial discrimination and left black townspeople to fend for themselves.

Even within Oberlin whites failed to challenge the emerging color line. In 1909 Byron Cherry, a sometime farmer who had attended the preparatory department of the college in the late 1850s, decided to sell forty-one acres of land that he owned north of West Lorain Street. He laid out streets for what he called the "Hollywood Addition," and with the help of the Smith Realty Company of Mount Vernon, Ohio, he arranged for the "Sale of Building Lots" at a three-day public auction in late May. Advertisements for the event highlighted the opportunity to "buy real estate if you wish to make money" and promised "Terms Very Liberal." To attract prospective buyers, Cherry arranged for "Free Carriages" to transport adults from the center of town to the auction site and offered "FREE PRESENTS," including the daily award of "a beautiful line of silverware, valued at $600.00." "You do not have to buy a lot to get a present," the promotional announcement said, "but you must be at the sale." The small print that followed added an overtly racist qualification: "No presents given to children or colored people." Moreover, not only were people of color ineligible to receive free gifts, they were also prohibited from buying into the Hollywood Addition. The deeds for the lots that Cherry offered for purchase contained a clause making it illegal for the "premises to be sold, rented, or conveyed to anyone belonging to the Negro or Colored Race."[60] Through this contractual mechanism, legal segregation came to Oberlin.

While formal racial covenants remained rare in early twentieth-century Oberlin, they codified a pattern that had been taking shape for many years. By 1900, Oberlin's people of color were highly concentrated in the southeast quadrant, while an entirely white enclave had matured west of Professor Street, bounded on the south by Morgan Street and on the north by Lorain Street, where Byron Cherry's house sat. Ironically, many of the most beautiful homes in this area were designed and built by the black-owned firm of Glenn and Copeland, the town's preeminent construction company during the late nineteenth century.[61] The restrictive covenants governing the properties sold in Cherry's Hollywood Addition were intended to ensure the perpetual whiteness of the Oberlin's west side.

Prominent whites knowingly acquiesced in the spread of racial segregation within the community. On June 30, 1913, real estate broker Louis E. Burgner sent a letter to college president Henry Churchill King requesting his views on "the colored person buying property in Oberlin residential districts." "Recently I have been importuned by one set of minds to sell to a colored man, a property on Forest Street, and by property owners to the contrary," Burgner wrote. "Is it right, in your judgment, for decent, clean, reputable, colored people to acquire real estate in good white neighborhoods?"[62] In his reply, King confessed to feeling ambivalent about how best to answer Burgner's question. From his personal point of view, King wrote, it appeared "right for decent, clean, reputable, colored people to acquire real estate in good white neighborhoods." Yet he also observed that "one cannot leave out of account the fact that, in view of prejudices in most communities, the financial value of other property in the vicinity of such a purchase is affected, and one may question whether he has a right to produce such an effect upon the property of others, tho[ugh] he feels the injustice of the general position taken."[63]

Frustrated by this ambiguous response, Burgner wrote King again, this time laying out explicitly his own views regarding racial integration in Oberlin. "On the colored question," Burgner explained, "I heartily feel that an agent has no right to introduce colored residents in white neighborhoods." He then proceeded to suggest that the college's own housing policies were inconsistent with its professed position on race. While the college "always takes a fine stand for the rights of the negro," Burgner asserted, it also "rents

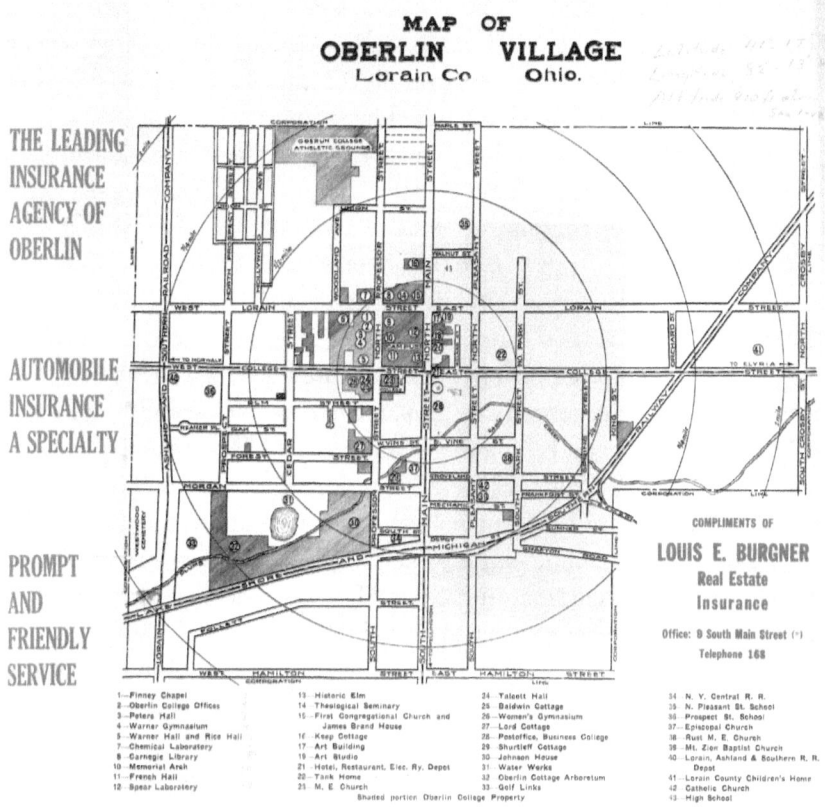

"Map of Oberlin Village," published for Louis E. Burgner, circa 1920.
Oberlin College Archives.

property in a white section for a colored boarding house."[64] By providing separate accommodations for black students in town rather than in integrated dormitories on the campus, he implied, the college failed to practice the racial egalitarianism that it preached.

King terminated the exchange by responding to Burgner's second missive with the insipid expression of his wish to achieve "as much mutual understanding as possible" and to "cooperate . . . for the good of both the College and the Town, whose interests I feel certainly cannot be separated."[65] He did not discuss whether the college would reconsider its housing policy for students of color. Instead, he used his copious diplomatic skills to maneuver around the increasingly controversial issue of residential integration.

Whatever his personal views on race, King had abandoned the antebellum notion that Oberlin—both the college and the community at large—had a moral responsibility to advocate forcefully for "the emancipation of the free colored man from the oppression of public sentiment."[66]

King's 1913 exchange with Burgner took place against the backdrop of an ongoing debate over race relations at the college.[67] More than a generation earlier, in 1882, when a group of white female students objected to dining alongside female students of color, Dean of Women Adelia Field Johnston and President James Harris Fairchild had acted quickly and firmly to uphold the tradition of integrated seating.[68] Florence Fitch, Johnston's successor as dean of women, was more sympathetic to white students who preferred not to mix with African Americans. In 1909, Fitch proposed separating the women's residences by race, calling the establishment of a segregated "colored house" her "chief immediate concern." President King was out of the country at the time. Acting in his stead, college librarian Azariah Root objected to Fitch's plan for pragmatic, if not principled, reasons. According to Fitch's account, Root asserted "that there would be a great deal of hard feeling on the part of many of the colored people and their friends if we had a separate college house for them."[69] Yet racial segregation prevailed in off-campus student housing during this era.[70]

"Oberlin College Turns on Negro," proclaimed a headline on the front page of the *Cleveland Plain Dealer* on April 20, 1910. "Undergraduates of Oberlin College are drawing sharp lines of discrimination against the negro," the newspaper reported. "Older alumni can hardly believe it. Professors and college officials nevertheless admit that race prejudice has slowly but surely eaten its way into the social vitals of the institution." In particular, the *Plain Dealer* alleged that white students had excluded students of color from the college's literary societies and discouraged black athletes from joining Oberlin sports teams. "College boarding houses no longer will allow the negro to eat at the same table as the white man," the paper added.[71]

"Some of the professors call the marked prejudicial attitude against the negro in Oberlin evidence of how race antipathy is growing in all colleges of the country," the *Plain Dealer* elaborated. "Then, too, it is said, the feeling against the African is shifting from the south to the north more and more." The paper asked presidential assistant Charles W. Williams for his interpretation of developments. Williams attributed the white students' "attitude . . . in a large measure to the position held by Booker T. Washington," who had declared that he would "not demand social equality between the negro and the white man until the negro has secured an economic status in society." Although Williams said that that he "deplores the recent move to ostracize the negro socially at the college," he also affirmed that he could "see the students' point of view" and signaled implicitly that college administrators would not take new steps to prevent racial discrimination at the institution.[72]

Many alumni responded to the news of Oberlin's retreat from egalitarian principles with alarm. Especially eloquent was a letter to the editors of the *Oberlin Alumni Magazine* from Lucien C. Warner, a white member of the class of 1865. "Can it be that the present generation of students and instructors have cut themselves loose from the past history and traditions of Oberlin so that they do not realize the foundations on which its present prosperity rests?" Warner asked rhetorically. "Must we say that the 'Brotherhood of Man' is all right as a doctrine for building up a college until it becomes strong and wealthy but then it must pass on to 'Higher Ideals?'" Warner urged the current student body "to be proud of the rich heritage of brotherhood and fellowship for which Oberlin has always stood," rather than "make colored men unwelcome now that other colleges gladly welcome them."[73]

Acting President Azariah Root responded by excusing both the college and its current students from any substantive responsibility for upholding Oberlin's historic mission: "As we draw from a far wider circle than in former years and from a generation which knows nothing of the anti-slavery discussion, it is probably not surprising that with the increasing color prejudice which seems to be developing throughout the North we should get some reflection of it in our student body." As to the troublesome reports of discriminatory conduct endured by Oberlin athletes of color, particularly at their away games, Root reiterated: "The difficulty arises from the prejudice which exists outside." He concluded by dismissing the option of resistance, instead counseling accommodation: "For this we cannot be responsible and must make such adjustments as are possible."[74]

On his return to Oberlin in late 1910, Henry Churchill King finally weighed in on the question of the college's color line. In a chapel talk titled "The College and Democracy" and subsequently published in the *Alumni Magazine*, he seemed to affirm a commitment to racial equality but in fact revealed a racial essentialism that precluded full integration and buttressed the status quo. "No more difficult, no more delicate, no more vital problem confronts the American people than the problem of the true solution to the relation of race to race in this nation," King asserted, and he opined that the key to racial harmony was the development of "self-respect on both sides."[75] Yet he also argued that the foundation for self-respect differed inherently from race to race. He urged the black man "not [to] allow himself to be betrayed into a mere imitation of the whites. . . . Let him take pride in his race's marked individuality," particularly "the singularly appealing power of the genuine negro melodies" and the "quaintness of humor and imagination" of black folklore. Rather than trying to emulate the "ungenerous, hard, selfish, domineering" qualities of whites, blacks should find self-respect in "a temperamental kindliness of disposition, a good nature, a readiness to make the most of a situation, and to find none insufferable," King advised.[76] While the white man "cannot keep his own self-respect . . . if he refuses complete justice to the negro," King explained, self-respecting persons of color "will not press the demand or make a bitter struggle for so-called social equality."[77]

To leave no ambiguity, King then quoted approvingly and extensively "that clear-sighted negro, Professor Kelly Miller," who, in a published essay, had asserted that the "negro's sense of self respect effectively forbids forcing himself upon any unwelcome associations. Household intercourse and domestic familiarity are essentially questions of personal privilege." King concluded his lengthy quotation with Miller's echo of Booker T. Washington: "In all purely personal and social matters let each, if he will, go unto his own company."[78] In King's view, by embracing their racially distinct character, Oberlin's people of color would willingly submit to their own segregation. Such was King's "Oberlin Compromise," designed to keep the peace, not to achieve social justice.[79]

King's position did not go unchallenged. In 1913, Mary Church Terrell, an 1884 graduate with a distinguished record of black activism, enrolled her two daughters at Oberlin, the older in the entering class at the college and the younger in the academy, as the preparatory department had come to be known. Terrell explained to King, a longtime friend, that she brought her girls to Oberlin to give them "the same chance of measuring arms with white youth that I myself had had."[80] But when the girls sought much-coveted housing in Talcott Hall for their second year, they came up against an unstated policy limiting the number of students of color allowed at one time in any women's dormitory. When Terrell protested, Dean of Women Florence Fitch tartly observed that Terrell failed to recognize that "Times have changed since her own student days."[81]

Terrell took her complaint next to George M. Jones, secretary of the college. After an appalling interview with Jones, she appealed to King. Terrell was irate, insisting that she "went to Mr. Jones feeling sure that [he] must regret the segregation of Colored students and the recrudescence of feeling against them, and was rendered almost speechless when he expressed himself so strongly against allowing them to board in any of the college dormitories and thus be brought into social contact with white students." Crushed, she wrote King: "[N]othing has come so near forcing me to give up hope, and resigning myself to the cruel fate which many people are certain awaits us, than the heart-breaking back-sliding of Oberlin College."[82] King replied defensively, "I am doing everything I know how to do to stand for fairness and justice, . . . and I do not believe that either Oberlin colored students or Oberlin colored residents will refuse to say that I have stood for fairness." He blamed the college's failure to do more for blacks on external forces, in particular "the large numbers [of white students] coming to us without any special training on this subject." "I can guess a little how hard the general situation in the country must often seem to colored people," he allowed, "but I hope that they will not make the mistake of turning against those who want to be their genuine friends."[83] Terrell's daughters did not return to Oberlin.

Changes at Oberlin College profoundly affected the local community of color. College attendance had always held the power to bestow the imprimatur of respectability on those who enrolled; educational achievement gave weight to claims for social status, for both white students and students of color. But in the early twentieth century, discrimination within the college subjected black students to embarrassment if not outright humiliation. Intolerant episodes on campus echoed through the local families of color; they aspired to send their children to the pre-collegiate academy, and the college, while also serving as hosts for out-of-town relatives, friends, and acquaintances whose offspring sought an Oberlin education. But they were powerless to defend against the racism of white students and the bias of administrators. Moreover, the tenuous ties to respectability frayed further as black enrollment in Oberlin College declined in the early twentieth century. Having peaked at nearly 8 percent during the decade after the Civil War, the proportion of students of color stood at less than 5 percent in 1907–1908, and that was the highest percentage of black students enrolled in any year during King's presidency. After the academy closed in 1916, the number of students of color at the institution dipped to only forty-nine, or just over 3 percent of the total enrollment.[84] The community of Oberlin had once touted education as a key path to racial equality and had taken great pride in a college that promoted black mobility; now few people of color found their way to its doors, and once inside, they learned that prejudice and differential treatment hampered their path. It was a setback for all black people in Oberlin who sought advancement and equality.

As the college retreated from its historic commitment to racial equality, the town pondered its educational responsibilities to people of color. Although they comprised one-fifth of the enrollment in the town's public schools between 1905 and 1913, black students lagged significantly behind their white counterparts in academic achievement. In 1914, Howard L. Rawdon, a 1906 graduate of the college who had become Oberlin's superintendent of schools in 1908, determined to use emerging social science methods to document and explain the reasons for blacks' notably greater failure to perform at grade level and the greater likelihood that they would be tardy, absent, held back, and drop out before high school graduation. Rawdon hoped his study would allow him to "suggest some things that might tend towards [the black child's] future welfare."[85]

Rawdon identified five factors that contributed to performance disparities. The first three reflected the impact of longstanding economic inequality: irregular parental employment, low parental educational achievement, and the necessity of both parents to be employed outside the home. Rawdon presented hard evidence of Oberlin's black poverty. Looking at the tax returns for 1913, when people of color represented about 18 percent of Oberlin's total population, he found they owned only 5 percent of the town's real property and less than 1 percent of local personal property. At $310, African Americans' per capita taxable wealth was less than one-fifth the comparable figure for whites, $1,610.[86]

Rawdon's fourth explanatory factor was the alleged moral deficiency of the black family. Analyzing the arrests recorded on the Mayor's Docket for 1912–1913 by race, he found that nearly 46 percent of the major offenses were attributed to people of color.[87] Cautiously but unambiguously, he concluded: "Though too much importance should not be attached to these statistics, doubtless the conclusion may be drawn that the moral status in the home is another reason why the scholarship of the colored pupils in general is lower than that of whites." In his view, the "degrading" moral environment in which people of color lived posed a major impediment to school achievement. Black culture, not just black poverty, was a major problem. Finally, Rawdon suggested that the four preceding factors combined to rob black students of ambition, the fifth reason they could not succeed. "All in all," he wrote, "the colored pupil's social and economic environment, and his outlook for the future afford him little incentive to make the most of his opportunities for an education."[88]

In light of these circumstances, Rawdon proposed a curricular innovation: vocational training, which, he averred, "will offer the greatest opportunities in the way of securing more steady employment at better wages." Like Booker T. Washington, Rawdon believed that African Americans should focus on the acquisition of practical skills with the goal of raising their standard of living, not challenging the fundamental structures of racial injustice. In particular, he recommended that Oberlin's schools help young people of color train to become cooks, seamstresses, dressmakers, carpenters, plumbers, masons, fruit growers, and gardeners. Local demand for workers in these occupations would, he believed, always ensure full employment.[89] By contrast, professional training for African Americans yielded little local benefit. The student of color "sees himself as handicapped as soon as he is through school in putting his education and practical training to use," Rawdon observed. "If he pursues a college course, he usually finds it necessary to go a long distance from home to enter the practice of his profession." Despite asserting that "Prejudice should be laid aside, for prejudice still exists," Rawdon did not question why career opportunities for educated people of color did not exist in Oberlin. Rather, he urged pragmatic efforts to improve the lives of students of color, and in so doing, further inscribed the pattern of racial differentiation that characterized Oberlin in the early decades of the twentieth century.[90]

Rawdon's assessment of the occupations available to Oberlinians of color accurately reflected reality; economic opportunities for blacks were narrowing. In 1910, only three of Oberlin's 102 households of color could be found among the highest quintile of property holders, and all derived their wealth from the building trades. Widowed Caledonia Mitchell had, for sixteen years, comfortably lived on the money left to her by her husband, Arthur Wellington Mitchell, the painting contractor and Oberlin town council member. George Quinn began as a brickmason and became a contractor. Similarly, Henson Tuck became a contractor after starting as a painter and wallpaper hanger. In the quintile below them, of the three persons of color listed, one,

Lizzie Jarvis, had inherited considerable property from her father, and another, Nettie Williams, appears to have been a dressmaker with a husband who had some success working as a mason. The third, George Shanks, had parlayed his work as a tinsmith into success in plumbing. Rising from artisans to small-scale entrepreneurs, Mitchell, Quinn, Tuck, and Shanks all followed the nineteenth-century path to economic security.[91]

But overall, people of color rarely found routes to prosperity in early twentieth-century Oberlin. Most of the wealth held by the overwhelmingly white top two quintiles of property holders belonged to merchants, retailers, and professionals. These occupations remained largely inaccessible to people of color. Nearly all of Oberlin's few black professionals were clergymen. No people of color found their way to the directorships of banks in this period, nor did they appear on local lists of major businessmen.[92] Oberlin's public schools did not employ a teacher of color until 1939, and Oberlin College hired its first black professor in 1948. In light of the limited opportunities for African Americans in the professions and in commerce, vocational education might seem a logical path to economic stability, if not social equality, for people of color.

Not everyone was satisfied with Washingtonian strategies, however. In September 1916, Harley J. Smith, an enterprising man of color, returned to Oberlin, his hometown, with a sense of mission. Inspired by developments in Cleveland, the thirty-eight-year-old Smith wrote to the national headquarters of the NAACP pledging "to take off my coat and go right to work to help organize a local branch" of the association. "I have interested some of our colored brethren in the necessity of such a helpful organization," Smith explained. "There are some five or six hundred colored people here, without any protection whatever for their children."[93]

Smith subsequently joined forces with Samuel Coleman, an African American steward at Oberlin College, and together they rallied twenty of the town's most respectable men of color to petition the national organization for authorization to form an Oberlin chapter.[94] The pastors of Mount Zion and Rust and physician S. W. Stevens topped the roster, with contractors George Quinn and William Madison Mitchell also lending their support to the cause. The remaining petitioners included a machinist, a teamster, a student, a watchman, and three janitors. Among them were the two living men of color who had served previously on Oberlin's town council and one who would run (but lose) in the next decade.[95] These were Oberlin's new "Talented Tenth."

At the NAACP's headquarters in New York City, Royal Nash, W.E.B. Du Bois's white assistant, responded enthusiastically to their petition. He remarked that a recent conversation with Mary Church Terrell had made him aware of issues in Oberlin, including that "colored girls in the college are discriminated against on every side." But Nash reminded his Oberlin correspondents that the NAACP was envisioned as an interracial organization, not one restricted to blacks. He therefore expressed his hope that there remained "several members of the faculty left who still cherished the old ideals" and urged the Oberlin organizers to enlist their support. In addition, he identified four Oberlin residents as "national members" of the association who should be contacted to secure their backing for a local chapter. One was Henry Churchill King, though—doubtless influenced by Terrell—Nash observed that "President King . . . is not a very staunch upholder of our principles."[96] The other three national members residing in Oberlin were Irving Metcalf, a former minister, founder of the Anti-Saloon League, and Oberlin College trustee who had become active in real estate and investments; Irving's brother Vernon Metcalf, a professor of chemistry at the college; and the prominent African American Elias Toussaint Jones, who with his wife, Blanche, had hosted the local meeting of the Niagara Movement in Oberlin nearly a decade before.[97]

Solicited directly by Nash himself, both King and Irving Metcalf responded with enthusiasm in favor of an Oberlin chapter to be headed by Reverend George Washington, pastor of Mount Zion Church. Metcalf wrote that Washington's leadership would ensure that the chapter was "wisely guided."[98] King patronizingly endorsed Washington as "one of the sanest colored leaders I know."[99] At age eighty-two, Elias Toussaint Jones conveyed his approval in an elegant, old-fashioned script. "I am glad if my name will help the group of Oberlin colored men to secure the charter applied for," Jones wrote. "Hope them success and will aid them in the cause."[100]

Chartered in January 1917, the Oberlin chapter published a notice of its founding in the local press, along with a statement of purpose and a list of officers—all persons of color.[101] Joining Washington on the executive committee were Vice President Harley J. Smith, Secretary Samuel Coleman, and Treasurer Hamilton Mosby, who had served for fifteen years as custodian at

Oberlin's Talcott Hall before becoming a janitor in the public schools; also on the committee were builder and former town councilman Thomas Bows, contractor Henson Tuck, and former councilman William Madison Mitchell, described by Coleman to his NAACP correspondent as "One of Oberlin's grand old men."[102]

The chapter launched a membership drive that brought in over one hundred new recruits by the fall of 1917—about one-quarter of them white. Among the white men who joined were five clergymen, including the pastors of First and Second Churches, and three professors at the college. Among the white women were several faculty wives and, perhaps surprisingly, the wife and daughter of Louis Burgner, the real estate agent who had sparred with President King over residential segregation.[103] Yet the vast majority of new members were people of color, most of them females. They included Margaret Sallee Barnes, past president of Oberlin's Women's Progressive Club and past vice president of the Ohio Federation of Colored Women's Clubs. Barnes had written to W.E.B. Du Bois as early as May 1914 to express her interest in founding a local branch of the NAACP.[104] She now signed up with enthusiasm and soon emerged as a major force within the Oberlin chapter.

In September 1918 Barnes and other representatives of the Colored Federated Clubs of Oberlin called for an NAACP investigation of the Student Army Training Corps (SATC) unit being established on the Oberlin College campus in response to American entry into World War I. At issue was the denial of applications by African Americans to join the unit. Barnes and her allies lamented the fact that young men of color traveled long distances to enlist at Oberlin "just to have them told they must go elsewhere" and expressed "their deep regret that such a policy should be enforced in the land of the free and the home of the brave." Yet in raising this concern, the black club women avoided placing direct blame on the college. Believing that the rejection stemmed from a War Department regulation, they observed with rueful dismay that "Oberlin who today knows no color or race must bow its head in humble submission to the powers that be, and turn colored youth away from its door."[105]

So it was with particular distress that the local NAACP learned in mid-October that—contrary to a statement by the college's acting president, Edward I. Bosworth—the War Department *had not* issued any orders preventing the enlistment of students of color at Oberlin.[106] The *Cleveland Advocate*, a black-owned Republican weekly, revealed that an advance copy of the War

Department memo advised local units: "Use tact and discretion in providing colored men with mess and quarters and in arranging such segregation as may be necessary under local conditions, cooperating with educational authorities in the matter."[107] Who, then, had determined that Oberlin's "local conditions" mandated racial separation? Evidence pointed to Francis Metcalf Root, the commandant of the Oberlin unit. A 1911 graduate of the college, Francis Metcalf Root was the son of college librarian Azariah Smith Root and a cousin of Irving W. Metcalf, the college trustee who had endorsed the founding of the Oberlin NAACP two years before. Francis Metcalf Root apparently had decided on his own that only white men would occupy the housing reserved for SATC recruits in the college's Men's Building. As he explained, "If enough Negro students had applied . . . I should certainly have recommended the formation of a Negro company, messed and quartered by itself." But he opposed integrated housing. Consequently he denied admission to the five African American students who applied to join the Oberlin unit and directed them to enlist instead at either Howard or Wilberforce, both all-black institutions.[108]

Even in retrospect, Acting President Bosworth insisted that Oberlin College was not at fault. By his account, representatives of the War Department in Ohio had originally informed the school that the department's regulations prohibited housing colored soldiers in the same barracks as white soldiers. Although he acknowledged that "Some weeks later these instructions were so modified as to permit the admission of colored soldiers," he suggested that by then it was too late for the college to change course. The issue became moot when the Great War ended in early November.[109] Yet college officials had never objected publicly to the construction of a segregated program on the Oberlin campus. Long gone was the notion that Oberlinians, black and white, should join together to push back vigorously against the discriminatory caste system of American society.

While continued tension characterized race relations at the college, the national NAACP proved reluctant to get involved. In April 1919, African American orator William Pickens, then a professor and dean at Morgan State College, spoke at Oberlin on "The Negro in Light of the Great War."[110] During his visit, Pickens learned from a college faculty member that the new dean of women, Frances Hosford, had, like her predecessor, sought "to exclude some colored girls from Oberlin College dormitories." According an account that Pickens dispatched to NAACP headquarters, after these black female students "drew lots [and] got high choices" in the campus housing lottery, Hosford asked them "not to accept what they are entitled to but to go out & hunt up a 'boarding house.'" Pickens called the situation a "flat *denial* of justice,—the plainest."¹¹¹ One of the aggrieved students, Beulah Tyrell, stated that Hosford "told us that we had been misinformed by Dr. Du Bois and other such men who were indeed intelligent but who were *themselves* misinformed in thinking we gained by forcing ourselves into [whites'] social circles." Tyrell, whose father was an honors graduate of Yale, reported that she in turn told Hosford that the dean herself was misinformed: "I thought if she knew the best people of my race she would find they were not after getting in their social circles, for they were quite satisfied with their own, but we *are* after our rights."¹¹²

Upon receiving Pickens's description of events, Mary White Ovington, national secretary of the NAACP, turned to Harry E. Davis, secretary of the association's Cleveland branch, for advice on how to deal with the Oberlin situation.¹¹³ Davis replied that "College Authorities have heretofore taken the right stand on matters of this kind" and counseled patience.¹¹⁴ In the end, as Davis anticipated, "The girls were allowed to exercise their rights."¹¹⁵ Beulah Tyrell testified afterward that "the big majority of the students are true to the traditions and history of Oberlin," but she also observed that "fourteen irreconcilables left these dormitories and went to a smaller house" rather than reside with persons of color.¹¹⁶

The decision of the national NAACP not to intervene in this Oberlin controversy reflected the organization's prioritization of combating lethal terror. In 1919 it published *Thirty Years of Lynching in the United States, 1888-1918*, a report documenting the racial violence that simmered nationwide and continued to erupt periodically with frightful force. The injustice of segregated college housing was a less urgent concern than the bloodthirsty aggression of seething white mobs. Yet the NAACP's national headquarters also appeared to be out of touch with the local Oberlin chapter, turning instead to the Cleveland branch for guidance.¹¹⁷ Oberlin's local chapter had bloomed, but only briefly. In March 1919 the local NAACP reported a membership of 150 and claimed for itself "the distinction of having the largest membership according to the ratio of the colored population."¹¹⁸ Yet, without explanation, it then abruptly vanished from public view and remained dormant for many years to come.¹¹⁹

Despite Oberlin's retreat from the founders' commitment to racial egalitarianism, the community continued to enjoy a special place in the imagination of racial progressives. When the NAACP held its annual convention in Cleveland during the summer of 1919, one thousand delegates and their guests journeyed out to Oberlin on a kind of pilgrimage. They toured the campus and ate lunch before assembling in Finney Chapel to hear Oberlin's mayor welcome them to the community and eighty-one-year-old Professor G. Frederick Wright reminisce "in an interesting fashion of civil war [sic] days and the Wellington rescue."[120] Oberlin's importance rested on its glorious nineteenth-century heritage. The delegates politely overlooked evidence of the recent retreat from the abolitionists' commitment to racial egalitarianism. At its sessions in Cleveland, the NAACP focused on violence in the South, the national campaign against lynching, and the multistate fight to maintain the vote.[121]

By the third decade of the twentieth century, Oberlin resembled numerous other small towns across America where racism went unchallenged. In her 1925 master's thesis titled "The Negro in Oberlin," Mildred Fairchild, a granddaughter of James Harris Fairchild, presented a depressing picture of demoralized blacks and disengaged whites. Mildred Fairchild drew a sharp contrast between what she called the "old Oberlin" and the "new Oberlin," describing "changes it is no longer possible to ignore even in Oberlin." By her account, "Men, whose fathers and predecessors spent their evenings teaching the illiterate blacks, are wearying of the work and turning away indifferent or hostile."[122] Without hope, black men and women abandoned their aspirations for self-improvement, upward mobility, and full equality with whites.

Fairchild identified as major causes of this predicament a "constant northward-drifting race-prejudice" and the "separation of contacts" between local whites and Oberlinians of color. "Much of this is class not racial hostility," she wrote, yet she added, "Its effect upon the less able group in either case must be the same."[123] Perhaps most important, according to Fairchild, was what she termed "The Economic Inadequacy of Oberlin." "In a town as nearly static for forty years as the Oberlin population indicates, the opportunity drops to a minimum," she explained. The most talented persons of color "necessarily seek their opportunity elsewhere," while the majority of African Americans remained stuck near the bottom of the local social order. In Fairchild's view, this situation was not inevitable. It was, instead, the result of "a deliberate policy on the part of . . . college officials and many townspeople" to keep the community small—a strategy which, she asserted, "from the view point of the negro community eventually may prove disastrous for the town."[124] Although she praised Howard Rawdon's effort to introduce vocational education, Fairchild suggested that Oberlin would need a much more ambitious program to promote demographic growth and economic development if it wished to enable the mass of its black residents to rise.

Fairchild hesitated to assign responsibility for Oberlin's predicament, however. In the introduction to her thesis, she declared, "Almost from the outset Oberlin has stood for justice and equality of opportunity for every man regardless of color." Yet she coupled this proud affirmation of Oberlin's heritage with an assertion that the community no longer had a special obligation to fight racial discrimination or advance the standing of African Americans. "With the granting of the opportunity, its responsibilities for the most part have ended," she opined, implying that nineteenth-century provisions of emancipation, civil equality, and voting rights had established an adequate foundation for racial equality. Summing up her perspective on contemporary Oberlin, she wrote, "We have no Utopia to observe . . . but a very ordinary town with ordinary problems, the usual successes and the usual failures, such as might be repeated in any locality in almost any state in the country."[125]

Oberlin's failure to confront the impact of reinscribed and self-reinforcing racial inequality in the early twentieth century is only surprising because the racial egalitarianism of its antislavery pioneers, black and white, represented in their day a boldness of vision that went beyond their descendants' ambivalent endorsement of equal opportunity. In 1835 the fledgling community declared itself committed not only to the emancipation of people of color from slavery, but also their emancipation "from the oppression of public sentiment." The achievement of racial equality, they asserted, required changing hearts and minds, eliminating the deep-seated racism that pervaded American society. Theirs was a utopian vision in the sense that it was a moral ideal that had never yet been realized; gradual emancipation in the American North and British emancipation in the West Indies offered models for freedom of the body, but not mass conversions of sentiment. The early residents of Oberlin had no practical program other than to live together in pursuit of this ideal and the transformation of their own characters. While the struggle against human bondage led them from a dedication to moral suasion into political engagement, and eventually into armed confrontation, the battle against racial prejudice was less straightforward.

Antebellum Oberlinians worked zealously to end slavery, which they believed caused prejudice and racial inequality. Whites as well as blacks bravely defied the Fugitive Slave Act of 1850 and fought valiantly in the Civil War. But after the Civil War townspeople struggled to comprehend the cause of the persistent social and economic inequality between the community's white majority on the one hand, and people of color on the other. White Oberlinians continued to encourage education, believing it would empower and equalize the races, thereby securing a more just distribution of wealth and influence. Like most Americans of their era, they firmly believed that hard work would be rewarded with material success. Holding on to these assumptions in the face of enduring racial disparities, white Oberlinians over time concluded that the source of persistent inequality lay in the dissolute character and behavior of African Americans, rather than the obstinacy of white bigotry and the tenacity of structural racism.

In 1926 Professor Kemper Fullerton told an Oberlin audience, "If the problem of the relationship of the white and colored race cannot be worked out in a just and satisfactory way in Oberlin, a place dedicated almost at its birth to the cause of emancipation, it cannot be worked out in the nation at large."[126] Yet Oberlin had already proved unequal to the task. Before and during the Civil War, the town modeled, albeit imperfectly, a racially integrated community based on a shared commitment to the abolition of American slavery and the eradication of racial prejudice. In 1863, Father Keep predicted that the economic gap between the races would close once emancipation ushered in a new era of upward mobility for blacks. But in the post–Civil War years, racial inequality deepened in Oberlin as members of the African American elite left town to pursue their prospects elsewhere and the local economy provided only modest opportunities for the advancement of ordinary people of color. White townspeople failed to heed the concerns of their black counterparts who worried about the virulent racism that resurged in the South and then spread northward. Embracing temperance as their new path to salvation, Oberlin's post–Civil War white reformers ignored a deepening racial divide within the community.

During the closing years of the nineteenth century, local black leaders adopted a strategy of respectability that proved an inadequate weapon with which to battle the condemnation of blackness that developed alongside the stigmatization of the poor.[127] Then, in the early twentieth century, white leaders of both the town and the college turned their backs on the pursuit of racial justice, declaring that they lacked the capacity to resist external social forces that brought the color line into Oberlin. Moreover, they no longer believed that the entrenched racial inequality they observed could be remedied by education, economic opportunity, religious conversion, or good will. In the face of neglect, exhaustion, and new local attitudes, Oberlin's black residents found themselves without power and with few white allies.

In the end, perhaps a fatal flaw was built into the original utopian vision articulated by the founders: the notion that the final step in the elimination of white supremacy was "the elevation of both [the emancipated slave and the free person of color] to an intellectual, moral, and political equality with the whites."[128] By making *white* achievement the standard, Oberlin's pioneering antislavery activists ignored both the necessity for black self-determination and the importance of black participation in the construction of goals to be pursued by a truly collaborative, egalitarian, multiracial community. This defect in the original vision was largely hidden so long as ending slavery remained the paramount concern. But in the years after the Civil War, the insensitivity of whites to the enduring obstacles facing blacks resulted in a process of self-reinforcing economic inequality as people of color long barred from remunerative work continued to arrive in Oberlin. Perhaps the outcome might have been different if Oberlin's original vision of a radical racial utopia had included reparations for the formerly enslaved, if community-wide celebrations of black culture and citizenship had highlighted achievement and autonomy, if political priorities had been set in consultations where the powerless invoked principles that provoked the powerful to act.

Could such a community have ever existed? And is it too late? Nestled into the flatlands of the Midwestern glacial plain, Oberlin has no hill upon which it might have perched itself as a model for the world. The quest for utopia nonetheless pushed many of the town's early residents to see beyond their present. While the history of race in Oberlin reminds us that well-meaning actions can have unintended consequences, amid today's continuing struggle for the conscience and soul of America, we need the courage to envision a future of racial justice, an inclusive and productive multicultural politics, an economy of abundance widely shared, and a society of mutual respect, generosity, and dignity. Dreams are dangerous, imperfect, and powerful. They are also elusive, as are the utopias we imagine.

EPILOGUE

On the morning of Thursday, May 4, 1944, as Americans eagerly awaited news of an impending Allied invasion of France in the global war against fascism, nine Oberlin College theology students publicly challenged the longstanding "whites-only" practices of local barbershops. Accompanied by the pastor of First Church, three students entered one shop, while six students went into another, each contingent including both white and black students. When chairs became available, the white students deferred to their black colleagues seeking service. But the barbers demurred, insisting "that technical difficulties were involved which would make it difficult for them to do successful work in hair cutting for a Negro." Without openly blocking access by other customers, the students drew the shops' proprietors into discussion and effectively prevented "business as usual." After about an hour, both shops suspended operations until, later in the day, an agreement was reached to open negotiations between the protesters and local barbers.[1] Oberlin's "barbershop controversy," at it came to be known, prompted a searching reevaluation of how people of color were treated in a community once fervently committed to the principle of racial equality.

Initial reaction to the students' protest was mixed. In a lengthy commentary published a week afterward, Charles Mosher, the editor of the *Oberlin News-Tribune,* sharply criticized the protesters' "unwise choice of tactics," which he complained were "too much like the methods of the posse, the vigilante, the Ku-Klux." Mosher also questioned whether, as temporary residents of Oberlin, the young men had a moral right "to foment troubles . . . and possibly nullify years of local progress toward better race relations, by one seemingly unnecessary and unwise act." Yet he acknowledged that the students' cause had merit. "[L]egally, logically and ethically, and particularly in the light of Oberlin's own traditions, no one can make a case in favor of discrimination against Negroes in barber shops," he wrote.[2] So what was to be done? Mosher offered a concrete proposal for collective action: "those who are interested in doing so [should] buy out one of the local barber shops and operate it on a bi-racial policy." He duly pledged his "own willingness to invest money and patronage in any such plan."[3]

On Sunday, May 14, Professor of Theology Walter M. Horton preached a guest sermon at First Church situating the barbershop controversy in the context of Oberlin's proud history. "Oberlin was planned and intended to be a New Jerusalem on the soil of Ohio, from the very first moment of its existence," he reminded his audience. "The founders of this community believed firmly in the equal rights of all human beings, male or female, Jew or Greek, white or colored." As a result, he reasoned, while elsewhere the "denial of barber service" on the basis of race might appear to be "a 'trivial' matter," in Oberlin it "constitutes a reversal of all the most sacred traditions and casts a cloud over the reputation for fair play for which we are famous."[4]

Horton portrayed the student protesters as champions of social justice in the activist tradition of the Lane Rebels and the Oberlin-Wellington Rescuers. "Is it not paradoxical for Oberlinites to point with pride to these perilous episodes in our past and then allow their teeth to chatter when a band of young theologs [sic] and a minister make an orderly demonstration in favor of the stricter observance of Ohio laws against racial discrimination?" he asked rhetorically. Horton endorsed Mosher's proposal to establish a "non-discriminating" barbershop in Oberlin, but he went one step further: he vowed to boycott the town's existing barbershops until they changed their policies. "Just what I'm to do now about a hair-cut, I don't know," Horton confessed. "But that is just the dilemma my Negro students and fellow-citizens are in. So long as they suffer, I intend to suffer with them."[5]

Over the next few weeks, a small Barber Shop Harmony Committee formed to explore "the possibilities of opening a barber shop which will give equal facilities to colored and white patrons."[6] Committee members included Walter M. Horton; Philip Bishop, a white professor in the Economics Department at the college; Normal C. Crosby, the black pastor of Mount Zion Church and a graduate of the Oberlin School of Theology; and Robert S. "Bob" Thomas, an African American clerk at the local post office. On June 19, the committee reported to a public meeting of "approximately 60 Oberlin citizens" at Mount Zion Church that it hoped to buy a barbershop on South Main Street and convert it into a nondiscriminatory enterprise.[7]

In mid-September, members of the Barber Shop Harmony Committee announced the formation of a corporation to establish the Cosmopolitan Barber Shop.[8] To raise capital for the enterprise, the corporation sold stock, pegging the price at only $1 per share to attract a wide array of subscribers—including women as well as men and out-of-towners as well as students and local residents. As the corporation explained in a public statement, the stock "is not offered as a security which will produce large dividends to stockholders; our investment is in the principle of racial equality."[9]

The next step, recruiting a barber to operate the shop, proved surprisingly difficult. In the early fall, after a barber from Washington, D.C., changed his mind about relocating to Oberlin, organizers searched for somebody else to take the job.[10] Thirty-five years later, Bob Thomas recalled that "[Philip] Bishop went as far away as Pittsburgh to try to get a barber; the black barbers wouldn't come because they said it wouldn't work."[11] Ultimately, Jerry Mizuiri, a Japanese American barber from California, accepted the position. Like thousands of other citizens of Japanese ancestry living on the West Coast, Mizuiri had been forcibly removed to an internment camp by presidential decree in 1942. He was later allowed to move to Cleveland, where he performed factory work in support of the war effort. On the recommendation of the federal War Relocation Authority, he began cutting hair at the Cosmopolitan Barber Shop in mid-November.[12]

The new enterprise got off to an uneven start. On the one hand, after six months revenues roughly matched expenses, demonstrating the financial viability of a nondiscriminatory barbering establishment.[13] On the other hand, the Cosmopolitan's customer base was disproportionately white. According to Bob Thomas's recollection, a short while after the shop opened, Philip Bishop said to him, "Bob, you know that only five percent of our business is Negroes." Thomas replied that black people felt highly uncomfortable about a person of Japanese descent "fooling around with their head with a razor."[14]

Black patronage of the Cosmopolitan increased after African American Robert L. Taliaferro succeeded Mizuiri as the shop's barber in the spring of 1945. Taliaferro had worked in Wooster, Wellington, and Cleveland before coming to Oberlin, and he was a Baptist minister as well as a barber. A year after his arrival, business was sufficiently robust that he hired a second barber, army veteran Gerald Scott, to help him.[15] Scott had lived in New York City before the war and had settled in Wooster after his discharge. While he was black, his wife was white, and their interracial marriage initially stirred some controversy in Oberlin. The barbershop corporation's officers stood by him, however, and Scotty, as he was commonly called, soon became a popular figure in the community.[16]

Two years after the Cosmopolitan Barber Shop's inception, shareholders were ready to declare their experiment a success and dissolve the corporation. In March 1947, after Taliaferro declined the opportunity, Gerald Scott bought the business and renamed it Scotty's Barber Shop and Shoe Shine Parlor. Five months later, under the headline "'All Races' Shop in Oberlin Hailed," the *Cleveland Plain Dealer* ran an article about Gerald Scott and his brother Charles, who worked alongside him. "We still are carrying out the original idea of the shop as carefully as possible," he explained in an interview. "We make a living, yes. We could do that anywhere. But we also are contributing toward racial harmony." The shop's clientele, he added, was "pretty evenly divided between the two races."[17]

Although the establishment of an integrated barbershop in the 1940s may seem like a small accomplishment when compared to the decision to admit students of color to the Oberlin Institute in the 1830s or the rescue of John Price from slave catchers in the 1850s, the success of the Cosmopolitan initiative was nonetheless significant. By renewing discussion of moral issues that had been largely neglected for decades and by effectively invoking Oberlin's distinctive egalitarian heritage, black and white activists rekindled the struggle for racial justice in their community.

In subsequent decades, interracial coalitions have continued to invoke Oberlin's antebellum heritage as they sought to dismantle the color line that took hold in the town after the Civil War. In the 1950s and early 1960s, town planners, activists, and dreamers worked together to reintegrate the city council, to desegregate new housing developments, and to enhance conditions for residents of Oberlin's traditionally black neighborhoods.[18] From the mid-1960s through the 1990s, black and white citizens demanded improvements in the education of African American students in the public schools and the adoption of affirmative action to promote local black employment. Yet economic inequality persisted. In 2000 the median annual income of black families in Oberlin was one quarter lower than the median annual income of the town's white families, and the poverty rate among black families was more than three times greater than that among white families. At the same time, only one-eighth of local African Americans aged twenty-five years or older were college graduates, compared to half of local whites in that age range.[19]

The quest for racial equality in Oberlin continues in the early twenty-first century. In 2008, a public celebration of the sesquicentennial of the Oberlin-Wellington Rescue brought together black and white residents to "testify to our great pride in our interracial antislavery heritage while recognizing that our community—like the nation at large—suffers from troubling racial divisions and racism in the present day." Organizers invited attendees to use the festivities "to renew our commitment to social justice and [to open] fresh dialogue among ourselves about how better to put progressive ideals into practice on a daily basis."[20] The persistent optimism in Oberlinians' intermittent rededications to the principle of racial equality is the closest thing to a happy ending that this study has to offer.

NOTES

INTRODUCTION

1. John Humphrey Noyes, *History of American Socialisms* (Philadelphia: J. B. Lippincott, 1870), 3.
2. Arthur Bestor, *Backwoods Utopias: The Sectarian Origins and the Owenite Phase of Communitarian Socialism in America, 1663-1829*, 2nd enlarged ed. (1950; reprint, Philadelphia: Univ. of Pennsylvania Press, 1970), 285; Donald E. Pitzer, ed., *America's Communal Utopias* (Chapel Hill: Univ. of North Carolina Press, 1997), 449-91; James M. Morris and Andrea L. Kross, *The A to Z of Utopianism* (Lanham, Md.: Scarecrow Press, 2009), 373-88.
3. Noyes, *History of American Socialisms*, 24-25.
4. Ibid., 26.
5. Ibid., 25.
6. Karl Mannheim, *Ideology and Utopia: An Introduction to the Sociology of Knowledge* (1936; reprint, New York: Harcourt, Brace and World, 1968), 205-6.
7. Covenant of Oberlin Colony, [1832], photocopy, Robert S. Fletcher Papers, ser. 1, subseries 4, box 19, Oberlin College Archives, Oberlin, Ohio.
8. Minutes, Feb. 10, 1835, Oberlin College Board of Trustees, ser. 2, subseries 2, box 1, Oberlin College Archives.
9. Quoted in J. W. Holton, *Holton's Semi-Centennial Directory and Guide to Oberlin, for 1883* (Oberlin, Ohio: News Office, 1883), 30.
10. Modern scholarly studies that focus on Oberlin's antebellum history include Robert Samuel Fletcher, *A History of Oberlin College from Its Foundation through the Civil War*, 2 vols. (Oberlin, Ohio: Oberlin College, 1943); William F. Cheek and Aimee Lee Cheek, *John Mercer Langston and the Fight for Black Freedom, 1829-65* (Urbana: Univ. of Illinois Press, 1989); Nat Brandt, *The Town that Started the Civil War* (Syracuse, N.Y.: Syracuse Univ. Press, 1990); J. Brent Morris, *Oberlin, Hotbed of Abolitionism: College, Community, and the Fight for Freedom and Equality in Antebellum America* (Chapel Hill: Univ. of North Carolina Press, 2014); Steven Lubet, *The "Colored Hero" of Harper's Ferry: John Anthony Copeland and the War against Slavery* (New York: Cambridge Univ. Press, 2015).

11. Books that concentrate mainly on the history of the college include Fletcher, *A History of Oberlin College from Its Foundation through the Civil War*; Donald M. Love, *Henry Churchill King, of Oberlin* (New Haven: Yale Univ. Press for Oberlin College, 1956); John Barnard, *From Evangelicalism to Progressivism at Oberlin College, 1866–1917* (Columbus: Ohio State Univ. Press, 1969); Cally L. Waite, *Permission to Remain among Us: Education for Blacks in Oberlin, Ohio, 1880–1914* (Westport, Conn.: Praeger, 2002); Geoffrey Blodgett, *Oberlin History: Essays and Impressions* (Kent, Ohio: Kent State Univ. Press, 2006); Roland M. Baumann, *Constructing Black Education at Oberlin College: A Documentary History* (Athens, Ohio: Ohio Univ. Press, 2010); Christi M. Smith, *Reparation and Reconciliation: The Rise and Fall of Integrated Higher Education* (Chapel Hill: Univ. of North Carolina Press, 2016). While William E. Bigglestone was the founding archivist at Oberlin College, he wrote about the history of the town in *Oberlin: From War to Jubilee, 1866–1883* (Oberlin, Ohio: Grady, 1983). Aaron Wildavsky, *Leadership in a Small Town* (1964; reprint, New Brunswick, N.J.: Transaction Publishers, 2004), focuses on political dynamics in the community during the mid-twentieth century.

12. Kemper Fullerton, "College or Cause," *Oberlin Alumni Magazine*, April 1926, 9.

13. Bernice Johnson Reagon, "Ella's Song," sung by Sweet Honey in the Rock, *Breaths* (Chicago: Flying Fish Records, 1988).

CHAPTER 1

1. Thomas Fairchild Sherman, *A Place on the Glacial Till: Time, Land, and Nature Within an American Town* (New York: Oxford Univ. Press, 1997), 60–78. For a fascinating study of the Great Lakes region as a whole during this period, see Richard White, *The Middle Ground: Indians, Empires, and Republics in the Great Lakes Region, 1650–1815* (Cambridge: Cambridge Univ. Press, 1991).

2. Sherman, *A Place on the Glacial Till*, 7, 40, 89–101.

3. Russia Township, Lorain County, Ohio, *Population Schedules of the Fifth Census of the United States, 1830* (National Archives Microfilm Publication M19), roll 135, pages 32A–33B.

4. Robert Samuel Fletcher, *A History of Oberlin College from Its Foundation Through the Civil War* (Oberlin, Ohio: Oberlin College, 1943), 1:58–66.

5. John J. Shipherd to Zebulon R. Shipherd, May 11, 1830, Oberlin College Office of the Treasurer, Letters Received by Oberlin College, Box 1, Oberlin College Archives, Oberlin, Ohio.

6. On the Rochester revival, see Paul E. Johnson, *A Shopkeeper's Millennium: Society and Revivals in Rochester, New York, 1815–1837* (New York: Hill and Wang, 1978).

7. Fletcher, *History of Oberlin College*, 1:67–68, 72.

8. Ibid., 1:84.

9. Ibid., 1:85–87.

10. Biographies of Oberlin include *The Life of John Frederic Oberlin, Pastor of Waldbach, in the Ban de La Roche* (Philadelphia: American Sunday School Union, 1830); John W. Kurtz, *John Frederic Oberlin* (Boulder, Colo.: Westview Press, 1976).

11. John J. Shipherd to Fayette Shipherd, Aug. 13, 1832, photocopy, Robert S. Fletcher Papers, ser. 3, subseries 1, box 9, Oberlin College Archives.

12. Ibid.

13. Fletcher, *History of Oberlin College*, 1:91.
14. Ibid., 1:91–92.
15. Ibid., 1:94.
16. Ibid., 1:101.
17. Covenant of Oberlin Colony, [1832], photocopy, Robert S. Fletcher Papers, ser. 1, subseries 4, box 19, Oberlin College Archives; David A. Weir, *Early New England: A Covenanted Society* (Grand Rapids, Mich.: Eerdmans, 2005); Kenneth A. Lockridge, *A New England Town: The First Hundred Years, Dedham, Massachusetts, 1636–1736* (New York: Norton, 1970), 4–7.
18. Covenant of Oberlin Colony.
19. Ibid.
20. John J. Shipherd to Fayette Shipherd, Dec. 10, 1832, photocopy, Robert S. Fletcher Papers, ser. 3, subseries 1, box 9; Fletcher, *History of Oberlin College*, 1:168–69.
21. Fletcher, *History of Oberlin College*, 1:96–97.
22. T. S. Ingersoll to John J. Shipherd, March 18, 1833, Oberlin College Office of the Treasurer, Letters Received by Oberlin College, box 1.
23. Fletcher, *History of Oberlin College*, 1:102–5.
24. Ibid., 1:104.
25. Covenant of Oberlin Colony; James Harris Fairchild, *Oberlin: The Colony and the College, 1833–1883* (Oberlin, Ohio: Goodrich, 1883), 36–37.
26. Quoted in Fletcher, *History of Oberlin College*, 1:127.
27. James Harris Fairchild, *Country Boy: Growing Up in Northern Ohio in the 1820s: A Historical Memoir,* ed. Geoffrey Blodgett (Elyria, Ohio: Lorain County Historical Society, 1993), 7–8.
28. Minutes, Oberlin Society, Oct. 15, 22, 1833, Oberlin College Office of the Treasurer, subgroup 1, ser. 7/1/3, box 1.
29. Quoted in Fletcher, *History of Oberlin College*, 1:121.
30. *New York Observer and Chronicle*, Aug. 24, 1833.
31. Ibid.; Paul Goodman, "The Manual Labor Movement and the Origins of Abolitionism," *Journal of the Early Republic* 13 (autumn 1993): 355–88.
32. Circular—Oberlin Collegiate Institute, March 8, 1834, Oberlin College Office of the Treasurer, subgroup 1, ser. 7/1/3, box 1.
33. Minutes, Oberlin Society, Dec. 23, 1833.
34. A Bill to Incorporate the Oberlin Presbyterian Society, Feb. 26, 1834, transcription, First and Second Congregational Churches of Oberlin Records, subgroup 1, ser. 1, box 1, Oberlin College Archives.
35. First Church Record Book 1, Aug.–Sept. 1834, First and Second Congregational Churches of Oberlin Records, subgroup 1, ser. 11, box 2.
36. Amy DeRogatis, *Moral Geography: Maps, Missionaries, and the American Frontier* (New York: Columbia Univ. Press, 2003), 37.
37. First Church Record Book 1, Sept. 13, 1834.
38. Robert S. Fletcher, "The Government of the Oberlin Colony," *Mississippi Valley Historical Review* 20 (September 1933): 179–90.
39. Fletcher, *History of Oberlin College*, 1:104; Wilbur H. Phillips, *Oberlin Colony: The Story of a Century* (Oberlin: Oberlin Printing Co., 1933), 21; Auditor's Duplicates for Oberlin

and Russia Township, 1835, Lorain County Records Retention Center, Elyria, Ohio; Fairchild, *Oberlin: The Colony and the College*, 32–48. On the social and cultural significance of the colony's layout, see DeRogatis, *Moral Geography*, 159–63.

40. Covenant of Oberlin Colony.

41. Auditor's Duplicates for Oberlin and Russia Township, 1835.

42. G. William Domhoff, *Who Rules America: Wealth, Income, and Power* (website), accessed Oct. 13, 2015, http://www2.ucsc.edu/whorulesamerica/power/wealth.html.

43. Gloria L Main, "Inequality in Early America: The Evidence from Probate Records of Massachusetts and Maryland," *Journal of Interdisciplinary History* 7 (spring 1977): 559–81.

44. *The First Annual Report of the Oberlin Collegiate Institute* (Elyria, Ohio, 1834), 11–12.

45. Ibid., 2; Fletcher, *History of Oberlin College*, 1:126–27.

46. Nathan P. Fletcher to Levi Burnell, Critical Letters, 1837, Letter No. 2, Oberlin College Office of the Treasurer, Administrative Files, ser. 7/1/3, box 4; Fletcher, *History of Oberlin College*, 1:140–41.

47. Fairchild, *Oberlin: The Colony and the College*, 46.

48. Fletcher, *History of Oberlin College*, 1:167–68.

49. On the radicalism of racial egalitarianism in the 1830s, see Paul Goodman, *Of One Blood: Abolitionism and the Origins of Racial Equality* (Berkeley: Univ. of California Press, 1998).

50. Fletcher, *History of Oberlin College*, 1:168.

51. The standard account of the controversy at Lane Seminary is Lawrence Thomas Lesick, *The Lane Rebels: Evangelicalism and Antislavery in Antebellum America* (Metuchen, N.J.: Scarecrow Press, 1980).

52. Robert H. Abzug, *Passionate Liberator: Theodore Dwight Weld and the Dilemma of Reform* (New York: Oxford Univ. Press, 1980), 47–50.

53. Ibid., 57–70.

54. Ibid., 86–89.

55. Theodore D. Weld to William Lloyd Garrison, Jan. 2, 1833, in *Letters of Theodore Dwight Weld, Angelina Grimké Weld and Sarah Grimké, 1822–1844*, ed. Gilbert Hobbs Barnes and Dwight Lowell Dumond (New York: D. Appleton-Century, 1934), 1:98.

56. [Henry B. Stanton et al.], *Debate at the Lane Seminary, Cincinnati—Speech of James A. Thome, of Kentucky, Delivered at the Annual Meeting of the American Anti-Slavery Society, May 6, 1834—Letter of the Rev. Dr. Samuel H. Cox, against the American Colonization Society* (Boston: Garrison and Knapp, 1834), [3]–5; Lesick, *The Lane Rebels*, 79–82.

57. Fletcher, *History of Oberlin College*, 1:154–55; Lesick, *The Lane Rebels*, 88–93.

58. Nikki M. Taylor, *Frontiers of Freedom: Cincinnati's Black Community, 1802–1868* (Athens: Ohio Univ. Press, 2005), 50–51, 64.

59. Fletcher, *History of Oberlin College*, 1:155–59; Lesick, *The Lane Rebels*, 95, 116–28.

60. Lesick, *The Lane Rebels*, 129–32.

61. *Liberator*, Jan. 10, 1835. Weld drafted the Rebels' statement. See Abzug, *Passionate Liberator*, 120.

62. Fletcher, *History of Oberlin College*, 168; Theodore D. Weld to John J. Shipherd, June 21, 1834, in Barnes and Dumond, eds., *Letters of Theodore Dwight Weld, Angelina Grimké Weld and Sarah Grimké, 1822–1844*, 1:152–53.

63. Asa Mahan, *Autobiography: Intellectual, Moral, and Spiritual* (London: T. Woolmer, 1882), 191–92; Edward H. Madden and James E. Hamilton, *Freedom and Grace: The Life of Asa Mahan* (Metuchen, N.J.: Scarecrow Press, 1982), 35–44.

64. Fletcher, *History of Oberlin College*, 1:168–69.

65. John J. Shipherd to Fayette Shipherd, Dec. 22, 1834, transcription, Robert S. Fletcher Papers, ser. 3, subseries 1, box 9.

66. Fletcher, *History of Oberlin College*, 1:169–73.

67. John J. Shipherd to Nathan P. Fletcher, Dec. 15, 1834, Oberlin College Office of the Treasurer Records, Administrative Files, ser. 7/1/5, subseries 1, box 1.

68. Nathan P. Fletcher to Levi Burnell, Critical Letters, Letter No. 3.

69. Fletcher, *History of Oberlin College*, 1:171.

70. For evidence of Keep's immediatist sentiments, see John Keep to Theodore Dwight Weld, Oct. 20, 1834, in Barnes and Dumond, eds., *Letters of Theodore Dwight Weld, Angelina Grimké Weld and Sarah Grimké, 1822–1844*, 1:173–74.

71. Students' Petition Regarding Admission of Persons of Color, Dec. 31, 1834, Miscellaneous Manuscripts, Oberlin College Archives; Roland M. Baumann, *Constructing Black Education at Oberlin College: A Documentary History* (Athens: Ohio Univ. Press, 2010), 20–21.

72. Petition Re: Colored Students, Jan. 1, 1835, Miscellaneous Archives, Oberlin College Office of the Treasurer, Oberlin College Archives; Baumann, *Constructing Black Education at Oberlin College*, 22–23.

73. Students' Petition Regarding Admission of Persons of Color; Petition Re: Colored Students; Baumann, *Constructing Black Education at Oberlin College*, 20–23.

74. Minutes, Jan. 1, 1835, Oberlin College Board of Trustees Records, ser. 2, subseries 2, box 1, Oberlin College Archives; Baumann, *Constructing Black Education at Oberlin College*, 24.

75. Nathan P. Fletcher to Levi Burnell, Critical Letters, Letter No. 3.

76. Minutes, Jan. 1, 1835, Oberlin College Board of Trustees Records.

77. Fletcher, *History of Oberlin College*, 1:172–75; J. Brent Morris, *Oberlin, Hotbed of Abolitionism: College, Community, and the Fight for Freedom and Equality in Antebellum America* (Chapel Hill: Univ. of North Carolina Press, 2014), 31–32.

78. John J. Shipherd to Trustees of the O. C. Institute, Jan. 19, 1835, photocopy, Robert S. Fletcher Papers, ser. 3, subseries 1, box 9.

79. Ibid.

80. Ibid.

81. Ibid.

82. John J. Shipherd to "all the beloved in Jesus Christ, whom I have gathered not only at Oberlin but in my *heart*," Jan. 27, 1835, transcription, Robert S. Fletcher Papers, ser. 3, subseries 1, box 9. For a slightly different version of this letter, see Fairchild, *Oberlin: The Colony and the College*, 337–46. Unfortunately, the original manuscript is missing.

83. Shipherd to "all the beloved in Jesus Christ, whom I have gathered not only at Oberlin but in my *heart*," Jan. 27, 1835.

84. Ibid.

85. Minutes, Feb. 9, 1835, Oberlin College Board of Trustees Records.

86. W. E. Bigglestone, "Irrespective of Color," *Oberlin Alumni Magazine* (spring 1981), 35–36; Milton Sernett, *Abolition's Axe: Beriah Green, Oneida Institute, and the Black Freedom Struggle*, paperback ed. (1986; reprint, Syracuse, N.Y.: Syracuse Univ. Press, 2004), 47, 52.

87. Minutes, Feb. 10, 1835, Oberlin College Board of Trustees Records.

88. Ibid. The board minutes do not include a record of the votes. Both James Harris Fairchild and Robert S. Fletcher assert that John Keep, in his role as chair, broke a 4–4 tie on the key resolution. See Fairchild, *Oberlin: The Colony and the College*, 64, and Fletcher, *History of Oberlin College*, 1:177.

89. Fletcher, *History of Oberlin College*, 1:179–80.

90. *New York Evangelist*, Feb. 28, 1835.

91. *Proceedings of the Ohio Anti-Slavery Convention—Held at Putnam, on the Twenty-Second, Twenty-Third, and Twenty-Fourth of April, 1835* ([Putnam, Ohio?]: Beaumont and Wallace, 1835), 40–41.

92. Ibid., 51.

93. Fletcher, *History of Oberlin College*, 1:182–83; Fairchild, *Oberlin: The Colony and the College*, 66–69.

94. *New York Evangelist*, Aug. 29, 1835.

95. Fletcher, *History of Oberlin College.*, 1:195; Fairchild, *Oberlin: The Colony and the College*, 71.

96. *Ohio Observer* (Hudson), July 9, 1835.

97. *New York Evangelist*, July 18, 1835.

98. *Liberator*, April 12, April 26, 1834; Constitution of the Oberlin Anti-Slavery Society, June 1835, Autograph File, Oberlin College Library Records, box 3, Oberlin College Archives.

99. Constitution of the Oberlin Anti-Slavery Society.

100. On white northerners' racial views in the early nineteenth century, see George M. Fredrickson, *The Black Image in the White Mind: The Debate on Afro-American Character and Destiny, 1817–1914* (New York: Harper and Row, 1972), 1–42; Reginald Horsman, *Race and Manifest Destiny: The Origins of American Racial Anglo-Saxonism* (Cambridge, Mass.: Harvard Univ. Press, 1981), 43–61, 81–157; James Brewer Stewart, "The Emergence of Racial Modernity and the Rise of the White North, 1790–1840," *Journal of the Early Republic* 18 (summer 1998): 181–217; Nicholas Guyatt, *Bind Us Apart: How Enlightened Americans Invented Racial Segregation* (New York: Basic Books, 2016), 247–80, 307–33.

101. David A. Gerber, *Black Ohio and the Color Line, 1860–1915* (Urbana: Univ. of Illinois Press, 1976), 3–4; Stephen Middleton, *The Black Laws: Race and the Legal Process in Early Ohio* (Athens: Ohio Univ. Press, 2005), 42–114.

102. Constitution of the Oberlin Anti-Slavery Society.

103. Ibid.

104. Ibid.

105. Appended to the manuscript copy of the Constitution in the Oberlin College Archives is a double-columned list of 379 names. The names are not actual signatures, however, and many of the names—mostly those of women—are crossed out. The figures in the text are based on an analysis of the first 230 names, including those crossed out.

106. Theodore D. Weld to Elizur Wright Jr., March 2, 1835, in Barnes and Dumond, eds., *Letters of Theodore Dwight Weld, Angelina Grimké Weld and Sarah Grimké, 1822–1844*, 1:206–7.

107. Theodore D. Weld to Lewis Tappan, Nov. 17, 1835, in Barnes and Dumond, eds., *Letters of Theodore Dwight Weld, Angelina Grimké Weld and Sarah Grimké, 1822-1844*, 1:242-45, quotation at 244.
108. *Oberlin Evangelist*, July 16, 1856.
109. Morris, *Oberlin, Hotbed of Abolitionism*, 43-48.

CHAPTER 2

1. John Keep to Gerrit Smith, Jan. 16, 1836, photocopy, Robert S. Fletcher Papers, box 19, Oberlin College Archives.
2. William F. Cheek and Aimee Lee Cheek, *John Mercer Langston and the Fight for Black Freedom, 1829-65* (Urbana: Univ. of Illinois Press, 1989), 85.
3. John Mercer Langston, *From the Virginia Plantation to the National Capitol* (1894; reprint, New York: Arno Press, 1969), 19; Cheek and Cheek, *John Mercer Langston and the Fight for Black Freedom*, 12-14.
4. Langston, *From the Virginia Plantation to the National Capitol*, 19-22; Cheek and Cheek, *John Mercer Langston and the Fight for Black Freedom*, 17.
5. Cheek and Cheek, *John Mercer Langston and the Fight for Black Freedom*, 19. Quarles had owned twenty-one slaves in 1830. By his will, he left twelve bondpeople to relatives and freed at least four others. Ibid., 15, 19.
6. Ibid., 20-21. William Langston was Lucy's son by a man other than Ralph Quarles.
7. Ibid., 30-33.
8. Ibid., 85; *Catalogue of the Trustees, Officers, and Students of the Oberlin Collegiate Institute; Together with the Second Annual Report* (Cleveland, Ohio, 1835), 13, 20.
9. Constitution of the Oberlin Anti-Slavery Society, June 1835, Autograph File (16/5), Oberlin College Library Records, box 3, Oberlin College Archives.
10. First Church Record Book 1, March 6, 1836, First and Second Congregational Churches of Oberlin Records, subgroup 1, ser. 11, box 2, Oberlin College Archives.
11. Cheek and Cheek, *John Mercer Langston and the Fight for Black Freedom*, 85.
12. James Bradley, "Brief Account of an Emancipated Slave," in *The Oasis*, ed. Lydia Maria Francis Child (Boston: B. C. Bacon, 1834), 106-7.
13. Ibid., 107-10.
14. [Henry B. Stanton et al.], *Debate at the Lane Seminary, Cincinnati—Speech of James A. Thome, of Kentucky, Delivered at the Annual Meeting of the American Anti-Slavery Society, May 6, 1834—Letter of the Rev. Dr. Samuel H. Cox, against the American Colonization Society* (Boston: Garrison and Knapp, 1834), 4.
15. Lawrence Thomas Lesick, *The Lane Rebels: Evangelicalism and Antislavery in Antebellum America* (Metuchen, N.J.: Scarecrow Press, 1980), 80-81.
16. Hiram Wilson to Amzi Barber, March 25, 1836. We thank George Dick for sharing images of this letter with us and for subsequently placing the original on deposit at the Oberlin College Archives.
17. Ibid. The authors have chosen throughout this volume to truncate the N-word when it appears in originals.

18. Ibid.

19. Robert Samuel Fletcher, *A History of Oberlin College from Its Foundation Through the Civil War* (Oberlin, Ohio: Oberlin College, 1943), 1:189; Ron Gorman, "James Bradley—From Hopeless Bondage to Lane Rebel," *Oberlin Heritage Center Blog* (website), posted Sept. 5, 2013, accessed Dec. 5, 2015, www.oberlinheritagecenter.org/blog/.

20. *Oberlin Evangelist*, Nov. 18, 1840; Henry Cowles, Catalogue and Record of Colored Students, 1835–1862, Minority Student Records, Oberlin College Archives.

21. Christopher P. Lehman, *Slavery in the Upper Mississippi Valley, 1787–1865: A History of Human Bondage in Illinois, Iowa, Minnesota and Wisconsin* (Jefferson, N.C.: McFarland, 2011), 33.

22. *Oberlin News*, March 19, March 26, 1897; William E. Bigglestone, *They Stopped in Oberlin: Black Residents and Visitors of the Nineteenth Century* (Scottsdale, Ariz.: Innovation Group, 1981), 59–61; Cheek and Cheek, *John Mercer Langston and the Fight for Black Freedom*, 286.

23. J. B. Meachum to Levi Burnell, May 29, 1839, photocopy, Oberlin College Treasurer's Office, Correspondence 1822–1897, box 5, Oberlin College Archives.

24. Bigglestone, *They Stopped in Oberlin*, 60; Oberlin College, *Alumni Register: Graduates and Former Students, Teaching and Administrative Staff, 1833–1960* (Oberlin, Ohio: Oberlin College, 1960), 349; *Oberlin News*, May 5, 1890.

25. The earliest known published account of this incident failed to mention Cox but established the year it took place. *New York National Anti-Slavery Standard*, Dec. 16, 1841.

26. A. L. Shumway and C. DeW. Brower, *Oberliniana: A Jubilee Volume of Semi-Historical Anecdotes Connected with the Past and Present of Oberlin College, 1833–1883* (Cleveland, Ohio: Home Publishing, 1883), 25.

27. Lewis Garrard Clarke and Milton Clarke, *Narratives of the Sufferings of Lewis and Milton Clarke, Sons of a Soldier of the Revolution, during a Captivity of More than Twenty Years among the Slaveholders of Kentucky, One of the So Called Christian States of North America—Dictated by Themselves* (Boston: B. Marsh, 1846), 86.

28. Shumway and Brower, *Oberliniana*, 26–27.

29. Ibid., 27; J. Brent Morris, *Oberlin, Hotbed of Abolitionism: College, Community, and the Fight for Freedom and Equality in Antebellum America* (Chapel Hill: Univ. of North Carolina Press, 2014), 200–203.

30. Bigglestone, *They Stopped in Oberlin*, 60–61; Oberlin Tax Map for 1851, Lorain County Auditor's Office, Elyria, Ohio.

31. Bigglestone, *They Stopped in Oberlin*, 75–76; Joseph Janey in 1830 U.S. Federal Census, Seneca, Seneca County, Ohio, M19, roll 140, page 151, *Ancestry.com*, accessed Dec. 6, 2015.

32. Enumeration of White Youth between the Ages of Four and Twenty One Years Residing in District No. 3 of the Township of Russia between the First and Twentieth of October 1843, Enumeration of White Youth between the Ages of Four and Twenty One Years Residing in District No. 3 of the Township of Russia between the First and Twentyeth of October 1848, Enumeration of Colored Youth between the Ages of Four and Twenty One Years Residing in District No. 3 of the Township of Russia between the First and Twentyeth of October 1848, Oberlin Public Schools, Oberlin Community, box 9, Oberlin College Archives; *General*

Catalogue of Oberlin College, 1833-1908, Including an Account of the Principal Events in the History of the College, with Illustrations of the College Buildings (Oberlin, Ohio: Oberlin College, 1909), 323.

33. *Oberlin Evangelist,* March 17, 1847.

34. Patricia Holsworth, "Oberlin Genealogical Database," 2012, in the authors' possession; Martha Gaskins in 1850 U.S. Federal Census, Russia Township, Lorain County, M432, roll 705, page 254A, image 30, *Ancestry.com,* accessed Dec. 6, 2015.

35. Russia Township, Lorain County, Ohio, *Population Schedules of the Sixth Census of the United States, 1840* (National Archives Microfilm Publication M704), roll 409, pages 161–167B; Russia Township, Lorain County, Ohio, *Population Schedules of the Seventh Census of the United States, 1850* (National Archives Microfilm Publication M432), roll 705, pages 242A–266B, images 6–55.

36. Oberlin was not unique among Midwestern towns in attracting African Americans from the Upper South during this period. For studies of other such communities, see Stephen A. Vincent, *Southern Seed, Northern Soil: African-American Farm Communities in the Midwest, 1765–1900* (Bloomington: Indian Univ. Press, 1999), and Sundiata Keita Cha-Jua, *America's First Black Town: Brooklyn, Illinois, 1830–1915* (Urbana: Univ. of Illinois Press, 2000).

37. "Early Years Tax Duplicates," *Lorain County Records Retention Center* (website), Russia Township, 1843, vol. 1, 268, accessed Feb. 2, 2013, www.loraincounty.us/commissioners-departments/records-center/records-search/early-tax-duplicates.

38. David Gordon in 1850 U.S. Federal Census, Russia, Lorain County, Ohio, M432, roll 705, page 246A, image 14, *Ancestry.com,* accessed Feb. 2, 2013.

39. William Gordon in 1830 U.S. Federal Census, Plymouth, Richmond County, Ohio, M19, roll 139, page 74, *Ancestry.com,* accessed Feb. 2, 2013.

40. David Gordon in 1860 U.S. Federal Census, Henrietta, Lorain County, Ohio, M653, roll 1002, page 290, image 220, *Ancestry.com,* accessed Feb. 2, 2013.

41. Barbara Fields, *Slavery and Freedom on the Middle Ground: Maryland during the Nineteenth Century* (New Haven: Yale Univ. Press, 1985), 1–6; T. Stephen Whitman, *The Price of Freedom: Slavery and Manumission in Baltimore and Early National Maryland* (Lexington: Univ. Press of Kentucky, 1997), 93–118. Until 1832, Maryland permitted freed blacks to remain in the state following manumission.

42. Bigglestone, *They Stopped in Oberlin,* 31–32; Jno Campton in 1840 U.S. Federal Census, Raleigh, Wake County, North Carolina, M704, roll 374, page 196, image 880, *Ancestry.com,* accessed Feb. 5, 2013; "Early Years Tax Duplicates," *Lorain County Records Retention Center* (website), Russia Township, 1843, accessed Jan. 23, 2013, www.lcrecordscenter.com/cgi-bin/early_tax.cgi.

43. John Campton in 1850 U.S. Federal Census, Russia, Lorain County, Ohio, M432, roll 705, page 254A, image 30, *Ancestry.com,* accessed Feb. 5, 2013; Oberlin Tax Map for 1851, Office of the Lorain County Engineer, Elyria, Ohio; Reference and Statistical Map of Oberlin, Lorain County, Ohio, 1857, Oberlin College Archives; Auditor's Duplicates for Oberlin and Russia Township, 1850, Lorain County Records Retention Center, Elyria, Ohio; *General Catalogue of Oberlin College, 1833–1908,* 158–59.

44. Bigglestone, *They Stopped in Oberlin,* 50, 123, 125.

45. Allen Jones—LifeStory, *Ancestry.com*, accessed Dec. 10, 2015; Bigglestone, *They Stopped in Oberlin*, 122; Steven Lubet, *The "Colored Hero" of Harper's Ferry: John Anthony Copeland and the War against Slavery* (New York: Cambridge Univ. Press, 2015), 35.

46. Allen Jones in "North Carolina, Index to Marriage Bonds, 1741–1868," bond date: Jan. 1, 1821, bond # 000154731, *Ancestry.com*, accessed Dec. 11, 2015.

47. Bigglestone, *They Stopped in Oberlin*, 122–23; Holsworth, "Oberlin Genealogical Database"; Allen Jones—LifeStory; Carol C. Bowie to Mercedes Holden Singleton, Oct. 30, 1960, photocopy, Ellen Lawson-Marlene Merrill Papers, box 3, Oberlin College Archives; Lubet, *The "Colored Hero" of Harper's Ferry*, 35.

48. Allen Jones—Family Emancipation Papers, *Ancestry.com*, accessed Dec. 10, 2015; Charles Jones—Bill of Sale, *Ancestry.com*, accessed Dec. 10, 2015; Lubet, *The "Colored Hero" of Harper's Ferry*, 35–36.

49. "Jones Family Tree," *Ancestry.com*, accessed Nov. 27, 2012; Allen Jones in 1840 U.S. Federal Census, Wake County, North Carolina, M704, roll 374, page 124, image 737, *Ancestry.com*, accessed Nov. 27, 2012.

50. *Raleigh Register*, April 8, 1842.

51. Ibid., Oct. 18, 1842.

52. John Hope Franklin, *The Free Negro in North Carolina, 1790–1860* (1943; reprint, Chapel Hill: Univ. of North Carolina Press, 1995), 92.

53. Bigglestone, *They Stopped in Oberlin*, 123.

54. *Raleigh Register*, Oct. 21, 1842.

55. Ibid., Dec. 6, 1842.

56. Holsworth, "Oberlin Genealogical Database"; Lubet, *The "Colored Hero" of Harper's Ferry*, 29–30.

57. Bigglestone, *They Stopped in Oberlin*, 50, 192; Leslie M. Kesler to Nancy Hendrikson, June 15, 2005, photocopy in the authors' possession; "Copeland Family Tree," *Ancestry.com*, accessed December 10, 2012; Jno Copeland in 1840 U.S. Federal Census, Raleigh, Wake County, North Carolina, M704, roll 374, image 196, *Ancestry.com*, accessed Nov. 28, 2012.

58. "Copeland Family Tree"; Bigglestone, *They Stopped in Oberlin*, 52, 202.

59. Bigglestone, *They Stopped in Oberlin*, 125.

60. *Oberlin Weekly News*, Aug. 19, 1881.

61. Bigglestone, *They Stopped in Oberlin*, 119; *Lorain County Exponent*, May 5, 1886; Henry Johnson in 1850 U.S. Federal Census, Russia, Lorain County, Ohio, M432, roll 705, page 249B, image 21, *Ancestry.com*, accessed Dec. 13, 2015; Henry Johnson in 1860 U.S. Federal Census, Russia, Lorain County, Ohio, M653, roll 1002, page 188, image 17, *Ancestry.com*, accessed Dec. 13, 2015.

62. *Oberlin Weekly News*, March 3, 1882.

63. Auditor's Duplicates for Oberlin and Russia Township, 1843, 1850.

64. Henry Johnson in 1850 U.S. Federal Census, Russia, Lorain County, Ohio.

65. Paul Heinegg, *Free African Americans of North Carolina, Virginia, and South Carolina from the Colonial Period to about 1820*, 5th ed. (Baltimore, Md.: Clearfield, 2005), 2:687.

66. Wm. Jarvis in 1810 U.S. Federal Census, York, Virginia, M252, roll 71, page 302, image 0181431, *Ancestry.com*, accessed Jan. 22, 2013; Wm. Jarvis in 1820 U.S. Federal Census,

NOTES TO PAGES 44–46

York, Virginia, M33, roll 135, image 166, *Ancestry.com*, accessed Jan. 22, 2013. On the status of free blacks in post-Revolutionary Virginia, see Eva Sheppard Wolf, *Race and Liberty in the New Nation: Emancipation in Virginia from the Revolution to Nat Turner's Rebellion* (Baton Rouge: Louisiana State Univ. Press, 2006), 85–161.

67. Luther Porter Jackson, *Free Negro Labor and Property Holding in Virginia, 1830-1860* (New York: D. Appleton-Century, 1942), 119, 209.

68. Thomas Jarvis in 1830 U.S. Federal Census, York County, Virginia, M19, roll 201, page 439, *Ancestry.com*, accessed Jan. 22, 2013; Thomas Jarvis in 1840 U.S. Federal Census, York County, Virginia, M794, roll 576, page 319, image 1280, *Ancestry.com*, accessed Jan. 22, 2013.

69. Bigglestone, *They Stopped in Oberlin*, 113–14.

70. On the motivations and behavior of black slaveholders in Virginia, see Philip J. Schwarz, "Emancipators, Protectors, and Anomalies: Free Black Slaveowners in Virginia," *Virginia Magazine of History and Biography* 95 (July 1987): 317–38.

71. Bigglestone, *They Stopped in Oberlin*, 113; Auditor's Duplicates for Oberlin and Russia Township, 1850.

72. *Oberlin Weekly News*, Oct. 31, 1872.

73. John Watson in 1850 U.S. Federal Census, Russia, Lorain County, Ohio, M432, roll 705, page 255A, image 32, *Ancestry.com*, accessed Dec. 15, 2015.

74. Ibid.; Charles R. Camp, *Camp's Directory of Oberlin, 1873-74: Comprising a Complete Directory of the Village of Oberlin, Including a History of the Business Men from the Foundation of Oberlin Up to the Present Time; Rates of Fare to All Points on the L.S. & M.S.R.R.* (Oberlin: Lorain County News Print, 1873), 9.

75. Bigglestone, *They Stopped in Oberlin*, 222.

76. Auditor's Duplicates for Oberlin and Russia Township, 1860.

77. "Robert and Margaret Van Vrankin," William E. Bigglestone Papers, ser. 3, subseries 1, box 11, Oberlin College Archives; Robert Vanwerker in 1830 U.S. Federal Census, Lansingburg, Rensselaer, New York, M19, roll 105, pages 87–88, *Ancestry.com*, accessed March 28, 2013; Robert Vanrankin in 1840 U.S. Federal Census, West Massilon, Stark County, Ohio, M704, roll 427, page 187, image 378, *Ancestry.com*, accessed March 28, 2013.

78. Auditor's Duplicates for Oberlin and Russia Township, 1843; Membership Register, First and Second Congregational Churches of Oberlin Records, subgroup 1, ser. 11, box 2, Oberlin College Archives.

79. Oberlin Tax Map for 1851.

80. Robert Vanvrankin in 1850 U.S. Federal Census, Russia, Lorain County, Ohio, M432, roll 75, page 261A, image 44, *Ancestry.com*, accessed Dec. 16, 2015.

81. For an overview of the black student experience at the Oberlin Institute, see Ellen N. Lawson and Marlene Merrill, "The Antebellum 'Talented Thousandth': Black College Students at Oberlin Before the Civil War," *Journal of Negro Education* 52 (spring 1983): 142–55.

82. William Cooper Nell, *The Colored Patriots of the American Revolution, with Sketches of Several Distinguished Colored Persons: To Which Is Added a Brief Survey of the Condition and Prospects of Colored Americans* (Boston: R. F. Wallcut, 1855), 181–88; Cheek and Cheek, *John Mercer Langston and the Fight for Black Freedom*, 88–89.

83. *General Catalogue of Oberlin College, 1833-1908*, 1005.

84. On the history and significance of First of August celebrations, see Edward Bartlett Rugemer, *The Problem of Emancipation: The Caribbean Roots of the American Civil War* (Baton Rouge: Louisiana State Univ. Press, 2008), 222–57.

85. *Oberlin Evangelist*, August 17, 1842.

86. R. J. M. Blackett, *Beating against the Barriers: Biographical Essays in Nineteenth-Century Afro-American History* (Baton Rouge: Louisiana State Univ. Press, 1986), 287–90; Todd Mealy, *Aliened American: A Biography of William Howard Day* (Baltimore, Md.: PublishAmerica, 2010).

87. Blackett, *Beating against the Barriers*, 290–92.

88. *Oberlin Evangelist*, Nov. 6, 1844.

89. Ibid., June 24, 1846.

90. Blackett, *Beating against the Barriers*, 295.

91. Philip S. Foner and George E. Walker, eds., *Proceedings of the Black State Conventions, 1840–1865* (Philadelphia: Temple Univ. Press, 1979), 1:226.

92. *Oberlin Evangelist*, July 17, 1844; Cheek and Cheek, *John Mercer Langston and the Fight for Black Freedom*, 113–16.

93. Blackett, *Beating against the Barriers*, 299.

94. Ellen NicKenzie Lawson and Marlene D. Merrill, *The Three Sarahs: Documents of Antebellum Black College Women* (New York: E. Mellen Press, 1984), 189, 193.

95. Ibid., 190–91.

96. Ibid., 191–92.

97. *Oberlin Evangelist*, Dec. 17, 1850.

98. Ibid., Nov. 6, 1850.

99. Cheek and Cheek, *John Mercer Langston and the Fight for Black Freedom*, 88–90.

100. Langston, *From the Virginia Plantation to the National Capitol*, 77.

101. Ibid., 78–79.

102. Ibid., 80–81, 89–90, 92.

103. Foner and Walker, *Proceedings of the Black State Conventions, 1840–1865*, 226.

104. U.S. Census Office, *The Seventh Census of the United States: 1850* (Washington, D.C.: R. Armstrong, 1853).

105. Russia Township, Lorain County, Ohio, *Population Schedules of the Seventh Census of the United States, 1850*; Auditor's Duplicates for Oberlin and Russia Township, 1850.

106. Russia Township, Lorain County, Ohio, *Population Schedules of the Seventh Census of the United States*.

107. Ibid.

108. Ibid.

109. Ibid.; Auditor's Duplicates for Oberlin and Russia Township, 1850.

110. Auditor's Duplicates for Oberlin and Russia Township, 1850; Holsworth, "Oberlin Genealogical Database."

111. U.S. Census Office, *Population of the United States in 1860: Compiled from the Original Returns of the Eighth Census, Under the Direction of the Secretary of the Interior* (Washington, D.C.: Government Printing Office, 1864), 386.

112. Bigglestone, *They Stopped in Oberlin*, 70, 110; "Evans Migration with Others," Bigglestone Papers, ser. 3, subseries 1, box 11.

113. Quoted in Robert Ewell Greene, *The Leary-Evans, Ohio's Free People of Color* (Washington, D.C.: Robert Ewell Greene, 1979), 46.

114. Bigglestone, *They Stopped in Oberlin*, 70.

115. Ibid., 69–70; Lubet, *The "Colored Hero" of Harper's Ferry*, 72–73; Rose Leary Love, "Plum Thickets and Field Daisies: My Father—John Sinclair Leary," *Charlotte-Mecklenburg Story* (website), accessed Dec. 19, 2015, www.cmstory.org/content/my-father-john-sinclair-leary. See also Elizabeth Dowling Taylor, *The Original Black Elite: Daniel Murray and the Story of a Forgotten Era* (New York: Amistad, HarperCollins, 2017), 40–42.

116. Henry Evans and Wilson Evans in "North Carolina, Marriage Index, 1741–2004" (database online), *Ancestry.com*, accessed Dec. 19, 2015.

117. For differing views on when Lewis Sheridan Leary journeyed to Oberlin, see Bigglestone, *They Stopped in Oberlin*, 164; Cheek and Cheek, *John Mercer Langston and the Fight for Black Freedom*, 355; Lubet, *The "Colored Hero" of Harper's Ferry*, 74–75.

118. Cheek and Cheek, *John Mercer Langston and the Fight for Black Freedom*, 355–56; Taylor, *The Original Black Elite*, 44.

119. Bigglestone, *They Stopped in Oberlin*, 163–64.

120. Ibid., 206–7; Daniel J. Sharfstein, *The Invisible Line: Three American Families and the Secret Journey from Black to White* (New York: Penguin Press, 2011), 28–29; Napoleon Wall in 1850 U.S. Federal Census, Chester, Clinton County, Ohio, M432, roll 668, page 291B, image 259, *Ancestry.com*, accessed Dec. 21, 2015.

121. Sharfstein, *The Invisible Line*, 34–38; Bigglestone, *They Stopped in Oberlin*, 207; Stephen Wall in "North Carolina, Wills and Probate Records, 1665–1998" (database online), *Ancestry.com*, accessed Dec. 21, 2015.

122. Bigglestone, *They Stopped in Oberlin*, 207; Cheek and Cheek, *John Mercer Langston and the Fight for Black Freedom*, 251–54; Sharfstein, *The Invisible Line*, 87–90; Oberlin College, *Alumni Register*.

123. Auditor's Duplicates for Oberlin and Russia Township, 1855.

124. Bigglestone, *They Stopped in Oberlin*, 207; John Wall in 1860 U.S. Federal Census, Oberlin, Lorain County, Ohio, M653, roll 1002, page 224, image 88, *Ancestry.com*, accessed Dec. 21, 2015; Albert Wall in 1860 U.S. Federal Census, Oberlin, Lorain County, Ohio, M653, roll 1002, page 225, image 90, *Ancestry.com*, accessed Dec. 21, 2015.

125. Holsworth, "Oberlin Genealogical Database"; Stanislas Etienne d'Anglas, *Quelques considérations sur l'hémoptysie* (Montpellier, France, 1825); Dr. J. D'Anglas in "New Orleans, Passenger Lists, 1813–1945" (database online), *Ancestry.com*, accessed Sept. 3, 2013; Elizabeth Shown Mills, "Certificates of Naturalization, Natchitoches Parish, Louisiana, 1820–1850," *Louisiana Genealogical Register* 21 (March 1974): 91.

126. Bigglestone, *They Stopped in Oberlin*, 176; Holsworth, "Oberlin Genealogical Database."

127. Doctor S. Danglass in 1840 U.S. Federal Census, M704, Natchitoches, Louisiana, roll 127, page 147, image 305, *Ancestry.com*, accessed March 6, 2013.

128. Holsworth, "Oberlin Genealogical Database."

129. Stanislaus Danglass in 1850 U.S. Federal Census, Natchitoches, Louisiana, M432, roll 233, page 46B, image 243, *Ancestry.com*, accessed March 7, 2013.

130. Stanislaus Dunglads [*sic*] in 1850 U.S. Federal Census—Slave Schedules, Natchitoches, Louisiana, M432, *Ancestry.com*, March 7, 2013.

NOTES TO PAGES 55–58

131. E. J. Miller to [President of Oberlin College], March 9, 1850, file 7/1/5, box 10, Oberlin College Archives; Bigglestone, *They Stopped in Oberlin*, 176; William Ingersoll in 1850 U.S. Federal Census, Russia, Lorain County, Ohio, M432, roll 705, page 254B, image 31, *Ancestry .com*, accessed March 6, 2013.

132. Bigglestone, *They Stopped in Oberlin*, 176; Holsworth, "Oberlin Genealogical Database"; Auditor's Duplicates for Oberlin and Russia Township, 1855.

133. Stanislas E. D'Anglas in "Oberlin Gravestone Inventory Database," *Oberlin Heritage Center: Oberlin Westwood Cemetery Transcription Project* (website), accessed Dec. 3, 2015, www.oberlinwestwood.org.

134. Stanislas E. Danglas, Will of Stanislas E. Danglas (Oberlin, Ohio, Jan. 30, 1854), Estate Case #751, microfilm, Lorain County Probate Court, Elyria, Ohio.

135. James S. Brawley, "Maxwell Chambers," in *Dictionary of North Carolina Biography*, ed. William Stevens Powell, vol. 1, *A–C* (Chapel Hill: Univ. of North Carolina Press, 1979), 351.

136. Cornelia Rebekah Shaw, *Davidson College, Intimate Facts* (New York: Fleming H. Revell Press, 1923), 87–88, n. 1.

137. Brawley, "Maxwell Chambers," 352.

138. Ibid., 351–52; Maxwell Chambers in North Carolina, Marriage Bonds, 1741–1868 (database online), *Ancestry.com*, accessed March 1, 2013.

139. Maxwell Chambers in 1850 U.S. Federal Census—Slave Schedules, Rowan County, North Carolina, M432, *Ancestry.com*, accessed Dec. 29, 2015.

140. Brawley, "Maxwell Chambers," 352.

141. Ibid.

142. [Maxwell Chambers], *Last Will of Maxwell Chambers* (Salisbury, N.C.: J. J. Bruner, 1856), 9.

143. *Salisbury (N.C.) Post*, July 12, 2015, online at www.salisburypost.com/2015/07/27/yesterday-the-freedom-document-for-slaves-of-maxwell-chambers/, accessed Dec. 29, 2015. Rymer appears to have been a Salisbury shoemaker. See *Carolina Watchman* (Salisbury, N.C.), May 13, 1852.

144. [Chambers], *Last Will of Maxwell Chambers*, 11; Bigglestone, *They Stopped in Oberlin*, 36.

145. Oberlin, Lorain County, Ohio, *Population Schedules of the Eighth Census of the United States, 1860* (National Archives Microfilm Publication M563), roll 1002, pages 199–226; Bigglestone, *They Stopped in Oberlin*, 38.

146. John E. Patterson in 1860 U.S. Federal Census, Oberlin, Lorain County, Ohio, M653, roll 1002, page 224, image 88, *Ancestry.com*, accessed Dec. 20, 2015.

CHAPTER 3

1. John Mercer Langston, *From the Virginia Plantation to the National Capitol* (1894; reprint, New York: Arno Press, 1969), 100.

2. Ibid., 102.

3. "The King Philosophy: The Beloved Community," *The Martin Luther King Jr. Center for Nonviolent Social Change* (website), accessed Jan. 25, 2016, http://www.thekingcenter.org/king-philosophy#sub4.

4. Zeruiah Porter Weed to S. S. Jocelyn, Dec. 21, 1859, transcription, Lawson-Merrill Papers, box 2, Oberlin College Archives, Oberlin, Ohio.

5. Delazon Smith, *Oberlin Unmasked: A History of Oberlin, or New Lights of the West. Embracing the Conduct and Character of the Officers and Students of the Institution; Together with the Colonists, from the Founding of the Institution* (Cleveland: S. Underhill and Son, 1837), 60.

6. *Ohio Statesman* (Columbus), March 19, 1841.

7. Langston, *From the Virginia Plantation to the National Capitol*, 101–2. See also J. Brent Morris, *Oberlin, Hotbed of Abolitionism: College, Community, and the Fight for Freedom and Equality in Antebellum America* (Chapel Hill: Univ. of North Carolina Press, 2014), 197.

8. *Liberator*, March 2, 1849.

9. *Oberlin Tribune*, July 4, 1901. We thank Roland Baumann for bringing this article to our attention.

10. "Local," *Oberlin Students' Monthly* 1 (Feb. 1859): 160.

11. U.S. Census Office, *Population of the United States in 1860: Compiled from the Original Returns of the Eighth Census, Under the Direction of the Secretary of the Interior* (Washington, D.C.: Government Printing Office, 1864), 386.

12. Stephen Middleton, *The Black Laws in the Old Northwest: A Documentary History* (Westport, Conn.: Greenwood Press, 1993), 34.

13. Ibid., 35, 34.

14. Ibid., 35; *Chalmers v. Stewart*, 11 Ohio 386 (1842); Paul Finkelman, "Race, Slavery, and Law in Antebellum Ohio," in *History of Ohio Law*, ed. Michael Les Benedict and John F. Winkler (Athens: Ohio Univ. Press, 2004), 762; Stephen Middleton, *The Black Laws: Race and the Legal Process in Early Ohio* (Athens: Ohio Univ. Press, 2005), 133–34. On the antebellum struggle for black education in Ohio, see Kabria Baumgartner, "Building the Future: White Women, Black Education, and Civic Inclusion in Antebellum Ohio," *Journal of the Early Republic* 37 (spring 2017): 117–45.

15. *Oberlin News*, Feb. 3, 1899.

16. Oberlin School District Minutes, 1834–51, Oberlin Public Schools, Oberlin Community, box 13, Oberlin College Archives.

17. Middleton, *The Black Laws in the Old Northwest*, 35.

18. Jonathan Entin, "An Ohio Dilemma: Race, Equal Protection, and the Unfulfilled Promise of a State Bill of Rights," *Cleveland State Law Review* 51 (Jan. 1, 2004): 404–5, available online at engagedscholarship.csuohio.edu/clevstlrev/vol51/iss3/6.

19. *Jeffries v. Ankeny*, 11 Ohio 372, at 375 (1842); *Oberlin Evangelist*, Feb. 1, 1843.

20. Among the "white youth" enumerated in Oberlin in 1843 were African Americans Richard Campton, [John] Anthony Copeland, George Copeland, Henry Copeland, Elizabeth Janey, Emeline Janey, Thomas Janey, and William Watson. Enumeration of White Youth between the Ages of Four and Twenty One Years Residing in District No. 3 of the Township of Russia between the First and Twentieth of October 1843, Oberlin Public Schools, Oberlin Community, box 9, Oberlin College Archives.

21. *American Freeman* (Prairieville, Wis.), Jan. 12, 1847. We are grateful to the late Ron Gorman for bringing this source to our attention.

22. Marlene D. Merrill, *Sarah Margru Kinson: The Two Worlds of an* Amistad *Captive* (Oberlin: Oberlin Historical and Improvement Organization, 2003), 1–8. Standard works

on the *Amistad* uprising include Howard Jones, *Mutiny on the* Amistad: *The Saga of a Slave Revolt and Its Impact on American Abolition, Law, and Diplomacy* (New York: Oxford Univ. Press, 1987), and Marcus Rediker, *The* Amistad *Rebellion: An Atlantic Odyssey of Slavery and Freedom* (New York: Viking, 2012). See also Benjamin N. Lawrance, *Amistad's Orphans: An Atlantic Story of Children, Slavery, and Smuggling* (New Haven, Conn.: Yale Univ. Press, 2014).

23. Quoted in Merrill, *Sarah Margru Kinson*, 8–9.

24. Middleton, *Black Laws in the Old Northwest*, 36–37.

25. Enumeration of White Youth between the Ages of Four and Twenty One Years Residing in District No. 3 of the Township of Russia between the First and Twentyeth of October 1848, Enumeration of Colored Youth between the Ages of Four and Twenty One Years Residing in District No. 3 of the Township of Russia between the First and Twentyeth of October 1848, Oberlin Public Schools, Oberlin Community, box 9, Oberlin College Archives.

26. Clayton S. Ellsworth, "Ohio's Legislative Attack upon Abolition Schools," *Mississippi Valley Historical Review* 21 (Dec. 1934): 379–86; Robert Samuel Fletcher, *A History of Oberlin College from Its Foundation Through the Civil War* (Oberlin, Ohio: Oberlin College, 1943), 1:442–43; Morris, *Oberlin, Hotbed of Abolitionism*, 1–2, 133–35.

27. Fletcher, *History of Oberlin College*, 2:887–88.

28. *Annual Catalogue of the Officers and Students of Oberlin College, for the College Year 1855–56* (Oberlin: James M. Fitch, 1855).

29. *Catalogue of the Officers and Students of Oberlin College, for the College Year 1850–51* (Oberlin: James M. Fitch, 1850); *Triennial Catalogue of the Officers and Students of Oberlin College, for the College Year 1851–52* (Oberlin: James M. Fitch, 1851); *Catalogue of the Officers and Students of Oberlin College, for the College Year 1852–53* (Oberlin: James M. Fitch, 1852); *Catalogue of the Officers and Students of Oberlin College, for the College Year 1853–54* (Oberlin: James M. Fitch, 1853); *Triennial Catalogue of the Officers and Students of Oberlin College, for the College Year 1854–55* (Oberlin: James M. Fitch, 1854); *Annual Catalogue of the Officers and Students of Oberlin College, for the College Year 1855–56*; *Annual Catalogue of the Officers and Students of Oberlin College, for the College Year 1856–57* (Oberlin: James M. Fitch, 1856); *Annual Catalogue of the Officers and Students of Oberlin College, for the College Year 1857–58* (Oberlin: James M. Fitch, 1857); *Annual Catalogue of the Officers and Students of Oberlin College, for the College Year 1859–60* (Oberlin: Shankland and Harmon, 1859).

30. Henry Cowles, Catalogue and Record of Colored Students, 1835–1862, RG 5/4/3—Minority Student Records, Oberlin College Archives; Russia Township, Lorain County, Ohio, *Population Schedules of the Seventh Census of the United States, 1850* (National Archives Microfilm Publication M432), roll 705, pages 242A–266B, images 6–55; Oberlin, Lorain County, *Population Schedules of the Eighth Census of the United States, 1860* (National Archives Microfilm Publication M653), roll 1002, pages 199B–226A.

31. For lists of students in the Collegiate and Ladies Literary Courses during the 1850s, see the catalogues cited in note 3.29. For a path-breaking article on black students who did college-level coursework at Oberlin before 1865, see Ellen N. Lawson and Marlene Merrill, "The Antebellum 'Talented Thousandth': Black College Students at Oberlin Before the Civil War," *Journal of Negro Education* 52 (spring 1983): 142–55.

32. John Morgan et al. to Asa Mahan, March 5, 1850, Miscellaneous Archives 1850–51, box 8, Asa Mahan Folder, Oberlin College Archives.

33. Thirza S. Pelton et al., To the Trustees of the O.C. Institute (petition), 1850, Miscellaneous Archives, 1850–52, box 8, Asa Mahan File, Oberlin College Archives.

34. John Campton et al., "Beloved and Rightly Esteemed President Mahan" (petition), 1850, Miscellaneous Archives, 1850–52, box 8, Asa Mahan File, Oberlin College Archives.

35. *Oberlin Evangelist*, Sept. 10, 1851.

36. Ibid., July 16, 1856; J. H. Fairchild, *Oberlin: Its Origin, Progress and Results. An Address, Prepared for the Alumni of Oberlin College, Assembled August 22, 1860* (Oberlin: Shankland and Harmon, 1860), 28.

37. Carol Lasser, "Enacting Emancipation: African American Women Abolitionists at Oberlin College and the Quest for Empowerment, Equality, and Respectability," in *Women's Rights and Transatlantic Antislavery in the Era of Emancipation*, ed. Kathryn Kish Sklar and James Brewer Stewart (New Haven, Conn.: Yale Univ. Press, 2007), 319–45.

38. Fairchild, *Oberlin: Its Origin, Progress and Results*, 28.

39. *Oberlin Evangelist*, July 17, 1844.

40. Ibid.

41. *Lorain County News* (Oberlin), Sept. 26, 1860.

42. *Liberator*, March 24, 1848; *North Star* (Rochester, N.Y.), March 31, 1848.

43. Langston, *From the Virginia Plantation to the National Capitol*, 101.

44. Edward Henry Fairchild, *Historical Sketch of Oberlin College* (Springfield, [Ohio]: Republic Printing, 1868), 25.

45. The Second Congregational Church of Oberlin was established in 1860 in order to relieve overcrowding at the original church. Wilbur H. Phillips, *Oberlin Colony: The Story of a Century* (Oberlin: Oberlin Printing, 1933), 97.

46. First Church Record Book 1, Aug. 19, 1834; June 17, 1836; May 26, 1837, First and Second Congregational Churches of Oberlin Records, subgroup 1, ser. 11, box 2, Oberlin College Archives.

47. Phillips, *Oberlin Colony*, 65–66.

48. Marlene Merrill, "First Church and Oberlin's Early African American Community" (Presentation to Oberlin African-American Genealogy and History Group, Oberlin, Ohio, Dec. 6, 2003), accessed March 3, 2016, www.oberlin.edu/external/EOG/FirstChurch/FirstChurch-Merrill.html.

49. Lawrence Thomas Lesick, *The Lane Rebels: Evangelicalism and Antislavery in Antebellum America* (Metuchen, N.J.: Scarecrow Press, 1980), 175–78.

50. As noted in chapter 2, Gideon and Charles Langston joined the Congregational Church in March 1836. First Church Record Book 1, March 6, 1836.

51. Seating Plan of First Church, 1844, First and Second Congregational Churches of Oberlin Records, subgroup 1, ser. 18, box 1, Oberlin College Archives.

52. *Liberator*, April 6, 1849.

53. Ibid., Oct. 10, 1856.

54. Members Register, 1857–1891, First and Second Congregational Churches of Oberlin Records, subgroup 1, ser. 11, box 2A, Oberlin College Archives; Cowles, Catalogue and Record of Colored Students, 1835–1862; Patricia Holsworth, "Oberlin Genealogical Database," 2012, in the authors' possession.

55. William F. Cheek and Aimee Lee Cheek, *John Mercer Langston and the Fight for Black Freedom, 1829–65* (Urbana: Univ. of Illinois Press, 1989), 293.

56. *Oberlin Evangelist*, Sept. 14, 1853.

57. Ibid.

58. On the emergence of scientific racism, see George M. Fredrickson, *The Black Image in the White Mind; the Debate on Afro-American Character and Destiny, 1817-1914*, Harper Torchbooks ed. (New York: Harper and Row, 1972); Reginald Horsman, *Race and Manifest Destiny: The Origins of American Racial Anglo-Saxonism* (Cambridge, Mass.: Harvard Univ. Press, 1981); Bruce R. Dain, *A Hideous Monster of the Mind: American Race Theory in the Early Republic* (Cambridge, Mass.: Harvard Univ. Press, 2002). On race as a social construction, see Michael Omi and Howard Winant, *Racial Formation in the United States: From the 1960s to the 1990s*, 2nd ed. (New York: Routledge, 1994).

59. *Oberlin Evangelist*, Sept. 14, 1853.

60. Ibid.

61. Sydney E. Ahlstrom, *A Religious History of the American People* (New Haven: Yale Univ. Press, 1972), 1:521-32; Christine Leigh Heyrman, *Southern Cross: The Beginnings of the Bible Belt* (New York: Knopf, 1997), 264-66.

62. Marcus Dale to American Missionary Association, April 2, 1861, photocopy, Lawson-Merrill Papers, box 3, Oberlin College Archives.

63. Ibid.

64. The federal census for 1860 lists no persons of color in Pittsfield Township, which is immediately south of Russia Township.

65. Oberlin, Lorain County, *Population Schedules of the Eighth Census of the United States, 1860* (National Archives Microfilm Publication M653), roll 1002, pages 199B-226A.

66. Ibid.; William E. Bigglestone, *They Stopped in Oberlin: Black Residents and Visitors of the Nineteenth Century* (Scottsdale, Ariz: Innovation Group, 1981), 222.

67. Oberlin, Lorain County, *Population Schedules of the Eighth Census of the United States, 1860*.

68. Ibid.

69. Ohio Constitution of 1803, *Ohio History Central* (website), accessed Sept. 12, 2014, www.ohiohistorycentral.org/w/Ohio_Constitution_of_1803_(Transcript)?rec=1858.

70. *Jeffries v. Ankeny*, 376. See also Dana Elizabeth Weiner, *Race and Rights: Fighting Slavery and Prejudice in the Old Northwest, 1830-1870* (DeKalb: Northern Illinois Univ. Press, 2013), 34-37.

71. *Cleveland Plain Dealer*, October 17, 1857.

72. Russia Township Records, vol. 3, Oct. 9, 1855, RG 31/11, Oberlin College Archives.

73. Ibid., April 6, 1857.

74. Cheek and Cheek, *John Mercer Langston and the Fight for Black Freedom*, 259-60, 296.

75. Langston, *From the Virginia Plantation to the National Capitol*, 162-63.

76. W. D. Patterson to William Patterson, January 31, 1853, Oberlin File, ser. II: Letters by Oberlin Students 1835-51, Oberlin College Archives.

77. Morris, *Oberlin, Hotbed of Abolitionism*, 197-98.

78. *Cleveland Herald*, Feb. 26, 1853.

79. Allen Jones—LifeStory, *Ancestry.com*, accessed Dec. 10, 2015; Steven Lubet, *The "Colored Hero" of Harper's Ferry: John Anthony Copeland and the War against Slavery* (New York, N.Y.: Cambridge Univ. Press, 2015), 35-39. See also chapter 2 above.

80. *Oberlin Weekly News*, Aug. 19, 1881.

81. Charles R. Camp, *Camp's Directory of Oberlin, 1873-74: Comprising a Complete Directory of the Village of Oberlin, Including a History of the Business Men from the Foundation of Oberlin Up to the Present Time; Rates of Fare to All Points on the L.S. & M.S.R.R.* (Lorain County News Print, 1873), 25.

82. *General Catalogue of Oberlin College, 1833-1908. Including an Account of the Principal Events in the History of the College, with Illustrations of the College Buildings* (Oberlin: Oberlin College, 1909), 529, 531, 534.

83. Carol C. Bowie to Mercedes Holden Singleton, Oct. 30, 1960, photocopy, Ellen Lawson-Marlene Merrill Papers, box 3, Oberlin College Archives.

84. *North Star*, Sept. 29, 1848.

85. *Cleveland Herald*, Aug. 28, 1856.

86. Denton J. Snider, *A Writer of Books in His Genesis; Written for and Dedicated to His Pupil-Friends Reaching Back in a Line of Fifty Years* (St. Louis, Mo.: Sigma Publishing, 1910), 102. On Snider's career, see *Dictionary of American Biography*, s.v. "Snider, Denton Jacques," and *The Dictionary of Modern American Philosophers*, s.v. "Snider, Denton Jacques."

87. Snider, *A Writer of Books*, 100.

88. Ibid., 103.

89. "James M. Jones," William E. Bigglestone Papers, ser. 3, subseries 1, box 11, Oberlin College Archives; Bigglestone, *They Stopped in Oberlin*, 124.

90. "Allen Jones," Bigglestone Papers, ser. 3, subseries 1, box 11.

91. On the concept of "seeing race," see Matthew Pratt Guterl, *Seeing Race in Modern America* (Chapel Hill: Univ. of North Carolina Press, 2013).

92. Clayton Sumner Ellsworth, "Oberlin and the Anti-Slavery Movement up to the Civil War" (Ph.D. diss., Cornell University, 1930), 115, n. 27.

93. Ibid., 131.

94. Ibid., 134.

95. Holsworth, "Oberlin Genealogical Database."

96. *Annals of Cleveland, 1818-1935: A Digest and Index of the Newspaper Record of Events and Opinions* (Cleveland, Ohio: Cleveland W.P.A. Project, 1936), 20:184; *Lorain Republican* (Elyria, Ohio), May 17, 1843.

97. Auditor's Duplicates for Oberlin and Russia Township, 1840, Lorain County Records Retention Center, Elyria, Ohio.

98. Holsworth, "Oberlin Genealogical Database."

99. *Cleveland Plain Dealer*, Sept. 18, 1857.

100. Ibid., Oct. 17, 1857.

101. *Elyria Republican*, May 17, 1900.

102. Holsworth, "Oberlin Genealogical Database."

103. Auditor's Duplicates for Oberlin and Russia Township, 1845.

104. Oberlin Tax Map for 1851, Lorain County Auditor's Office, Elyria, Ohio; James Harris Fairchild, *Oberlin: The Colony and the College, 1833-1883* (Oberlin: E. J. Goodrich, 1883), 237; *Elyria Courier*, Jan. 5, 1853.

105. *Elyria Courier*, Jan. 5, 1853.

106. *Cleveland Plain Dealer*, Dec. 19, 1856.

107. Holsworth, "Oberlin Genealogical Database."

108. On "colorphobia," see "An Address Delivered at Oberlin, Ohio, by Miss Sally Holley, daughter of Myron Holley, of Rochester, N.Y.," published in *North Star,* Jan. 23, 1851.

109. Langston, *From the Virginia Plantation to the National Capitol,* 158.

110. Ibid., 159.

111. C. S. Williams, *Williams' Medina, Elyria and Oberlin City Directory, City Guide, and Business Mirror* (n.p., 1859); Oberlin, Lorain County, *Population Schedules of the Eighth Census of the United States, 1860*; Auditor's Duplicates for Oberlin and Russia Township, 1860; Oberlin, Part of Map of Lorain County, 1857, GR case 4, drawer 1, Oberlin College Archives.

112. Douglas S. Massey, *American Apartheid: Segregation and the Making of the Underclass* (Cambridge, Mass: Harvard Univ. Press, 1993), 21.

113. James Oliver Horton and Lois E. Horton, *Black Bostonians: Family Life and Community Struggle in the Antebellum North* (New York: Holmes and Meier, 1979), 6.

114. Langston, *From the Virginia Plantation to the National Capitol,* 158.

115. Zeruiah Porter Weed to S. S. Jocelyn, December 21, 1859.

116. Middleton, *The Black Laws,* 250–51.

117. Smith, *Oberlin Unmasked,* 58.

118. *Lorain County News,* May 7, 1862.

119. Bigglestone, *They Stopped in Oberlin,* 119–20; Henry Johnson in 1850 U.S. Federal Census, Russia, Lorain County, Ohio, M432, roll 705, page 249B, image 21, *Ancestry.com,* accessed Dec. 13, 2015; Holsworth, "Oberlin Genealogical Database."

120. Bigglestone, *They Stopped in Oberlin,* 73–74; Holsworth, "Oberlin Genealogical Database"; Elizabeth Fox in "U.S., Find a Grave Index, 1600s-Current" (online database), *Ancestry.com,* accessed March 16, 2016.

121. Lorain County, Ohio, Abstract of Wills, 1824–1865 from Probate Court Records, Court House, Elyria, Ohio, typescript (1962), Lorain County Historical Society, Elyria, Ohio; Stanislas E. Danglas, Will of Stanislas E. Danglas (Oberlin, Ohio, Jan. 30, 1854), Estate Case #751, microfilm, Lorain County Probate Court, Elyria, Ohio; *Elyria (Ohio) Independent Democrat,* Feb. 13, 1856.

122. Holsworth, "Oberlin Genealogical Database"; B. F. Adair in 1850 U.S. Federal Census—Slave Schedules, Spring Creek, Phillips County, Arkansas, M432, *Ancestry.com,* accessed Sept. 8, 2014.

123. Benjamin Adair in 1860 U.S. Federal Census, Oberlin, Lorain County, Ohio, M653, roll 1002, page 203, image 47, *Ancestry.com,* accessed Sept. 8, 2014; Auditor's Duplicates for Oberlin and Russia Township, 1860.

124. "Benjamin F. Adair and Family," Bigglestone Papers, ser. 3, subseries 1, box 11.

125. Holsworth, "Oberlin Genealogical Database"; Bigglestone, *They Stopped in Oberlin,* 215; Carl G. Jahn, ed., *Ohio Nisi Prius and General Term Reports* (Columbus, Ohio: Carl G. Jahn, 1896), 3:197.

126. Jahn, ed., *Ohio Nisi Prius and General Term Reports,* 3:196; Ellen Warren in 1850 U.S. Federal Census, Madison, Jefferson County, Indiana, M432, roll 154, page 42B, image 89, *Ancestry.com,* accessed March 18, 2016.

127. M. Warren to Ellen, Mary et al. (Emancipation Deed), entered Sept. 9, 1860, Miscellaneous Records 1, 1848–73, pages 295–96, Lorain County Recorder's Office, Elyria, Ohio.

128. Quoted in Bigglestone, *They Stopped in Oberlin*, 215.
129. Ibid.; *Lorain County News*, Feb. 9, 1871.
130. Nat Brandt, *The Town That Started the Civil War* (Syracuse, N.Y.: Syracuse Univ. Press, 1990), 55–58.
131. *Lorain County News*, Nov. 14, 1860.
132. *Ohio Statesman* (Columbus), Nov. 10, 1860.
133. Malachi Warren's failure to marry Ellen haunted the town for decades after his death in 1862, leading to a legal battle over the property on which Ellen and the children lived. See *Oberlin Weekly News*, March 27, 1890.

CHAPTER 4

1. This chapter's title pays tribute to Aileen S. Kraditor's classic study *Means and Ends in American Abolitionism: Garrison and His Critics on Strategy and Tactics, 1834–1850* (New York: Pantheon Books, 1969).
2. Constitution of the Oberlin Anti-Slavery Society, June 1835, Autograph File, Oberlin College Library Records, box 3, Oberlin College Archives, Oberlin, Ohio.
3. For a comprehensive study of American abolitionism that foregrounds the critical role of African American activists, see Manisha Sinha, *The Slave's Cause: A History of Abolition* (New Haven: Yale Univ. Press, 2016).
4. K. Stephen Prince, "Oppression Shall Not Always Reign: The Evolution of Christian Antislavery in Oberlin, 1835–1863" (honors thesis, Oberlin College, 2004), 15–35; J. Brent Morris, *Oberlin, Hotbed of Abolitionism: College, Community, and the Fight for Freedom and Equality in Antebellum America* (Chapel Hill: Univ. of North Carolina Press, 2014), 89–95.
5. *Ohio State Journal and Columbus Gazette*, Dec. 18, 1835.
6. Memorial of Ladies of Oberlin praying Congress to reject all proposals for the annexation of Texas, presented Sept. 26, 1837 (SEN25A-Hi), 25th Cong., 1st sess., Records of the U.S. Senate, RG 46, box 122, National Archives, Washington, D.C.; *Philanthropist* (Cincinnati), Dec. 7, 1842. We thank Ben Weber for his extraordinary work tracking down Oberlin petitions held by the National Archives.
7. *Oberlin Evangelist*, Sept. 30, 1846; Clayton Sumner Ellsworth, "Oberlin and the Anti-Slavery Movement up to the Civil War" (Ph.D. diss., Cornell University, 1930), 118–23, n. 33; Stacey M. Robertson, *Hearts Beating for Liberty: Women Abolitionists in the Old Northwest* (Chapel Hill: Univ. of North Carolina Press, 2010), 138–41; Morris, *Oberlin, Hotbed of Abolitionism*, 123–31. As Morris points out, Douglass switched sides on this issue soon afterward.
8. *Oberlin Evangelist, Extra*, [July 6, 1848].
9. Morris, *Oberlin, Hotbed of Abolitionism*, 143.
10. *Oberlin Evangelist*, Aug. 16, 1848.
11. Ibid., Sept. 27, 1848.
12. Ellsworth, "Oberlin and the Anti-Slavery Movement up to the Civil War," 114, n. 25.
13. Stephen E. Maizlish, *The Triumph of Sectionalism: The Transformation of Ohio Politics, 1844–1856* (Kent, Ohio: Kent State Univ. Press, 1983), 124–42; Frederick J. Blue and Robert McCormick, "Norton S. Townshend: A Reformer for All Seasons," in *The Pursuit of*

Public Power: Political Culture in Ohio, 1787-1861, ed. Andrew R. L. Cayton and Jeffrey Paul (Kent, Ohio: Kent State Univ. Press, 1994), 146-48; Paul Finkelman, "Race, Slavery, and Law in Antebellum Ohio," in *History of Ohio Law*, ed. Michael Les Benedict and John F. Winkler (Athens: Ohio Univ. Press, 2004), 767.

14. *Liberator*, March 2, 1849.

15. Ibid.

16. *Oberlin Evangelist*, Feb. 28, 1849.

17. Ibid.

18. *Report of the Debates and Proceedings of the Convention for the Revision of the Constitution of the State of Ohio, 1850-51*, ed. J. Victor Smith (Columbus: S. Medary, 1851); Frank U. Quillin, *The Color Line in Ohio: A History of Race Prejudice in a Typical Northern State* (Ann Arbor, Mich.: G. Wahr, 1913), 60-87.

19. "Fugitive Slave Act 1850," *Avalon Project*, accessed September 12, 2014, http://avalon.law.yale.edu/19th_century/fugitive.asp; Don E. Fehrenbacher, *The Slaveholding Republic: An Account of the United States Government's Relations to Slavery* (New York: Oxford Univ. Press, 2001), 231-35.

20. *Oberlin Evangelist*, Oct. 9, 1850.

21. *Oberlin Tribune*, July 4, 1901.

22. Ron Gorman, "The Secret Rooms of the Fitches," *Oberlin Heritage Center Blog*, posted Oct. 20, 2013, accessed April 11, 2016, www.oberlinheritagecenter.org/blog/2013/10/the-secret-rooms-of-the-fitches/.

23. *Oberlin Tribune*, July 4, 1901.

24. Ibid.

25. *Oberlin Evangelist*, July 16, 1856.

26. Young Men's Anti-Slavery Society Record Book, Oct. 1, 1852, Student Life: Activist/Political Organization, Oberlin College Archives; William F. Cheek and Aimee Lee Cheek, *John Mercer Langston and the Fight for Black Freedom, 1829-65* (Urbana: Univ. of Illinois Press, 1989), 209.

27. *Oberlin Evangelist*, Oct. 13, 1852.

28. *Elyria (Ohio) Independent Democrat*, Nov. 10, 1852.

29. David M. Potter, *The Impending Crisis, 1848-1861* (New York: Harper and Row, 1976), 152-67; Michael F. Holt, *The Political Crisis of the 1850s* (New York: Wiley, 1978), 144-47.

30. *Oberlin Evangelist*, June 7, 1854.

31. Ibid., June 21, 1854.

32. Ibid., Aug. 2, 1854.

33. Ibid., Aug. 16, 1854.

34. Ibid., Aug. 30, 1854.

35. Maizlish, *The Triumph of Sectionalism*, 203; *Cleveland Plain Dealer*, Oct. 20, 1855.

36. James Monroe, *Oberlin Thursday Lectures, Addresses and Essays* (Oberlin: E. J. Goodrich, 1897), 118-20; Catherine M. Rokicky, *James Monroe: Oberlin's Christian Statesman and Reformer, 1821-1898* (Kent, Ohio: Kent State Univ. Press, 2002), 33-36; *Acts of the State of Ohio* 53 (Columbus, 1856): 61-63.

37. *Ashland (Ohio) Union*, July 30, 1856.

38. Cheek and Cheek, *John Mercer Langston and the Fight for Black Freedom*, 322.

39. Paul Finkelman, *Dred Scott v. Sandford: A Brief History with Documents* (Boston: Bedford Books, 1997), 61.
40. *Oberlin Evangelist*, March 18, 1857.
41. Cheek and Cheek, *John Mercer Langston and the Fight for Black Freedom*, 296.
42. Rokicky, *James Monroe*, 44; William Cox Cochran, *The Western Reserve and the Fugitive Slave Law: A Prelude to the Civil War* (Cleveland, Ohio: Western Reserve Historical Society, 1920), 118; Morris, *Oberlin, Hotbed of Abolitionism*, 184–85.
43. Cochran, *The Western Reserve and the Fugitive Slave Law*, 118–21.
44. Jacob R. Shipherd, *History of the Oberlin-Wellington Rescue* (1859; reprint, n.p.: Qontro Historical Reprints, Filiquarian Publishing, 2009), 175.
45. Cochran, *The Western Reserve and the Fugitive Slave Law*, 123.
46. Cheek and Cheek, *John Mercer Langston and the Fight for Black Freedom*, 316–17; Nat Brandt, *The Town That Started the Civil War* (Syracuse, N.Y.: Syracuse Univ. Press, 1990), 54, 113–14; Steven Lubet, *The "Colored Hero" of Harper's Ferry: John Anthony Copeland and the War against Slavery* (New York: Cambridge Univ. Press, 2015), 67–69.
47. *Cleveland Leader*, Sept. 10, 1858.
48. Brandt, *The Town That Started the Civil War*, 63–69, 122; Lubet, *The "Colored Hero" of Harper's Ferry*, 91–92.
49. Shipherd, *History of the Oberlin-Wellington Rescue*, 23, 36.
50. Brandt, *The Town That Started the Civil War*, 69–86; Morris, *Oberlin, Hotbed of Abolitionism*, 209; Lubet, *The "Colored Hero" of Harper's Ferry*, 92–93.
51. Shipherd, *History of the Oberlin-Wellington Rescue*, 105; Brandt, *The Town That Started the Civil War*, 87–111, quotation at 105.
52. Shipherd, *History of the Oberlin-Wellington Rescue*, 105; Lubet, *The "Colored Hero" of Harper's Ferry*, 95.
53. Shipherd, *History of the Oberlin-Wellington Rescue*, 106.
54. Brandt, *The Town That Started the Civil War*, 87–111; Lubet, *The "Colored Hero" of Harper's Ferry*, 95–96, 100–101.
55. *New-York Daily Tribune*, Sept. 18, 1858.
56. Shipherd, *History of the Oberlin-Wellington Rescue*, 106.
57. Ibid.
58. *Oberlin Evangelist*, Sept. 29, 1858.
59. *Cleveland Plain Dealer*, Sept. 21, 1858.
60. Lubet, *The "Colored Hero" of Harper's Ferry*, 108–9.
61. *Cleveland Plain Dealer*, Nov. 9, 1858.
62. Ibid., Dec. 10, 1858. See also *Cleveland Leader*, Dec. 14, 1858.
63. *Cleveland Herald*, Dec. 7, 1858; *Cleveland Plain Dealer*, Dec. 7, 1858.
64. *Cleveland Plain Dealer*, Dec. 7, 1858; William E. Bigglestone, *They Stopped in Oberlin: Black Residents and Visitors of the Nineteenth Century* (Scottsdale, Ariz: Innovation Group, 1981), 111–12; Daniel J. Sharfstein, *The Invisible Line: Three American Families and the Secret Journey from Black to White* (New York: Penguin Press, 2011), 87–88; Patricia Holsworth, "Oberlin Genealogical Database," 2012, in authors' possession.
65. Russia Township Records, vol. 3, Oct. 9, 1855, RG 31/11, Oberlin College Archives; Russia Township, Lorain County, Ohio, *Population Schedules of the Seventh Census of the United*

States, 1850 (National Archives Microfilm Publication M432), roll 705, pages 242A–266B, images 6–55.

66. Shipherd, *History of the Oberlin-Wellington Rescue*, 4; Brandt, *The Town That Started the Civil War*, 126.

67. Shipherd, *History of the Oberlin-Wellington Rescue*, 4–5; Brandt, *The Town That Started the Civil War*, 126–29; Lubet, *The "Colored Hero" of Harper's Ferry*, 110–11.

68. *Oberlin Evangelist*, Jan. 19, 1859; "Local," *Oberlin Students' Monthly* 1 (Feb. 1859): 160. In 1908 Elias Toussaint Jones recalled that he had been "secretary of an Anti-Slavery Association of coloured people, in Oberlin, which had no white members, and which held weekly meetings in a hall that belonged to the negroes which they called 'Liberty School House'—This association kept a fund, fed by fines, dues, etc—for the helping of fugitive slaves." Interview with Elias Jones by K[atherine] M[ayo], Dec. 9, 1908, Oswald Garrison Villard [Collection of] John Brown Manuscripts, Rare Book and Manuscript Library, Columbia University, photocopy in Oberlin College Archives.

69. Shipherd, *History of the Oberlin-Wellington Rescue*, 5–6.

70. Ibid., 5–11; *Cleveland Leader*, Jan. 13, 1859.

71. *Oberlin Evangelist*, Jan. 19, 1859; *Cleveland Leader*, Jan. 14, 1859.

72. Shipherd, *History of the Oberlin-Wellington Rescue*, 13–88; Brandt, *The Town That Started the Civil War*, 145–58.

73. Paul Finkelman, "A Political Show Trial in the Northern District: The Oberlin-Wellington Fugitive Slave Rescue Case," in *Justice and Legal Change on the Shores of Lake Erie: A History of the United States District Court for the Northern District of Ohio*, ed. Paul Finkelman and Roberta Sue Alexander (Athens: Ohio Univ. Press, 2012), 54.

74. *Cleveland Leader*, April 16, 1859; Shipherd, *History of the Oberlin-Wellington Rescue*, 88–89; Brandt, *The Town That Started the Civil War*, 158–61.

75. *Cleveland Herald*, April 18, 1859; Jacob R. Shipherd, *History of the Oberlin-Wellington Rescue*, 90.

76. *The Rescuer* (Cleveland), July 4, 1859; Brandt, *The Town That Started the Civil War*, 196–99.

77. Brandt, *The Town That Started the Civil War*, 177–78, 195.

78. Shipherd, *History of the Oberlin-Wellington Rescue*, 175–78.

79. Ibid., 178, 170.

80. Brandt, *The Town That Started the Civil War*, 203–21; Morris, *Oberlin, Hotbed of Abolitionism*, 217–20.

81. Brandt, *The Town That Started the Civil War*, 221.

82. *The Rescuer* (Cleveland), July 4, 1859.

83. Brandt, *The Town That Started the Civil War*, 222–34. Bushnell was released on July 11 and received a hero's welcome upon his return to Oberlin. But he was unable to pay his fine and died penniless in 1861. Ibid., 240, 245–46.

84. Shipherd, *History of the Oberlin-Wellington Rescue*, 265–66.

85. Ibid., 266.

86. Ibid., 267.

87. Ibid., 268.

88. Ibid., 269–70.

89. Ibid., 270.

90. Ibid., 275.

91. For an alternative assessment that equates nonviolence and moderation, see Roland M. Baumann, *The 1858 Oberlin-Wellington Rescue: A Reappraisal* (Oberlin: Oberlin College, 2003), especially page 8.

92. Robert E. McGlone, *John Brown's War against Slavery* (New York: Cambridge Univ. Press, 2009), 220–328 passim.

93. Bigglestone, *They Stopped in Oberlin*, 50–52; Rose Leary Love, "A Few Facts about Lewis Sheridan Leary Who Was Killed at Harpers Ferry in John Brown's Raid," *Negro History Bulletin* 6 (June 1943): 198; Holsworth, "Oberlin Genealogical Database"; Lubet, *The "Colored Hero" of Harper's Ferry*, 30–39, 72–75, 78–80, 91–99.

94. Lubet, *The "Colored Hero" of Harper's Ferry*, 154–55.

95. *Oberlin Evangelist*, Nov. 9, 1859.

96. Lubet, *The "Colored Hero" of Harper's Ferry*, 134–36.

97. John Mercer Langston, *From the Virginia Plantation to the National Capitol* (1894; reprint, New York: Arno Press, 1969), 191–96; Cheek and Cheek, *John Mercer Langston and the Fight for Black Freedom*, 353–54; Lubet, *The "Colored Hero" of Harper's Ferry*, 129–30. Lubet hypothesizes that Copeland had already learned of Brown's plan from his friend James Monroe Jones, Allen Jones's son, when he accompanied John Price to Chatham, Canada, in the fall of 1858.

98. Cheek and Cheek, *John Mercer Langston and the Fight for Black Freedom*, 358; Lubet, *The "Colored Hero" of Harper's Ferry*, 164.

99. *Cleveland Plain Dealer*, Nov. 18, 1859.

100. *Oberlin Evangelist*, Nov. 9, 1859.

101. *Oberlin Students' Monthly* 2 (Jan. 1860): 93.

102. *Cleveland Leader*, Dec. 12, 1859.

103. Ibid., Dec. 16, 1859.

104. Ibid., Dec. 28, 1859.

105. *Oberlin Students' Monthly* 2 (Jan. 1860): 93.

106. Monroe, *Oberlin Thursday Lectures*, 158–61; Benjamin Quarles, *Allies for Freedom: Blacks and John Brown* (New York: Oxford Univ. Press, 1974), 140; Lubet, *The "Colored Hero" of Harper's Ferry*, 203–4.

107. Monroe, *Oberlin Thursday Lectures*, 162–84; *Oberlin Evangelist*, Jan. 4, 1860; Lubet, *The "Colored Hero" of Harper's Ferry*, 204–7.

108. Monroe, *Oberlin Thursday Lectures*, 174–75; *Liberator*, Jan. 13, 1860.

109. A. N. Beecher et al., "A Monument, To Commemorate the Manly Virtues of Those Noble Representatives of the Colored Race of the Nineteenth Century, John A. Copeland, Lewis Leary, and Shields Green, who, for the Cause of Freedom, laid down their lives at Harper's Ferry and Charlestown, Va., October 17, and December 16, 1859" (Oberlin, Ohio: n.p., Dec. 29, 1859), in *American Missionary Association Manuscripts*, microfilm, Amistad Research Center, Ohio roll 9. The text of this circular was published in the *Liberator*, Jan. 13, 1860, and *Weekly Anglo-African*, Jan. 14, 1860.

110. *Liberator*, Jan. 13, 1860. The monument to Oberlin's martyrs at Harpers Ferry was erected after the Civil War and stands today in Martin Luther King Jr. Park on East Vine Street.

CHAPTER 5

1. *Oberlin Evangelist,* May 23, Sept. 12, 1860; *Cleveland Herald,* Nov. 7, 1860.
2. *Lorain County News* (Oberlin), Feb. 6, 1861.
3. John Carey Leith to J. S. Leith et al., April 14, 1861, John C. Leith Papers, box 1, Oberlin College Archives.
4. Lucien C. Warner, *Personal Memoirs of Lucien Calvin Warner during Seventy-Three Eventful Years, 1841–1914* (New York: Association Press, 1915), 33.
5. *Cleveland Leader,* April 19, 1861; *Lorain County News,* April 24, 1861.
6. J. M. Guinn, "The Monroe Rifles," in *The Hi-o-Hi* (Oberlin, Ohio: n.p., 1894), 226–28; Theodore Wilder, *The History of Company C, Seventh Regiment O.V.I.* (Oberlin: J. B. T. Marsh, 1866), 6–9; Robert Samuel Fletcher, *A History of Oberlin College from Its Foundation Through the Civil War* (Oberlin, Ohio: Oberlin College, 1943), 2:845–46.
7. *Lorain County News,* April 24, 1861.
8. Ibid., May 1, 1861.
9. Ibid.; William E. Bigglestone, *They Stopped in Oberlin: Black Residents and Visitors of the Nineteenth Century* (Scottsdale, Ariz: Innovation Group, 1981), 215–17.
10. Guinn, "The Monroe Rifles," 228.
11. Bigglestone, *They Stopped in Oberlin,* 217.
12. *Lorain County News,* April 24, 1861; *Cleveland Leader,* April 23, 1861.
13. Fletcher, *History of Oberlin College,* 2:881.
14. William F. Cheek and Aimee Lee Cheek, *John Mercer Langston and the Fight for Black Freedom, 1829–65* (Urbana: Univ. of Illinois Press, 1989), 383–84.
15. Richard Donegan, comp., "Oberlin Civil War Soldiers Database," *Oberlin Heritage Center* (website), accessed Dec. 3, 2014, http://www.oberlinheritagecenter.org/researchlearn/civilwardatabase.
16. *Oberlin Evangelist,* July 16, 1862; *Lorain County News,* July 23, 1862.
17. Cheek and Cheek, *John Mercer Langston and the Fight for Black Freedom,* 387.
18. *Lorain County News,* Aug. 6, 1862.
19. "Edmonia Lewis," *Wikipedia, the Free Encyclopedia,* accessed March 16, 2015, http://en.wikipedia.org/w/index.php?title=Edmonia_Lewis&oldid=651704730; John Mercer Langston, *From the Virginia Plantation to the National Capitol* (1894; reprint, New York: Arno Press, 1969), 171–80.
20. Langston, *From the Virginia Plantation to the National Capitol,* 172. Although Langston did not name Lewis's accusers, Geoffrey Blodgett identified them as Maria Miles and Christina Ennes. He identified the family with whom the women resided as the Keeps. Geoffrey Blodgett, *Oberlin History: Essays and Impressions* (Kent, Ohio: Kent State Univ. Press, 2006), 62–63.
21. Langston, *From the Virginia Plantation to the National Capitol,* 173–75.
22. Ibid., 176–77.
23. Ibid., 177.
24. Ibid., 175, 178–79.
25. Scholarly accounts of the Lewis case include Blodgett, *Oberlin History,* 61–74; Cheek and Cheek, *John Mercer Langston and the Fight for Black Freedom,* 302–4; Kirsten Pai Buick,

Child of the Fire: Mary Edmonia Lewis and the Problem of Art History's Black and Indian Subject (Durham, N.C.: Duke Univ. Press, 2010), 8-10.

26. *Lorain County News*, April 4, 1866, Feb. 6, 1867, Jan. 1, 1868.
27. Ibid., April 30, 1862.
28. Ibid., July 9, 1862.
29. Ibid., Aug. 6, 1862.
30. Ibid., Sept. 24, 1862.
31. Ibid., Jan. 7, 1863.
32. Ibid.
33. Ibid..
34. Ibid..
35. Cheek and Cheek, *John Mercer Langston and the Fight for Black Freedom*, 390-93.
36. *Lorain County News*, April 15, 1863. The black enlistees included John Barker, Falding Brown, Leander Howard, William Mitchell, Harrison Nichols, H. I. Patterson, Henry Peet, H. N. Rankin, Oliver Ridgway, William Rutledge, Samuel Smith, John Wall, Isaiah Wilson, and Simpson Younger.
37. Bigglestone, *They Stopped in Oberlin*, xx, 237-42; Donegan, "Oberlin Civil War Soldiers Database."
38. Oberlin, Lorain County, *Population Schedules of the Eighth Census of the United States, 1860* (National Archives Microfilm Publication M653), roll 1002, pages 199B-226A; Donegan, "Oberlin Civil War Soldiers Database"; Patricia Holsworth, "Oberlin Genealogical Database," 2012, in authors' possession.
39. Fletcher, *History of Oberlin College*, 2:850-75 passim; J. Brent Morris, *Oberlin, Hotbed of Abolitionism: College, Community, and the Fight for Freedom and Equality in Antebellum America* (Chapel Hill: Univ. of North Carolina Press, 2014), 233-38.
40. Fletcher, *History of Oberlin College*, 2:865-66.
41. Bigglestone, *They Stopped in Oberlin*, xx.
42. *Lorain County News*, Aug. 20, 1862. On the college's ownership of the hotel that Palmer operated, see Charles R. Camp, *Camp's Directory of Oberlin, 1873-74: Comprising a Complete Directory of the Village of Oberlin, Including a History of the Business Men from the Foundation of Oberlin Up to the Present Time; Rates of Fare to All Points on the L.S. & M.S.R.R.* (Oberlin, Ohio: Lorain County News Print, 1873), 19.
43. *Lorain County News*, July 17, 1861, July 20, 1864, June 2, 1870.
44. Ibid., March 22, 1865.
45. Ibid., April 5, 1865.
46. Ibid.; Fletcher, *History of Oberlin College*, 2:882.
47. *Lorain County News*, April 12, 1865; W. G. Ballantine, ed., *The Oberlin Jubilee 1833-1883* (Oberlin, Ohio: E. J. Goodrich, 1883), 220; Fletcher, *History of Oberlin College*, 2:882.
48. *Lorain County News*, April 19, 1865.
49. John G. Fraser, "Diary and Notes of John G. Fraser 1865-67," April 16, 1865, transcription, Robert S. Fletcher Papers, ser. 3, subseries 1, box 6, folder 12, Oberlin College Archives.
50. Eric Foner, *Reconstruction: America's Unfinished Revolution, 1863-1877* (New York: Harper and Row, 1988), 181-82, 221-22.
51. *Lorain County News*, July 25, 1865; *Cleveland Leader*, July 20, 1865.

52. *Lorain County News*, June 14, 1865; Cheek and Cheek, *John Mercer Langston and the Fight for Black Freedom*, 430–33, 439.

53. *Lorain County News*, July 25, 1865.

54. Ibid.

55. *Cleveland Leader*, July 20, 1865.

56. Gene Schmiel, *Citizen General: Jacob Dolson Cox and the Civil War Era* (Athens: Ohio Univ. Press, 2014), 6–9, 14–16, 18–19, 29–175 passim.

57. Ibid., 186.

58. Charles F. Cox to Jacob Dolson Cox, July 22/24, 1865, Jacob Dolson Cox Papers, ser. 1, box 1, Oberlin College Archives.

59. *Lorain County News*, Aug. 9, 1865; Jacob D. Cox, E. H. Fairchild, and Samuel Plumb, *Reconstruction and the Relations of the Races in the United States: Letter from a Committee at Oberlin to Gen. J. D. Cox, the Union Candidate for Governor: Gen. Cox's Response* (Columbus: Ohio State Journal Steam Press, 1865), 3–4.

60. Cox, Fairchild, and Plumb, *Reconstruction and the Relations of the Races in the United States*, 4–5, 6.

61. Ibid., 9–10.

62. Ibid., 8 (italics in the original).

63. Ibid., 11. For an insightful analysis of Cox's proposal in historical context, see Nicholas Guyatt, "'An Impossible Idea?': The Curious Career of Internal Colonization," *Journal of the Civil War Era* 4 (June 2014): 234–63.

64. *Lorain County News*, Aug. 9, 1865.

65. *General Catalogue of Oberlin College, 1833–1908, Including an Account of the Principal Events in the History of the College, with Illustrations of the College Buildings* (Oberlin, Ohio: Oberlin College, 1909), 665; Approved Pension Applications of Widows and Other Dependents of Civil War Veterans Who Served between 1861 and 1910, Application No. WC120522, National Archives, *Fold3 by Ancestry*, accessed June 2, 2017, https://www.fold3.com/image/305953080.

66. *Lorain County News*, Aug. 18, 1865.

67. Ibid., Aug. 23, 1865.

68. *Cleveland Leader*, Aug. 15, 1865.

69. *Liberator*, Sept. 15, 1865.

70. *Lorain County News*, Aug. 23, 1865.

71. *Cleveland Leader*, Aug. 22, 1865.

72. Ibid., Aug. 23, 1865.

73. Ibid.

74. *Lorain County News*, Aug. 23, 1865. See also *New York Times*, Aug. 27, 1865.

75. *Cleveland Leader*, Aug. 23, 1865.

76. *Lorain County News*, Aug. 23, 1865.

77. *Liberator*, Sept. 15, 1865.

78. *Lorain County News*, Oct. 11, 1865.

79. *Cleveland Plain Dealer*, Nov. 27, 1865.

80. *Lorain County News*, Oct. 18, 1865.

81. *Journal of the House of Representatives of the State of Ohio,* 57th General Assembly, Jan. 24, 1866, vol. 62, page 90; *Lorain County News,* Feb. 7, 1866.

82. G. Frederick Wright, *A Standard History of Lorain County, Ohio; an Authentic Narrative of the Past, with Particular Attention to the Modern Era in the Commercial, Industrial, Civic and Social Development. a Chronicle of the People, with Family Lineage and Memoirs* (Chicago: Lewis Publishing Company, 1916), 572–74; Nat Brandt, *The Town That Started the Civil War* (Syracuse, N.Y.: Syracuse Univ. Press, 1990), 135, 257.

83. *Lorain County News,* March 7, 1866.

84. Ibid., April 18, 1866.

85. Ibid., Jan. 24, 1866.

86. Ibid., March 7, 1866.

87. Ibid., March 21, 1866.

88. Ibid., Feb. 14, 1866.

89. Ibid., May 9, 1866.

90. Ibid., May 23, 1866.

91. Ibid., Aug. 8, 1866.

92. Ibid., Aug. 15, Aug. 29, 1866.

93. Ibid., Sept. 26, 1866.

94. Ibid., Oct. 3, 1866.

95. *Elyria (Ohio) Independent Democrat,* Oct. 17, 1866.

96. *Lorain County News,* Oct. 17, 1866.

97. Ibid., Dec. 12, 1866.

98. Robert D. Sawrey, *Dubious Victory: The Reconstruction Debate in Ohio* (Lexington, Ky.: Univ. Press of Kentucky, 1992), 102; *Lorain County News,* Feb. 6, 1867.

99. Sawrey, *Dubious Victory,* 102–6.

100. *Lorain County News,* April 10, 1867.

101. Joseph Patterson Smith, *History of the Republican Party in Ohio* (Chicago: Lewis Publishing Company, 1898), 2:234–38.

102. *Lorain County News,* June 26, 1867.

103. Ibid., July 10, 1867.

104. *New Orleans Tribune,* July 31, 1867.

105. *Lorain County News,* July 3, 1867.

106. Ibid., July 17, 1867.

107. Ibid., Aug. 14, 1867.

108. Ibid., Sept. 25, 1867.

109. Ibid., Oct. 2, 1867.

110. *Elyria (Ohio) Independent Democrat,* Oct. 16, 1867.

111. Eugene H. Roseboom, *The Civil War Era, 1850-1873* (1944; reprint, Columbus: Ohio State Archaeological and Historical Society, 1968), 462.

112. *Lorain County News,* Oct. 16, 1867.

113. George Henry Porter, *Ohio Politics during the Civil War Period* (New York: Columbia University, Longmans, Green, 1911), 251–53.

114. *Lorain County News,* Oct. 13, 1869.

NOTES TO PAGES 132-150

115. Porter, *Ohio Politics during the Civil War Period*, 254; Roseboom, *The Civil War Era, 1850-1873*, 471.
116. *Lorain County News*, April 14, 1870.
117. Ibid.
118. Ibid.
119. Ibid.
120. Marilyn Wainio, "R. J. Robinson: A Wellington Treasure—Hidden in Plain View," presentation to the Oberlin African-American Genealogy and History Group, Oberlin, Ohio, Feb. 6, 2016.
121. *Lorain County News*, April 14, 1870.
122. Catherine M. Rokicky, *James Monroe: Oberlin's Christian Statesman and Reformer, 1821-1898* (Kent, Ohio: Kent State Univ. Press, 2002), 79-110.
123. *Lorain County News*, April 14, 1870.
124. William Cheek and Aimee Lee Cheek, "John Mercer Langston: Principle and Politics," in *Black Leaders of the Nineteenth Century*, ed. Leon Litwack and August Meier (Urbana: Univ. of Illinois Press, 1988), 103-28.
125. *Lorain County News*, July 3, 1867.
126. Ibid., Feb. 17, 1870.

CHAPTER 6

1. *Lorain County News*, April 14, 1870.
2. For a helpful summary on the shifting relationship of northern blacks to the Republican Party in this period, see David A. Gerber, "A Politics of Limited Options: Northern Black Politics and the Problem of Change and Continuity in Race Relations Historiography," *Journal of Social History* 14 (winter 1980): 235-55.
3. *Lorain County News*, April 5, 1865.
4. Ibid., April 3, 1867.
5. *Oberlin Weekly News*, April 8, 1875.
6. A movement to abandon the caucus began in 1897 according to Wilbur H. Phillips, *Oberlin Colony: The Story of a Century* (Oberlin, Ohio: Press of Oberlin, 1933), 173. But Oberlin newspapers continued to cite the caucus at least through 1905 for the town (see *Oberlin News*, Oct. 3, 1905) and through 1925 for the township (see *Oberlin News*, Sept. 3, 1925).
7. *Oberlin Weekly News*, April 11, 1879.
8. On Cox, see, for example, *Oberlin Weekly News*, July 8, 1875, April 4, 1879, Aug. 5, 1881, Aug. 8, 1884.
9. *Lorain County News*, Jan. 6, 1869.
10. Braden Paynter, comp., Roster of Oberlin Town Council Members, 1865-1955, unpublished spreadsheet in the authors' possession.
11. Petition from citizens of Oberlin praying for passage of Charles Sumner's bill supplementary to the civil rights bill, presented Jan. 8, 1872 (HR 42A-H8.10), 42nd Cong., 2nd sess., Records of the U.S. House of Representatives, RG 233, National Archives, Washington, D.C.
12. See, for example, *Lorain County News*, May 20, July 25, Oct. 27, 1872.

13. *Cleveland Herald*, Aug. 6, 1872.

14. *Lorain County News*, Sept. 5, 1872. On supporting Grant out of fear that Greeley's victory would undermine the rights of freedmen, see ibid., July 5, 1872; on denouncing Sumner, see ibid., Aug. 8, 1872, and Aug. 22, 1872. Interestingly, former Oberlin College president Asa Mahan weighed in to support Greeley because of his temperance stand. Ibid., Aug. 22, 1872.

15. *Lorain County News*, Nov. 14, 1872.

16. For discussions about the appeal of black political independence at the state level, see Lawrence Grossman, *The Democratic Party and the Negro: Northern and National Politics, 1868–92* (Urbana: Univ. of Illinois Press, 1976), 80–81; Nikki M. Taylor, *America's First Black Socialist: The Radical Life of Peter H. Clark* (Lexington: Univ. Press of Kentucky, 2013), 116–21.

17. On the statewide convention, see Taylor, *America's First Black Socialist*, 117–25; *Lorain County News*, Sept. 11, 1873. The men who issued the call were Henry Lee, W. Mendenhall, Garrison Chambers, Thomas Janey, Alfred Monroe, M. Goosland, T. P. Smith, R. J. Robinson, C. H. Johnson, John C. Copeland, Abraham Chambers, Levi Newsom, Fenderson Copes, T. H. Mumford, R. Reeves, J. Fox, J. A. Warring, A. T. Mitchell, and J. W. Brown.

18. Ibid., Sept. 18, 1873.

19. Ibid., Nov. 27, 1873.

20. William E. Bigglestone, *They Stopped in Oberlin* (Scottsdale, Ariz.: Innovation Group, 1981), 127–28.

21. *Lorain County News*, Feb. 8, 1865.

22. William F. Cheek and Aimee Lee Cheek, *John Mercer Langston and the Fight for Black Freedom, 1829–65* (Urbana: Univ. of Illinois Press, 1989), 430–35.

23. Bigglestone, *They Stopped in Oberlin*, 128–31.

24. William H. Rogers, *Senator John P. Green, and Sketches of Prominent Men of Ohio* (Washington, D.C.: Arena Publishing, 1893), 65–70.

25. *Christian Recorder* (Philadelphia), Feb. 2, 1867.

26. *Lorain County News*, July 31, 1867, Jan. 8, 1868.

27. Ibid., May 20, Sept. 7, 1868.

28. Ibid., Dec. 8, 1869; *Proceedings of the Colored National Labor Convention held in Washington, D.C., on December 6th, 7th, 8th, 9th, and 10th, 1869* (Washington, D.C.: Office of the New Era, 1870), 12. See also Philip S. Foner and Ronald L. Lewis, eds., *The Black Worker: A Documentary History from Colonial Times to the Present* (Philadelphia: Temple Univ. Press, 1978–84), 2:32–33.

29. *Cleveland Herald*, March 14, 1872.

30. Ibid., May 16, 1872.

31. *Lorain County News*, April 24, 1873.

32. Ibid., May 22, 1873; *Western Reserve Chronicle* (Warren, Ohio), May 21, 1873.

33. Taylor, *America's First Black Socialist*, 117–20; Hugh Davis, *"We Will Be Satisfied with Nothing Less": The African American Struggle for Equal Rights in the North during Reconstruction* (Ithaca, N.Y.: Cornell Univ. Press, 2011), 103–6.

34. *Oberlin News*, Jan. 1, 8, 1874.

35. Ibid., Jan. 1, 1874.

36. Ibid., Jan. 8, 1874.

37. Ibid., Jan. 22, 1874.

38. *Oberlin Weekly News,* March 19, 1874.
39. Ibid., March 26, 1874.
40. Ibid., May 7, 1874; *Cleveland Herald,* May 7, 1874.
41. *Cleveland Herald,* May 9, 1874. On John Patterson Green, see Kenneth L. Kusmer, *A Ghetto Takes Shape: Black Cleveland, 1870–1930* (Urbana: Univ. of Illinois Press, 1978), 118–21; Rogers, *John P. Green, and Sketches of Prominent Men of Ohio*; and "Green, John Patterson," *Encyclopedia of Cleveland History* (website), case.edu/ech/articles/g/green-john-patterson/.
42. The *Cleveland Herald,* May 18, 1874, reported the race of the young women, who were called simply "young ladies" without specification of color in the *Oberlin Weekly News,* May 21, 1874.
43. *Oberlin Weekly News,* May 21, 1874.
44. Davis, *"We Will Be Satisfied with Nothing Less,"* 103.
45. *Oberlin Weekly News,* May 21, 1874.
46. Ibid., July 30, Sept. 24, 1874.
47. Ibid., Oct. 8, 1874.
48. Ibid., Dec. 10, 1874.
49. Ibid., Dec. 31, 1874.
50. *Journal of the House of Representatives of the United States,* 43rd Cong., 2nd sess., Jan. 6, 1875, 125.
51. *Oberlin Weekly News,* Jan. 14, 1875.
52. Joseph H. Battle received his bachelor's degree from Oberlin in 1871, and in 1873 he identified himself as a "Business Man" in Oberlin. He coedited the local paper with George Pratt from December 1873 to January 1875, when Pratt retired and Battle turned to his father, cattle dealer William Battle, for support. Battle's editorship ended in July 1876. He later did work for the *Cleveland Leader* and the *Youngstown Evening News* before moving to St. Louis, where he performed clerical work. For information on Battle, see Former Student File for Joseph Hall Battle, Alumni and Development Records, box 55, Oberlin College Archives; *History of Lorain County, Ohio, with Illustrations and Biographical Sketches of Some of Its Prominent Men and Pioneers* (Philadelphia: Williams Brothers, 1879), 6; Patricia Holsworth, "Oberlin Genealogical Database," 2012, in authors' possession.
53. *Oberlin Weekly News,* April 15, 1875.
54. Ibid., Aug. 19, 1875. On Langston's earlier support for Grant, see Douglas Egerton, *The Wars of Reconstruction: The Brief, Violent History of America's Most Progressive Era* (New York: Bloomsbury Press, 2014), 281–82.
55. *Oberlin Weekly News,* April 6, 1876.
56. Ibid.
57. *Boston Daily Advertiser,* May 31, 1867. See also Andy Hall's three posts about Hatton available on Ta-Nehisi Coates's blog for the *Atlantic*: www.theatlantic.com/national/archive/2011/01/george-w-hatton-soldier/69659/, www.theatlantic.com/national/archive/2011/01/george-w-hatton-politician/69692/, www.theatlantic.com/national/archive/2011/01/george-w-hattons-long-road/69924/.
58. On John Craven Jones, see Bigglestone, *They Stopped in Oberlin,* 122–24, and "John Craven Jones," William E. Bigglestone Papers, ser. 3, subseries 1, box 11, Oberlin College Archives.
59. Information on marriage and births of children gleaned from Gibbs Family Tree, *Ancestry.com,* accessed June 15, 2017.

60. *Pacific Appeal* (San Francisco, Calif.), April 8, 1876. On the travels of M. W. Gibbs, see his autobiography, *Shadow and Light: An Autobiography with Reminiscences of the Last and Present Century* (1902; reprint, Lincoln: Univ. of Nebraska Press, 1995).

61. *Inter-Ocean* (Chicago), April 7, 1876.

62. *Pacific Appeal*, April 29, 1876, emphasis added. Yet the April 15, 1876, *Pacific Appeal* quoted Edward Shaw, editor of the *Memphis Planet*, who cautioned that "if the convention passed a series of resolutions pledging the colored people to a fixed policy, it fixed the color line in the South."

63. *Pacific Appeal*, April 29, 1876.

64. *Oberlin Weekly News*, April 6, 1876.

65. Ibid.

66. *Oberlin Weekly News*, May 4, 1876. For Scott's authorship, see *Oberlin Weekly News*, May 25, 1876. Biographical details on Scott can be found in Bigglestone, *They Stopped in Oberlin*, 183–85.

67. *Oberlin Weekly News*, May 4, 1876.

68. Ibid., May 11, 1876.

69. Ibid.

70. Ibid., May 25, 1876.

71. Ibid., June 13, 1876.

72. Ibid., June 29, 1876.

73. Ibid., Aug. 31, 1876.

74. Ibid., Aug. 24, 31, 1876.

75. Ibid., Nov. 9, 1876.

76. Ibid., Jan. 25, Feb. 8, March 15, 1877.

77. Ibid., March 5, 1877.

78. See David Gerber, *Black Ohio and the Color Line, 1860–1915* (Urbana: Univ. of Illinois Press, 1976), 224–25.

79. On Williams, see John Hope Franklin, *George Washington Williams: A Biography* (Durham, N.C.: Duke Univ. Press, 1998), especially 48–49; for Green and other state politicians, see Gerber, *Black Ohio and the Color Line*, 226–28.

80. *Oberlin Weekly News*, April 26, 1877.

81. Ibid., Aug. 27, Sept. 20, 1877.

82. Ibid., Oct. 18, 1877, Oct. 4, 1875.

83. Gerber, *Black Ohio and the Color Line*, 226.

84. See also Rayford W. Logan, *The Betrayal of the Negro: From Rutherford B. Hayes to Woodrow Wilson*, enlarged ed. (1954; New York: Collier Books, 1965), 12–37.

85. *Oberlin Weekly News*, Jan. 4, 1878. On Watkins, an 1878 Oberlin College graduate, see Former Student File for Solomon Glenn Watkins, Alumni and Development Records, box 1087, Oberlin College Archives. See also Thomas C. Cox, *Blacks in Topeka, Kansas, 1865–1915: A Social History* (Baton Rouge: Louisiana State Univ. Press, 1982), 182.

86. *Oberlin Weekly News*, Dec. 28, 1877, Jan. 4, 1878; "Green, John Patterson," *Encyclopedia of Cleveland History* (website), accessed June 18, 2017, case.edu/ech/articles/g/green-john-patterson/.

87. *Oberlin Weekly News*, Jan. 4, 1878.

88. Ibid.
89. Ibid.
90. Ibid.
91. Ibid., April 20, 1867.
92. James Harris Fairchild, *Oberlin: The Colony and the College, 1833-1883* (Oberlin, Ohio: E. J. Goodrich, 1883), 107.
93. See chapter 3 above for the efforts of Marcus Dale. Evidence of racial integration at First Methodist Episcopal in its early years comes from newspaper coverage of the accident that befell several church members engaged in building the church when its scaffolding collapsed; see *Oberlin Weekly News*, April 20, 27, 1871. The race of the church members was verified in Patricia Holsworth, "Oberlin Genealogical Database," 2012, in the authors' possession.
94. On Goosland, see Bigglestone, *They Stopped in Oberlin*, 86-87.
95. *Oberlin Weekly News*, July 21, 1882.
96. Grace Hammond, Elizabeth Harrison, and Jennifer Ni, "Rust United Methodist Church: A Brief History," fall 2003, in Electronic Oberlin Group, *Oberlin Through History* (website), accessed June 18, 2017, www.oberlin.edu/external/EOG/AfAmChurches/Rust.htm. Mrs. Goosland remained associated with Second Methodist by, for example, holding a fund-raiser at her house in July 1879; see *Oberlin Weekly News*, July 4, 1879. Oberlin-born Alfred Vance Churchill (1864-1949) remembered "Mammy Goosland" [*sic*] as "the best cook in town" and described her "marvelous figure. She was about five feet one in height, weighed between two hundred and fifty and three hundred pounds, and was exquisitely gowned in a delicate lilac-colored textile with white trimmings, while her head was swathed in a smooth white napkin. She looked like the domes of St. Mark." Alfred Vance Churchill, "Midwestern: The Colored People," *Northwest Ohio Quarterly* 25 (summer 1953): 173.
97. On Hatton, see *Boston Daily Advertiser*, May 31, 1867, and Andy Hall's posts about Hatton on Ta-Nehisi Coates's blog for the *Atlantic* (see note 57 above).
98. *Oberlin Weekly News*, July 27, 1876.
99. Ibid., Aug. 17, 1876.
100. Ibid., Dec. 28, 1876. On the African Methodist Episcopal Church in Oberlin, see William E. Bigglestone, *Oberlin: From War to Jubilee, 1866-1883* (Oberlin, Ohio: Grady Publishing, 1983), 57-58. For the sale of Hatton's effects by Constable Whitney to pay debts, see *Oberlin Weekly News*, May 17, 1878.
101. Bigglestone, *Oberlin: From War to Jubilee*, 143-45. Lee fought on for over a month, with the quarterly meeting finally confirming his expulsion in September; see *Oberlin Weekly News*, Aug. 16, 23, 30, Sept. 13, 1878. Lee sued the church for funds owed to him and eventually won $337.14. See *Oberlin Weekly News*, July 30, 1880.
102. On the endless permutations of the Omnibus War, see, for example, *Oberlin Weekly News*, Oct. 25, Dec. 20, 1878; March 21, April 11, 1879; March 19, 26, April 2, 16, 23, June 4, 11, Oct. 1, 29, 1880; Jan. 14, Nov. 11, 1881; Feb. 3, 17, 24, 1882; April 20, 1883; July 11, 1884; Feb. 19, March 5, May 14, Oct. 7, Nov. 4, 1886; April 14, 1887; June 28, 1888; April 25, 1889.
103. Ibid., Feb. 3, 10, 1882.
104. On Clark, see Taylor, *America's First Black Socialist*, 135-53; Foner and Lewis, *The Black Worker*, 2:242-48, 268-69.

105. *Oberlin Weekly News*, May 17, Sept. 20, 1878.
106. Ibid. Oct. 18, 1878.
107. Ibid., Oct. 11, 1878.
108. Ibid.
109. Ibid., Oct. 17, 1879. Jackson operated as a political player in both racially distinct and integrated settings. Indeed, he was prominent enough in the Ohio Republican Party that he was tapped later that year to provide the second for the nomination of Ohio Republican gubernatorial candidate Charles Foster. The honor's going to Jackson also served as a recognition to the importance of courting African American voters. *Oberlin Weekly News*, June 6, 1879, and *Inter-Ocean*, May 29, 1879. The Oberlin A.M.E. Church also hosted Jackson in November 1879; see *Oberlin Weekly News*, Nov. 14, 1879. On Jackson, see Richard R. Wright, *Centennial Encyclopaedia of the African Methodist Episcopal Church* (Philadelphia: Book Concern of the A.M.E. Church, 1916), 127.
110. On Taylor, see George Washington Williams, *History of the Negro Race in America from 1619 to 1880* (New York: G. P. Putnam's Sons, 1883), 2:469–74; *Oberlin Weekly News*, Feb. 28, 1879.
111. *Oberlin Weekly News*, Aug. 27, Sept. 3, 1880.
112. Ibid., Sept. 24, Oct. 1, 1880.
113. Ibid., Oct. 8, 1880.
114. Ibid., Nov. 5, 1880.
115. Ibid., March 18, 1881. On the Wynns and Cowan, see Bigglestone, *They Stopped in Oberlin*, 231–32, 59.
116. *Oberlin Weekly News*, Sept. 23, 1881.
117. Gerber, *Black Ohio and the Color Line*, 230–43.
118. *Oberlin Weekly News*, April 29, June 3, 1875, June 13, 1879.
119. Ibid., Feb. 20, 1880.
120. Ibid., April 25, 1879.
121. Ibid., Oct. 13, 1882; *Cleveland Herald*, Nov. 14, 1882.
122. *Oberlin Weekly News*, Dec. 22, 1882.
123. W. E. Bigglestone, "Oberlin College and the Negro Student, 1865–1940," *Journal of Negro History* 56 (July 1971): 200. See also Cally L. Waite, *Permission to Remain Among Us: Education for Blacks in Oberlin, Ohio, 1880–1914* (Westport, Conn.: Praeger, 2002), 82–88.
124. *Oberlin Review*, Feb. 3, 16, 1883.
125. Ibid., March 3, 1883.
126. *Oberlin Weekly News*, March 16, 1883.
127. Bigglestone, "Oberlin College and the Negro Student," 201.
128. *Oberlin Weekly News*, Nov. 3, 1882, April 19, 1883; William G. Ballantine, ed., *The Oberlin Jubilee, 1833–1883* (Oberlin, Ohio: E. J. Goodrich, 1883), passim.
129. Judson Smith, "The Future Work of Oberlin," in Ballantine, ed., *The Oberlin Jubilee*, 328.
130. Ibid, 336.
131. Ibid, 337–38.

CHAPTER 7

1. *Lorain County News*, Jan. 7, 1863. For the source of Father Keep's address, see *Springfield (Mass.) Republican*, Dec. 24, 1862.

2. *Lorain County News*, Jan. 7, 1863.

3. Oberlin, Lorain County, Ohio, *Population Schedules of the Ninth Census of the United States, 1870* (National Archives Microfilm Publication M593), roll 1235, pages 628A–664A; Enumeration Districts 90–91, Russia Township, Lorain County, Ohio, *Population Schedules of the Twelfth Census of the United States, 1900* (National Archives Microfilm Publication T623), roll 1294, pages 218A–258B.

4. Heather Cox Richardson, *The Death of Reconstruction: Race, Labor, and Politics in the Post–Civil War North, 1865–1901* (Cambridge, Mass: Harvard Univ. Press, 2001).

5. W. E. Burghardt Du Bois, "The Talented Tenth," in Booker T. Washington et al., *The Negro Problem: A Series of Articles by Representative American Negroes of Today* (New York: J. Pott, 1903), 31–75.

6. *Lorain County News* (Oberlin), Sept. 12, 1872.

7. William Cheek and Aimee Lee Cheek, "John Mercer Langston: Principle and Politics," in *Black Leaders of the Nineteenth Century*, ed. Leon F. Litwack and August Meier (Urbana: Univ. of Illinois Press, 1991), 103–26.

8. Langston, *From the Virginia Plantation to the National Capitol*, 97–103, 524–28.

9. Daniel J. Sharfstein, *The Invisible Line: Three American Families and the Secret Journey from Black to White* (New York: Penguin Press, 2011), 129–33, 151–67; Kate Masur, *An Example for All the Land: Emancipation and the Struggle over Equality in Washington, D.C.* (Chapel Hill: Univ. of North Carolina Press, 2010), 159–60; Elizabeth Dowling Taylor, *The Original Black Elite: Daniel Murray and the Story of a Forgotten Era* (New York: Amistad, HarperCollins, 2017), 68, 73–74.

10. Auditor's Duplicates for Oberlin and Russia Township, 1870, 1875, Lorain County Records Retention Center, Elyria, Ohio; Henry Evans in 1880 U.S. Federal Census, Washington, D.C., T9, roll 121, page 158C, image 0802, *Ancestry.com*, accessed Dec. 19, 2015; Taylor, *The Original Black Elite*, 58–59.

11. William E. Bigglestone, *They Stopped in Oberlin: Black Residents and Visitors of the Nineteenth Century* (Scottsdale, Ariz.: Innovation Group, 1981), 70.

12. Willard B. Gatewood, *Aristocrats of Color: The Black Elite, 1880–1920* (1990; reprint, Fayetteville: Univ. of Arkansas Press, 2000), 40–41, 104, 237, 324, 337. On Anna Evans and Daniel Murray, see Taylor, *The Original Black Elite*, passim.

13. On the Gibbs family, and especially Ida Gibbs Hunt, see Adele Logan Alexander, *Parallel Worlds: The Remarkable Gibbs-Hunts and the Enduring (In)significance of Melanin* (Charlottesville: Univ. of Virginia Press, 2010). The purchase of the Langston home is mentioned on page 62. See also Mifflin Wistar Gibbs, *Light and Shadow: An Autobiography* (Washington, D.C.: n.p., 1902), which tells his story at great length.

14. Alexander, *Parallel Worlds*, passim. The residence of Ida with her classmate appears on pages 69–70. For more on Cooper, see her *A Voice from the South* (Xenia, Ohio: Aldine Publishing House, 1892) and Frances Richardson Keller, "Cooper, Anna Julia Haywood,"

NOTES TO PAGES 180–182

American National Biography Online, posted Feb. 2000, accessed July 28, 2017, www.anb.org/articles/09/09-00197.html.

15. Bigglestone, *They Stopped in Oberlin*, 164–65. See also Former Student File for Mary Jane Patterson, Alumni and Development Records, box 790, Oberlin College Archives.

16. *Oberlin Weekly News*, Oct. 23, 1890, Feb. 21, 1891, Oct. 29, 1891, Sept. 8, 1892, Oct. 27, 1892. On Stephen Wall's later life and his transition from "black" to "white," see Sharfstein, *The Invisible Line*, 253–71.

17. Mark Scott, "Langston Hughes of Kansas," *Kansas History* 3 (spring 1980): 3–13; Arnold Rampersad, *The Life of Langston Hughes* (New York: Oxford Univ. Press, 1986), 1:5–10; Richard B. Sheridan, "Charles Henry Langston and the African American Struggle in Kansas," *Kansas History* 22 (winter 1999): 273–82; Mary Langston in "U.S. Find a Grave Index, 1600s-Current," *Ancestry.com*, accessed June 27, 2015.

18. Rampersad, *The Life of Langston Hughes*, 1:7. Langston Hughes donated the shawl to the Ohio Historical Society in 1943. "History Blog: An Ordinary Shawl with an Extraordinary Story," *Ohio History Connection* (website), posted Feb. 20, 2014, accessed Aug. 29, 2017, https://www.ohiohistory.org/learn/collections/history/history-blog/2014/february-2014/an-ordinary-shawl-with-an-extraordinary-story.

19. Langston Hughes, *The Big Sea: An Autobiography* (1940; reprint, New York: Hill and Wang, 1993), 17.

20. B. F. Adair in 1850 U.S. Federal Census—Slave Schedules, Spring Creek, Phillips County, Arkansas, M432, *Ancestry.com*, accessed March 17, 2016; Benjamin Adair in 1860 U.S. Federal Census, Oberlin, Lorain County, Ohio, M653, roll 1002, page 203, image 47, *Ancestry.com*, accessed June 7, 2014; "Arkansas, County Marriages, 1837–1957," *FamilySearch* (website), accessed June 28, 2015; "Benjamin F. Adair and Family," William E. Bigglestone Papers, ser. 3, subseries 1, box 11, Oberlin College Archives; Judith Kilpatrick, "(Extra)ORDINARY MEN: African-American Lawyers and Civil Rights in Arkansas before 1950," *Arkansas Law Review* 53 (2000): 331, 345.

21. Former Student File for Joseph E. Wiley, Alumni and Development Records, box 276, Oberlin College Archives.

22. *Oberlin Weekly News*, Dec. 8, 1887, Aug. 22, 1889; *Oberlin News*, April 30, 1891, Dec. 17, 1891, Sept. 21, 1893.

23. *Oberlin Weekly News*, Dec. 25, 1890.

24. *Oberlin News*, March 29, 1894.

25. Fifty-nine African American females from Oberlin had attended the college by the end of 1883. Of the thirty-five with identifiable occupations, thirty-one were teachers. See "Catalog and Record of Colored Students," *Oberlin College Archives* (website), accessed Aug. 1, 2017, www2.oberlin.edu/archive/oresources/minority/index.html. See also Carol Lasser, "Enacting Emancipation: African American Women Abolitionists at Oberlin College and the Quest for Empowerment, Equality, and Respectability," in Kathryn Kish Sklar and James Brewer Stewart, eds., *Women's Rights and Transatlantic Antislavery in the Era of Emancipation* (New Haven: Yale Univ. Press, 2007), 319–45.

26. Former Student File for John Charles Fremont Jackson, Alumni and Development Records, box 522, Oberlin College Archives.

27. Former Student File for William Montgomery Jackson, Alumni and Development Records, box 312, Oberlin College Archives; Former Student File for Martha Rebecca Jackson, Alumni and Development Records, box 523, Oberlin College Archives. See also *Oberlin Weekly News*, Dec. 2, 1886.

28. Former Student File for Joseph Russell, Alumni and Development Records, box 221, Oberlin College Archives.

29. Former Student File for Carrie Anna Burnett/Mrs. Henry Ellis, Alumni and Development Records, box 297, Oberlin College Archives; Ella Jane Burnett/Mrs. Spencer H. Harris, Alumni and Development Records, box 307, Oberlin College Archives; Former Student File for Mary Morris Burnett/Mrs. William H. Talbot, Alumni and Development Records, box 1019, Oberlin College Archives; Bigglestone, *They Stopped in Oberlin*, 24–25.

30. Mason subsequently worked as a bookkeeper in the Chicago store of her first husband, William Price, and then, after marrying baseball star Moses Fleetwood Walker, helped him run his opera house in Cadiz, Ohio. Former Student File of Ednah Jane Mason/Mrs. Moses Fleetwood Walker, Alumni and Development Records, box 1076, Oberlin College Archives. See also David W. Zang, *Fleet Walker's Divided Heart: The Life of Baseball's First Black Major Leaguer* (Lincoln: Univ. of Nebraska Press, 1995).

31. Former Student File of Mary A. Campton/Mrs. Robert Tate, Alumni and Development Records, box 338, Oberlin College Archives; Former Student File of Alice L. Simms, Alumni and Development Records, box 231, Oberlin College Archives; Former Student File of Samantha C. Tuck/Mrs. Alexander Vivian, Alumni and Development Records, box 261, Oberlin College Archives.

32. *Oberlin Weekly News*, March 15, 1888; *Oberlin News*, May 15, 1896, June 5, 1896.

33. Former Student File of Alice Alexander/Mrs. James Augustus Davis, Alumni and Development Records, box 64, Oberlin College Archives; Former Student File of Sarah Jane Evans/Mrs. Thomas Sewell Inborden, Alumni and Development Records, box 517, Oberlin College Archives.

34. *New National Era*, Nov. 23, 1871.

35. Ibid., Dec. 14, 1871. An extraordinary and committed educator, Fanny Jackson remained principal of the Institute for Colored Youth in Philadelphia even after her marriage to AME minister Levi Jenkins Coppin in 1881. See Linda M. Perkins. "Coppin, Fanny Jackson," *American National Biography Online*, accessed Aug. 1, 2017, www.anb.org/articles/09/09-00202.html.

36. Oberlin, Lorain County, Ohio, *Population Schedules of the Eighth Census of the United States, 1860* (National Archives Microfilm Publication M653), roll 1002, pages 199B–226A; Oberlin, Lorain County, Ohio, *Population Schedules of the Ninth Census of the United States, 1870* (National Archives Microfilm Publication M593), roll 1235, pages 628A–664A, images 199475–202330; Enumeration District 181, Oberlin, Lorain County, Ohio, *Population Schedules of the Tenth Census of the United States, 1880* (National Archives Microfilm Publication T9), roll 1042, pages 592A–624A, images 0533–0597.

37. Oberlin, Lorain County, Ohio, *Population Schedules of the Eighth Census of the United States, 1860*; Oberlin, Lorain County, Ohio, *Population Schedules of the Ninth Census of the United States, 1870*.

38. Oberlin, Lorain County, Ohio, *Population Schedules of the Ninth Census of the United States, 1870*; Enumeration District 181, Oberlin, Lorain County, Ohio, *Population Schedules of the Tenth Census of the United States, 1880*.

39. Oberlin, Lorain County, Ohio, *Population Schedules of the Eighth Census of the United States, 1860*; Enumeration District 181, Oberlin, Lorain County, Ohio, *Population Schedules of the Tenth Census of the United States, 1880*.

40. Auditor's Duplicates for Oberlin and Russia Township, 1865, 1870, 1875, 1880, 1885, 1890, Lorain County Records Retention Center, Elyria, Ohio. The race of household heads was determined by record linkage with Patricia Holsworth, "Oberlin Genealogical Database," 2012, in the authors' possession.

41. Auditor's Duplicates for Oberlin and Russia Township, 1865, 1870, 1875, 1880, 1885, 1890; Holsworth, "Oberlin Genealogical Database."

42. Abraham Lincoln, *Speeches and Writings 1859-1865: Speeches, Letters, and Miscellaneous Writings, Presidential Messages and Proclamations*, ed. Don E. Fehrenbacher (New York: Literary Classics of America, 1989), 296.

43. William Fleming Robinson, "A Life Sketch of William Fleming Robinson, April 10, 1832-June 21, 1928," undated typescript. This wonderful source was kindly made available to the authors by Maggie Robinson, a descendant.

44. Ibid., 1-2.

45. Ibid., 2-4; Simon Luttrell in 1830 U.S. Federal Census, Eastern Division, Mason, Kentucky, M19, roll 39, page 211, *Ancestry.com*, accessed August 10, 2015.

46. William Fleming Robinson, "Life Sketch," 5-6.

47. Ibid., 7-9.

48. Ibid., 10-11.

49. George Robinson, William Robinson, and Sarah Baker in 1860 U.S. Federal Census, Oberlin, Lorain County, Ohio, M653, roll 1002, page 220, *Ancestry.com*, accessed June 13, 2017; William Fleming Robinson, "Life Sketch," 11.

50. William Fleming Robinson, "Life Sketch," 12; Nora Nowel in 1850 U.S. Federal Census, Regiment 22, Mecklenburg, Virginia, M432, roll 960, page 98, image 198, *Ancestry.com*, accessed August 12, 2015.

51. William Robinson in 1880 U.S. Federal Census, Enumeration District 180, Russia, Lorain, Ohio, roll 1042, page 581C, image 0511, *Ancestry.com*, accessed August 12, 2015.

52. William Fleming Robinson, "Life Sketch," 12; *Oberlin News*, June 28, 1928.

53. "Oberlin, Ohio: City Directory Spreadsheet," *Oberlin Heritage Center* (website) accessed August 12, 2015, www.oberlinheritagecenter.org/researchlearn/directories.

54. Holsworth, "Oberlin Genealogical Database"; Auditor's Duplicates for Oberlin and Russia Township, 1890.

55. William Fleming Robinson, "Life Sketch," 12.

56. "Oberlin, Ohio: City Directory Spreadsheet"; William F. Robinson in 1900 U.S. Federal Census, Enumeration District 0089, Russia, Lorain County, Ohio, roll 1294, page 9B, *Ancestry.com*, accessed Aug. 12, 2015; Auditor's Duplicates for Oberlin and Russia Township, 1900.

57. Holsworth, "Oberlin Genealogical Database."

58. *Oberlin News*, June 28, 1928.

59. Bigglestone, *They Stopped in Oberlin*, 82; James Glenn in 1840 U.S. Federal Census, Monroe, Virginia, M704, roll 56, page 151, image 667, *Ancestry.com*, accessed August 12, 2015.

60. George Glenn in 1850 U.S. Federal Census, Chillicothe, Ross County, Ohio, M432, roll 725, page 53B, image 112, *Ancestry.com*, accessed August 13, 2015.

61. Bigglestone, *They Stopped in Oberlin*, 82.

62. David A. Gerber, *Black Ohio and the Color Line, 1860–1915* (Urbana: Univ. of Illinois Press, 1976), 27.

63. George Glenn in 1860 U.S. Federal Census, Marion, Allen County, Ohio, M653, roll 929, page 355, image 193, *Ancestry.com*, accessed Nov. 1, 2015.

64. *The Owl* (Oberlin, Ohio), Feb. 22, 1896; Bigglestone, *They Stopped in Oberlin*, 82.

65. *Oberlin News*, Jan. 17, 1896; Bigglestone, *They Stopped in Oberlin*, 83.

66. *Oberlin Tribune*, April 28, 1916.

67. Quoted in Bigglestone, *They Stopped in Oberlin*, 84.

68. *Oberlin News*, May 3, 1916; Bigglestone, *They Stopped in Oberlin*, 84.

69. *Commemorative Biographical Record of the Counties of Huron and Lorain, Ohio* (Chicago: J. H. Beers, 1894), 993; *Oberlin News*, May 19, 1896.

70. *Oberlin News*, Sept. 15, 1920.

71. Ibid.; Jordan Dodd, ed., "Ohio, Marriages, 1803–1900" (online database) *Ancestry.com*, accessed Aug. 19, 2015; Bigglestone, *They Stopped in Oberlin*, 150.

72. Auditor's Duplicates for Oberlin and Russia Township, 1880; William M. Mitchel in 1880 U.S. Federal Census, Oberlin, Lorain, Ohio, T9, roll 1042, page 603C, ED 181, image 0555, *Ancestry.com*, accessed August 19, 2015.

73. *Oberlin News*, Sept. 15, 1920.

74. Ibid.

75. Edith Campton Mitchell in "Oberlin Gravestone Inventory Database," *Oberlin Heritage Center: Oberlin Westwood Cemetery Transcription Project* (website), www.oberlinwestwood.org, accessed Aug. 19, 2015.

76. The publication of Stephan Thernstrom, *Poverty and Progress: Social Mobility in a Nineteenth Century City* (Cambridge, Mass.: Harvard Univ. Press, 1964), prompted a raft of quantitatively oriented social mobility studies by American historians over the next fifteen years. For useful reviews of this literature, see Edward Pessen, "Social Mobility in American History: Some Brief Reflections," *Journal of Southern History* 45 (May 1979): 164–84; Howard P. Chudacoff, "Success and Security: The Meaning of Social Mobility in America," *Reviews in American History* 10 (Dec. 1982): 101–12. Our approach to the analysis of economic mobility has been influenced by Gregory Acs and Seth Zimmerman, "Like Watching Grass Grow? Assessing Changes in U.S. Intragenerational Economic Mobility over the Past Two Decades" (Washington, D.C.: Urban Institute and Economic Mobility Project of the Pew Charitable Trusts, 2008).

77. Auditor's Duplicates for Oberlin and Russia Township, 1865, 1870, 1875, 1880, 1885, 1890. The race of household heads was determined by record linkage with Holsworth, "Oberlin Genealogical Database."

78. Auditor's Duplicates for Oberlin and Russia Township, 1865, 1870, 1875, 1880, 1885, 1890; Holsworth, "Oberlin Genealogical Database."

79. Auditor's Duplicates for Oberlin and Russia Township, 1865, 1870, 1875, 1880, 1885, 1890; Holsworth, "Oberlin Genealogical Database."

80. Auditor's Duplicates for Oberlin and Russia Township, 1865, 1870, 1875, 1880, 1885, 1890; Holsworth, "Oberlin Genealogical Database."

81. Auditor's Duplicates for Oberlin and Russia Township, 1860, 1900.

82. C. S. Williams, *Williams' Medina, Elyria and Oberlin City Directory, City Guide, and Business Mirror* (s.l., 1859); Oberlin, Lorain County, *Population Schedules of the Eighth Census of the United States, 1860*; Auditor's Duplicates for Oberlin and Russia Township, 1860; Oberlin, Part of Map of Lorain County, 1857, GR Case 4, drawer 1, Oberlin College Archives; Enumeration Districts 90–91, Russia Township, Lorain County, Ohio, *Population Schedules of the Twelfth Census of the United States, 1900*.

83. Enumeration Districts 90–91, Russia Township, Lorain County, Ohio, *Population Schedules of the Twelfth Census of the United States, 1900*.

84. *Oberlin Record*, Nov. 23, 1889.

85. Stewart E. Tolnay and E. M. Beck, *A Festival of Violence: An Analysis of Southern Lynchings, 1882–1930* (Urbana: Univ. of Illinois Press, 1995), 29–32; Amy Kate Bailey and Stewart E. Tolnay, *Lynched: The Victims of Southern Mob Violence* (Chapel Hill: Univ. of North Carolina Press, 2015), 11–17.

86. James W. Loewen, *Sundown Towns: A Hidden Dimension of American Racism* (New York: New Press, 2005), 9–10, 24–38.

87. Jack S. Blocker Jr., *A Little More Freedom: African Americans Enter the Urban Midwest, 1860–1930* (Columbus: Ohio State Univ. Press, 2008), 224–25, 39–50, 112–18.

CHAPTER 8

1. *Oberlin Weekly News*, March 10, 1882.

2. On different methodologies for converting past dollars into current dollars, see the website *MeasuringWorth.com*.

3. *Oberlin Weekly News*, March 10, 1882.

4. Covenant of Oberlin Colony, [1832], photocopy, Robert S. Fletcher Papers, ser. 1, subseries 4, box 19, Oberlin College Archives; *Oberlin Weekly News*, March 5, 1874.

5. *Lorain County News*, Oct. 25, 1865. The Oberlin College faculty voted at their meeting of Oct. 7, 1868, to "prohibit students from visiting Munson's Saloon, where cigars and billiards only are found." Faculty Minutes, Oct. 7, 1868, William E. Bigglestone Papers, ser. 3, subseries 2, box 14, Oberlin College Archives.

6. *Lorain County News*, March 31, 1869.

7. Ibid., July 28, 1869.

8. William E. Bigglestone, *Oberlin: From War to Jubilee, 1866–1883* (Oberlin, Ohio: Grady Publishing, 1983), 83. On Jenkins's encounters with the law, see, for example, *Lorain County News*, March 17, Dec. 1, 1870, and *Oberlin Weekly News*, April 15, 1881.

9. Record Book 1, Oberlin Temperance League/Alliance Records, box 1, Oberlin College Archives. The signatures appear on pages 1–3 and were matched against information on race gleaned from Patricia Holsworth, "Oberlin Genealogical Database," 2012, in the authors' possession.

10. Quotation from handbill titled "Oberlin Temperance League" and attached to page 10 of Book 1, Oberlin Temperance League/Alliance Records.

11. For an excellent description of reformers' transition from persuasion to legal strategies, see Jack S. Blocker Jr., *American Temperance Movements: Cycles of Reform* (Boston: Twayne Publishers), 1989.

12. On the Adair Law and its limited effectiveness, see Jack S. Blocker Jr., *"Give to the Winds Thy Fears": The Women's Temperance Crusade, 1873-1874* (Westport, Conn.: Greenwood Press, 1985), 127-33. On the passage of Oberlin's temperance ordinance, see *Lorain County News*, July 28, 1869.

13. *Lorain County News*, June 30, 1870.

14. Record Book 1, March 19, 1877, May 20, June 17, Sept. 16, 1878, July 21, Sept. 15, 1879; Jan. 19, Feb. 9, 1880, Jan. 21, 1881, Oberlin Temperance League/Alliance Records. For typical efforts to strengthen the law, see ibid., Aug. 10, 1874, when temperance forces rallied to defeat a licensing clause in the proposed state constitution, which, as they saw it, would have provided incentives for the sale of alcoholic beverages by giving the state the tax revenue thereby generated. From 1876 to 1880, the Temperance League regularly appealed to the state legislature to allow prohibition as a local option. The legislature refused. See ibid., Feb. 1, 27, 1876, Feb. 26, 1877, Jan. 28, 1878, June 17, 1878, Jan. 20, 1879, Dec. 16, 1880.

15. *Oberlin Weekly News*, April 29, 1875.

16. Record Book 1, April 26, 1875, Oberlin Temperance League/Alliance Records.

17. James Harris Fairchild, *Woman's Right to the Ballot* (Oberlin, Ohio: G. H. Fairchild, 1870), 55-58.

18. "Annual Report of Secretary, Mrs. Hand," May 11, 1879, in Secretary's Book of the Ladies Temperance League, Oberlin Woman's Christian Temperance Union (WCTU) Records, box 1, Oberlin College Archives.

19. W. W. Wright to his son, April 5, 1874, Bigglestone Papers, ser. 3, subseries 2, box 14.

20. *Oberlin Weekly News*, March 26, 1874.

21. Record Book 1, March 20, 1882, Oberlin Temperance League/Alliance Records.

22. *Oberlin Weekly News*, March 26, 1874; Record Book 1, March 26, 1874, Oberlin Temperance League/Alliance Records.

23. Blocker, *"Give to the Winds Thy Fears,"* 94.

24. Eliza Jane Trimble Thompson et al., *Hillsboro Crusade Sketches and Family Records* (Cincinnati: Jennings and Graham, 1906), 59.

25. Blocker, *"Give to the Winds Thy Fears,"* 7-30.

26. Secretary's Book of Ladies Temperance League, March 13, 1874.

27. Ibid., March 14, 1874.

28. Ibid., Aug. 9, 1881.

29. Minute Book 1, Aug. 13, 1889, Oberlin WCTU Records, box 1, Oberlin College Archives. As will be discussed later in this chapter, the Oberlin Ladies Temperance League became the Oberlin WCTU in 1882.

30. Secretary's Book of Ladies Temperance League, March 31, 1874.

31. Ibid., Dec. 1874.

32. Ibid., March 12, 1874. Black River is now Lorain, Ohio.

33. Ibid., April 23, March 25, 1874.

34. Ibid., April 24, 1874.

35. See Secretary's Book of Ladies Temperance League, March 12, 1877, for a list of the vice presidents by name, and April 9, 1878, for a reference to "different pastors wives—Vice Pres[ident]s." Although Mary Goosland, wife of the first pastor of the Second Methodist Episcopal Church, was among the women who came together in 1874 to form the league, at this point no black church was represented.

36. Secretary's Book of Ladies Temperance League, March 8, 1881.
37. *Oberlin Weekly News*, April 8, 1881.
38. Minute Book 1, Oct. 9, 1883, Oberlin WCTU Records.
39. Mary F. Eastman, *The Biography of Dio Lewis* (New York: Fowler and Wells, 1891), 206.
40. *Oberlin Weekly News*, Dec. 21, 1877.
41. H. M. Whitney, "The Analogy of Slavery and Intemperance Before the Law," *New Englander* 3 (May 1880): 376.
42. *Oberlin News,* June 11, 1874.
43. Ibid., June 18, 1874.
44. Secretary's Book of Ladies Temperance League, Nov. 8, 1880.
45. Ibid., Nov. 14, 1880.
46. Ibid., Jan. 11, 1880.
47. Ibid., Oct. 10, 1882.
48. Bigglestone, *Oberlin: From War to Jubilee*, 91.
49. Secretary's Book of Ladies Temperance League, May 11, 1880.
50. Record Book 1, Feb. 9, 1880, Oberlin Temperance League/Alliance Records.
51. *Oberlin Weekly News*, Aug. 19, 1878.
52. Ibid., July 12, 1878.
53. Ibid., Aug. 26, 1881.
54. Mary Shurtleff to Giles Shurtleff, Aug. 24, 1881, Giles Waldo and Mary E. Shurtleff Papers, Oberlin College Archives. Mary A. Keep was married to the late John Keep's son, Theodore.
55. Thad H. Rowland to the people of Oberlin, Aug. 1881, James Harris Fairchild Papers, ser. 5, box 2, Oberlin College Archives; *Oberlin Weekly News*, Sept. 9, 1881.
56. *Oberlin Weekly News*, Sept. 9, 1881.
57. Record Book 1, Oct. 25, 1881, Dec. 28, 1881, Oberlin Temperance League/Alliance Records; *Oberlin Weekly News*, Dec. 30, 1881.
58. *Oberlin Weekly News*, Dec. 23, Dec. 30, 1881, Jan. 13, 1882.
59. *The Whole Story: History of the Oberlin Temperance War, 1882* (Cleveland: Leader Printing, 1882), 7.
60. Ibid., 7, 15.
61. Ibid., 9.
62. Ibid., 12.
63. Ibid., 9.
64. Ibid., 12.
65. Ibid., 11.
66. *Oberlin Weekly News*, May 20, 1881.
67. Ibid., May 20, June 10, Dec. 2, 9, 1881.

68. Ibid., Feb. 24, 1882.

69. Ibid., March 3, 1882, quoting the *Cleveland Leader,* Feb. 20, 1882, and citing the response that originally appeared in the *Cleveland Leader,* Feb. 22, 1882.

70. *Oberlin Weekly News,* March 3, 1882.

71. *The Whole Story: History of the Oberlin Temperance War,* 10.

72. A. L. Shumway and C. DeW. Brower, *Oberliniana: A Jubilee Volume of Semi-Historical Anecdotes Connected with the Past and Present of Oberlin College, 1833-1883* (Cleveland: Home Publishing Company, 1883), 168–69.

73. On undercover work, see "Confidential," Oberlin Temperance Alliance to G. W. Shurtleff, March 9, 1882, loose sheet inserted in Record Book 1, Oberlin Temperance League/Alliance Records. On legal prosecution, see *The Whole Story: History of the Oberlin Temperance War,* 15.

74. *The Whole Story: History of the Oberlin Temperance War,* 16.

75. Ibid., 20.

76. *Oberlin Weekly News,* March 24, 1882.

77. Ibid., March 31, 1882.

78. Ibid., July 9, 1880.

79. Ibid., July 23, 1881.

80. *National Prohibition Reform Party: Its Candidates, Platform, Address, and Some Reasons Why It Is Pre-eminently Deserving the Support of the People of the United States* (Detroit: William A. Scripps, 1876), 10, quoted in Lisa Anderson, *The Politics of Prohibition: American Governance and the Prohibition Party, 1869-1933* (New York: Cambridge Univ. Press, 2013), 51.

81. *Oberlin Weekly News,* Sept. 22, 1882, Aug. 2, 1888.

82. J. R. Meader, *The Cyclopedia of Temperance and Prohibition* (New York: Funk and Wagnalls, 1891), 106–8.

83. Ohio election results can be found at "Political Party Strength in Ohio," *Wikipedia* (website), accessed Aug. 1, 2017, en.wikipedia.org/wiki/Political_party_strength_in_Ohio.

84. Lawrence Grossman, *The Democratic Party and the Negro: Northern and National Politics, 1868-92* (Urbana: Univ. of Illinois Press, 1976) 82; *Oberlin Weekly News,* Oct. 3, 1884; David Gerber, *Black Ohio and the Color Line, 1860-1915* (Urbana: Univ. of Illinois Press, 1976), 238–43.

85. Record Book 2, May 24, 1893, Oberlin Temperance League/Alliance Records.

86. *Oberlin News,* June 8, 1893.

87. Record Book 2, March 14–Sept. 22, 1893, Oberlin Temperance League/Alliance Records.

88. Secretary's Book of Ladies Temperance League, Aug. 10, 1880.

89. Minute Book 1, Nov. 14, 1882, Oberlin WCTU Records.

90. Ibid., Jan. 8, 1884.

91. Ibid., May 13, 1884.

92. *Oberlin Weekly News,* May 16, 23, 1884, June 5, 1885.

93. Minute Book 1, July 8, 1884, Oberlin WCTU Records.

94. Minute Book 1, July 10, 1882, Oberlin WCTU Records.

95. *Oberlin Weekly News,* Oct. 12, 1883.

96. Relating a confrontation over suffrage with her son William Goodell Frost, Maria Goodell Frost wrote Ohio's state suffrage organizer Frances Jennings Casement: "I very sin-

cerely repeated some [of a speech you gave in Springfield, Ohio] to my son, and he was the angriest man I ever saw. He said I would 'break up his family.' . . . [H]e said I should 'never speak of it in his house,' and was so excited I had to leave. . . . It is well I am not dependent upon him. His father was the greatest tyrant that ever lived on earth." Maria Goodell Frost to Frances Jennings Casement, Oct. 10, 1887, Frances Jennings Casement Papers, box 1, folder 30, Ohio Historical Society, Columbus, Ohio.

97. *Oberlin Weekly News*, Oct. 10, 1884.

98. Ibid., March 29, 1888.

99. Ibid., March 31, 1887. It appears that the first sham voting was held in November 1886. See Aurelia Webster to Frances Jennings Casement, Nov. 5, 1886, Frances Jennings Casement Papers, box 1, folder 33. (Webster was superintendent of the Lorain County WCTU.)

100. Amelia Webster to Frances Jennings Casement, Nov. 18, 1887, in Frances Jennings Casement Papers, box 1, folder 33.

101. *Oberlin Weekly News*, Nov. 8, 1888.

102. Ibid., March 15, 1888.

103. Ibid., June 7, 1888.

104. Minute Book 1, May 1888, Oberlin WCTU Records. The advent of Oberlin's Non-Partisan WCTU preceded the formation of a National Non-Partisan WCTU by more than one year—and it would survive past the national reconciliation. The Oberlin College Archives has records of the group from 1897 to 1924.

105. See Estelle Freedman, *Redefining Rape: Sexual Violence in the Era of Suffrage and Segregation* (Cambridge, Mass.: Harvard Univ. Press, 2013), 120–22.

106. Alison Parker, *Articulating Rights: Nineteenth-Century Women on Race, Reform and the State* (DeKalb: Northern Illinois Univ. Press, 2010), 141–44.

107. *Oberlin News*, May 2, 1895.

108. Ibid., Oct. 31, 1895.

109. Minute Book 1, Feb. 1, 19, 1895, Oberlin WCTU Records. Swing's father, Hiram Mead, had served on the faculty of the Oberlin Theological Seminary, 1869–1881; her brother was the philosopher George Herbert Mead. The family history is summarized in Penina Migdal Glazer, "Mead, Elizabeth Storrs Billings," *American National Biography Online*, posted Feb. 2000, accessed June 23, 2017, www.anb.org/articles/09/09-00936.html.

110. *Oberlin News*, March 21, April 4, 1895. On the eve of the election, the *Oberlin News* advised women to remember that "they are doing the voting and not their husbands. They should therefore give their own names and not the names of their husbands. . . . If you lose your head when you get behind the curtain and forget what to do, you may ask the judges to show you how to mark a ballot. . . . vote just like an intelligent man." *Oberlin News*, March 28, 1895.

111. Mary Burton Shurtleff to Giles Shurtleff, April 14, 17, 1877, Giles Waldo and Mary E. Burton Shurtleff Papers, 1846–1930, box 5, Oberlin College Archives; Freed Woman's Aid Society Record Book, Dec. 1878, First and Second Congregational Church Records, subgroup 1, ser. 14, box 5, Oberlin College Archives.

112. Secretary's Report—Annual Meeting, Dec. 16, 1891, Ladies Aid Society Record Book, First and Second Congregational Church Records, subgroup 1, ser. 14, box 3. That the society sent rugs to a renowned source of floor coverings is baffling.

113. Ladies Aid Society Record Book, July 20, 1892, March 21 1894.

114. Annual Report for 1893, Ladies Aid Society Record Book.

115. J. D. Smith to Julia F. Monroe, Nov. 28, 1888, George B. Buzelle to Julia F. Monroe, Dec. 5, 1888, Oberlin Associated Charities Records, Julia Finney Monroe Papers, ser. 6, box 2, Oberlin College Archives.

116. For financial backing, Monroe turned to Rebecca A. Johnson, the wife of a local bank president, and Ida Shearman, whose husband represented the railroad in Oberlin. Oberlin Associated Charities Records, Julia Finney Monroe Papers, ser. 6, box 2, Oberlin College Archives.

117. Memoranda for First Meeting of the Friendly Visitors, Oberlin, Ohio, 1889, Oberlin Associated Charities, Julia Finney Monroe Papers, ser. 6, box 2, Oberlin College Archives. The number of Friendly Visitors from the churches were as follows: First Congregational Church, 19; Second Congregational Church, 16; First Methodist, 6; Baptist, 4; Episcopal, 3. Branch of Ass[ociated] Charities Work—Acquaintance with our own Poor—List of Friendly Visitors, Oberlin Associated Charities Records, Julia Finney Monroe Papers, ser. 6, box 2, Oberlin College Archives.

118. Report of Committee on Work Rooms for Women, Nov. 21, 1889; Report of H. J. Clark, Treas. of the Associated Charities of Oberlin for the Year Ending Nov. 21, 1889, Oberlin Associated Charities Records, Julia Finney Monroe Papers, ser. 6, box 2, Oberlin College Archives.

119. Handwritten addition to Memoranda for First Meeting of the Friendly Visitors, Oberlin, Ohio, 1889, Oberlin Associated Charities, Julia Finney Monroe Papers, ser. 6, box 2, Oberlin College Archives.

120. Report of Committee on Work Rooms for Women, Nov. 21, 1889, Oberlin Associated Charities Records, Julia Finney Monroe Papers, ser. 6, box 2, Oberlin College Archives.

121. Associated Charities of Oberlin Secretary's Book, Charitable Organizations, Oberlin Community, box 1, Oberlin College Archives.

122. Report of the Committee on Work Room for Women, Nov. 21, 1889. Monroe did make a note to consult the pastors of Rust and Mount Zion about the presence of a "mutual relief society among the colored people."

123. Report of the Committee on Work Room for Women, Nov. 21, 1889. The records of the group are not complete enough to provide a racial profile of the clients.

124. Associated Charities of Oberlin Secretary's Book, April 1, 26, 1889. The Associated Charities also took charge of paying the expenses for the loss of a foot by his son George. Associated Charities of Oberlin Secretary's Book, Nov. 11, 1891.

125. Associated Charities of Oberlin Secretary's Book, April 14, 1894.

126. Ibid., May 5, 1894.

127. Ibid., May 25, 1892.

128. *Oberlin News*, April 7, 1892.

129. Ibid., April 14, 1892.

130. For a biographical sketch of Shaw, see William H. Rogers, *Senator John P. Green, and Sketches of Prominent Men of Ohio* (Washington, D.C.: Arena Publishing, 1893), 37–62. Shaw's mother was the black concubine of a plantation owner in Louisiana made famous by Solomon Northrup in *Twelve Years a Slave*. See David Fiske, "Oberlin Has Tie to '12 Years a Slave' Character," *Oberlin Heritage Center Blog*, posted Jan. 8, 2014, accessed June 24, 2017, www.oberlinheritagecenter.org/blog/tag/daniel-webster-shaw/. Shaw's wife was Alice Bookram.

131. Rogers, *Senator John P. Green, and Sketches of Prominent Men of Ohio*, 58. On Shaw's activities, see, for example, *Oberlin Weekly News*, June 9, 1887, Sept. 9, 1887, Oct. 18, 1888, for literary society; Jan. 19, 1888, for Shakespeare productions; April 7, 1887, for Young People's Literary Society; Feb. 2, 28, 1889, for "colored voters political club."

132. *Oberlin News*, April 21, 1892.

133. Ibid., May 25, 1893.

134. On the founding of Mount Zion and B. B. Hill's pastorate, see also Fred L. Steen, "A Brief History of Mount Zion Church," Miscellaneous Churches Collection, Oberlin College Archives, quoted in Lee Davis, Alison Dennis, and Satoko Kanahara, "Mount Zion Church: A History," in *Oberlin's Sacred Heritage: The African-American Tradition*, ed. Carol Laser (Oberlin, Ohio: Oberlin African-American Genealogy and History Group, 2004), 33–34, and posted online at www2.oberlin.edu/external/EOG/AfAmChurches/default.html.

135. *Oberlin News*, June 28, 1894.

136. Ibid., July 12, 1894.

137. Ibid.

138. Ibid., June 29, 1893.

139. Ibid., Aug. 10, 1893, April 4, 1895, Dec. 19, 1902.

140. Ibid., Jan. 24, 1895.

141. Oberlin Mayor's Criminal Dockets, 1886–1890, 1890–1894, 1894–1897, City of Oberlin Records, 1858–2007, subgroup 2, ser. 4, boxes 2–4, Oberlin College Archives. The race of those arrested was determined by record linkage with Patricia Holsworth, "Oberlin Genealogical Database," 2012, in the authors' possession.

142. As Kali N. Gross has observed, "Crime and criminal offending germinate from both the perpetrators and the society in which they live." See her *Colored Amazons: Crime, Violence and Black Women in the City of Brotherly Love, 1890–1910* (Durham, N.C.: Duke Univ. Press, 2006), 155. On how crime statistics fueled debate over the so-called "Negro Problem" in the late nineteenth century, see Kalil Gibran Muhammad, *The Condemnation of Blackness: Race, Crime, and the Making of Modern Urban America* (Cambridge, Mass.: Harvard Univ. Press, 2010), 15–87.

143. Secretary's Book No. 2, Oct. 5, 1897, Oberlin Non-Partisan Woman's Christian Temperance Union Records, box 1, Oberlin College Archives.

144. *Oberlin News*, May 18, 1897.

145. Ibid., Oct. 5, May 18, 1897.

146. Ibid., May 18, 1897.

147. Mildred Fairchild, "The Negro in Oberlin" (Master's thesis, Oberlin College, 1925), 41. Even after the kindergarten program was absorbed into the Oberlin Public Schools, it continued to hire only white teachers. Indeed, the exclusion of black teachers in any part of the Oberlin schools remained local policy until the 1940 appointment of Elizabeth Glenn, who taught a majority black kindergarten class that year in the same—now quite dilapidated—Centennial Building, still a school attended primarily by children of color. *Oberlin News Tribune*, April 9, Nov. 5, 1940.

148. See, for example, *Oberlin News*, March 12, 1886, April 19, 1888, June 27, 1889, Aug. 21, 1890, Feb. 14, 18, May 26, Sept. 15, 1892, Feb. 9, 1893, March 29, 1894, June 20, 1895, Jan. 24, 1896, March 27, 1900.

149. Ibid., June 22, 1897.
150. See, for example, ibid., Jan. 26, Feb. 5, 1897, Nov. 25, 1898.
151. Ibid., Jan. 23, 1898.
152. *Cleveland Gazette*, Feb. 2, 1898. Scott went on to assert the importance of black agency: "Mr. Raynor says the white race freed the colored people but . . . they helped to free themselves. . . . I thank God we are rising above the oppression we have received." Ibid.
153. *Oberlin News*, June 21, 24, 1898.
154. Delavan L. Leonard, *The Story of Oberlin: The Institution, the Community, the Idea, the Movement* (Boston: Pilgrim Press, 1898), 381.

CHAPTER 9

1. *Oberlin News*, June 2, 1899.
2. Ibid., Dec. 2, 1898, June 2, 1899.
3. Lee's conflicts with the minister at the Second Methodist Episcopal Church are covered in chapter 6 above; see, for example, *Oberlin Weekly News*, Aug. 16, 23, 30, Sept. 6, 13, 1878.
4. For a sampling of this dispute, see *Oberlin Weekly News*, Oct. 25, 1878, April 2, 1880, Feb. 3, 1882, May 14, 1886, June 28, 1888.
5. For her public denial, see *Oberlin Weekly News*, Oct. 19, 1880.
6. See, for example, *Oberlin News*, March 26, 1897.
7. William E. Bigglestone, *They Stopped in Oberlin* (Scottsdale, Ariz.: Innovation Group, 1981), 131–32.
8. Quoted in William H. Rogers, *Senator John P. Green, and Sketches of Prominent Men of Ohio* (Washington, D.C.: Arena Publishing, 1893). 72. On the importance of the Avery Fund, see Christi M. Smith, *Reparation and Reconciliation: The Rise and Fall of Integrated Higher Education* (Chapel Hill: Univ. of North Carolina Press, 2016), 180–81.
9. *Cleveland Gazette*, May 26, 1894. The "Park" was a skating rink.
10. Rogers, *Senator John P. Green, and Sketches of Prominent Men of Ohio*, 70; *Oberlin News*, June 2, 1899.
11. *Oberlin News*, January 10, 1896; William E. Bigglestone, *They Stopped in Oberlin: Black Residents and Visitors of the Nineteenth Century* (Scottsdale, Ariz.: Innovation Group, 1981), 102–3.
12. Patricia Holsworth, "Oberlin Genealogical Database" (2012), in authors' possession; Bigglestone, *They Stopped in Oberlin*, 148.
13. Bigglestone, *They Stopped in Oberlin*, 110.
14. *Oberlin News*, May 3, 1916, March 19, March 26, 1897; Bigglestone, *They Stopped in Oberlin*, 83.
15. *Oberlin News*, Sept. 15, 1920; Bigglestone, *They Stopped in Oberlin*, 150–51.
16. Geoffrey Blodgett, *Oberlin Architecture: A Guide to Its Social History* (Oberlin: Oberlin College, 1985), 143, 145; *Oberlin News*, March 16, 1897.
17. T. N. Carver to John Spencer Bassett, April 2, 1895, General Correspondence, box 15, folder 8, John Spencer Bassett Papers 1770–1928, Manuscripts Division, Library of Congress, Washington, D.C. We thank Craig Thompson Friend for sending us a copy of this letter.

18. City Council Minute Book 3, City of Oberlin Records, subgroup 1, ser. 2, box 1, Oberlin College Archives, entry April 21, 1897.

19. *Oberlin Tribune,* Dec. 3, 17, 1931.

20. Braden Paynter, comp., Roster of Oberlin Town Council Members, 1865–1955, unpublished spreadsheet in the authors' possession; Aaron Wildavsky, *Leadership in a Small Town* (Totowa, N.J.: Bedminster Press, 1964), 110–11. Wade Ellis, the college's first African American professor, was elected to the Oberlin City Council in 1957.

21. *Oberlin News,* Feb. 13, 1903.

22. Ibid., Jan. 2, 1900.

23. Ibid., Nov. 26, July 2, Dec. 3, 1901.

24. Ibid., May 30, 1899.

25. Ibid., Sept. 17, 1901.

26. Ibid., Oct 14, 1904, April 4, 1905.

27. Ibid., Aug. 11, 1908, Aug. 19, 1909.

28. Ibid., Sept. 10, 1907.

29. Ibid. On Mrs. Ramey, see *Cleveland Gazette,* Sept. 20, 1902, Aug. 6, 1910.

30. Biographical information on Blanche Harris Brooks Jones was gathered from Former Student File for Blanche Harris/Mrs. Elias Toussaint Jones, Alumni and Development Records, box 543, Oberlin College Archives.

31. Monroe Alpheus Majors, *Noted Negro Women* (Jackson, Tenn.: M. V. Lynk Publishing House, 1893), 30–32.

32. Former Student File for Elias Toussaint Jones, Alumni and Development Records, box 543, Oberlin College Archives; Bigglestone, *They Stopped in Oberlin,* 122–24; Former Student File for Blanche Harris/Mrs. Elias Toussaint Jones, Alumni and Development Records, box 543, Oberlin College Archives.

33. *Oberlin News,* May 23, June 28, May 9, 1898, Nov. 11, 17, 1899.

34. Ibid., Sept. 3, 1901.

35. Ibid., March 21, 1899, March 13, 1900.

36. Ibid., Aug. 25, 1903.

37. Ibid., Aug. 29, 1908; *Oberlin Tribune,* Aug. 28, 1908.

38. W.E.B. Du Bois, *The Autobiography of W.E.B. Du Bois: A Soliloquy on Viewing My Life from the Last Decade of Its First Century* (New York: International Publishers, 1968), 248, 250. See also Angela Jones, *African American Civil Rights: Early Activism and the Niagara Movement* (Santa Barbara, Calif.: Praeger, 2011).

39. For a classic analysis of the debate between Du Bois and Washington, see August Meier, *Negro Thought in America, 1880–1915: Racial Ideologies in the Age of Booker T. Washington* (Ann Arbor: Univ. of Michigan Press, 1963), especially 161–247.

40. *Oberlin News,* Feb. 19, 1897.

41. Ibid., May 13, 1904.

42. Gary Gerstle, *American Crucible: Race and Nation in the Twentieth Century* (Princeton, N.J.: Princeton Univ. Press, 2001), 62–63.

43. *Oberlin News,* Sept. 2, 1908.

44. Ibid., Sept. 4, 1908.

45. Ibid.

46. Hale lauded "right thinking, energetic colored men and women, constructive members of their communities, [who] have put their shoulder to the wheel to help the party lift up the masses here and elsewhere," and he concluded ominously, "You must leave your manhood behind whenever you enter the domain" of the Democratic Party. *Oberlin News,* Sept. 9, 1908; *Oberlin Tribune,* Sept. 11, 1908.

47. *Oberlin News,* Oct. 21, 1908.

48. Ibid., Oct. 28, 1908.

49. Booker T. Washington's third wife, Margaret Murray Washington, spoke in Oberlin in March 1914 (*Oberlin News,* April 1, 1914). Oberlin marked Washington's death with a memorial tribute in November 1915 (*Oberlin News,* Dec. 1, 8, 1915). Du Bois returned to Oberlin several times after this, including in late 1910 (*Cleveland Gazette,* Dec. 17, 1910), again in July 1919 with the NAACP (*Oberlin News,* July 2, 1919), and once more in March 1922 (*Oberlin News,* March 29, 1922).

50. *Oberlin News,* Aug. 26, 1908. On the historical origins and significance of "racial uplift ideology," see Kevin K. Gaines, *Uplifting the Race: Black Leadership, Politics, and Culture in the Twentieth Century* (Chapel Hill: Univ. of North Carolina Press, 1996), 1–46 and passim.

51. *Oberlin News,* Sept. 23, 1908.

52. Oberlin women and their allies had played important founding roles in the black women's club movement. Mary Church Terrell served as the original NACWC president, with 1865 Oberlin graduate Frances Jackson Coppin as the founding first vice president. Mary Burnett Talbert, the Oberlin barber's daughter who helped establish the Niagara Movement, would serve as president of the national organization from 1916 to 1920. On the NACWC, see Nikki L. M. Brown, *Private Politics and Public Voices: Black Women's Activism from World War I to the New Deal* (Bloomington: Indiana Univ. Press, 2006).

53. "Calendar of the Women's Progressive Club for the Year 1912," Oberlin Women's Progressive Club Records, Oberlin Community Record Group, box 25, Oberlin College Archives.

54. By 1915, they attracted at least forty-five women to a regular meeting. *Cleveland Gazette,* January 23, 1915.

55. *Cleveland Gazette,* July 5, 1913.

56. "Year Book of the Mutual Improvement Club, Oberlin, Ohio, 1913–14," Mutual Improvement Club of Oberlin Records, box 1, Oberlin College Archives.

57. *Oberlin News,* April 5, 1916.

58. The "respectability politics" practiced by Oberlin women had both the radical edge and the conservative implications discussed by Evelyn Higginbotham, *Righteous Discontent: The Women's Movement in the Black Baptist Church, 1880–1920* (Cambridge, Mass.: Harvard Univ. Press, 1993), 14–15. For other discussions of respectability politics, see (among the vast literature) Paisley Harris, "Gatekeeping and Remaking: The Politics of Respectability in African American History and Black Feminism," *Journal of Women's History* 15 (May 2003): 212–20; Frederick Harris, "The Rise of Respectability Politics," *Dissent* 61 (winter 2014): 33–37.

59. *Oberlin News,* Aug. 19, 1908.

60. See *Oberlin News,* May 19, 21, 1909, for the advertisement. Coverage of the auction can be found in *Oberlin News,* June 2, 1909. For an example of the Hollywood Addition covenant, see Warranty Deed 53351, Lorain County Deed Books, vol. 114, page 418, Lorain County Re-

corder's Office, Elyria, Ohio. See also Robert Q. Thompson, *Hollywood Street, Oberlin, OH: A Centennial History* (Columbus, Ohio: Zip Publishing, 2009).

61. Information on the role of Glenn and Copeland in building many homes, especially on Elm Street, was compiled from the *Oberlin News*. See also Geoffrey Blodgett, *Oberlin Architecture*, 143, 145, 158.

62. Louis E. Burgner to Henry Churchill King, June 30, 1913, typescript copy, Henry Churchill King Papers, Correspondence, box 12, Oberlin College Archives.

63. Henry Churchill King to Louis E. Burgner, Aug. 14, 1913, typescript copy, ibid.

64. Louis E. Burgner to Henry Churchill King, received Sept. 20, 1913, ibid. The residence may have been the "Holly Tree Inn" at 42 South Cedar Street. See W. E. Bigglestone, "Oberlin College and the Negro Student, 1865–1940," *Journal of Negro History* 56 (July 1971): 210, n. 47.

65. Henry Churchill King to Louis E. Burgner, Sept. 24, 1913, typescript copy, Henry Churchill King Papers, Correspondence, box 12, Oberlin College Archives.

66. Constitution of the Oberlin Anti-Slavery Society, June 1835, Autograph File, Oberlin College Library Records, box 3, Oberlin College Archives.

67. For an insightful sociological account of the retreat of Oberlin College from its support of what she calls "interracial coeducation," see Smith, *Reparation and Reconciliation*, 174–83 and 186–88. In Smith's analysis, loss of external support for its "anti-caste" mission pushed Oberlin College to redefine itself as an elite institution that also enrolled a handful of students of color. Our work does not contradict her findings but rather places them in the context of a complex historical narrative about not only the college but also the town, founded as a utopia with a distinctive radical racial egalitarian vision.

68. Bigglestone, "Oberlin College and the Negro Student," 200.

69. Florence Fitch to "Dear Ones at Home," Feb. 28, 1909, Florence Mary Fitch Papers, ser. 3, subseries 1, box 7, Oberlin College Archives.

70. Bigglestone, "Oberlin College and the Negro Student," 207.

71. *Cleveland Plain Dealer*, April 20, 1910.

72. Ibid. See also *Cleveland Gazette*, April 23, 1910.

73. Lucien Warner, "Letters to the Editor," *Oberlin Alumni Magazine* 6 (April 1910): 253.

74. "Review of the Year," *Oberlin Alumni Magazine* 6 (July 1910): 443–45.

75. Henry Churchill King, "The College and Democracy," *Oberlin Alumni Magazine* 7 (Dec. 1910): 96.

76. Ibid., 97–98.

77. Ibid., 101, 99.

78. Ibid. Miller's essay originally appeared in *National Magazine* (Feb. 1905), 524–29.

79. "Oberlin Compromise" is the authors' term, not King's, and deliberately echoes the "Atlanta Compromise" associated with Booker T. Washington.

80. Mary Church Terrell, *A Colored Woman in a White World* (1940; reprint, Amherst, N.Y.: Humanity Books, 2005), 284.

81. Quoted in Cally L. Waite, *Permission to Remain among Us: Education for Blacks in Oberlin, Ohio, 1880–1914* (Westport, Conn.: Praeger, 2002), 108.

82. Mary Church Terrell to Henry Churchill King, Jan. 26, 1914, Henry Churchill King Papers, Correspondence, box 72, Oberlin College Archives. A digitized and annotated version of this letter can be found at "'You Can't Keep Her Out': Mary Church Terrell's Fight for Equality

in America," *Digitizing American Feminisms*, Document 2, online at americanfeminisms.org/ayou-cant-keep-her-out-mary-church-terrells-fight-for-equality-in-america/document-2-segregation-in-oberlin-college-dormitories/#footnotes.

83. Henry Churchill King to Mary Church Terrell, Feb. 4, 1914, unsigned copy, Henry Churchill King Papers, Correspondence, box 72, Oberlin College Archives.

84. Bigglestone, "Oberlin College and the Negro Student," 98–99.

85. Howard L. Rawdon, "The Colored Pupil in the Oberlin Public Schools" (Master's thesis, Oberlin College, 1914), 1–2.

86. Ibid., 29.

87. Rawdon's figures suggest a disturbing change. One decade earlier, people of color accounted for just over one-third of all arrests for serious crimes recorded on the Mayor's Docket (see chapter 8); the increase to 46 percent is notable.

88. Rawdon, "The Colored Pupil in the Oberlin Public Schools," 33–34.

89. Ibid., 38–39.

90. Ibid., 34.

91. 1910 Tax Duplicates for Oberlin, Range 18, vols. 2, 4, Town 5, Lorain County Records Retention Center, Elyria, Ohio, and available for download at www.loraincounty.us/commissioners-departments/records-center/records-search/early-tax-duplicates.

92. This analysis rests on tax lists, census records, Holsworth's "Oberlin Genealogical Database," and lists of people in business in 1910 in Wilbur H. Phillips, *Oberlin Colony: The Story of a Century* (Oberlin, Ohio: Oberlin Printing Company, 1933), 318.

93. Harley J. Smith to "Sir," Sept. 18, 1916, in National Association for the Advancement of Colored People Records, Part I: Branch Files, 1910–1947, box I:G167, Library of Congress, Washington, D.C., digital copy in Oberlin College Archives.

94. Samuel Coleman to "Sirs," Feb. 18, 1917, ibid.

95. This tally combines the names on a typescript list that Smith sent to Nash dated October 12, 1916, with the signatures on the application for a charter, stamped with the date November 16, 1916, both in ibid. The former councilmen were William Madison Mitchell and Thomas A. Bows. Henson Tuck ran and lost in 1925; his son Archibald Tuck ran and lost in 1933.

96. Royal Nash to H. J. Smith, Oct. 6, 1916, NAACP Records, Part I: Branch Files, 1910–1947, box I:G167, digital copy in Oberlin College Archives.

97. Ibid.

98. Irving Metcalf to Roy Nash, Nov. 29, 1916, ibid.

99. Henry Churchill King to Roy Nash, Dec. 2, 1916, ibid.

100. Elias T. Jones to Roy Nash, Dec. 9, 1916, ibid.

101. Samuel Coleman to Roy Nash, Jan. 17, 1917, ibid.

102. Samuel Coleman to "Sirs," Jan. 17, 1917, ibid.

103. Membership Report, Sept. 26, 1918, ibid.

104. "There are splendid reasons why we need it," Barnes stated in 1914, asking, "Are we desirables?" Barnes intended to "arouse and benefit our people." Margaret S. Barnes to W.E.B. Du Bois, May 5, 1914, ibid.

105. Resolutions of the Colored Federated Clubs of Oberlin, Sept. 23, 1918, typescript, NAACP Records, Part I: Branch Files, 1910–1947, box I:G167, digital copy in Oberlin College Archives; *Oberlin News*, Oct. 2, 1918.

106. *Ohio State Monitor* (Columbus), Oct. 19, 1918; *Cleveland Advocate*, Oct. 19, 1918.
107. *Cleveland Advocate*, Oct. 19, 1918.
108. See Bigglestone, "Oberlin College and the Negro Student," 207.
109. *Annual Reports of the President and the Treasurer of Oberlin College for 1917–18* (Oberlin, Ohio: Oberlin College, 1918), 11.
110. *Oberlin News*, April 30, 1919.
111. William Pickens to "Dear Friends," April 28, 1919, NAACP Papers, Part I: Branch Files, 1910–1947, box I:G167, digital copy in Oberlin College Archives.
112. Beulah Tyrell to William Pickens, April 29, 1919, ibid.
113. William Pickens to Dean Bosworth, May 1, 1919, and William Pickens to Frances Hosford, May 1, 1919, both in ibid.
114. Mary White Ovington to Beulah Tyrell, May 7, 1919, ibid.
115. William Pickens to Mary White Ovington, May 9, 1919, ibid.
116. Beulah Tyrell to Mary White Ovington, May 15, 1919, NAACP Records, Part I: Administrative Files, 1885–1949, Subject File: Discrimination, Education, Oberlin Univ. [*sic*] 1919, file 15, Library of Congress. (This letter is not included in the digital copies of NAACP Records at the Oberlin College Archives.)
117. According to William W. Giffin, the Cleveland chapter "was the most vital NAACP affiliate in the state." Giffin, *African Americans and the Color Line in Ohio, 1915–1930* (Columbus: Ohio State Univ. Press, 2005), 66.
118. *Elyria Chronicle-Telegram*, March 26, 1919.
119. In the NAACP Records archived at the Library of Congress, there appears to be no surviving documentation of an Oberlin chapter between 1919 and 1948. Yet there is mention of "the Oberlin N.A.A.C.P." in Caroline Wasson Thomason, "Will Prejudice Capture Oberlin?" *The Crisis* (Dec. 1934), 361.
120. *Oberlin News*, July 2, 1919.
121. On the conference sessions in Cleveland, see *Cleveland Advocate*, June 28, July 5, 1919.
122. Fairchild, "The Negro in Oberlin," 62–63.
123. Ibid., 63.
124. Ibid., 65.
125. Ibid., 1.
126. Kemper Fullerton, "College or Cause," *Oberlin Alumni Magazine* (April 1926), 9.
127. For a brilliant analysis of the condemnation of blackness as a social and ideological process in late nineteenth- and early twentieth-century America, especially the North, see Kalil Gibran Muhammad, *The Condemnation of Blackness: Race, Crime, and the Making of Modern Urban America* (Cambridge, Mass.: Harvard Univ. Press, 2010).
128. Constitution of the Oberlin Anti-Slavery Society.

EPILOGUE

1. *Oberlin News-Tribune*, May 11, 1944. The catalyst for the May 4 protest was an evening conversation among theological students from which a black student excused himself to go get a haircut. A white student asked him where he could get a haircut at that hour, and the

black student explained that there was a college employee—Walker Pair—who cut black hair at his house at night. Evidently the white students involved in the conversation had not previously known that the town's regular barbershops refused to serve men of color. Oscar Fox, who worked during the week in Elyria, cut black hair in Oberlin on Saturdays, however. Oral history interview with Robert Thomas by Peter Way, April 19, 1979, transcribed by Marlene Merrill, Oberlin Oral History Project, held by the Oberlin Heritage Center, Oberlin, Ohio; oral history interview with George T. Jones, Betty Thomas, and Bob Thomas by Allan Patterson, Nov. 17, 1984, Oberlin Oral History Project; Mary Manning, "Integrating Oberlin's Barber Shops, 1944–45," *Oberlin Heritage Center Blog*, posted Feb. 25, 2016, and accessed July 26, 2017, www.oberlinheritagecenter.org/blog/2016/02/integrating-oberlins-barber-shops-1944-45/.

2. *Oberlin News-Tribune*, May 11, 1944.
3. Ibid.
4. Ibid., May 18, 1944.
5. Ibid.
6. Ibid., June 15, June 22, 1944. See also Manning, "Integrating Oberlin's Barber Shops, 1944–45."
7. *Oberlin News-Tribune*, June 22, 1944. Although the shop's owner, Victor Rodriguez, was himself a person of color, he would not cut black hair at his shop, at least during regular business hours. Oral history interview with Gerald Scott by Mildred Chapin, Nov. 14, 1986, transcribed by Amy Zeigle, Oberlin Oral History Project.
8. *Oberlin News-Tribune*, Sept. 21, 1944; *Oberlin Review*, Sept. 22, 1944.
9. "Oberlin Cosmopolitan Barber Shop Incorporated," mimeographed sheet, Oct. 26, 1944, in August Meier Papers, ser. 3, box 4, Oberlin College Archives.
10. *Oberlin News-Tribune*, Nov. 2, 1944.
11. Oral history interview with Robert Thomas by Peter Way, April 19, 1979.
12. *Oberlin News-Tribune*, Nov. 16, 1944. See also "Tonsorial Tolerance," *Time*, Nov. 27, 1944, 46.
13. *Oberlin News-Tribune*, May 17, 1945.
14. Oral history interview with George T. Jones, Betty Thomas, and Bob Thomas by Allan Patterson, Nov. 17, 1984.
15. Manning, "Integrating Oberlin's Barber Shops, 1944–45"; oral history interview with Gerald Scott by Mildred Chapin, Nov. 14, 1986.
16. Oral history interview with Gerald Scott by Mildred Chapin, Nov. 14, 1986; oral history interview with Robert Thomas by Peter Way, April 19, 1979.
17. *Cleveland Plain Dealer*, Aug. 25, 1947.
18. Aaron Wildavsky, *Leadership in a Small Town* (1964; reprint, New Brunswick, N.J.: Transaction Publishers, 2004), 44–47, 83–126 passim.
19. U.S. Census Bureau, "Profile of Selected Economic Characteristics: 2000," "Poverty Status in 1999 of Families and Nonfamily Householders: 2000," "Profile of Selected Social Characteristics: 2000," *American FactFinder* (website), accessed Aug. 28, 2014, factfinder2.census.gov.
20. *Oberlin-Wellington Rescue Celebration 2008 Events* (Oberlin, Ohio: Oberlin-Wellington Rescue Coalition, 2008), brochure in the authors' possession.

INDEX

Italicized page numbers refer to illustrations.

abolitionism in Oberlin, 84, 86–87, 95, 171; as shared goal of the community, 2–3, 26–27, 29–31, 32, 251; and electoral politics, 85–86, 89–90, 91, 92; racial differences in, 86–87, 96, 99, 103, 105; and defiance of Fugitive Slave Act, 88–89 (*see also* Oberlin-Wellington Rescue); interracial solidarity in, 89, 99, 103–4, 107, 109; during Civil War, 111, 115–20; and black suffrage, 120–26, 132–33; compared to temperance movement, 203–4

Adair, Benjamin Franklin, 81, 181, 191

Adair, Charlotte, 81, 181

Adair, Docia Wright, 181

Adair, Frank (Benjamin Franklin Adair, Jr.), 181

African American leadership in Oberlin: antebellum, 46, 47–48, 63–64, 98–99; and community celebrations, 46, 47, 98–99, 155, 162–64; attrition of, through moves to other cities, 48, 134, 178–83, 230, 251; and national politics, 147–48, 150–56, 157–61, 166–67, 224–25; town offices held by, 149, 162, 179 (*see also* Oberlin town council: African American members of); clergymen in, 222, 245; and quest for respectability, 224, 228–30, 251; women in, 228–30, 246

African Methodist Episcopal Church (Oberlin), 165, 167, 204–5

American Anti-Slavery Society, 31, 34, 46

American Colonization Society, 20–21, 56

Andrew, John A., 117

Associated Charities of Oberlin, 195, 216–17, 220

Avery, Henry, 202, 205

Bagby, Robert B., 153

Baker, Ella, 8

Baker, Sarah, 187

Barber, Amzi, 36–37

"barbershop controversy," 253–57, 311–12nn1,7

Bardwell, John P., 128

Barnes, Margaret Sallee, 234, 246

Battle, Joseph H., 156–57, 159, 160, 170, 290n52

Beabout, John N., 88–89

Beecher, A. N., 108, 109

Beecher, E. N., 206

Beecher, Lyman, 20, 21

Berry, John, 180

INDEX

Bigelow, Isaac, 98
Bishop, Philip, 254, 255
Black Laws (in Ohio), 52, 86–87, 163
Black Lives Matter movement, 7
Black River, Ohio, 203
black suffrage: nationally, 120–26, 127–29, 132–34 (*see also* Fifteenth Amendment); in Ohio, 71–72, 87–88, 120, 126–27, 129–32
Blake, Mary J., 217
Bosworth, Edward I., 246, 247
Bows, Thomas, 227, 233, 246
Boynton, Lewis D., 76–77, 111, 127
Boynton, Ruth, 76
Boynton, Shakespeare, 127
Boynton, Washington Wallace (W. W.), 126–27
Bradley, Dan F., 208
Bradley, James, 35–37
Branch, Lauretta, 62
Brand, James, 201, 206, 219
Breckinridge, John C., 76
Broadwell, John H., 205, 206
Bronson, Frank, 206–9
Brooks, Maude Rebecca, 229
Brooks, William Lafayette, 229
Brough, John, 120
Brown, John, 104. *See also* Harpers Ferry raid
Brown, John (Oberlin resident), 48
Brown, John, Jr., 105–6
Brown, Margaret. *See* Van Rankin, Margaret Brown
Buchanan, James, 76, 77, 92, 93
Burgner, Louis E., 236–38, 246
Burnett, Cornelius J., 154, 182, 199, 231
Burnett, Mary. *See* Talbert, Mary Burnett
Burton, Julius, 233
Bushnell, Simeon, 99, 100, 101, 102, *139*, 282n83
Butler, Benjamin, 129

Calkins, Storrs S., 133
Campton, Edith. *See* Mitchell, Edith Campton

Campton, John, 40, 63, 71, 199
Campton, John R. (son of John and Mary Campton), 191
Campton, Mary, 40, 63
Campton, Mary A. (daughter of John and Mary Campton), 182, 191
Canada, 75, 95, 158, 182, 229; as refuge for escaped slaves, 38, 43, 48, 59, 89, 94, 95, 187
Cannon, J. C., 128
Carr, Elizabeth, 165
Carver, Thomas Nixon, 226–27
Cass, Lewis, 86
caucus system, 131, 148–49, 162, 226, 227, 230
cemetery (Westwood Cemetery), 119, 156, 169
Centennial Building, 220, 230
Chambers, Augustus, 93
Chambers, Garrison, 132–33
Chambers, Maxwell, 55–56, 57; slaves freed by, 55–56, 169
Charitable Organization Society, 230
charitable work, 215–23, 230; "scientific" basis for, 195, 209, 216; racial condescension in, 216–17; 219–23; and black churches, 217–18, 219, 220
Chase, Salmon P., 76, 86, 89
Cherry, Byron, 235–36
Chesnutt, Charles W., 232
Chillicothe, Ohio, 34, 39, 49, 189
Cincinnati, Ohio, 19–23, 80. *See also* Lane Seminary
Civil Rights Act of 1875, 156, 157
Civil War, 4, 110–20, 124, 160, 174, 190, 251
Civil War amendments, 134. *See also* Fifteenth Amendment; Fourteenth Amendment; Thirteenth Amendment
Clark, Lewis, 163
Clark, Peter H., 153, 166
Cleveland, Ohio, 48, 112, 152, 157; former Oberlin residents in, 48, 155, 218, 255; national reform conventions in, 74, 211, 214, 249; Oberlin-Wellington Rescue

INDEX

trial in, 96, 100–102; black politics in, 152, 162, 163; temperance movement in, 211, 214, 228–29; NAACP in, 244, 248, 249
Cleveland Advertiser, 59
Cleveland Advocate, 246–47
Cleveland Gazette, 222
Cleveland Herald, 73, 74–75, 100, 154–55, 170
Cleveland Leader, 98–100, 102, 122, 126, 207, 208
Cleveland Plain Dealer, 71, 76–77, 96, 97, 106, 238–39, 256
Cochran, William, 93
Coleman, Samuel, 244, 245
Colored Federated Clubs of Oberlin, 246
Colored Law and Order League, 233
Colored Men's National Council, 153
"color line," 6, 169–70; emergence of, in Oberlin, 3, 5, 147, 223; black responses to, 159, 228, 232; at Oberlin College, 170–71, 238–41; in housing, 234–38; emerging challenges to, post–World War II, 252–57
Compromise of 1877, 162
Congregational Church. *See* First Church in Oberlin
Cooper, Anna Julia, 180
Copeland, Delilah Evans, 42, 53, 108
Copeland, Frederick, 189, 226. *See also* Glenn and Copeland firm
Copeland, John, 42–43, 63, 71, 108; family of, 42–43, 53 (*see also* Copeland, Delilah Evans; Copeland, Frederick; Copeland, John Anthony)
Copeland, John Anthony, 95, 97, 105, *140*, 189; and Harpers Ferry raid, 104, 105, 107, 108–9
Copeland, John, Jr. *See* Copeland, John Anthony
Coppin, Fanny Jackson, 180, 183, 187, 296n35, 308n52
Cosmopolitan Barber Shop, 255–56
Covenant of Oberlin Colony, 2, 12–13, 17–18, 25, 198

Cowan, James, 169
Cowan, John, 157
Cowles, Henry, 64, 87, 105, 106, 116
Cox, Helen Finney, 122
Cox, Jacob Dolson, 122–26, 129, 130
Cox, Sabram, 37–39, 149, 155, 204; in antislavery movement, 38–39, 87, 109, 117; in town politics, 148, 149, 151, 153–54, 161, 162
crime, 218–19, 242, 310n87
Crosby, Norman C., 254
Crummell, Alexander, 125

D'Anglas, Belinda, 54, 55
D'Anglas, Diza, 54–55, 70, 81
D'Anglas, Mary Louisa, 54, 55
D'Anglas, Stanislas, 54–55, 81
Dale, Marcus, 69, 164
Dascomb, James, 202
Dascomb, Marianne Parker, 202, 203
Davis, Alice Alexander, 182
Davis, Harry E., 248
Day, William Howard, 45, 46–48, 50, 74, 87
Dayton, Anson P., 93–94, 95, 96
Democratic Party supporters in Oberlin, 75–77, 93–94, 149; as small minority in presidential elections, 90, 92, 168. *See also* Wack, Chauncey
Dennison, William, 130
Dickinson, R. L., 218
Douglas, Stephen, 76, 90
Douglass, Frederick, 74, 85, 163, 186, 214
Dred Scott decision (1857), 92
Dresser, Amos, 42
Du Bois, W.E.B., 178, 233, 245, 246, 248; and Niagara Movement, 182, 230, 231, 232; in Oberlin, 231, 232, 308n49
Durham family, 207
Dyer, Alfred J., 155, 199
Dyer, George, 217

Echols, W. C., 165
economic mobility. *See* social mobility
Edwards, Andrew, 133

315

Ellis, John M., 122, 133
Elyria, Ohio, 10–11, 23–24, 26, 38, 131, 233
Emancipation Proclamation, 111, 116, 117, 163–64, 173
English, William H., 168
Evans, Anna. *See* Murray, Anna Evans
Evans, Delilah. *See* Copeland, Delilah Evans
Evans, Delilah (niece of Delilah Evans Copeland), 179
Evans, Eliza Colwell, 212
Evans, Henrietta Leary, 53, 179
Evans, Henry, 70, 109, 199; background of, 53; family of, 53, 179, 212 (*see also* Evans, Wilson Bruce); status of, in Oberlin, 70, 71, 115, 119; and Oberlin-Wellington Rescue, 97, 98, 103, 115, *139*
Evans, Lewis Sheridan, 179
Evans, Sarah, 179
Evans, Sarah Jane Leary, 53
Evans, Wilson (nephew of Wilson Bruce Evans), 179
Evans, Wilson Bruce, 53, 179, 210, 212; status of, in Oberlin, 71, 154; and Oberlin-Wellington Rescue, 97, 98, *139*

Fairchild, Edward Henry, 116; on race relations in Oberlin, 66, 80–81; and black suffrage, 121, 122–23, 125
Fairchild, James Harris, 65, 106, 121, *138*; reminiscences by, 14, 32, 164, 198; and fugitive slaves, 88, 89, 95, 96; as Oberlin College president, 155, 170, 182–83, 238; and temperance, 200, 201
Fairchild, Mildred, 249–50
Fauver, Alfred, 218
Ferris, William, 39
Fifteenth Amendment, 3, 111, 132, 147, 150, 159; celebrations of, 132–33, 152, 154–55
5th U.S. Colored Troops, 117–18, 128, 160
Finney, Charles Grandison, 1–2, 39, 125, *138*, 216; and Second Great Awakening, 10, 12; and Oberlin Institute, 22, 24, 27, 28–29; as abolitionist, 27, 31, 116; as pastor in Oberlin, 49, 67, 69, 116, 120

Finney, Julia. *See* Monroe, Julia Finney
Finney, Lydia, 31
Finney Chapel, 232, 249
fire companies, 169
First Church in Oberlin (known until 1860 as the Congregational Church or the Oberlin Church), 66–67, 74, 106, *135*, 169–70, 254; founding of, 16–17; pastors of, 49, 66, 67, 69, 116, 120
—public meetings at, 131, 231; antislavery, 84, 102–4, 108, 116–17; during the Civil War, 111, 116–17, 173; for black suffrage, 125–26, 129, 133–34, 155–56; for temperance, 201, 221
—black participation in, 189, 190–91, 205, 212, 215–16; before 1860, 34, 45, 59, 67–69
First Methodist Church (Methodist Episcopal Church), 164, 218–19
First of August celebrations, 46, 47, *137*
Fisher, Cordelia Quinn, 234
Fitch, Florence, 238, 240
Fitch, James M., 89, 96, 106, 108, 109; and Oberlin-Wellington Rescue, 99, 101, 102, 103, *139*
Fitch, Jane, 89
Fletcher, Nathan P., 22, 23, 24
Florence Nightingale Association, 113
Foster, Stephen, 85
Fourteenth Amendment, 3, 129, 150, 159
Fox, Elizabeth Sullivan, 81
Fox, Jeremiah (Jerry), 81, 97, 150
Free Democratic Party, 89–90
Freedman's Western Educational Society, 225
Freedmen's Bureau, 128, 179
Freedmen's Relief Association of Oberlin, 116–17
freemasonry, 228
Free Soil Party, 47, 85–86, 89
Free Territory Convention (1848), 85–86
Frémont, John C., 77, 92
French, William C., 133
Frost, William Goodell, 195, 213, 302–3n96

INDEX

Fugitive Slave Law (1850), 52, 60, 88, 92; defiance of, in Oberlin, 88–89 (*see also* Oberlin-Wellington Rescue)
Fullerton, Kemper, 7, 251

Gardner, J. M., 205–6
Garfield, James, 122, 130, 168, 169
Garrison, William Lloyd, 20, 21, 46, 85, 119
Gaskins, Godfrey, 39
Gibbs, Harriet Althea, 180
Gibbs, Ida, 179–80
Gibbs, Maria Alexander, 158, 179, 212
Gibbs, Mifflin Wistar, 158, 179
Gibson, W. H., 203
Glenn, Augusta Louisa König, 189
Glenn, Charles H., 189, 220, 233. *See also* Glenn and Copeland firm
Glenn, George Mathewson, *144*, 188–89, 191, 226
Glenn, William H., 233
Glenn and Copeland firm, 189, 236
Goodrich, E. J., 206
Goosland, Matthew, 155, 164, 165, 204, 292n96
Gordon, David, 39–40
Grant, Ulysses S., 120, 150, 161, 179
Greeley, Horace, 76, 150, 158, 163
Green, John Patterson, 155, 162, 163–64, 166, 226
Green, Shields, 108–9
Greenback Party, 166, 168
Grimes, Solomon, 98, 109
Guinn, James M., 112

Hale, John P., 89–90
Harper, Frances E. W., 212
Harpers Ferry raid (1859), 105–9; Oberlin and, 5, 53, 84, 95, 104–9, 283n10
Harris, Blanche Virginia. *See* Jones, Blanche Virginia Harris Brooks
Hatton, George W., 158, 161, 165
Hayes, Rutherford B., 130, 131, 160, 161, 162
Henderson, Robert C., 157
Henderson, William T., 133, 155, 168, 215, 226

Hendry, Samuel, 111, 112
Hicks, Richard, 217
Hill, B. B., 218, 219
Holley, Sallie, 126
"Hollywood Addition," 235–36
Home Missionary Society, 215
Hopkins, Chellas S., 61
Horton, Walter M., 254
Hosford, Frances, 222, 247–48
Hughes, Langston, 181
Hughes, Samuel, 12, 14, 18

Imes, Benjamin A., 157, 168, 171
Impartial Suffrage Committee, 129–30
Inborden, Sarah Jane Evans, 182
Ingersoll, Theodore S., 14
Ingersoll, William, 55
interracial marriage, 25, 26, 80–82, 189, 211, 256

Jackson, Andrew, 43
Jackson, Andrew (Oberlin resident), 154, 182, 226
Jackson, Fanny M. *See* Coppin, Fanny Jackson
Jackson, George, 182
Jackson, T. H., 167, 293n109
Jackson, William Montgomery, 180, 182
Janey, Joseph, 39
Janey, Martha, 39
Janey, Thomas Jefferson, 39, 61, 97
Jarvis, Lizzie, 243–44
Jarvis, Nancy, 44
Jarvis, Thomas, 63, 70, 71, 173, 199
Jarvis, William, 43–44
Jeffries v. Ankeny (1842), 61, 71
Jenkins, William O., 199, 202, 220
Jennings, Anderson, 94–95
Johnson, Andrew, 120–21, 127, 129
Johnson, Anna, 81
Johnson, Henry, 43, 81
Johnson, Matthew, 97, 99–100
Johnston, Adelia Field, 170, 190, 238
Jones, Allen, 41–42, 53, 72, 73–75, 149, 158, 229

Jones, Blanche Virginia Harris Brooks, *143*, 229–30, 245
Jones, Elias Toussaint, 74, *142*, 229–30, 245
Jones, George M., 241
Jones, John Craven, 72, 158, 159, 160, 161, 166
Jones, Temperance (Tempe), 41–42, 229
Jones, William, 158
Jubilee celebration (1883), 171–72, 225

Kansas, 163, 170, 180–81; and slavery conflict, 76, 90–91, 92
Kansas Emigration Aid Association of Northern Ohio, 91
Kansas-Nebraska Act (1854), 90–91
Keep, John ("Father Keep"), 49, 121, 134, 195; as Oberlin Institute trustee, 23–24, 27, 33, 98, 264n88; as abolitionist, 23, 98, 102, 106; optimism of, at end of Civil War, 173–74, 175, 178, 195, 251
Keep, Mary A., 206, 301n54
Keep, Theodore, 188
Kelley, Abbey, 85
Kellogg, William E., 109
King, Henry Churchill, *146*, 238; and racial issues, 231, 236–38, 239–41, 245
Kinney, George, 109
Kinson, Sarah Margru, 48, 61
Knapp, A. D., 206
König, Augusta Louisa. *See* Glenn, Augusta Louisa König

Ladies Aid Society of First Church, 215–16
Ladies Literary Course, 40, 48, 54, 63, 229
Ladies Literary Society, 48, 113
Lane, John, 40, 42–43, 47, 53, 71
Lane Rebels, 21–22, 31, 36, 106, 124; influence of, on Oberlin Institute, 21–22, 26, 27; invoking of, in later years, 171, 254
Lane Seminary, 20–21, 29, 35–36; secession from, *see* Lane Rebels
Langston, Arthur, 161
Langston, Caroline Mercer, 181

Langston, Caroline Wall, 54, 65, 178
Langston, Charles, 33–35, 37, 49, 93, 100, 106, 117, 180–81; and Oberlin-Wellington Rescue, 93, 95, 97, 99, *139*
Langston, Dessalines, 181
Langston, Gideon, 33–35, 37, 49
Langston, John Mercer, *138*; background of, 49, 70; family of, 49, 161, 178 (*see also* Langston, Charles; Langston, Caroline Wall); on race relations in Oberlin, 58, 66, 78, 113–14, 155; as part of African American elite in Oberlin, 70, 71, 72; and electoral politics, 72, 89, 92, 131, 150, 153, 157; and fugitive slaves, 73, 82, 95, 99; and Harpers Ferry raid, 105–6, 108, 109; during Civil War, 111, 113–15, 116, 117, 119; and black suffrage, 121–22, 124, 125, 130, 131; in Washington, DC, 134, 155, 178; and National Equal Rights League, 151, 152
Langston, Mary Patterson Leary, 53, 180–81
Langston, Nathaniel Turner, 181
Leary, Lewis Sheridan, 53, 104–5; and Harpers Ferry raid, 53, 57, 104–5, 106, 108–9, 180
Leary, Louise, 181
Leary, Mary Sampson Patterson. *See* Langston, Mary Patterson Leary
Lee, Henry, *142*, 151–54, 155, 224–25, 226; family of, 151, 152, 182; in political quarrels, 152, 153, 158, 160, 162; in Second Methodist Episcopal Church, 158, 165–66, 225, 292n101; and "Omnibus War," 166; and temperance, 204, 207, 210; death of, 204
Lee, Robert E., 105, 120
Leonard, Delavan, 222–23, 227–28
Lewis, Dio, 201, 203
Lewis, Mary Edmonia, 113–15
Lexington Methodist Conference, 165
Liberator, 66, 119
Liberty Party, 47, 85, 86
Liberty School, 48, 65–66, 187

Lincoln, Abraham, 110, 112–13, 163, 185–86; and Emancipation Proclamation, 111, 115–17, 173; assassination of, 120

Literary Course. *See* Ladies Literary Course

Lorain County News, 112, 120, 132, 147, 150, 151; during Civil War, 112, 116–17, 119–20; on electoral politics, 123–24, 126, 129, 130, 131, 147; on black suffrage, 123–24, 128, 130, 131, 132, 133, 134; on postwar South, 127–29; *Oberlin News* as successor to, 149

Love, Richmond, 54

Lovejoy, Elijah, 37

Lowe, Jacob, 94, 95

Lyman, Ansel W., 94, *139*

Macdonald, A. J., 1

Mahan, Asa, 21–22, 27–28, 87, 152; as Oberlin Institute president, 22, 24, 28, 29, 63–64, 87; and antislavery movement, 27–28, 31, 85

Mahan, Mary, 31

Majors, Monroe Alpheus, 229

Mannheim, Karl, 2

Marsh, J.B.T., 126

Marshall, Napoleon Bonaparte, 180

Mason, Ednah Jane, 182, 296n30

Mason, Missouri Ann. *See* Mitchell, Missouri Ann Mason

McKinley, William, 158, 228

Meachum, Climson, 37

Meachum, John B., 37

Meachum, Nathaniel, 37

Mead, Hiram, 201

Metcalf, George P., 209. *See also* Metcalf bill

Metcalf, Irving W., 245, 247

Metcalf, Vernon, 245

Metcalf bill (in Ohio legislature), 209, 210

Mexican-American War, 85

Michener, William P., 124

migrants to Oberlin: white, 10, 33, 184; black, 4, 33–49, 57, 183, 233

Miller, Kelly, 240

Minor, Patrick, 61

minstrelsy, 167

Missouri Compromise (1821), 90

Mitchell, Arthur, 182

Mitchell, Arthur Wellington, 226, 233, 243, 244

Mitchell, Caledonia, 243

Mitchell, Edith Campton, 191

Mitchell, Edward Wellington, 233

Mitchell, Ida de France, 182

Mitchell, Missouri Ann Mason, 190

Mitchell, William Madison, 190–91, 226, 244, 246

Mizuiri, Jerry, 255

Monroe, James, 96, 109, 111–12, *138*, 216; in state legislature, 92–93, 111–12, 120, 122; as public speaker, 102, 108, 134; "Monroe Rifles" named after," 112; in Congress, 136; and temperance movement, 206, 210

Monroe, Julia Finney, 216, 219–20

Monroe, Mary, 187

"Monroe Rifles," 112

Morgan, John, 22, 24, 26, 27, 28, *38*

Mosby, Hamilton, 245–46

Mosher, Charles, 253–54

Mount Zion Baptist Church of Oberlin, 218, 226, 227, 228, 255; founding of, 217–18; pastors of, 218, 244, 245, 254

"mulattoes," 40, 45, 60, 70–71, 183; as census category, 39, 40, 45, 70–71, 183–84; legal status of, 61, 71–72

Munson, Edward F., 77

Munson, Samuel, 198–99, 200

Murray, Anna Evans, 179

Murray, Daniel, 179

Muse, James H., 108

Mutual Benefit Association, 220, 230

NAACP, 244–48, 249

Nash, Royal, 245

National Association of Colored Women's Clubs (NACWC), 233–34

INDEX

National Black Convention (1964), 151
National Colored Convention (1876), 157–59
National Colored Labor Union, 152
National Convention of the Colored Freemen (1848), 74
National Equal Rights League, 121, 152, 160
Nell, William, 67
New National Era, 182
New Orleans race riot (1866), 128–29
New York Evangelist, 27, 29
New York Witness, 160
Niagara Movement, 231–32; Oberlin connections of, 182, 230, 231, 232
Nichols, Albert, 200
Non-Partisan Woman's Christian Temperance Union (NPWCTU), 214, 303n104. *See also* Woman's Christian Temperance Union (WCTU)
North Star, 66
Nowell, Nora Jane. *See* Robinson, Nora Jane Nowell, 187–88
Noyes, John Humphrey, 1–2

Oberlin, John Frederic, 11
Oberlin Academy, 222, 240, 241. *See also* Oberlin College: preparatory department of
Oberlin Alumni Magazine, 239
Oberlin Anti-Slavery Platform (1854), 91
Oberlin Anti-Slavery Society, 29–31, 32, 34, 84, 88, 91, 98; second incarnation of, 98, 99
Oberlin charter, 16, 17, 63
Oberlin Church. *See* First Church in Oberlin
Oberlin Citizens Aid Society, 216
Oberlin College (known as Oberlin Collegiate Institute until 1850); and abolitionism, 27–28, 31–32, 46, 89, 98, 106–7, 108; renaming of, 40, 63; size of, 63; longtime all-white faculty of, 167, 244; Jubilee celebration of (1863), 171–72, 225; and temperance, 208; presidents of: *see* Fairchild, James Harris; Finney, Charles Grandison; King, Henry Churchill; Mahan, Asa
—founding of, 13, 14, 15–16; decision of, to admit black students, 2–3, 22, 24–28
—black students in, 40, 80–81, 113–15, 163, 168, 179–80, 188, 191, 225; in preparatory department, 34–35, 37, 38, 40, 49–50, 54, 66, 151, 181; before 1860, 45–50, 54, 63, 64–65, 74–75, 158; as proportion of all students, 63, 241–42; discrimination against, 64–65, 170–71, 182–83, 225, 236–41, 246–48
—preparatory department of (later renamed Oberlin Academy), 63, 66, 99, 182, 222; black students in, 34–35, 37, 38, 40, 49–50, 54, 66, 151, 181
Oberlin Council of Colored Women, 234
Oberlin Equal Rights League, 121, 131
Oberlin Evangelist, 39, 46, 86, 92; on race relations in Oberlin, 61, 67–69, 87, 90–91; on resistance to Fugitive Slave Law, 95, 98, 104; on Harpers Ferry raid, 105, 106
Oberlin Freed Woman's Aid Society, 215
Oberlin Kindergarten Association, 220–21, 230
Oberlin Kindergarten Training School, 220–21
Oberlin Ladies Temperance League, 202–3, 204–5, 212, 301n35
Oberlin Mutual Improvement Club, 234
Oberlin News, 149, 164, 170, 188, 198, 219; as successor to *Lorain County* News, 149; on race relations in Oberlin, 149, 170, 227–28, 234–35; racial condescension of, 153–54, 156–57, 159, 160, 162, 221; and civil rights legislation, 155–56; Joseph Battle and, 156–57, 160, 162, 170; on electoral politics, 159, 161, 162, 167, 168; on temperance movement, 213, 214
Oberlin News-Tribune, 253–54
Oberlin Review, 170–71
Oberlin School Board, 178, 215, 225, 230
Oberlin Students' Monthly, 107

320

INDEX

Oberlin Telegraph Company, 170
Oberlin Temperance League, 199
Oberlin town council, 148–49, 162, 166; African American members of, 148, 149, 155, 189, 226–27, 233, 244–45, 246, 256; and temperance, 196, 200
Oberlin Unmasked (Smith), 59, 80
Oberlin Young Men's Anti-Slavery Society, 89
Oberlin-Wellington Rescue (1858), 4, 60, 94–95, 104, 119, 127, 256; charges resulting from, 45, 96–102, 111, 115, 124, *139*, 159; interracial nature of, 94, 97, 99, 235; popular support for, 95, 98–99, 102–4; in town memory, 133, 190, 232, 254, 257
occupations, 34, 45, 50, 57, 71, 101–2, 188, 243–44; racial disparity in, 50, 175–78, 244
Ohio Anti-Saloon League, 211, 221, 245
Ohio State Convention of Colored Men, 130–31
Ohio state legislature, 85, 86–87, 93, 162, 211; and Oberlin charter, 16, 17, 63; Oberlin representatives in, 86, 92, 111–12, 155; and black suffrage, 120, 126–27, 130, 131–32; and temperance, 209
Ohio Supreme Court, 60–61, 71–72, 101, 120
"Omnibus War," 166
Ovington, Mary White, 248

Palmer, Henry, 118–19
Palmer House hotel, 95, 98, 118–19
Parker, Hale G., 232
Patterson, Henry, 71, 180
Patterson, John E., 56–57, 70, 199
Patterson, Katharine, 180
Patterson, Mary Jane, 180
Patterson, W. D., 72–73
Pease, Hiram, 133
Pease, Peter Pinder, 14
Peck, Henry E., 97, 106–7, 108, 119, 134; and Oberlin-Wellington Rescue, 96, 97, 98, 103, 107, *139*
Peck, Medora Eliza Wack, 220
Peterson, M. C., 170

Pickens, William, 247–48
Pierce, Franklin, 76, 90
Pinchback, P.B.S., 158–59
Plessy v. Ferguson (1896), 221, 224
Plumb, Ralph, 96, 106, 122–23, 124; and Oberlin-Wellington Rescue, 102–3, 124, *139*
Plumb, Samuel, 98, 106, 109, 121
poverty, black, 186, 190, 193, 242, 256–57; prejudiced views of, 3, 198, 221, 242–43
Price, John, 94–95, 205. *See also* Oberlin-Wellington Rescue
Prohibition Party, 168, 209–11, 213, 214, 226
property ownership, 51–52; in early years, 18–19; racial differences in, 43–44, 51–52, 70, 174–75, 184–85, 193–94, 242, 243–44; differences in, within black community, 43–44, 55, 70–71, 83, 183, 243–44
public schools, 3, 169, 242, 256; antebellum, 30, 39, 48, 55, 60–62, 187; longtime lack of black teachers in, 244, 305n147

Quarles, Ralph, 33–34, 265n5
Quinn, George, 243, 244

racial stigmatization, 218, 222, 224, 227, 251; temperance movement's unwitting role in, 5, 198, 207–8
Ramey, Katie, 228
Rawdon, Howard L., 242–43, 250
Raynor, Gilbert, 221–22
Reagon, Bernice Johnson, 8
Reconstruction, 120–21, 123–24, 127–28, 148, 150, 178, 179
Redington, Eliphalet, 12, 14
Republican Party: in antebellum period, 91, 92, 122; faded loyalty of, to equal rights, 126, 150, 162, 167, 178; black debates about, 147–48, 150–52, 153–54, 159–61, 166–67, 224–25; and temperance, 210, 213
Rescuer, The, 101–2

321

residential segregation in Oberlin, 78–80, 194–95, 235–38, 256; and restrictive covenants, 235–36; in Oberlin College, 236–41, 247–48
respectability, 241; racialization of, 157, 198, 199, 223, 224; black elite and, 212, 222, 224, 225–26, 228–29, 234, 251
restrictive covenants, 235–36
Robinson, Amanda Scott, 188
Robinson, George, 186–88, 191
Robinson, Robert J., 133–34
Robinson, R. P., 228
Robinson, William F., 186–88, 191
Roosevelt, Theodore, 231
Root, Azariah Smith, 211, 213, 238, 239, 247
Root, Francis Metcalf, 247
Rose, C. J., 217, 218
Rowland, Thad, 205, 206, 208
Russell, Joseph, 182
Russia Township: relation of, to town of Oberlin, 11, 53, 69
Rust, Richard, 165
Rust Methodist Episcopal Church (known as Second Methodist Episcopal Church until 1882), 163–66, 167–68, 169, 217, 220, 228, 231; pastors of, 158, 165, 218, 222, 228, 244; renaming of, 165, 217
Rutledge, William, 98
Rymer, Moses, 56

Schenck, Robert, 130
school board. *See* Oberlin School Board
schools. *See* Liberty School; public schools; Oberlin School Board; Oberlin College: preparatory department of
"scientific charity," 195, 209, 216
"scientific" racism, 5, 68
Scott, Amanda. *See* Robinson, Amanda Scott
Scott, Charles, 256
Scott, Gerald, 255–56
Scott, John H., 53, 103, *139*, *141*, 233; as harness maker, 53, 155; in postbellum politics, 153, 159–61, 166, 168, 210; and temperance, 199, 204, 210, 222
Scott, Winfield, 90
Scrimgeour, William D., 96
Second Congregational Church, 164, 246, 275n45; pastors of, 218, 246
Second Great Awakening, 10, 16, 20
Second Methodist Episcopal Church. *See* Rust Methodist Episcopal Church
sewers, 219
Shanks, George, 244
Shaw, Daniel Webster, 218, 304n130
Sheffield, Ohio, 35, 37
Sheldon, William, 205, 206
Shipherd, Esther, 10
Shipherd, Jacob R., 95, *139*
Shipherd, John Jay, 10–11, 19, 66–67, 95; background of, 10–11; and founding of Oberlin colony, 11–14; and Oberlin Collegiate Institute, 14, 15–16, 19, 24–28; as champion of racial equality, 21–22, 24–28, 29
Shurtleff, Giles W., 129–30, *140*, 171; in Civil War, 112, 117–18, 171; and temperance, 198, 206, 208, 211
Shurtleff, Mary Burton, 215
Siddall, James F., 187
Simms, Alice, 182
Simms, Lizzie, 182
Smith, Amanda, 204
Smith, Delazon, 59, 80
Smith, Gerrit, 33, 86
Smith, Harley J., 244, 245
Smith, James, 94
Smith, Judson, 133, 172, 206
Snider, Denton J., 75
social mobility, 185–91; ideals of, 173, 185–86, 242, 251; racial differences in, 191–92, 249, 251
Stanton, Lucy A., 45, 48–49
Stevens, S. W., 244
Stewart, Philo P. 11–12, 14, 23, 24, 28, 31
Still, William, 125

INDEX

Stone, Frank, 207
Stone, Lucy, 67
Storer, Bellamy, 121
Story of Oberlin, The (Leonard), 222–23
Street, Titus, 12, 14, 18
Strieby, Michael, 2–3
Stuart, Charles, 20
Student Army Training Corps (SATC), 246–47
Sumner, Charles, 150, 154, 163; civil rights bill sponsored by, 150, 152, 154, 155–56
Swing, Alice Mead, 215

Taft, Alfonso, 168
Taft, William Howard, 168, 232
Talbert, Mary Burnett, 182, 231
Talbert, William H., 182
"Talented Tenth," 178, 183, 245
Taliaferro, Robert L., 255–56
Talley, Alfred M., 205, 206
Tambling, Croydon, 210, 213
Taney, Roger, 92
Tappan, Arthur, 21–22, 24, 27
Tappan, Lewis, 21–22, 24, 27, 31, 62
Tappan Square, 120, 134
Taylor, Marshall W., 168
Taylor, Zachary, 86
temperance movement in Oberlin, 5, 196–215; undercutting of racial egalitarianism by, 5, 169, 195, 198, 209, 214; and racial stigmatization, 5, 198, 207–8; white men in, 196, 198–99, 200, 201, 206, 213; white women in, 196, 198, 200–203, 204–5, 209, 211–15; establishments targeted by, 196, 198–99, 200, 202, 205–8; and fire of 1882, 196–97, 208–9; black participation in, 199, 204, 211, 212; compared to abolitionism, 203–4; and woman suffrage, 212–14
Tenney, H. M., 218
Terrell, Mary Church, *145*, 180, 240–41, 245, 308n52
Thirteenth Amendment, 3, 111, 159

Thomas, Robert S. "Bob," 254, 255
Thome, James A., 65, 106
Thompson, Eliza, 201
Thompson, Lucy, 212–13
Thompson, Uriah, 106–7
Tod, David, 113
Torrey, Charles T., 47
town council. *See* Oberlin town council
Townshend, Norman S., 86
Tuck, Henson, 233, 243, 244, 246
Turner, Nat, 34, 181
Tyrell, Beulah, 248

Union Campaign Club, 131
upward mobility. *See* social mobility
U.S. Congress, 127; and slavery, 60, 88, 90, 91, 115; petitions to, 85, 150, 156; and civil rights bills, 127, 132, 150, 152, 154, 155–56, 157
U.S. Supreme Court, 61–62, 92, 221, 224

Van Buren, Martin, 85–86
Van Rankin, Margaret Brown, 45
Van Rankin, Robert, 45
Vashon, George, 45–46, 49
Vashon, John B., 45–46
Vetter, John, 128

Wack, Chauncy, 76, 77, 132, 162, 205, 220
Wack, Mary Ann Brown, 77
Wack, Medora Eliza. *See* Peck, Medora Eliza Wack
Wagoner family, 94
Walker, Moses Fleetwood, 163, 296n30
Wall, Amanda, 179–80, 181
Wall, Caroline. *See* Langston, Caroline Wall
Wall, O.S.B., 54, 70, 111, 173, 178–79, 180; and Oberlin-Wellington Rescue, 97, 111, 119, *139;* in Civil War, 117, 119, 178–79
Wall, Sarah, 54
Wall, Stephen, 54
Wall, Stephen (son of O.S.B. and Amanda Wall), 180

INDEX

Warner, Lucien C., 239
Warren, Ellen, 81–82, 112
Warren, Jim, 112
Warren, Malachi, 81–82, 112, 279n133
Washington, Booker T., 238–39, 240, 243; and Oberlin, 231, 232–33, 308n49
Washington, George, 107
Washington, Rev. George, 245
Watkins, Solomon Glenn, 163
Watson, David, 97, *139*
Watson, John, 44–45, 47, 130; and resistance to Fugitive Slave Law, 60, 89, 94, 97, 98, *139;* status of, in Oberlin, 70, 71, 109, 132, 173; as public speaker, 98, 103, 108
Watson, Margaret, 44–45
wealth. *See* property ownership
Weed, Zeruiah Porter, 58–59, 69, 80
Weld, Theodore Dwight, 20, 21, 29, 31–32, 124–25
Wellington, Ohio, 255. *See also* Oberlin-Wellington Rescue
Wells, Ida B., 214
Western Reserve, *9*, 10, 17, 93
West Indies, 46, 250. *See also* First of August celebrations
Westwood Cemetery, 119, 156, 169
Wheeler, William A., 161
Whipple, George, 49–50
White, Armstead, 187
Whitney, Levi, 206
Wightman, David L., 100
Wiley, Joseph, 181
Willard, Frances, 213–14
Williams, Charles W., 238–39
Williams, George Washington, 162, 168
Williams, Nettie, 244
Williston, J. P., 46–47
Willson, Hiram V., 98, 99, 100, 101, 102
Wilson, Hiram, 36–37
Woman's Christian Temperance Union (WCTU), 211–14, 216, 220, 229, 230. *See also* Non-Partisan Woman's Christian Temperance Union (NPWCTU)
woman suffrage, 202, 212–14
Wood, J. E., 222
World War I, 246–47
Wright, G. Frederick, 249
Wynn, Alexander, 169
Wynn, Carolyn Dyer, 169
Wynn, Edward, 181–82

www.ingramcontent.com/pod-product-compliance
Lightning Source LLC
Chambersburg PA
CBHW021342300426
44114CB00012B/1042